Arts 2

Understanding Adaptation
Drama, Fiction, Film – A Casebook

Understanding Adaptation
Drama, Fiction, Film – A Casebook

James R. Russo

ISBN 978-1-84890-404-0

College Publications
Scientific Director: Dov Gabbay
Managing Director: Jane Spurr

http://www.collegepublications.co.uk

Cover produced by Laraine Welch

v

Table of Contents

Introduction: Fiction into Film
Fiction into Film

Preface

What follows is an adaptation-studies textbook that contains seventy essays on eighty geographically diverse, historically significant novels, short stories, and plays that have been adapted to film. In each instance, the film's year, director, and primary performers have been provided, along with the date and author of the source work. (Complete credits for every film discussed may be found online at the Internet Movie Database.) A comprehensive critical apparatus, together with selected images and an exhaustive index, supplements the model essays. The reader is referred to this book's two concluding bibliographies, as well as to Internet resources, for lists either of films based on musicals and stage plays— including Shakespeare's—or of films based on novels and short stories.

There will be no focus in *Understanding Adaptation* on films literally adapted from other films, rather than from original sources. These would include many works of Japanese horror and such oddities as George Sluizer's *The Vanishing* (1988, 1993) and Michael Haneke's *Funny Games* (1987, 2014). Neither will there be any focus in this book on the many movies that have been adapted from video games since the 1990s, or on podcasts that are now being adapted into films and streaming series. There will be no attention paid here, either, to the adaptation of popular motion pictures to the stage, usually as Broadway shows like *The Lion King* (screen, 1994; stage, 1997), *Beauty and the Beast* (1991, 1994), *The Little Mermaid* (1989, 2008), and *Aladdin* (1992, 2011).

Written with university students (and possibly also advanced high school students) in mind, the analytical essays in *Understanding Adaptation* cover some of the central works treated, and central formalistic (not theoretical) issues raised, in today's adaptation-studies courses and will provide students with practical models to help them improve their own writing and analytical skills—in literature and theater as well as film studies. This volume is aimed not only at students, but also at teachers and aficionados with an interest in the practice of screen adaptation, as well as at those educated readers with an interest in global cinema in general and film studies in particular.

Almost all adaptation-studies texts are books about the methods and techniques of adaptation and contain few (if any) actual analyses of fiction or drama into film. *Understanding Adaptation* describes the methods and techniques of adaptation at the same time as it provides numerous examples of such analysis. The list of films treated includes a number of noted artistic works, immediately recognized by the keen student or enthusiast: *A Passage to India, Lord Jim, Women in Love, Tropic of Cancer, The Unbearable Lightness of Being, The Age of Innocence, Where Angels Fear to Tread, The Portrait of a Lady, Mrs. Dalloway, The Remains of the Day, Dangerous Liaisons, A Room with a View, The Brothers Karamazov, The Sun Also Rises, The Great Gatsby, The Red Badge of Courage, Moby Dick, Electra, The Glass Menagerie, Cyrano de Bergerac, The Elephant Man, The Crucible, Miss Julie, The Cherry Orchard, A Doll's House, Saint Joan, Henry V, Hamlet, Richard III, The Merchant of Venice, Love's Labour's Lost, A Midsummer Night's Dream, Death of a Salesman*, and *Long Day's Journey into Night*.

As the above list shows, my focus is on Anglo-American, or English-language, film adaptations (even when the original dramatic or literary work is in a different language), not out of any desire to exclude but to play to my own strengths as well as to the viewing habits of many, if not all, readers. English, after all, is the second language of the world in the majority of places, and in a number of those places it is the first language (does this even need stating?); therefore, worldwide—I am talking here about the total numbers of movies made in addition to their wide distribution—most adaptations come in the English language. Hence, again, my focus.

My other focus, or perhaps bias, the non-theoretical one, is less easily explained but nonetheless explicable. This book favors the student and the non-specialist, or a "populist" critical frame that ignores the so-called epistemic advances that Translation-Adaptation Studies has made as a discipline, and the ways in which such studies have drawn on poststructuralist ideas (including intertextuality and reader-response theory). I did not miss those post-1960s debates that questioned and scrambled the original/imitation-translation-adaptation "binaries," but I do think that such debates tended to reinvent the wheel, if you will, to talk in circles, to state the obvious, or to create straw-man arguments (in a misguided attempt to create intellectual legitimacy, and scholarly activity, for a new subject area?). Three examples: "Every adaptation is an instance of textual *in*fidelity" (Carroll, 1); "adaptation" is an expression "of how art creates art" (Sanders, 1).

I save the third and best example for last:

> For many people the comparison of a novel [or a play] and its film version results in an almost unconscious prioritizing of the fictional origin over the resulting film, and so the main purpose of comparison becomes the measurement of the success of the film in its capacity to realize what are held to be the core meanings and values of the originary text. (Cartmell & Whelehan, 3)

Yes, this is true; it is also obvious: the novel or play came first, and comparison is inevitable. (Why shouldn't it be?)

It is equally true that a film adaptation can be so different from the original source, so reconceived or reconfigured, that the new work takes on an independent, fully realized artistic life of its own. Needless to say—and contrary to what many theorists *think* an "originalist" or formalist like me thinks—there's nothing wrong with that. Why should there be? Good art is welcome in any form. The only real questions in the end are quality, not "fidelity"; coherence or unity, not "omission" or "addition." The reader is urged, therefore, not only to see as many of the films discussed as possible, but also to read the original play, novel, or short story. Seeing is a kind of reading, to be sure, yet reading is also a kind of seeing. Which comes first is up to the individual to decide, but ideally, over time, the acts of seeing and reading will merge in the single, attentive mind intent on understanding a work of filmic, literary, or dramatic art—again, in any form.

Finally, *Understanding Adaptation* is one of the few books to consider, implicitly or explicitly, the contemporaneous threat of cinema, by way of the Internet, to the very existence of literature and the theater. Indeed, one could argue that the Internet is equally the enemy of all three—drama, books, *and* cinema—and that streaming video on the Internet can be viewed as the apotheosis of cinema. Hence (paradoxically), the death of cinephilia (see Sontag in Works Cited) by oversupply of the filmic product, as well as the decomposition of cinema by disappearance of its infrastructure—movie theaters and all those who program, supply, attend, or service them. I used to be one of those people, in every capacity.

Works Cited

Carroll, Rachel, ed. *Adaptation in Contemporary Culture: Textual Infidelities*. New York: Continuum, 2009.

Cartmell, Deborah, & Imelda Whelehan, eds. *Adaptations: From Text to Screen, Screen to Text*. London: Routledge, 1999.

Sanders, Julie. *Adaptation and Appropriation*. London: Routledge, 2006.

Sontag, Susan. "The Decay of Cinema." *New York Times*, Sec. 6 (Feb. 25, 1996): 60.

ELEMENTS OF PLAY ANALYSIS

I. Analysis of Plot and Action

1. What are the given circumstances of the play's action? Geographical location? Historical period? Time of day? Economic environment? Political situation? Social milieu? Religious system?

2. From what perspective do we see the events of the play? Psychological? Ethical? Heroic? Religious? Political?

3. What has the dramatist selected of the possible events of the story to put into actual scenes? Which events are simply reported or revealed through exposition?

4. Drama is action and the essence of action is conflict. Insofar as a situation contains conflict, it is dramatic: no conflict, no drama. Drama is the process of *resolving* conflict, or of suggesting that the conflict will continue. (For example, in the last scene of *Hamlet*, Fortinbras of Norway will now be the ruler of Denmark, as the entire Danish royal family has been wiped out by its own internecine conflict. But for many readers or viewers, this conclusion is inconclusive: will the Danes accept Norwegian suzerainty?) What is most important in script analysis is to perceive the conflict inherent in the play. Conflict creates characters, or characters—their opposing desires or needs—create conflict. To understand a dramatic text or playscript, it is necessary to discover and expose the conflict. What, then, is the conflict in the play in terms of opposing principles? What kinds of qualities are associated with either side, or with *all* sides? Or, considering the principal characters as "ideas" or ethical/moral agents, into what sort of dialectic can you convert the plot? What is opposing what?

5. Where has the dramatist pitched the emphasis in his or her story, as an unfolding action? (For example, the long and careful approach to the "kill" in *Hamlet* versus the relatively quick "kill" followed by the long and haunted aftermath in *Macbeth*.) What has happened before the play, and what happens during the play? (For instance, the late point of attack in *Oedipus Tyrannos*, whose plot has a considerable past, versus the early point of attack in *King Lear*, in which the past is virtually non-existent.)

6. How many acts and scenes are there? Did the play's author note them or were these divisions added later? What motivates the divisions of the play and how are they marked (curtains, blackouts, etc.)?

7. Are there subplots? If so, how is each related to the main action?

8. What alignments, parallels, or repetitions do you notice? (For example, the triple revenge plot in *Hamlet*; the blind Teiresias who can really "see" from the start as contrasted with the blind Oedipus who can really "see" only at the end of the play.)

9. What general or universal experience does the plot seem to be dramatizing?

II. Analysis of Character

1. Assuming that each character is *necessary* to the plot, what is the dramatic function of each? (For instance, why does Shakespeare give Hamlet a close friend, but no friend to Macbeth or Othello?)

2. Do several characters participate in the same "flaw" or kind of fallibility? (For example, Gloucester and Lear are both blind to the true nature of filial love.)

3. Is there a wide range of character "positions" respecting such antitheses as innocence-guilt, good-evil, honorableness-dishonorableness, reason-irrationality, etc.?

4. What qualities or aspects of character are stressed: the physical, the social, the psychological, or the moral or ethical? (For instance, Ibsen's "ethical" character versus Chekhov's character of "mood" or frustrated sensibility: Aeschylus's "grand," sculptural character versus Euripides' "psychopathic" character.)

5. How is character revealed? By symbols and imagery (Macbeth's preoccupation with blood and time)? By interaction with various other characters (Hamlet with Horatio and Ophelia)? By what the character says? By what others say about the character? By what the character does? (the most important). By descriptions of the character in the stage directions?

6. How do character traits activate the drama? (Note how a character's traits are invariably involved in his or her acts as motives for, or causes of, those acts.)

7. Consider each character as a "voice" in the play's overall dialectic, contributing to theme, idea, or meaning.

8. What evidence of change can you detect? What seems to have been the source of this change, and what does it signify for the play's theme or the final nature of the character's identity?

9. How is the character's change expressed dramatically? (For example, in a "recognition" speech, in a newfound attitude, in a behavioral gesture, etc.)

III. Analysis of Language

1. The dialogue is the primary means by which a play implies the total makeup of its imaginative world and describes the behavior of all the characters that populate that world. For any one passage of dialogue in a play, ask yourself the following questions:

    a.   What happens during this dialogue and as a result of this dialogue?

b. What does this passage reveal about the inner life and motives of each character?
c. What does this scene reveal about the relationships of the characters to each other?
d. What does this section reveal about the plot or about any of the circumstances contributing to the complication or resolution of the plot?
e. What are the most notable moments or statements in this dialogue?
f. Are there any implicit or unspoken matters in this scene that deserve attention?
g. What facial expressions, physical gestures, or bodily movements are implied by the dialogue?
h. What props or set pieces are explicitly or implicitly called for in the dialogue or the stage directions?
i. What vocal inflexions or tone of voice does a line suggest?
j. Where might the characters increase or decrease the volume or speed of their delivery?
k. Where might the characters pause in delivering their lines?
l. Where might the characters stand onstage and in relation to each other at the beginning of the scene and at later points in the same scene?

2. Do all the characters use language in much the same way, or does each have his or her own verbal characteristics?

3. What are the dominant image patterns? (For instance, disease-decay-death imagery in *Hamlet*.)
Do characters seem to share a particular pattern, or is it exclusive to one character? (For example, Othello gradually begins to pick up Iago's sexual-bestial imagery as he becomes more convinced of Desdemona's guilt.)

4. What combinations or conflations of image patterns can you detect? (For instance, in *Hamlet*, in the lines "By the o'ergrowth of some complexion, / Oft breaking down the pales and forts of reason," the imagery of cancer, or pollution by "overgrowth," is conflated with military imagery.)

5. Explain the presence of such rhetorical devices as: sudden shifts from verse to prose; rhymed couplets, which indicate the conclusion of a particular scene; "set" speeches that give the appearance of being standard or conventional (Polonius's advice to Laertes in *Hamlet*); choral speeches; formal "debates"; etc. These devices are often used to emphasize, or italicize, certain aspects of meaning and theme. Since Shakespeare's stage, for one, had no curtain, rhyming couplets performed its function, as in these lines from *Macbeth*: "Fair is foul, and foul is fair: / Hover through the fog and filthy air."

6. How, generally, would you distinguish the use of language and imagery in any play under consideration from that of other plays? (For example, dramatic verse speech tends, on the whole, to "recite" the content directly and faithfully, presenting all the implications on the word-surface; but as dialogue in plays becomes more realistic—becomes prose, that is—particularly from the

nineteenth century forward, there is an increasing rift between what is actually said and what is implied, or latent, in the language.)

7. In what ways does the language of the play—its imagery; style; tempo or rhythm; tone; descriptive, informational, or ideational content; and level of probability or internal consistency—help to create the sense of a unique "world," or circumscribed space, appropriate to this play and no other? (For instance, *Macbeth*'s dark, "metaphysical" space versus *Hamlet*'s dense and various world of objects, people, animals, and processes.)

IV. General Analysis

1. What is the dramatist's attitude toward the materials of his or her play? What tone does he or she take toward the action and the characters? (Skeptical? Critical? Ironic? Sympathetic? Neutral or objective? Etc.)

2. What features or elements of the play seem to be the source of the dramatist's attitude? (A reasonable or reasoning character you can trust? A choral element? A didactic voice detectable in the content as a whole? An allegorical quality? The way in which the incidents are arranged? A set of symbols? A balance or equilibrium of opposed readings of the world?)

3. What is the nature of the play's world order? (Fatalistic? Benign? Malignant? Just? Neutral?) Another way of asking this: Are there *operative* gods, and what share of the responsibility for events do they hold?

4. What is the source of your impression of this world order? Remember that meaning in drama is usually *implied*, rather than stated directly. It is suggested by the relationships among the characters; the ideas associated with unsympathetic and sympathetic characters; the conflicts and their resolution; and such devices as spectacle, music, and song. What, then, is the source of your impression of the play's meaning?

5. If the play departs from realism or representationalism, what devices are used to establish the internal logic of the action?

6. Are changes in the dramatic action paralleled by changes in visual elements such as lighting, costume, make-up, and scenery? How important is such visual detail to the dramatic action?

7. For what kind of theatrical space was the play intended by its author? Are some of the play's characteristics the result of dramatic conventions in use at the time the work was written?

8. How extensive are the stage directions? Were they written by the author or interpolated by someone else? What type of information do they convey? Are they important to the dramatic action?

9. Is the play a translation? Can you compare it to the original? Can you compare it with other translations? Are there significant differences between the source and a translation, such as the rendering of the author's original French verse in English prose?

10. Is there any difference between playing time (the time it takes to perform the play) and illusory time (the time the action is supposed to take)? What is the relationship between the two, if any?

11. Is there anything special about the title? Does it focus on a character, the setting, or a theme? Is it taken from a quotation or is it an allusion? Does the title contain a point of view, suggest a mood, or otherwise "organize" the action of the play?

12. Does the play clearly fall into one of the major dramatic categories (tragedy, comedy, etc.)? What conventional features of its type does the play exhibit (subject matter, situations, character types)? Does knowledge of the genre contribute to an understanding of this play?

ELEMENTS OF FICTION ANALYSIS

THEME: The theme, sometimes called the central idea, refers to the author's main point or purpose in writing the narrative. The theme is more than an indication of the narrative's subject; it is also the author's statement (implicit or explicit) about that subject. If the subject of the narrative is maturity, for example, the central idea could be that maturity is a product of one's actions and attitudes, not one's age and possessions.

Questions to consider:

- What was the writer's purpose in writing the narrative? What does the title itself suggest about the narrative?
- What is the theme of the narrative? Is it implicit or explicit?
- Does the central idea offer a new insight into the human condition or human experience?
- What message or lesson, if any, does the writer wish the reader to take from the narrative?
- How is the central idea expressed? Through the narration, the dialogue, the characterization, the imagery, or a combination of all of these?
- Are any elements repeated in the narrative as a way of suggesting the theme?
- Is there more than one theme?

PLOT: The plot is the main sequence of events that make up the narrative. The turning point is the moment where the action undergoes a major change in direction, as the narrative moves from its midpoint toward its conclusion. The climax is the point of greatest tension or intensity in the plot, usually coming toward the end.

Questions to consider:

- What is the most important event in the action?
- How is the plot structured? Is it linear and chronological, or does the action move around in time (and place)?
- Does the writer use flashback? If so, how and why?
- Does the writer use flashforward? If so, how and why?
- How does the writer create suspense, if he creates any at all?
- What is the turning point of the narrative? What is the climax?
- Is the plot believable? Fantastic? Surreal? Etc.

CHARACTER: Character refers to the people or forces that inhabit a narrative. Each narrative has a central character and some minor characters. Characters have certain qualities and behaviors that help to illustrate the central idea. The main character, or protagonist, will often have one initial key trait or value that is out of balance. The key trait is more than an emotion, an occupation, or an external characteristic: examples of a key trait might include immaturity, conceitedness, self-denial, arrogance, fear of change, sexual frustration, or a variety of other human attributes.

In any analysis of character, the student should be most concerned with the static or dynamic nature of the main character. Is the main character's initial key trait changed by the end of the narrative? A character whose initial key trait is changed at the end is said to be dynamic. A character whose beginning key trait is remains unchanged at the end is said to be static.

Questions to consider:

- What does the character say and do? What does his dialogue or behavior tell you about his values, beliefs, interests, and motives?
- How does the character look? What does her appearance suggest about the character?
- How does the main character change as the narrative progresses? Is he a static/flat character who does not change, or a dynamic/round character who *does* change?
- Who is the villain or antagonist in the narrative? Why?
- Who is the protagonist in the narrative? Why?
- Has the author described the characters not only by physical appearance, but also by thoughts and feelings (either stated or reported) as well as interaction with other characters? Or has the author used a combination of all three of these?
- What types of characters are deployed in the narrative? What qualities stand out? Are they stereotypes?
- Are the characters believable? Need they be on this case?

CONFLICT: Conflict refers to the various problems or difficulties a character encounters in a narrative. The main character will usually face one major conflict and several minor conflicts (called complications). Conflicts are of three general types: one individual vs. another individual; the individual vs. the cosmos; and the individual vs. himself. At the climax of a narrative, some critical decision is made or some critical action is taken by the central character, as the "winner" of the major conflict becomes apparent. The resolution of the major conflict then produces a new state of affairs. In most substantial narratives, the major conflict is internal (the individual vs. himself), and it relates to a key character trait (usually belonging to the protagonist) that is out of balance.

Questions to consider:

- How would you describe the major conflict?
- What conflicts does the main character experience? How does the character deal with these conflicts?
- Is there an internal conflict in the main character?
- Is there an external conflict caused by the surroundings or environment in which the main character finds himself?
- What other types of conflict occur during the narrative?

SETTING: Setting in a narrow sense refers to the physical location and time period of the narrative, the "where" and the "when." It can also refer to the cultural, historical, economic, or social circumstances of the action. The setting is, in a sense, the world through which the characters journey, encountering problems along the way. On a surface level, the setting of a narrative may sometimes seem insignificant. On an underlying level, though, the setting is often thematically connected to the important events in the narrative.

Questions to consider:

- What is the setting of the narrative?
- Does the setting function as an antagonist in the narrative? If so, how?
- How does the setting contribute to or impact on the narrative? In other words, what role does the setting play? Is it an important part of the plot or theme? Or is the setting just a backdrop against which the action takes place?
- How does the writer use setting to create a narrative that is believable (or fantastic, as the case may be)?
- How does the setting impact the protagonist in the narrative?
- What is the mood throughout the narrative, and how does the setting affect that mood?
- How is the setting created? Consider geography, weather, season, time of day, living conditions, type of room or building, etc.
- When was the narrative written?
- Does the narrative take place in the present, the past, or the future?
- How does the time period of the narrative affect its language, atmosphere, and political circumstances?

PERSPECTIVE: Perspective or point of view refers to the position from which the narrative is seen or related. This position determines the manner or light in which the reader views the characters and events of the narrative. The narrative voice is a *persona* the author assumes to tell the story; the author is not the narrator. This voice can be that of a character in the narrative (first-person); a semi-detached observer (third-person limited); or a detached observer (third-person omniscient/third-person objective). The narrative voice may have a certain sensibility or world view that can in some way color the reader's perception of the story. Be aware that point of view in the analysis of literary art has nothing to do with a settled opinion or a persuasive (not to say propagandistic) perspective.

Questions to consider:

- What point of view or perspective does the writer use? Who is the narrator or speaker in the story?
- Are the narrator and the main character the same person?
- What does the narrator know about the characters in the narrative?
- Does the author use perspective to reveal or conceal?

- How does the narrator or point of view impact the narrative? For instance, the first-person narrator knows only what she sees or hears. But the third-person-omniscient narrator is all-knowing and therefore can reveal what all the characters are thinking and doing at all times and in all places.
- Why did the author choose the particular perspective used in the narrative?
- Does the author speak through the main character, who thus functions as a kind of *raisonneur* or mouthpiece?

LANGUAGE: This term refers to a variety of figurative and literary devices used in a narrative. In most cases, the author's intent in using these devices is to compare dissimilar objects or evoke secondary, non-literal associations for thematic effect. The word "style" is often used to refer to a writer's choice of language and sentence structure.

Questions to consider:

- What types of diction does the writer use? Slang? Formal? Profanity? How does the diction impact the narrative? How does it impact you as the reader?
- What types of sentences does the writer use? Fragments? Simple sentences? Complex? Rhetorical? How does the sentence structure impact the narrative?
- Does the writer use simile? Why is it used?
- Does the writer use metaphor? Why?
- Does the writer use personification? Why?
- What types of imagery does the writer use? How does the imagery make the narrative believable or effective? How does it affect the mood of the narrative?
- What sorts of symbols are used by the writer?
- Do any characters act as symbols? How and why?
- Do elements of the narrative's setting appear symbolic? How and why?
- Is one symbol used throughout the narrative? Or do the symbols change as the narrative progresses? ("Motifs" are repeated patterns in a narrative that are often symbolic.)

TONE: Tone refers to the author's emotional attitude toward the narrative and the characters. The reader gauges tone through his own emotional response to the narrative, which is partly determined by its mood or atmosphere. If the author is successful in creating tone, then tone and mood should be intimately connected. The reader's response to tone is the *reader's*—not any character's response; the *reader* determines the "feel" of the narrative. A narrative's tone should be expressed as an adjective: for example, "The tone of the narrative is sad." Tone can also be ironic, humorous, cold, or dramatic, among other designations.

Questions to consider:

- What is the writer's attitude toward the characters and events in the narrative?
- What is the writer's attitude toward the readers? Condescending? Ironic? Empathic?
- How does the tone of the narrative impact your reading? For instance, do you laugh? Do you cry? Or are you neutral to the point of being indifferent?

ELEMENTS OF FILM ANALYSIS

If one is preparing to write about a film, one should aim to:

Investigate background information on the film one is writing about, such as the film's historical, cultural, and stylistic contexts, or its production history. This kind of background material can prove useful in one's analysis, evaluation, and general understanding of the film because, even if one's assignment does not ask that one explicitly write about the film in relation to the era in which it was made, knowledge of that history will deepen one's critical awareness of other aspects of the film. Examining the film as a process that has been shaped by different types of events—historical, contemporary, and individual or personal— can lead to one's having one's own ideas about the film.

Explore the individual and collaborative factors that affected the film's final form so that one can better understand the aesthetic and cinematic decisions the director made. The final images one views on screen come from an extended creative process, involving the influence of the director, screenwriter, and cinematographer (among others), as well as the relevant conditions during the making of the film (including financing, casting, weather, illness, etc.).

Find out who the film's director is and what other films he has made. By viewing some of the director's other films, one will have a better understanding of the film one is writing about as one develops a larger picture of the themes that have inspired the director, the genres and techniques he has preferred, and the consistency (or lack thereof) in storytelling method over the course of his career.

Be selective in one's approach to elements of film composition, as production includes everything from lighting and sound, to wardrobe and editing, to special effects. The more specific the focus, the closer one can analyze one's chosen area of investigation and relate that analysis to a thesis about the particular cinematic work as a whole.

Think comprehensively about the film's story and characters. Cinematic images do not merely represent a single dimension of a subject, such as just the narrative or just the characters. All feature films tell stories and have characters, but the way in which the narratives and their protagonists are presented to us can vary greatly in style, tone, and technique from film to film and filmmaker to filmmaker. Film analysis is concerned with *how* these various elements help tell the story and create the characters.

Watch films with critical awareness, just as one would actively read and annotate a book one was preparing to write about; one should make note of a film's striking features and ask relevant questions. After an initial viewing, if possible one should watch the film a second time, taking notes and letting one's general, preliminary questions evolve into more specific ones. If one is writing about a film that one can view only once, the initial groundwork will be essential to the success of one's paper. One should be aware, too, that doing research beforehand can play a significant role in freeing the viewer to experience the film with purposeful observation and informed note-taking.

Guide oneself to a focused topic through one's questions, and continue to narrow one's approach as one decides which questions can be grouped together under a shared idea concerning the theme of the film, the function of its characters, or the nature of its technical and formal features.

Ask oneself the following questions as one analyzes any film:

Background

Who is the writer of the film? Has the screenplay been adapted from another work?

Who is the director?

When was the film made?

How might industrial, social, and economic factors have influenced the film's making? Did conditions in the filmmaking industry at the time limit the way in which the film could represent particular subjects? Does the film follow or critique the dominant ideologies of its period? Does it reflect and even shape particular cultural tensions?

Form/Narrative/Perspective

What "happens" in the plot? In considering the narrative structure, note whether the film follows a standard chronological narrative, and how time is used. (That is, how is the story told: linearly; with flashbacks or flash-forwards; or episodically?) What are the key moments and how are they established? What are the climaxes and anti-climaxes? How far ahead is the audience in understanding what is happening to the characters than the characters themselves are? What propels the story forward? What is the pace of the narrative? How do earlier parts of the narrative set up later parts? Where do the key emotive moments occur—that is, when the audience is frightened, enraged, enraptured, avenged, etc.—and how has the narrative helped to establish these emotions on the part of the audience? Note when there is a *change of knowledge* (when characters or audience members become aware of new information) that shifts the *hierarchy of knowledge* (the relative amount of knowledge characters have, as opposed to what knowledge the audience has). Does the narrative have a coherence or unity, or does it leave the audience feeling unfulfilled or confused?

Is the film told, in general, from a particular character's point of view, or is it "objective"? Is the film's perspective primarily intellectual or emotional, visionary or realistic? Within the film, are particular shots shown from this or that character's point of view (in a "subjective shot"), and how does the camera technically reinforce such a point of view? On whom is the audience meant to be focusing at particular moments?

What does the title mean in relation to the film as a whole? Consider alternative titles and why this particular title was chosen; also, consider any ambiguities in the title. The opening credits themselves establish a tone and often are used to foreshadow events, themes, or metaphors, so one should pay careful attention from the very beginning of any film. How are the opening credits presented? Are they connected to the film's meaning in any way?

Why does the film's action begin in the way that it does?

Are there any linguistic or visual motifs that are repeated during the film? What purpose do they serve?

Which three or four sequences are the most important in the film? Why?

Is sound used in any vivid ways to enhance the film's drama, heighten tension, disorient the viewer, etc.?

How does the film use color or light-and-dark to suggest tone and mood in different scenes?

Are there any striking uses of perspective (through camera angle or placement)? How does this relate to the meaning of the scene in question?

How and when are scenes cut? Is there any meaningful pattern to the way the editing is carried out?

What specific scene constitutes the film's climax? How does this scene resolve the central issue of the film?

Does the film leave any disunities or loose ends at its conclusion? If so, what does this suggest?

Why does the film conclude on this particular image and not some other one?

Theme

What is the film's central theme, idea, or generative principle? That is, from an intellectual perspective, what is the motivating force behind the film?

Does the film present a clear-cut point-of-view on its particular subject? How so, and to what end?

Are there any aspects of the film's theme that are left ambiguous at the conclusion? Why?

How does this film measure up to literary texts you have read on the same subject?

Characterization

Who are the central characters? How are minor characters used? Are characters thinly or fully drawn, and why? Who in the audience is meant to relate to which characters, and what sort of emotion (fear, pleasure, anxiety) are audience members meant to feel on account of this identification? Is there a clear-cut hero or villain, or do these figures remain ambivalent in the film? What values do the characters represent, and do the characters change in the course of the action? Are the characters meant to play a particular "type" and do they play *against* type at any time? Do different characters use different kinds of language? Do certain characters speak through their silences?

What is the acting style of the performers: mannered ("classical"); intense and psychologically driven ("Method"); or less affected and more "natural"? Do particular actors have their own recognizable style or type, and how do the filmmakers integrate the various acting styles of different performers? What expectations do audiences have of "star" actors? Do the stars, in this instance, fulfill or challenge the expectations of the audience as they perform their roles?

Mise-en-scène/Montage

Is the setting realistic or stylized? What atmosphere does the setting suggest? Do particular objects in the setting serve a symbolic function? Does the setting itself serve such a function?

How are the characters costumed and made up? What does their clothing or makeup reveal about their social standing, ethnicity, nationality, gender, or age? How do costume and makeup convey character? How are characters contrasted by means of costume?

What in the film is well-illuminated and what is in shadow? How does the lighting scheme shape our perception of character, space, or mood? How are colors used? Is there a pattern or scheme to the use of color? That is, is color used symbolically in the film?

What shot distances are used? Does one notice a movement from longer to closer shots? When in particular are the various shot distances used (e.g., the opening of a scene, during a conversation, etc.)? What purposes do the long shots, medium shots, and close-ups serve?

How do camera angles function? How do they shape the audience's view of characters, spaces, or actions?

How do camera movements function? What information do they provide about characters, objects, and locations? Do the camera movements guide the viewer's eye toward particular details? Do they align the viewer's perspective with that of a character?

Editing ("cuts") creates continuities (or discontinuities), juxtapositions, and overall narrative structure in a film. What types of cuts are used? How are the cuts used: to establish rhythm, shift the viewer between characters, create transitions between spaces, mark the passage of time? Does the film's editing comment on the relationships between characters or spaces?

What is the purpose of the film's music? How does it direct our attention within the image? How does it shape our interpretation of the image? How are sound (including dialogue) and sound effects used, in general, in the film?

Was the film shot in a studio, on a soundstage, or was it shot on location? How is the setting integrated into the action, both the larger background of that setting and its smaller foreground (including props)? How is the setting used in composing shots (verticals and horizontals, windows and doors, shades and mirrors, etc.)? How do particular settings (a vast mountain range, a cluttered urban setting) function as signs in order to convey narrative or psychological information to the viewer?

CHARACTERISTICS OF THEATER, FICTION, & FILM

Characteristics of Theater

1. A three-dimensional, ephemeral performance of events.
2. Continuous, "big" acting aimed at a live audience; does not employ amateur actors.
3. Immediate relationship between the actors and the audience, both of whom are physically present in the same space at the same time.
4. Except in rare cases, has no narrator.
5. Relatively active audience that must choose for itself where to look or what to see; what the audience sees is unmediated by a camera.
6. A verbal art primarily, but it also has a visual component (through costumes, sets, lights, choreography, and action itself).
7. A collaborative art, with the actor finally in control on the stage.
8. A total work of art or *Gesamtkunstwerk*, but not quite to the extent that film is.
9. Irreducible: to have theater, you must have living actors performing before a real audience in a more or less demarcated space.
10. A group experience, as it occurs in a theatrical auditorium of one kind or another.
11. The most popular art form of the nineteenth century and before.
12. Its essence consists of human beings in conflict with each other or themselves.
13. The descriptive linguistic term belonging to the theater is "therefore" rather than "then"; in other words, the theater gives primacy to causality more than it does to succession.
14. Deals with the relationship between people.
15. There is only one "shot": the full picture of the stage.
16. Intermissions are common, and scene changes (as well as costume, make-up, and lighting changes) can be slow and laborious. Space is therefore less manipulable and time is less flexible.
17. The dramatic text is an independent artwork that can be read *or* performed.
18. Usually dramatizes the *consequences* of action; characters are often victims of their pasts.

Characteristics of Fiction

1. With a strong emphasis on character development, fiction describes what characters do, say, think, feel, or believe.
2. Can feature multiple plots or actions, with their concomitant characters.
3. Plot elements (including the ending) may remain unresolved and ambiguous, or may simply be left to the reader's interpretation.
4. Has a narrator.
5. Can explore large philosophical themes regarding the human condition and the nature of the universe, as well as major developments in recent history and contemporary culture.
6. A verbal art that can consist of dialogue as well as narration.

7. "Collaborative" only in the sense that the reader's imagination collaborates with the writer's art.
8. A "partial" work of art, rather than a *Gesamtkunstwerk*, in the sense that it does not combine different art forms—such as music, photography, dance, etc.—into one; and in the sense that fiction is almost always produced by a single author, not multiple collaborators.
9. Is "reducible" only in the sense that the physical book, or story collection, can become a virtual one on the Internet.
10. Reading fiction is chiefly a solitary experience, but it can also be a group experience (at fiction readings, for example).
11. Time is highly elastic or flexible in fiction.
12. Can feature multiple settings.
13. The descriptive linguistic terms belonging to fiction are both "then" and "therefore"; in other words, fiction gives primacy to succession as well as to causality.
14. Deals with the relationship between people, as well as with the relationship of people to things, places, *and themselves*.
15. Can contain ample symbolism, metaphor, allegory, and allusion.
16. "Intermissions" or breaks whenever the reader wishes, as a work of fiction can be experienced over several, even many, days.
17. Complete when written (and published), as an independent artwork; the only performance involved might be in the case of a public reading by the author or someone comparable.
18. Can concentrate on action *per se*, even when this action is "interior" or psychological; can also dramatize the *consequences* of action.

Characteristics of Film

1. A two-dimensional, permanent visual record of a performance.
2. Discontinuous, "smaller" acting aimed at the camera lens; can employ amateur actors.
3. No immediate or physical interrelationship between the actors and the audience.
4. Has a narrator: the camera.
5. Relatively passive audience for whom the camera chooses what will be seen.
6. A visual art primarily, but also a dramatic art that enacts stories (with words once the sound era begins) and a narrative art that tells those stories through the mediation of the camera.
7. A collaborative art, with the director ultimately in control.
8. A total work of art, or *Gesamtkunstwerk*.
9. Reducible to DVD, video, television, etc.
10. Can be a solitary experience, especially if you are watching a film alone at home.
11. The most popular art form of the twentieth century and beyond.
12. Can dispense with overt conflicts, climaxes, and even plots; indeed, can be almost completely non-theatrical or -dramatic.

13. The descriptive linguistic term belonging to the cinema is "then" rather than "therefore"; in other words, the cinema gives primacy to succession more than it does to causality.
14. Deals with the relationship of people not only to other people, but also to things and places.
15. The camera can provide the viewer with multiple visual perspectives, through different shots.
16. Intermissions are rare, and scenes changes (as well as costume, make-up, and lighting changes) are accomplished swiftly and easily through cuts or editing. Space is therefore manipulable and time is flexible.
17. The film script is not an independent artwork and cannot be read by itself fruitfully, nor can its words be "performed" as a play's words could be; a screenplay is a preparatory sketch for a future art work, a fully realized cinematic experience.
18. Usually concentrates on action *per se*, even when this action is "interior" or psychological; characters are often makers of their own destinies in the present.

Introduction: Drama into Film

As long as people lack original ideas for a movie or are in a hurry to come up with a script, they will turn to adaptations. Short stories, novels, and especially plays are grist for the adapters' mills, which, unlike God's, grind fast and exceeding coarse. Theater, since the dawn of cinema, was considered the ideal source for photoplays, as moving pictures used to be called with *nouveau-riche* pretension. The prestigious thing for the movies was to capture some New York stage star in a hit vehicle for transfer to the screen; nowadays the traffic tends to be reversed, as Hollywood blockbusters are turned into Broadway musicals, and big- and small-screen stars are coaxed into offering themselves up live to their hungry fans.

Yet movie adaptations of plays have presented, from the beginning, pitfalls galore. Film is a restless medium, suffering from acute dromomania, and can stay put for any length of time only with great difficulty—or great directorial know-how. Conversely, theater, though it too enjoys an outing or a change of scene, is perfectly content to tarry among the same three walls for an entire evening. Though in need of some action, theater dotes on talk; whereas nothing seems to make movies more nervous than public speaking. I could list further differences, but all this is well-known to everyone except the unfortunates who keep making movies out of plays.

Let me begin, nonetheless, by saying something practical about the adaptation of drama to film, mainly because so little is understood about the process of adaptation by even the educated filmgoer. Many people (especially those outside the entertainment professions) still cling to the naïve belief that drama and film, for example, are two aspects of the same art, except that drama is "live" while movies are "recorded." Certainly there are undeniable similarities between the two forms. Most obviously, both employ action as a principal means of communication: that is, what people *do* is a major source of meaning. Live theater and movies are also collaborative enterprises, involving the coordination of writers, directors, actors, designers, and technicians. Drama and film are both social arts in that they are exhibited before groups of people and are therefore experienced publicly as well as individually. But films are not mere recordings of plays. The language systems of these two art forms are fundamentally different, and movies have a far broader range of techniques at their disposal.

The usual solution to the problem of adaptation, of course, is to "open up" the play: to fill in the scenes merely reported or mentioned in the stage version, or invent new ones out of whole cloth for the celluloid version. This tends to be risky: the rhythms, strategies, cohesion of the play are tampered with; it is at the very least as if a drawing in charcoal on paper were translated into one in chalk on a blackboard. Say something in the enclosed space of a stage box, where the viewer sees the entire cast of reacting characters all the time, then say it on screen in a close-up or two-shot—even in a long shot showing everyone present—and you always end up getting unsettlingly more or less than the play-in-the-theater did. (The classic case of trying to remain faithful to a play is Hitchcock's *Rope* [1948], from Patrick Hamilton's 1929 stage thriller, where, after a scene on a park bench, the action stays within an apartment. But, in this case, the play had scant literary merit, and the film adds little to it save technical bravura.)

Indeed, the surest sign of the clichéd mind in filmmaking is a feeling of obligation to open up plays when they become films and a conviction that this process proves superiority, that a play really comes into its own when it is filmed. We can really go to Italy in Franco Zeffirelli's film of *Romeo and Juliet* (1968), so for some people this picture automatically supersedes stage-bound theatrical productions. We can dissolve and cross-fade more easily in the movie of *Death of a Salesman* (1951, Laszlo Benedek), therefore the theater proves yet again just a tryout place for later perfect consummation on screen—despite, in this case, the theater's superior ability to suggest the childishness of Willy's sons (by having the adult actors of Biff and Happy play their boyhood selves) and the momentousness of Willy's adultery (by having it occur, not on location in Boston, but on the forestage—right in the Lomans' living room, as it were). And we can go outside in Mike Nichols' film of *Who's Afraid of Virginia Woolf?* (1966), so once more the theater is shown up as cribbed or confined, if not superficially realistic, even though the claustrophobic nature of George and Martha's single-set living room on the stage is part of the point of this long night's journey into day.

The trouble here is a confusion in aesthetic logic, an assumption that we are comparing apples and apples when we are really comparing apple and pears. Fundamentally, film takes the audience to the event, shifting the audience continually; theater takes the event to the audience, shifting it never. Just as the beauty of poetry often lies in tensions between the free flight of language and the molding capacity of form, so the beauty of drama often lies in tensions between imagination and theatrical exigency. To assume that the cinema's extension of a play's action is automatically an improvement is to change the subject: from the way theater builds upwards, folding one event upon another in almost perceptible vertical form, to the way film progresses horizontally. Figuratively speaking, theater works predominantly by building higher and higher in one place; film, despite the literally vertical progress of planes in the image, works predominantly in a lateral series of places. In this way, action in the cinema is more of a journey in the present than a confrontation based on the past (the usual form of tragedy in drama): the one is filled with possibility or promise, the other with suspense or foreboding. By its very form, it can then be said, film reflects for spectators in the twenty-first century the belief that the world is a place in which a person can leave the past behind and create his or her own future—hence one of the reasons the cinema took such a foothold, so early, in the history of the United States.

"Opening up" a play may be desirable, but it must be part of a total rethinking of the way the space is to be used in the new medium. It can be successful when the filmmaker knows clearly what he is doing and treats his film as a new work from a common source, as Richard Lester did in his admirable 1965 film of Ann Jellicoe's *The Knack*. Or consider the instance of a film's improving on a play: David Lean's *Brief Encounter* (1945,); but Noël Coward's 1936 play was a one-act that could use expansion, and Coward himself wrote the screenplay. (Moreover, one seldom if ever sees the original play, titled *Still Life*, acted by the likes of the movie's Trevor Howard and Celia Johnson.) Still, most adapters seem to think that any banal set of film gimmicks constitutes a liberation for which the poor cramped play ought to be grateful. I shall not be discussing here, therefore, which form is superior, theater or cinema—an issue, at this point, about as meaningful as the old debate on art versus science. The old strictures about films as *against the theater* are still valid, however.

To wit: a film is created almost as much by technicians (cinematographers and cutters) as by artists (actors, writers, directors). The cinema is essentially not congenial to language. (All the Shakespeare films prove this.) Film does not permit sustained acting; further, skillful directors and editors can synthesize a performance where the talent is minimal. (Marilyn Monroe could not have sustained a ten-minute vaudeville sketch, but Billy Wilder wrung a few hundred snippets of scenes out of her and wove them into her amusing vocalist in *Some Like It Hot* [1959].)

But, true though these strictures are, all they do is compare cinema with the theater, and we can no longer use theatrical standards to judge films. To do so is a historical fallacy. Film, as we all finally know, must be judged by an aesthetic that is consonant with its resources, methods, and highest potentials. To refute the strictures above by *appropriate* argument: there are indeed more technicians in a movie, but the notion that this means the mechanical deep-freeze of art is about as sound as saying that good writing cannot be done on a typewriter. The theater uses some technicians; the cinema uses more. At what precise number does art die? Obviously all that matters is the result. If our bosoms are truly wrung, it is irrelevant to dismiss the work because the sound engineer and special-effects man contributed. We should know how it happened; but how can we claim it *didn't* happen?

By now, moreover, it has become an unwritten law that film is a director's medium and the theater is a writer's medium; but all unwritten laws ought to be written down once in a while so that they can be examined. Some plays make the second part of the proposition worth examining. At least they show how much the playwright is at the mercy of his director, a mercy that is sometimes hard and sometimes helpful. In conventional theater, plays do not begin without a script. Between us and the author are the performers, as boon or blockade; and in the past 150 years or so, the controlling figure of the director has arisen (incidentally, soon after the rise of the virtuoso musical conductor). Nowadays no dramatist comes to us except through the mind and sensibilities of a director. This does not make the theater as much a director's medium as the cinema; one has only to compare film scripts and play scripts to see this quite clearly. But it does often make the director the decisive element in theatrical performance, for good or less good. One advantage of the theater over films— and a factor that swings the theater's balance to the writer—is that a play can survive one production to be produced again. (Hollywood remakes of earlier movies are not really a relevant analogy.)

As for language, if film is not its best medium, still a film can be well written (Orson Welles's *Citizen Kane* [1941]) always immediately to come to mind); and film has non-verbal languages of its own that the theater is denied. They include montage; metaphors of motion by which the audience can be transported as easily as the actors; and the art wrung from sheer physical action—from the elemental chase to the scurrying of the tiny car in Jacques Tati's *Mr. Hulot's Holiday* (1953) to Max von Sydow's ritualistic bath-cum-revenge in Ingmar Bergman's *The Virgin Spring* (1960).

However, it is the matter of acting that, even today, is the heart of the theater's assumed superiority. If Monroe's voice in a play could not puff past the

3

tenth row, why is that a relevant criterion for her performances in films? Many a fine singer can "act" well in his singing but is hopelessly ham in his actual acting; no one thinks that nullifies his validity in his own medium. The superiority of theater acting over film acting—sustained work over "piece" work done out of sequence—rests on the false assumption that if acting is not done in the theater *per se*, it is not acting. Film underplaying itself is not, by definition, easier than most contemporary stage playing; it is simply more internal, not non-existent. The ability to jump into the middle of a scene, without build-up, does not demand the power of sustenance of the stage, but it does demand keen powers of concentration and imagination, as any stage actor can testify who has been interrupted in rehearsal, then asked to resume in mid-scene.

Most conclusively, again, the results speak for themselves. The techniques of film may aid screen actors in ways that the stage actor, coached by his director but now alone, is not aided. But the performances of the best film actors are *performances*—designed, projected work, fired by empathy and imagination and the talent of re-creation. I cite, among many from the past, the film acting of Paul Newman, Marcello Mastroianni, Toshiro Mifune, even the underrated Jean Simmons. (A double bill of two inferior films, Mervyn LeRoy's *Home Before Dark* [1958] and Stanley Donen's *The Grass Is Greener* [1960], would show how sadly Simmons was underrated.)

In 1936, the film critic Otis Ferguson wrote the following in *Theatre Arts*:

> The movies have had a hard time in the court of criticism, finding themselves generally in the position of being guilty until they prove themselves innocent. . . . The prosecution can always cite ten bad pictures to the one good picture found by the defense . . . Hence pictures as art are simply not, not nearly; and there is nothing left for the defense to say except that art shall not live by its bad works alone, and that anyone in the more established fields who squinted down the tradition and saw only the fertilizer and not the flower would be punished horribly. (Ferguson, 137)

This statement could almost be applied to contemporary theater. But never mind, for the theater has always been judged by its best achievements, its potentialities. A case could be made that serious plays, tragic *or* comic, are not wanted by our society today. The writing talents of our time, whether they could succeed dramatically or not, are rarely drawn to plays because they cannot feel that the theater is penetrable by them or important to the audience they want to reach.

Positively speaking, by contrast, the attractions of film to serious writing, directing, and acting talents increased in the second half of the twentieth century because, in the United States and abroad, there was a sense of social response to film, a sense that it was wanted, that it was acutely attuned to the age. The historical fact seems to be that, when a society wants an art form, talent arises to supply the need (painting in the Renaissance, opera in nineteenth-century Italy). With the interplay of timeliness and talent, all things—though doubtless difficult—were, and are, possible.

To put the matter negatively, as film stands now, most of its works are (as ever) ephemeral and bad, as are most works in all arts. Cinema may be free of the shadow of its antecedent art, but its future, once at least as bright as the theater's, is now hamstrung by cable television, digital widescreens, and the rise of the computer, together with the Internet, live-streaming, social media, iPhones, YouTube—as well as the consequent, inevitable disappearance of movie theaters if not of DVDs themselves. The bonds of commercialism thus are no longer worse in the theater than in the cinema.

I'd like to close this section not by arguing for the overall superiority of film as an art form—it is superior to the theater in some ways, inferior in others, which have been carefully left out of this discussion. In a sense, I examine screen adaptations of drama here precisely because such works exist in a state of aesthetic limbo that precludes absolute or purist judgment.

Work Cited

Ferguson, Otis. "The Screen Presents—Hollywood's Gift to Broadway." *Theatre Arts Monthly*, 20.2 (Feb. 1936): 136-143.

"Placing Drama on Film: Seven Adaptations, 1962-1999"

Let me look here at seven Euro-American adaptations of plays to film during what I call the Golden Age of Cinema, from the post-World War II period (starting with the rise of Italian neorealism, otherwise not treated here) to the invention and subsequent development first of the videocassette, in 1971, and then of the digital video or versatile disc (DVD) in 1995. I emphasize, in the previous sentence, Golden Age of *Cinema*, for, by contrast, none of the following adaptations is a superior filmic work of art unto itself: by and large, each is too dependent on the form from which it is derived. I treat these works here because, analytically speaking, they reveal as much about the drama as the cinema.

The plays adapted are as follows: Euripides' *Electra* (413 B.C.), Jean Genet's *The Balcony* (1956), Peter Shaffer's *Equus* (1973), Bernard Pomerance's *The Elephant Man* (1977), Arthur Miller's *The Crucible* (1953), Strindberg's *Miss Julie* (1888), and Chekhov's *The Cherry Orchard* (1904) as well as *The Sea Gull* (1896).

Electra (1962, Michael Cacoyannis)

In the early 1960s the question of adaptation broadened out from a matter of form, purely, to include style, as from Greece came two films adapted from classic plays: *Antigone* (1961) and then *Electra* (1962). The second is the more successful because Michael Cacoyannis, its director, is more aware of its inappropriateness. Euripides' play (413 B.C.) was designed for performance (in masks) to an audience of many thousands, some of whom were a hundred yards away, to be declaimed to music with formal movement, with its cast always seen at one fixed, great distance; the film is seen in distances varying from long shot to close-up, with mixed movements and rhythms and the camera's motion added, with photography insisting on the realism of the individual rather than his or her symbolic reality. Texture is thus drastically altered; the chorus— which, besides its dance and dramatic aspects, was a kind of amplifying system for the back rows—becomes merely a nuisance; and the gods, whose appearance was fitting in the abstraction of the theater and necessary to the themes of any Greek drama, are eliminated as *ex machina*.

In making *Antigone*, the director George Tzavellas himself clung fairly closely to the original of Sophocles and achieved sincere stiltedness. Cacoyannis, a more talented film director, foresees this pitfall and tries to "lick" Euripides. He slims down the dialogue (although he added some reviling of her mother's body by Electra) and beefs up the physical movement wherever possible—even to the point of taking us into the peasant's house with Clytemnestra. (Euripides was a daring innovator but he would have been horrified by that.) Cacoyannis also attempts to preserve style by using attitudes and stately groupings derived from Greek bas-reliefs and urns, but the more he tries, the more it all looks like pretty posing, too studied and statuesque for the busybody camera. Only some arts and styles—ballet, opera, classic theater—were designed to exist at a remove from the audience, in conventions too large for intimacy.

Walter Lassally, the cameraman of Tony Richardson's socially realistic *A Taste of Honey* (1961) and *The Loneliness of the Long Distance Runner* (1962), makes a considerable journey eastward and back in time to photograph *Electra* in steely sun and muted shadows, and gives us the austerity of the Greek landscape. (Some of the scenes in palaces and temples seem odd, however. These buildings weren't ancient at the time; they must have looked new.) Irene Papas, distinguished and smoldering, does her best to sustain a high Handelian line as Electra, as she tried in Tzavellas's *Antigone*, but is cramped and harried by the form itself. Some of her moments, though—like the recognition of Orestes (Yannis Fertis)—strike home.

None of this is to argue that the film form is incapable of tragedy or to say that the cinema will necessarily always be inferior to the great Greek theater. It is only to note—in formal and stylistic comparison—that *Electra* on film is basically as incongruous as Antonioni on stage. One can understand that a Greek film director was tempted by his nation's heritage, even as the English have been tempted by Shakespeare. But from Laurence Olivier's *Henry V* (1944) we remember most vividly the flight of the arrows and the charge of the horses at Agincourt, from *Electra* the stony, shadowed mountains—not Shakespeare or Euripides. Billy Wilder's *Some Like It Hot* (1959) is better, as film, than either.

The Balcony (1963, Joseph Strick)

Jean Genet's play *The Balcony* had a considerable history of adaptation in its early life. It was first published in 1956 in fifteen scenes; the play was subsequently published in a second, longer version in 1960; then it appeared in a third, shorter rendition (nine scenes) in 1962. (Bernard Frechtman's first English translation [published in 1958] was based on Genet's second version, while Frechtman's second, revised English translation [published in 1966] was based on Genet's third version.) Its first production was in English—London, 1957—over the author's violent protests about the way it was produced. *The Balcony* was first presented in New York, Off-Broadway, in March of 1960 and was condensed before the opening; it was presented in France the following May and was again condensed—after the opening. In 1963 it was radically adapted for the screen and filmed Off-Hollywood, so to speak.

The Balcony is the name of a brothel in an unidentified country that is torn by revolt. This brothel, an imaginatively equipped palace of illusion, is an observation post from which the bloodshed and struggle can be watched; and the fantasies that the clients act out with the girls are caricatures of the world outside. Three regular customers have always enacted a bishop, a judge, and a general, and in a moment of crisis they have to masquerade as such in the real world. The chief of police, busy suppressing the rebels, himself takes time to visit the madam, who is his mistress. One of his frustrations is that no client has yet wanted to impersonate him. The rebel leader appears toward the end and asks to impersonate the chief. At the conclusion of his scene with a girl, the leader castrates himself. The characters disperse. The revolt is either a success or a failure; it is not clear. The madam addresses the audience: "You must now go home, where everything—you can be quite sure—will be even falser than here" (Genet, 96).

Even this stripped-down summary discloses that the play is a fantasy on themes of power and relative values, as mirrored in extreme rituals of sex. Genet's plays were once shoved into the hastily convoked Theater of the Absurd, but they do not belong there. Both before and after *The Balcony*, he showed himself to be a poetic dramatist of social protest. The modes of meaninglessness—of Samuel Beckett, Eugène Ionesco, Harold Pinter, Arthur Adamov—were remote from this man, whose life and work were acts of assault, hatred of degraded ideals. There was cruelty in the Absurdists, but there was little hate. Hate is impossible without ideals, and ideals were not possible in the theater's *reductio ad Absurdum*.

The screenplay of *The Balcony* (1963), by Ben Maddow, tries to slice down to the themes of the original, articulating them somewhat differently. In a narrow sense the script is an improvement. Genet poses vivid situations, then does not develop them dramatically. For example, each of the clients' scenes begins startlingly, but after one has perceived both the fetish and its symbolism, which takes about a minute, nothing further comes of the scene but verbal embroidery on the initial situation. On a larger scale the play could be summed up in the same way: it is a basically startling and promising image that is not successfully developed. One does not ask for copybook maxims from a poetic drama, but, on Genet's own terms, the metaphors do not generate sufficient tension, do not grow and burst, as the act of drama should. The best effects here are those of lyric poetry, which has only to establish striking figures in apposition and need not do much more with them.

Maddow, sensing this, has tried to impose stricter form and direction on the material, has shortened and simplified. Thus some of the theatrical tedium has been excised, but, inevitably, so has much of the imagery and idea. If Genet had shaped the work better, it would be a better play; Maddow's shaping only makes it more streamlined. And, while altering, Maddow has added mere gags (some of which date: the general settles his bill with a credit card); and he has disrupted the tone of the work by fluctuating between bitter fantasy and broad satire. The police chief gives a nonsensical radio address; the three fake officials make a farcical, triumphant tour by car and pay a meaningless visit to the morgue; the castration is omitted, and the chief and the rebel fight—stopped only by the whores' stripping them naked at the madam's orders.

Yet this same script might have become a more satisfying film in the hands of a more gifted director. Joseph Strick, who previously made the sophomoric *Savage Eye* (1960) and *The Big Break* (1953), has little knowledge of acting, a trite pictorial eye, and less sense of tone than his scriptwriter. Under the titles we see a montage of newsreel shots: street riots, raging mobs. From this scary reality we switch to the brothel, which does not seem to be related even in fantasy to this grainy newsreel world. (When the three fakers later ride through the streets, the newsreel shots, which had previously been used with the grimmest reality, are used for Chaplinesque effects.) Within the chimerical brothel itself, the film is handled without evocative poetic effect. The camera is factual, yet it needed the touch of a Jean Cocteau.

Strick cannot help insecure actresses like Joyce Jameson and Arnette Jens, and he has miscast Ruby Dee. Peter Falk, an actor of guttural capabilities, is never allowed to make the police chief either a power symbol with comic facets or a Marx Brothers butt. Shelley Winters, the madam, is much too earthbound to be an Earth Mother; we could believe her as a madam in Toledo or Tulsa, but not as the archetypal madam of Nowhere and Everywhere. However, the film does give substantial opportunity to that shamefully neglected actress, Lee Grant, who

8

plays the madam's lesbian friend. How prodigally wasteful our theater and cinema were (and are), not to have offered fuller scope to this fine actress.

The merits of the picture, which exist, must not be scanted. It is worth applauding the elementary fact that *The Balcony* was made, that something was done at the time—even if it was adapting a French play—to keep American films at least vaguely in touch with what was happening in the rest of the world. (The New American Cinema, only a few years later, would do more such "outreach" in films like *The Pawnbroker* [1965, Sidney Lumet], *The Graduate* [1967, Mike Nichols], and *Medium Cool* [1969, Haskell Wexler].) More positively, after all the faults have been noted, the picture contains a residuum of the suggestive ambiguities of Genet's play. And it conveys some sense of sex as ambience, sex not merely as the pleasures of the bed but as a pervasive force, a medium for mysteries, revelations, fulfillments.

Equus (1977, Sidney Lumet)

Peter Shaffer's 1973 play *Equus* had been a tremendous success in London at the National Theatre, had been hailed in New York even before it arrived for its middle-seriousness, and had then opened in the City to praise and profits. It's probably still being revived somewhere in the United States. What bothered me was not the play's success—success or failure is not my professional interest—but its ecstatic critical reception. Like all serious critics, I remain naïve in at least one respect: I can never reconcile myself to the fact that inferior work often gets high praise. (I've never known a serious critic who was truly cynical in this regard. The good ones are outraged by bad criticism the thousandth time as much as the first time.)

At least Sidney Lumet's film of *Equus* (1977) exposes the play for the artistic mediocrity—or less—that it is. I had no clue at the time as to whether the film would be a commercial success (it was not), but I risked one prediction: the film would impose less than the play. The acting, even Sidney Lumet's direction, might be praised, but the dubiousness of the material would be more apparent. And this drew me to think of past occasions when transposition to film had been like an acid bath revealing the lead in allegedly golden plays—Arthur Miller's *Death of a Salesman* (1949; filmed 1951, Laszlo Benedek) and Arthur Kopit's *Indians* (1968; filmed 1976 as *Buffalo Bill and the Indians*, Robert Altman) are only two examples—and then to explore why this happens.

I don't mean plays that make bad films because they're badly filmed: Terrence McNally's *The Ritz* (1975; filmed 1976, Richard Lester), for one, is a better-than-average farce, but its better-than-average film director, Richard Lester, didn't know how to handle stage material. I mean plays that make bad or lesser films because they are bad or lesser plays; I'm talking about the way in which film form searches out flabbiness and thinness in subject matter that, in the theater, has been thought substantial. Often this is because techniques that seemed impressive in the theater are stripped away or reduced to commonplaces by the very form of film. The time-interweavings in *Salesman*, the heavy-breathing sleight of hand in *Indians*—these are such commonplaces of film discourse that they couldn't possibly aggrandize the material on screen. So, in the cases of Miller and Kopit, the film medium revealed that the content under the wrappings was: (a) separable from the wrappings, which in good art would not be the case; (b) less than it had seemed when wrapped.

In *Equus* on the stage, the central metaphor was a boxing ring, into which the actors for each scene stepped from the sidelines. The encounters between the psychiatrist and the boy who had blinded six horses were seen as bouts, probably—since the recurrent motif in the doctor's mind is ancient Greece— intended to have some of the flavor of classic pugilism. The horses were represented by six young men in skin-tight costumes with wire-frame horse heads, and all this symbolic accoutrement was necessity-changed-into-device. The boxing ring was a way of theatrical containment and of abstraction. And, since six real horses were somewhat out of the question, the men-as-horses suggested both the sleek physicality of the beasts and the underlay of unacknowledged homosexuality that pervaded the boy's problem.

These devices gave the play, for many, an air of the poetically profound; but these devices were ruled out by the transposition to film. Symbolism has often been used in films and sometimes by masters—Cocteau and Ingmar Bergman come to mind—but usually it has been symbolism conceived in cinematic modes, and it has very rarely been used in expensive pictures aimed at the "massiest" of mass markets. The mass *theater* audience is not only much smaller numerically than the mass film audience, it also begins at a somewhat higher stratum of intellectual-artistic sophistication. (As has often been noted, there is no longer a truly popular theater audience corresponding in kind to the immense broad base of the film audience.) Indeed, the Broadway audience and its counterparts elsewhere rather enjoy, from time to time, a bit of comfy derrière-garde experimentation and non-realism—Michael Cristofer's *The Shadow Box* (1977; filmed 1980, Paul Newman) was a contemporaneous instance. One of the reasons for the success of the play *Equus*, I'm convinced, was its assurance to theater audiences that they had been tested imaginatively—and had passed!

There's none of this in the film version. Not only because the biggest part of the audience would be discomfited by it but also because the film medium itself would be discomfited by it. Nothing is easier to the cinema than to include many places, so the boxing-ring idea would seem artificial. And real horses, easy to manage with cutting and re-takes, push the idea of symbolic horses into the trashcan. Even the most subtle viewer would find these symbols hard to credit in a film. So the film of *Equus* is stripped of its theater paraphernalia.

The script must therefore rearrange the time planes. For the most part we don't get the past as, for the most part, we got it in the play: through the boy's remembering "now" of what happened "then." The film goes to the past in conventional flashback, converting the past into another "now." This makes patent nonsense of what was dreamily disguised nonsense in the play. We see the boy—again, as in the play, well-acted by Peter Firth—behaving moonily and loonily with real horses *before* he commits the atrocities, instead of remembering his past acts moonily and loonily after he commits them. This is to make the boy a very visible clinical case right from his first appearance. He is so immediately weird that his parents seem dense not to notice it, and the girl's sexual interest in him becomes highly bizarre. The film thus changes the play's intended mystery about the boy's violent explosion into a flat inevitability, highly predictable by everyone around.

The film does even worse, in a different way, for the psychiatrist. (He is played by Richard Burton with more to work on than in the contemporaneous *Exorcist II* [1977, John Boorman], but with about equal professional sincerity.) The play's various devices tried to give the doctor at least a base for his own agony—his envy of the boy's passion. In the film the present-tense re-creation of the past makes the doctor's envy, which was clearly silly to some of us in the theater, now glaringly clear. Here is a doctor a great deal sicker than his patient—not deprived of passion but sick. Because what the doctor is envying here, obviously, is not passion but psychosis. And the loading of the medical dice by the author, Peter Shaffer, is much more conspicuous on screen: the boy has been assigned to a doctor who is having a frigid marital life. In the play it was plain enough that if the doctor were happily married, the whole thesis would crumble. In the movie version, the contrivance of choosing just this one doctor seems much clumsier, and the whole jerry-built pseudo-Lawrentian comment on the lack of ecstasy in modern life utterly collapses.

But the film medium reveals the spuriousness in spurious plays by more than the stripping away of theatrical devices. Sometimes a poor play has no such devices: it tries to make its way by conviction of realism. Then we get such films as *The Subject Was Roses* (1968, Ulu Grosbard) and *The Effect of Gamma Rays on Man-in-the-Moon Marigolds* (1972, Paul Newman)—each made from a Pulitzer-Prize-winning play by Frank D. Gilroy (1964) and Paul Zindel (1970), respectively—where what seemed like verisimilitude in the theater shows up as artifice, or mere banality, on screen. The film medium *begins* realer than the theater: it eats such plays for breakfast before it gets down to the day's realistic work. Before the digital era, it would have been like putting a ten-power photograph under a 1,000-power viewer and discovering that the photo was insufficiently microscopic or even touched up. With *Equus*, it isn't a case of beginning with gritty realism. The necessities of film "reduced" the play to realism, and that second-stage realism simply doesn't stand up under the camera. Put another way, if there had never been a play called *Equus*, the film still wouldn't ring true.

What does this mean about the relative truth and value of the two arts as such? Absolutely nothing. Some good plays become good films (*The Homecoming*, 1973, Peter Hall, from Harold Pinter's 1965 play); some good plays become bad films (*Long Day's Journey into Night*, 1962, Sidney Lumet. from Eugene O'Neill's 1941 drama); some bad plays become good films (*Way Down East*, 1920, D. W. Griffith, from the 1897 play by Lottie Blair Parker). About the reverse flow—from film to stage—there's much less to say for the obvious reason that, in historical sequence, the theater has been much more of a source for films than vice versa. The few instances I know of the reverse flow have been deplorable: *Sweet Charity* (1966, Bob Fosse, from Federico Fellini's film *Nights of Cabiria* [1957]), *Sugar* (1972, Gower Champion, from Billy Wilder's film *Some Like It Hot* [1959]), *Rashomon* (1959, Michael Kanin, from Akira Kurosawa's film *Rashomon* [1950]), and *A Little Night Music* (1973, Harold Prince, from Ingmar Bergman's film *Smiles of a Summer Night* [1955]; Prince then adapted his stage version to the screen in 1977). They showed, not surprisingly, that the cinema has its own untranslatable systems of felicities and disguises, that the theater's peculiar strengths can sometimes cripple even a healthy film script. But a trash-detection factor in the theater, analogous to what I've been discussing above, doesn't really apply because I can't think of an original screenplay as poor as the *Equus* film adaptation that has been reworked for the stage.

The aesthetic relations/differences between theater and film aside, a basic duality has increasingly been growing in creative people. Talents coming to maturity these days do not often think of themselves arbitrarily as either playwrights or screenwriters: both arts seem linked, interactive, wonderfully identical, wonderfully different. Even if a writer does choose one or the other, the basic linkage must remain in the twenty-first century. No matter how much a playwright may loathe film, he cannot write for the theater today without awareness of the cinema's effect on vision, rhythm, and realism. No matter how much a screenwriter may disregard the theater, he cannot (if he's serious) disregard what the best modern dramatists have wrought—in strophes of dialogue, surgeries of character, spectrums of imagination. To go back to when this phenomenon began, several decades ago, I can't imagine that Terrence Malick's script for *Badlands* (1973) or Eric Rohmer's scripts for some of his *Moral Tales* (1963-72) would be as they are if Samuel Beckett and the so-called Theater of the Absurd hadn't existed.

So the subject is rosy. And it has really only begun to be cultivated. I describe it here to prevent any misconception about the intent of this piece. I'm not remotely interested in ranking the two arts of drama and cinema. I am interested, and *Equus* brings it up again, in this X-ray detector action of film form on some overrated plays: in showing up the outlines of *papier-mâché* arty décor, in penetrating the surface of superficial realism. The film of *Equus* may have failed at the box office for other reasons, but the adaptation surely showed a lot of people that there is less in the work than met the theater audience's eye.

The Elephant Man (1980, David Lynch)

The first minute of the film of *The Elephant Man* (1980) is awful. So it's a surprise that the next half hour or so is pretty good. But the rest of the picture is almost as bad as the opening.

That first minute shows us, mistily, John Merrick's mother being frightened by an elephant when she was pregnant. As an explanation of her son's disfigurement—which *he* believes—it's scientifically loony, and, as cinema, it's ludicrous. Then, for a while, the camera of Freddie Francis, guided by the director David Lynch, gives us a "breather": the dank brick of Victorian London is depicted so graphically that we feel rubbed against it. (Francis and Lynch clearly studied Victorian photographs carefully, and the result is that, properly, the whole film is in black and white.)

Through this section, the screenplay by Christopher De Vore, Eric Bergren, and Lynch is laying out its ground vividly enough; but when it wants to swing into action, it doesn't. It repeats and drags, seems only tenuously impelled by an idea, and is written in flabby language. Indeed, the screenplay's dialogue has no flavor at all: it's merely loose or misdirected talk. In the film of *The Elephant Man*, you can hear "contact" used as a verb in 1884. There's also a reference to the "London *Times*"—in London. And the visits of the star actress, Mrs. (Madge) Kendal, to Merrick, which in the play were at least theatrically effective, are stupid—especially once Anne Bancroft, as Mrs. Kendal, opens her mouth. (Bancroft sounds as if she's just come right off the Bronx subway, and there's no way to explain this except to reveal that her husband, Mel Brooks, was one of the movie's backers.)

The script of Lynch's *Elephant Man* is not based on Bernard Pomerance's now well-known, 1977 play of the same name; both works, however, are derived from the same factual sources: *The Elephant Man and Other Reminiscences* (1923), by Frederick Treves, and *The Elephant Man: A Study in Human Dignity* (1971), by Ashley Montagu. The play of *The Elephant Man*, I continue to think, has merit, despite some patness in arrangement and imbalance in structure. (The real drama is in Treves, the doctor, not in Merrick, who is only a victim without possibilities; but Merrick is so much more eye-catching, especially on screen, that Treves fades.) Some of that merit derives from the playwright's use of deft ellipses and neat irony—for instance, in Merrick's building of a model of the church across the way; and much of Pomerance's dialogue, despite occasional sogginess, is astringent, tart, suggestive.

The play, well or less well, grapples with an immense theme: the arbitrariness of life, its lack of design or reason, posed against what we are capable of expecting. Man's great blessing—or curse—the gift of logic, thus keeps ramming into the illogic of human existence. Lynch's film, nebulously, barely visibly, is about a lesser but good idea: man's fear of that arbitrariness, a fear that can take derisive, "scientific," or sanctimonious form. Treves gets professional status, for example, by discovering and exhibiting Merrick, and Treves's hospital gets renown by sheltering the Elephant Man. Society, even royalty, brings gifts to the patient and feels noble about it. By contrast, the night porter at Merrick's hospital sells places to pub pals to peer at the Elephant Man. (The direction in those scenes is dreadfully heavy-handed.) All these are ways of gaping in fear at a gap in the design of existence. But this theme is not cultivated and harvested. After it's set, it's just reiterated over and over until the fact of iteration obscures it. (And what was the significance of all that smoke issuing from factories and trains and steamers? Is *any* visual motif a valid theme these days? How about Merrick's building of the church model? Why was it left to become just another hobby on his part?)

John Hurt, behind a swollen helmet of makeup, does as well as possible in the title role, though his inflections are a bit subtle for a man who has spoken so little. Pomerance's play deals better with both face and voice. The stage Merrick wears no makeup at all: he contorts his body to suggest disfigurement. Thus we avoid getting used to the horror, and thus, symbolically, we can accept Merrick's supple discourse as being derived from its flip side—intractable grotesqueness. In the film he could not be barefaced: the camera leaves no room for that kind of imagining; yet his lumpy, twisted head soon becomes just one more horror-flick getup, and the drawing-room dialogue issuing from his mouth begins to take on an air of the faintly comic.

What the film of *The Elephant Man* proves, I think, is that this idea really belongs in the theater—where, in fact, it had already found a home.

The Crucible (1996, Nicholas Hytner)

"At a moment when we are all being 'investigated,' or imagining that we shall be, it is vastly disturbing to see indignant images of investigation on the other side of the footlights" (Miller, *Crucible*: 204). So wrote Eric Bentley in February of

1953, reviewing Arthur Miller's *The Crucible* (1953) in *The New Republic*. Bentley's widely discussed review then commented on the play's implied parallel between the communist witch-hunt in the early 1950s and the Salem witch-hunt in 1692:

> [The parallel] is true in that people today are being persecuted on quite chimerical grounds. It is untrue in that communism is not, to put it mildly, merely a chimera. (Miller, 1996: 205)

The above criticism is still haunting Miller. In a 1996 *New Yorker* article about the writing of *The Crucible*, a moving article generally, he refers to this point (without mentioning Bentley) and replies that the existence of witches, in the seventeenth century, "was never questioned by the loftiest minds in Europe and America" (Frankel, 45). But this is no reply: neither Bentley nor anyone else had questioned that witchcraft was taken seriously in 1692. The real objection was that McCarthyism, as Miller certifies in his article, was what spurred him to write his play and that the analogy with the Salem witch-hunt was specious.

Paradoxically, this forty-year-old argument was all the more interesting in 1996 because, at that moment, it was irrelevant. (The argument is highly relevant today, in 2022, as the Democratic Party of the United States continues what former President Donald Trump calls its witch-hunt against him and a number of his high-level supporters.) Presented as a film in that year, *The Crucible* was actually helped by the fact that no topical analogy applied. (Diabolist circles don't signify politically.) With no need to weather the political-analogy test, freed too of the gratitude of a 1950s audience hungry for anti-McCarthyism, the play stands on its own and is better for it. I shall now look at it from this 1996 perspective rather than from the vantage point of 2022.

John Proctor is a farmer in the Massachusetts colony; he and his wife, Elizabeth, have two sons. (Reduced, for some reason, from the three sons in the play.) Some months before the start, Elizabeth had discharged their maid, Abigail Williams, because she thought—justly—that something sexual was brewing between her husband and the maid. Now Abigail, living with her clergyman uncle, dances at night in the woods with other girls her age, eighteen or so, more to vent sexual steam than anything else. They are discovered by her uncle, who is enraged. This turmoil leads to brief hysterical paralysis in two of the girls, and this in turn leads to charges that they have been bewitched. Accusations of witchcraft increase.

After a chain of connections, Abigail sees a way, through more accusations of witchcraft, to get rid of Elizabeth so that she can have John. She doesn't see that John, too, will be involved. A cloudburst of panic breaks over the village. (Abigail's uncle presses witchcraft charges against some men because he wants to acquire their land.) A prominent judge is brought in, and trials are held, all of them recorded. Eventually nineteen people are hanged as witches, including Proctor. He is given a chance to clear himself by signing a confession— to acts he did not commit. He signs; then, like Joan of Arc, he tears up his confession and chooses death. (Abigail had arranged for him to escape with her; he refused, and she fled alone.)

Miller says that he saw his way into the historical material, as a playwright, when he read in the record about a gesture of Abigail's toward John, a gesture revealing tenderness. Thus the play became possible for him when he saw sex as a motivation for Abigail's charges, to which he added land-greediness in others. (When Jean-Paul Sartre wrote the first screenplay of *The Crucible* in 1957, called *The Witches of Salem* [Raymond Borderie], he saw the drama baldly as class war.) No one can quarrel with the possible truth of Miller's interpretation, but it's noteworthy that he couldn't envision his play until he saw it in sexual and material terms, which were not at all the supernatural terms in which the colonists and those "loftiest minds" saw the matter.

Besides these mundane reductions of motive, there are other points to consider. Once the characters are arranged in relation to one another, we simply watch the play unfold predictably. Of course this is also true of great tragedy, but *The Crucible*, as it moves along, seems more the fulfillment of an author's pattern than the grinding of an inexorable fate. And in that pattern there is a gap. Abigail, the Iago of the piece, runs away. And Miller does not follow; he merely drops her when he has no further need of her—not exactly a Shakespearean tactic. Still, this is the best Arthur Miller work that I know.

First, the dialogue. In Miller's modern plays, the dialogue sometimes sounds like squeaky shoes, stiff, uncomfortable. His writing seems much more at ease, more easily figurative and less dragooned into poetry, in the formalities of the seventeenth century. (Miller acknowledges the help of a poet friend with the dialogue.) As for the wholeness of *The Crucible*, there's no point in comparing it with such moribundities as *After the Fall* (1964), *Incident at Vichy* (1964), *The Price* (1968), *The American Clock* (1980), or *Broken Glass* (1994). The two comparable works are *A View from the Bridge* (1955) and *Death of a Salesman* (1949). But the former is ultimately a bit of police news decked out with tragic garlands; and the latter does not, as it claims, dramatize the fall of a man, under worldly pressures, into self-delusion. Willy Loman is deluded from the beginning.

Unlike *A View from the Bridge* and *Death of a Salesman*, *The Crucible* has sinew. Despite Miller's compression of the metaphysical theme into sweaty contrivings, this is the play of his that comes closest to naked, ancient drama. Decades after it was written, shorn of contemporary "utility," the play stands a bit taller, especially toward the end (in Act IV), where Proctor must make his gaunt choice. When he rips up his false and cowardly confession, thus choosing the gallows, his wife, weeping, throws herself on him. He looks at the judges and says: "Give them no tear. Show honor now, show a stony heart and sink them with it" (Miller, *Crucible*: 144).

Miller made his own screen adaptation and, considerably experienced in this work, did it deftly. He has pruned his play for the sake of cinematic movement and expanded it for the same reason. (For instance, to let us see the girls dancing in the woods.) I don't understand why John and Elizabeth have their last private conversation on a beach, with the jailers a hundred yards away, when all they had wanted was to be alone; and I much prefer the way the drama ends, with Elizabeth's closing lines after John leaves ("He have his goodness now. God forbid I take it from him!" [Miller, *Crucible*: 145]), to the film's finish on the gallows. But Miller has clearly had a fresh look at his work and has restructured *The Crucible* as if he had conceived it for the screen; he hasn't been content to saw up his play and re-tack it together.

15

Nicholas Hytner, the director, is less limber here than he was with the earlier *Madness of King George* (1994). Once in a while he indulges in stage "pictures" rather than film flow; and once in a while he misses the center of the action. Early on, when one of the pseudo-paralyzed girls sits up, she is just discernible at the bottom left corner of the screen. Hytner also "missed" the music, which is characterized by many tympani and therefore much heaviness. The score he commissioned from George Fenton sounds as if the composer had been listening to Leonard Bernstein's score for *On the Waterfront* (1954, Elia Kazan)—another allegorical work about communist witch-hunts.

Miraculously, however, Hytner has evoked something like a performance from Winona Ryder as Abigail. She doesn't reveal a burning talent, but at least here she is not the star of a college show. Daniel Day-Lewis, as Proctor, gets better the less he has to be a believable farmer and the more he becomes the protagonist of a moral drama. Joan Allen, who at the time was Mrs. Nixon in *Nixon* (1995, Oliver Stone), has always been a rather cool actress, so the part of Elizabeth Proctor fits her. Paul Scofield is the senior judge and speaks his lines adequately. Scofield is of course a highly accomplished actor, but in some roles he does little more than burnish his lines carefully and serve them up on the silver salver of his experience: no bother about creating a man behind the lines. That's what Scofield did as the King of France in Kenneth Branagh's *Henry V* (1989), and that's what he does here. He gets away with it; the film itself does better.

Miss Julie (1999, Mike Figgis)

It would have been odd to predict good work from Mike Figgis. To wit: in the 1990s, this British director was best known in the United States for *Stormy Monday* (1988), an imitation American gangster flick set in a small English city, and *Leaving Las Vegas* (1995), a contraption in which an alcoholic man and a hooker find sudsy bliss together. Certainly, Figgis is not a man from whom we would have expected a film of August Strindberg's *Miss Julie*—at all. Or that it would turn out to be (even) as good as it is. Surprises are not often pleasant in the film world, yet, in 1999, Figgis served up a double pleasure.

Comment on any production of this play must start with the cast. Either the two principals are excellent, or the enterprise is doomed. Figgis has cast those two roles superbly, with two British actors little-known in the United States. Saffron Burrows is Julie and has precisely the face and temperament that the role needs, a beauty that promises trouble—for herself as well as others. When she sweeps in, the moody, tyrannical, teasing daughter of a nineteenth-century Swedish count, she brings an immediate air of class that is both her weapon and her prison, along with a sexual drive that we can almost hear seething. The best Julie I had previously seen (I think, since I was a teenager at the time) was the Swedish actress Inga Tidblad, who came to New York with the Royal Dramatic Theatre of Stockholm in 1962 and scintillated in the role (as directed by Alf Sjöberg), though she was sixty-one at the time. Burrows, in her twenties, as she would have to be on screen, plunges just as daringly into the middle of the storm and swirls through it to the play's catastrophe.

Peter Mullan is the count's valet, Jean. (Strindberg gives this Swedish servant a French name to mark him as a man who is all too well aware of his class and is unquiet in it.) The best Jean I had previously seen was Christopher Walken, in 1973 at the Long Wharf Theatre in New Haven. Mullan, though quite dissimilar in timbre, matches Walken in tacit, smoldering strength and insolent competence. One not-so-minor point: Mullan is shorter than Burrows. Figgis thus deliberately defies the theater-film convention that a man must be taller than the woman who plays opposite him. Yet with a grim blend of reserve and drive, Mullan towers.

The third character, Christine, the cook who has been Jean's lover, is played by Maria Doyle Kennedy, a quite competent actress who doesn't quite fit. Kennedy, fine-featured, looks more like a cousin of Miss Julie than the earthy working-class woman that Strindberg presumably had in mind as contrast to her mistress. But Christine is a lesser role: the excellence of the two chief actors propels the drama.

Strindberg's play, in one long act, was written in 1888. (Why the opening legend moves the film ahead to 1894 is a mystery.) It is set in the large kitchen of the count's country residence on Midsummer Eve, an annual festival of song and dance with a smack in it of pre-Christian fertility rites. In the celebration outside, the twenty-five-year-old Julie has been dancing with the thirty-year-old Jean. Her excitement and heat drive her to follow him into the kitchen, where he has withdrawn to avoid the trouble he senses may come from her. In the first section of the play, the two of them play their class roles, but they also frivol and flirt, and quarrel and reminisce, and thus draw closer to each other. When the servants are heard approaching with song and dance—salacious in tone—Jean takes Julie into his bedroom to avoid the others. There the pair make love. (In the film, the place where it happens is less luxe than a bed.)

After the servants leave the kitchen and the lovers return, the play explodes in lightning ashes of harmony and quarrel, of possibly feeling together abroad, of some disgust in each for the other, of pity, of despair, of perception of the bleak future—at least for Julie. At the end, exhausted, hollowed, she asks Jean to order her what to do. She knows what he will say. With cool, god-like dispensation, he hands her his razor, and she goes to her suicide. Some years ago a theater director who was planning to produce *Miss Julie* told me that his basic underlying design was to have Julie consciously-unconsciously headed for that razor from the moment that she first enters in high spirits. This, of course, is the quintessence of the tragedy.

In his epochal foreword to *Miss Julie*, Strindberg explains his view of characterization in the play: he maintains that contradictions and variations, rather than consistencies, are the core of human behavior. Though he was hardly the first dramatist to perceive it, his use of this truth advances the play through its reality more than its plot. This makes it a groundbreaking work, formally as well as characterologically. Eric Bentley says of *Miss Julie* that Strindberg "destroyed the French 'well-made' play that had been the technical basis of later Ibsenism" (Bentley, 61). Henrik Ibsen's *A Doll House* (1879) and *Hedda Gabler* (1890), though revolutionary in idea and intent, are molded in popular theater structures of the day; *Miss Julie* is not. The Strindberg scholar Evert Sprinchorn writes: "Whereas Ibsen's plays are all exposition, *Miss Julie* is all climax and catastrophe" (Sprinchorn, 36). Thus the play's very organism becomes part of what it is about.

What it is about, at its very base, is history. The transgression of class boundaries occurs here as much because of the century in which Julie and Jean live as because of their present actions. Without in the least being mere signet figures, they arise out of a Europe roiling after 1848. And as part of its historical relevance, this pre-Freud play is startling in its sexual insights. (Not incidentally, it is the first play I know of that mentions menstruation.) We hear about Julie's games with a whip that she played with her former fiancé, her dream of being atop a pillar, Jean's boyhood escape from the count's garden through an outhouse, his childhood sense of filth in relation to Julie's purity, his revenge for his pollution—which is what we witness. All these elements can be found in the Freudian index.

Helen Cooper, who wrote the screen adaptation of *Miss Julie* from a translation that she had done for theater production, obviously understands all these matters. She has tried to sustain them, but by her rearrangement and condensation—for cinematic fluency, as she saw it—she has hobbled them somewhat. (I remember being bothered by Sjöberg's 1951 film of the play, as well.) Cooper's version moves the action outside once in a while; further, she— or Figgis—includes a number of fades to black, apparently to denote brief passages of time. But this is precisely what Strindberg did not want—time-lapses or shifts of locale to divert the play from its dynamics. *Miss Julie* takes place, except for the offstage sex, in one room and in real time: interruptions and rearrangements interfere with its almost Sophoclean wholeness.

The very existence of this film involves a collision of two arts, much more jarring than with most films of great plays. The difference is as much phenomenological as aesthetic. In the theater, part of the play's power is that it happens in the real time that passes for us, too, as we are sitting there. This not only gives the play a temporal shape, it heightens the *agon* of Jean and Julie, for we see them going through it minute by minute. But any film, we know, is made over a period of time. Even if Figgis's picture was done in weeks, instead of the usual months, on screen it was still performed in distended time; and the fade-outs only increase our awareness of this fact. To see a good performance of the play is, in an almost literal sense, to endure it—for an hour and a half. This experience is intrinsically impossible with a film because we know that it is composed of scenes shot over many days. And this fact detracts, too, from the effect of the acting, as compared with theatrical performance. At the finish of a stage production of *Miss Julie*, the actors seem almost heroic for having passed through the fire—continuously—before our eyes. This precise effect is not achievable in a film.

Figgis does all he can do, and it is a lot, to controvert this ineluctable fact. With the lithe and darting camera of Benoît Delhomme, he keeps close to his people, pressing us against them so often and so intensely that we seem to feel their bodies and breath. (Figgis did some of the shooting himself, and he did all the music [which is apt and helpful] for *Miss Julie*—even as he has composed the score for some of his previous films.) Throughout, we sense that Figgis wants to beat his film's innate handicap, to give it a victory over its sensory difference from the theater. Yet for all his fervor, for all the fine acting he has evoked, when the picture is done, we miss the arc, the trajectory, of the play. It would have been pretty lame to nail the camera down and perform Strindberg's whole drama in

18

front of it, but a cinematic adaptation of this particular work seems like the old sci-fi device of trying to transfer a soul from one body to another.

The Cherry Orchard (1999, Michael Cacoyannis) & The Sea Gull (1968, Sidney Lumet)

All great plays suffer in some measure when adapted for film, because they are great plays—because they are *already* great—but Anton Chekhov's plays suffer more than most. Of all great dramatists, Chekhov is one of the least amenable to screen adaptation. He often seems to be one of the easiest: he seems so modern, in many ways so immediate. But in terms of form and concept, he is more distant from cinema than many other dramatists, even some earlier ones.

Michael Cacoyannis undertook the Chekhovian transfer with *The Cherry Orchard* in 1999. This Greek director had been absent from the screen and the American stage for many years, but long ago he did much honorable work: films in Greece (*Stella* [1955], *A Girl in Black* [1956]), Greek classics Off-Broadway, the movie of *Zorba the Greek* (1964), ancient Greek adaptations (*Electra* [1962], *The Trojan Women* [1971], *Iphigenia* [1977]), and more. One might think that if a Chekhov play was to be filmed, Cacoyannis (in his seventies at the time) was as likely an adapter-director as could be. But Chekhov resists, simply by being what he is—a unique dramatist.

The largest difficulty with *The Cherry Orchard* (1904) is that, like all this dramatist's major plays, it was conceived in four acts. Such an arrangement is not, for Chekhov, a typographical matter or a theater convenience: it is absolutely integral to his work. Most plays are written in acts that the author uses as building blocks; only a few playwrights conceive those acts doubly—as building blocks, certainly, but also as entities in themselves, burnished and whole, even though they are parts of a larger work. For Chekhov, to whom form is not constraint but beauty, the theater presented the chance to create a work in separate yet cumulative entities. For such authors—Chekhov prime among them—the acts of a play are like movements of a symphony, whole in themselves yet cumulative. *The Cherry Orchard* is not divided into four acts: it is an organism built of four related organisms. "The structure of each act," says Francis Fergusson, "is based upon a more or less ceremonious social occasion" (Fergusson, 177). Each of those occasions is the armature of the act, separate from but preceding or following other social occasions.

A film cannot solve this four-act problem merely by inserting three intermissions along the way, because the film adapters usually feel there must be rearrangements of the material and interpolations. The result, as in this *Cherry Orchard*, is like playing a symphony with its four movements intermingled a bit and with some riffs added. For me, the only truly successful film of a Chekhov play is Louis Malle's *Vanya on 42nd Street* (1994). This is not only because Malle filmed a theater production of *Uncle Vanya* (1898) that André Gregory and his ensemble had been working on for the previous five years—yes, five years—but because Malle's film is not an adaptation. It is Gregory's theater production dexterously photographed, with the play's architecture emphasized by brief intermissions. Free of the stilting that theater-on-film often entails, Chekhov's play, as a play, courses through a film channel; and the result is transfiguring.

Malle's comprehension of form gives his film of *Vanya* a rare depth: it enters the most profound mystery of Chekhov, which is open to good theater production of his plays but eludes most films of them. Three elements compose this mystery. First, there is what we see and hear, the action—life as it flows before us, in all its currents and colors. This flow discloses the subtext beneath the action, the large theme or themes of the play. And beyond that subtext, we come to a stillness, absolute stillness. The text and the subtext, as sculpted in four sections by the author, ultimately lead to a quiet at the center of the whirlpool, a halting of breath, an immobile purity, a fixing of melancholy, a whisper of mortality. Without the shape of the play as Chekhov shaped it, this stillness is out of reach.

In *The Cherry Orchard*, he used a unique device to emphasize this stillness. In Act II, most of the characters are lounging in a meadow at the edge of the orchard. They fall comfortably silent. Here is Chekhov's next stage direction, in Ann Dunnigan's translation: "All sit lost in thought. . . . Suddenly a distant sound is heard, as if from the sky, like the sound of a snapped string mournfully dying away" (Chekhov, 1739). They all wonder what that sound was: several of them guess at it. (Cacoyannis doesn't use a snapped string: he puts in a distant rumble like a jet plane high above, so the various guesses don't remotely apply.) For me, that distant sound, never really explained, is Chekhov's means of underscoring the play's central stillness—not the momentary silence of these characters but the play's crystalline core. Since Cacoyannis's film is never near this core, that mysterious sound underscores nothing and is irrelevant.

Quite in disregard of Chekhov's design, this adaptation of *The Cherry Orchard* frequently bows to the supposed gods of screen adaptation. In the first instance, though the play is utterly Russian—about the sale of an estate in Russia and the complex meanings of that sale—the film begins in Paris. Anya, the daughter of Madame Ranyevskaya, the estate's owner, has gone there to bring her extravagant mother home. In Act I of the play itself, all of which takes place on the estate, Anya tells us that she made this trip; but Cacoyannis "opens up" the play by beginning in Paris. This attempted flexing into cinematic form breaches the enclosure of place, of specific place, that Chekhov intended. (Theatrically speaking, it also injures Ranyevskaya's entrance. In the film we see her sitting in her Paris attic, amid friends, placid. In the play we first see her returning to her home after a five-year absence, savoring her return both truthfully and histrionically.) Such an alteration also ignores a basic aesthetic difference between film and theater. Film ventures forth, finding and following action. In the theater, the action arrives: the theater does not go looking for it. For Chekhov, this theater principle is essential.

Here's another instance of ill adaptation in the film of *The Cherry Orchard*. In Act III, as Chekhov planned it, Madame Ranyevskaya is giving a party that she can ill afford, at the same time that elsewhere her estate is being put up at auction. Again Cacoyannis cannot resist the temptation to cinematize: he intercuts these simultaneous events. Thus the quasi-suicidal bustle of the party is interrupted, and when the affluent peasant Lopahin breaks into the party to announce that he has bought the place, the impact of his announcement is diminished.

A paradox, an additional pity, clings to Cacoyannis's film: most of the actors are exceptionally good. Charlotte Rampling, at the time blossoming in mid-career, decks Ranyevskaya with nobility and with a profligacy that belongs to the past. Alan Bates, another actor who kept growing, plays Gayev, her lazy, endearing brother, dispensing elegance and kindly imperception. Katrin Cartlidge, as Ranyevskaya's adopted daughter Varya, gives tacit pain to a frustrated marriage. As the student Trofimov, who came to the estate to tutor Ranyevskaya's son and stays around after the boy's death, Andrew Howard amply provides the fire with which his character sees the future. Owen Teale is Lopahin, the peasant who was not even allowed in the kitchen when he was a boy and who now owns the place. The tearful-joyful outburst in which he announces his purchase is one of the pinnacles of dramatic literature; Teale almost attains it. (My measure of Lopahin is James Earl Jones, who was superb in an all-black production of the play [also directed by Jones] in New York in 1972.) Of the capable others, I note only Michael Gough, who, after being the valet in *Batman* (1989, Tim Burton), turns up here as another valet, doddering old Firs, who is forgotten at the end when everyone else moves on.

With this cast and even with this adaptation, Cacoyannis could have done better. Chekhov called *The Cherry Orchard* a comedy—in my view, he insisted on this point because, fearing the slow and mournful tempo he knew Stanislavsky (the director of the premiere) would try to achieve, he wanted to prod him to keep things moving. With Cacoyannis, the phrase "slow and mournful" is almost vivacious. The pauses, the slow pick-up of cues, are examples of what is often assumed to be Chekhovian style but is only a facile dolor that hurts the work's true gravity.

I must add that the difficulties mentioned above apply only to Chekhov's plays. His stories, for formal reasons, are much more congenial to the screen. One of the most beautiful films that I know is Josef Heifitz's adaptation of *The Lady with the Dog*, made in the Soviet Union in 1959. I should say that "I knew," though I obviously can still see Heifitz's film today on a television screen, even on a digital, wide-screen, high-definition TV. I don't think, however, that the likes of such a film (adaptation though it may be) will appear again in anybody's neighborhood, university, or art-house cinema any time soon. For cinephilia as we once knew it, during the Golden Age of Cinema, began decaying in the late 1990s (and may now in fact be dead)—precisely when Cacoyannis's *The Cherry Orchard*, about decay and death of another kind, was made.

The 1968 film adaptation of *The Sea Gull* is another, worse matter. From the very first moment , it's clear that Sidney Lumet doesn't know what to do with Anton Chekhov's 1896 play and so is going to do lots and lots of things. Long shots of scenery, followed by a girl—presumably Nina—galloping a horse on the other side of the lake. Insecure, irrelevant, just pretty stuff. Then, in utter distortion of the play, we see Masha and Medvedenko in a little sexual tussle on the grass. Somehow they manage to slide from this tussle into the somber opening lines of the play, and we are off. Far off. Lumet apparently wanted to make his outdoor scenes Beautiful. (This time he's imitating *Elvira Madigan* [1967, Bo Widerberg].) Mostly he makes them look like indoor sets. And the post-recording of the outdoor scenes has a dead, studio sound.

Lumet's furiously energetic, tin cleverness would be partially redressed if the performances were good. They are not. As Madame Arkadina, Simone Signoret (peace to the ashes of her earlier self) is ludicrous, a plump lady who cannot speak English and who, in close-up, looks like a badly painted clown.

James Mason, at his most profound, makes Trigorin sound merely peevish. Harry Andrews, as Sorin, barks as if he were still at the Battle of Balaclava in *The Charge of the Light Brigade* (1968, Tony Richardson). David Warner, the Treplev, continues to mistake biliousness for sensitivity. Denholm Elliott is unfocused as Dorn (and is atrociously wigged). Kathleen Widdoes and Alfred Lynch, as Masha and Medvedenko, are acceptable. Ronald Radd, as her father, is not.

The major disappointment is Vanessa Redgrave's Nina. I had read of her in the part on the London stage in the early 1960s and looked forward to seeing her in this picture. But by 1968 she was too old to play Nina—on film, at any rate. Redgrave has the technique and range to cope with what few modern actresses could manage: the high-flying play-within-a-play in *The Sea Gull*. And her confession to Treplev of her love for Trigorin, after what the latter has done to her, is moving. But most of the time I felt that she was trying for the girlishness, the *newness*, of Nina, and the strain seemed to unsettle her.

The poor performances, combined with Lumet's defective rhythmic sense and camerawork (cinematographer: Gerry Fisher), make the film tedious. As Cacoyannis showed three decades later, this isn't hard with Chekhov, who is far from actor-proof even on the stage—where he belongs; but it makes this film dislocation all the more gratuitous.

For a last treat Lumet distorts the ending. Dorn discovers Treplev's body outside, then he returns to the group sitting about the table. The camera moves slowly from face to face as everyone's unspoken knowledge of the tragedy is implied. Chekhov wanted only a moment of apprehension as Dorn goes out to investigate the noise; when he returns and lies about the cause, the triviality of the lotto game is to continue, while Dorn takes Trigorin aside and tells him quietly what has happened. Lumet gives us a general Great Realization. Chekhov wanted life resumed with the fact of death slipped in on the periphery. But since Lumet began with a distortion, why shouldn't he end with one?

Chekhov, anyone? (*Sans* Lumet, *sans* Cacoyannis, *sans* cinema.)

Works Cited

Bentley, Eric. *The Playwright as Thinker*. 1946. Minneapolis: University of Minnesota Press, 2010.

Chekhov, Anton. *The Cherry Orchard*. Trans. Ann Dunnigan. In *Understanding Literature: An Introduction to Reading and Writing*. Ed. Walter Kalaidjian, Judith Roof, & Stephen Watt. Boston: Houghton, Mifflin, 2004. 1720-1760.

Fergusson, Francis. *The Idea of a Theater: A Study of Ten Plays*. Garden City, N.Y.: Doubleday, 1949.

Frankel, Benjamin. *History in Dispute: The Red Scare after 1945*. Detroit: St. James Press, 2004.

Genet, Jean. *The Balcony*. Trans. Bernard Frechtman. 1958. New York: Grove Press, 1966.

Kauffmann, Stanley. "The Film Generation." In Kauffmann's *A World on Film: Criticism and Comment*. New York: Harper & Row, 1966. 415-428.

Miller, Arthur. *The Crucible*: Text and Criticism. Ed. Gerald Weales. 1971. New York: Penguin, 1996.

----------. "Why I Wrote *The Crucible*." *New Yorker* 72.3726 (Oct. 21 & 28, 1996): 158-160, 162-164.

Sprinchorn, Evert. *Strindberg as Dramatist*. New Haven, Conn.: Yale University Press, 1982.

"Drama into Film and Filmic Drama: The Cases of *The Little Foxes*, *Betrayal*, and *Edmond*"

The films discussed in the following essay are William Wyler's *The Little Foxes* (1941), from the 1939 play by Lillian Hellman; David Jones's *Betrayal* (1983), from the 1978 play by Harold Pinter; and Stuart Gordon's *Edmond* (2005), from the 1982 play by David Mamet.

The Little Foxes (1941, William Wyler)

One film that respects its dramatic source almost completely and is nevertheless cinematic is William Wyler's *The Little Foxes* (1941). Lillian Hellman's play from 1939 has undergone nearly no adaptation: for instance, there are no exterior scenes of dramatic action in the film—precisely the kind of scene, I have been arguing, that most directors would have deemed necessary in order to introduce a little "cinema" into this intractable theatrical mass.

The majority of the action in Wyler's film takes place on the same, totally neutral set, the ground-floor living room of a huge colonial house. At the back, a staircase leads to the second-floor bedrooms of Regina and Horace Giddens, which adjoin each other. (Regina and Horace are played by Bette Davis and Herbert Marshall respectively, and I shall use the actors' names in my discussion of the film version.) Nothing picturesque adds to the realism of this somber place, which is as impersonal as the setting of classical tragedy. The characters have a credible, if conventional, reason for confronting one another in the living room, whether they come from the outdoors or from their bedrooms; they can also plausibly linger in the living room. The staircase at the back plays a role similar to the one it would in the theater: it is purely an element of dramatic architecture, which in this case will be used to set off the characters in the vertical space of the frame. Let's look at the central scene of the film, the death of Herbert Marshall, which happens to take place in the living room and on the staircase. An analysis of this scene will reveal that to be cinematic a film adaptation not only doesn't have to go outdoors, it also doesn't have to feature either a mobile camera or lots of cutting.

First let me summarize the action of *The Little Foxes* up to and just beyond this point, which occurs toward the end. We are in the South at the turn of the century, where and when middle-class capitalism-cum-materialism has more than begun to eclipse aristocratic feudalism-cum-agrarianism. Two brothers, Ben and Oscar Hubbard, believe they can make a fortune by establishing the first mill in their town, which is surrounded by cotton plantations. Lacking the $75,000 needed for the venture, they seek the partnership of their sister, Regina Giddens, who, eager to share in the profits, promises to get the money from her wealthy husband, Horace, president of the local bank. Having just been brought home from the hospital in Baltimore by his devoted daughter, Alexandra, Horace has only a short time to live and refuses to become involved. Therefore, to help his father, Oscar's son, Lee, a clerk in Horace's bank, steals $80,000 in bonds from Horace's safe-deposit box, on the assumption that his uncle will not check the box for six months; and Ben and Oscar complete their business deal. Horace discovers the theft but tells Regina that he will not prosecute her brothers. On the contrary, he will call the theft a loan and make a new will in which Regina will receive only $80,000 in bonds, the exact amount of the theft. Thus Regina will share neither in her husband's fortune nor in the fortune the mill will make. While the two quarrel, Horace suffers a heart attack, but Regina refuses to administer a reviving drug and cold-bloodedly stands by as he dies. With her knowledge of the theft, she then blackmails her brothers into assigning her a 75% interest in the mill, lest she prosecute them. Our scene is the quarrel between Regina and Horace, or, to switch back to the actor's names, between Bette Davis and Herbert Marshall, who has revealed to her the theft of his bonds.

Bette Davis is sitting in the middle ground facing the viewer, her head at the center of the screen; the lighting enhances the brightness of her heavily made-up face. In the foreground Herbert Marshall sits in three-quarter profile. The ruthless exchanges between husband and wife take place without any cutting from one character to the other, since the very positions of Davis and Marshall emphasize their separation and antagonism. Then comes the husband's heart attack, during which he begs his wife to get him his medicine from upstairs. From this instant all the drama in this scene derives from the immobility of both Bette Davis and the camera. Marshall is forced to stand up and go get the medicine himself, and this effort will kill him as he climbs the first few steps of the staircase.

In the theater, this scene would most likely have been staged in the same manner. A spotlight could have been focused on Bette Davis, and the spectator would have felt the same horror at her criminal inaction, the same anguish at the sight of her staggering victim. Yet, despite appearances, William Wyler's directing makes as extensive use as possible of the means offered him by the camera and the frame. Bette Davis' position at the center of the screen endows her with privilege and power in the geometry of the dramatic space. The whole scene revolves around her, but her frightening immobility takes its full impact only from Marshall's double exit from the frame, first in the foreground on the right, then in the mid-background on the left. Instead of following him in this lateral movement, as any less intelligent director would have done, Wyler's camera remains imperturbably immobile. When Marshall finally enters the frame for a second time and begins to climb the stairs, the cinematographer, Gregg Toland, acting at Wyler's request, is careful not to bring into focus the full depth of the image, so that Marshall's fall on the staircase and his death will not be clearly visible to the viewer. This artificial blurring augments our feeling of anxiety: as if over the shoulder of the dominant Bette Davis, who faces us and has her back toward her husband, we have to discern in the distance the outcome of a drama whose protagonist is nearly escaping us.

This analysis of Marshall's death in *The Little Foxes* clearly reveals how Wyler can make a whole scene revolve around one actor. Bette Davis at the center of the screen is paralyzed, like a hoot owl by a spotlight, and around her the staggering Marshall weaves as a second—this time mobile—pole, whose shift first out of the frame and then into the background, draws with it all the dramatic attention. In addition, this shift creates tremendous suspense because is consists of a double disappearance from the frame, and because the focus on the staircase at the back is imperfect. One can see here how Wyler uses depth of field: as I've indicated, the director elected to have Toland envelop the character of the dying Marshall in a certain haziness, to have his cinematographer, as it were, befog the back of the frame. This was done to create so much anxiety in the viewer that he should almost want to push the immobile Bette Davis aside to have a better look. The dramatic development of this scene does indeed follow that of the dialogue and of the action itself, but the scene's cinematic expression superimposes its own evolution upon the dramatic development: a second action, as it were, that is the very story of the scene from the moment Marshall gets up from his chair to his collapse on the staircase.

We can see here everything that the cinema adds to the means of the theater, and we can also see that, paradoxically, the highest level of cinematic art coincides with the lowest level of *mise-en-scène*. Nothing could better heighten the dramatic power of this scene than the absolute *immobility* of the camera. Its slightest movement, which is a less skillful director would have deemed the right "cinematic" element to introduce, would have decreased the dramatic tension. Furthermore, the camera does not follow the path of the average viewer's eyes by cutting from Bette Davis to the frantic Marshall; instead, it obstructs our vision merely by recording, without full depth of field, the same scene in one continuous take. It is the stationary camera itself, in other words, that organizes the action in terms of the frame and the ideal coordinates of its two-dimensional geometric space. By means of the cinema, William Wyler has mined the artistic depths of this scene at the same time that he has respected its theatrical appearances.

To the real looks the actors would direct at one another on stage, one must add here the virtual "look" of the camera with which our own identifies. Wyler excels in making us sensitive to his camera's gaze. In *Jezebel* (1938), for example, there is the low-angle shot that clearly points the lens directly at Bette Davis's eyes looking down at the white cane that Henry Fonda holds in his hand with the intention of using it. We thus follow the dramatic line between the character and the object much better than we would have if, by the rules of conventional cutting, the camera had shown us the cane from the point of view of Bette Davis herself.

A variation on the same principle: in *The Little Foxes*, in order to make us understand the thoughts of the character who notices the small steel box in which the stolen bonds were locked and whose absence from the box is going to indicate theft, Wyler placed it in the foreground with the camera being this time at eye-level and at the same distance from the box as the eyes of the character. Our eyes no longer meet the character's eyes directly through the beheld object, as in the above-mentioned scene from *Jezebel*, but as if through a mirror. The angle of incidence of our own view of the object is, as it were, equal to the angle of reflection of the character's view, which angle takes us to this person's eyes. In any case, Wyler commands our mental vision according to the rigorous laws of an invisible dramatic optics.

Paradoxically, insofar as Wyler has never attempted to hide the novelistic of theatrical nature of most of his scripts, he has made all the more apparent the cinematic phenomenon in its utmost purity. Not once has the *auteur* of *The Best Years of Our Lives* (1946), *Jezebel*, or *The Little Foxes* said to himself *a priori* that he had to have a "cinematic look"; still, nobody can tell a story in cinematic terms better than he. For him, the action is expressed first by the actor. Like a director in the theater, Wyler conceives of his job of enhancing the action as beginning with the actor. The set and the camera are there only to permit the actor to focus upon himself the maximum dramatic intensity; they are not there to create a meaning unto themselves. Even though Wyler's approach is also that of the theater director, the latter has at his disposal only the very limited means of the stage. He can manipulate his means, but no matter what he does, the text and the actor constitute the essence of theatrical production.

Film, then, is not at all magnified theater on screen, the stage viewed constantly through opera glasses. The size of the image or unity of time has nothing to do with the matter. Cinema begins when the frame of the screen and the placement of the camera are used to enhance the action and the actor. In *The Little Foxes*, Wyler has changed almost nothing of the dramatic text or even of the set: one could say that he limited himself to directing the play in the way that a theater director would have directed it; and, furthermore, that he used the frame of the screen to *conceal* certain parts of the set and used the camera to bring the viewer closer to the action. What actor would not dream of being able to play a scene, immobile on a chair, in front of 5,000 viewers who don't miss the slightest movement of an eye? What theater director would not want the spectator in the worst seat at the back of the house to be able to see clearly the movements of his actors, and to read with ease his intentions at any moment in the action? Wyler didn't choose to do anything other than realize on film the essence of a theatrical *mise-en-scène* that would not use the lights and the set merely to ornament the actor and the text. Nevertheless, there is probably not a single shot in *The Little Foxes* that isn't pure cinema. Indeed, there is a hundred times more cinema, and better cinema at that, in one fixed shot of *The Little Foxes* than in all the exterior traveling shots, in all the natural settings, in all the geographical exoticism, in all the shots of the reverse side of the set, by means of which up to now the screen has ingeniously attempted to make us forget the stage.

Betrayal (1983, David Jones)

I'd now like to treat Harold Pinter's play *Betrayal* (1978) because, along with Pinter's *No Man's Land* (1975) and *Old Times* (1971) and quite unlike Hellman's *The Little Foxes*, it has often been described as "cinematic" in its use of time-jumping or time-eliding strategies more common to film. In this connection, the three plays exhibit some of the impact of Pinter's work as a screenwriter on his playwriting. In fact his movie career has included screen adaptations of some of his plays (*The Caretaker* [1963, Clive Donner] and *The Homecoming* [1973, Peter Hall]), as well as of such novels as Robin Maugham's *The Servant* (1963), Nicholas Mosley's *Accident* (1967), L. P. Hartley's *The Go-Between* (1971), John Fowles's *The French Lieutenant's Woman* (1981), and Ian McEwan's *The Comfort of Strangers* (1990). In the case of each of the novels, Pinter exploited the structural flexibility of film to make a more complex narrative out of a conventional one, or to find an equivalent in film for the book's narrative voice and deployment of time.

The playwright's foremost achievement in this regard is his 1977 adaptation of *A Remembrance of Things Past* (literally, and better, titled *In Search of Lost Time*), Marcel Proust's fictional reminiscence about childhood, love, and sexual awakening. Pinter did the adaptation between his writing of *Old Times* and *No Man's Land*, which, taken together with *Betrayal*, form a trilogy on the nature of memory and the play of time; and, where those works bear the imprint of the dramatist's experience as a film scenarist, so too does Pinter's interest in Proust's novel gain significance in light of his own memory plays, including *Landscape* (1968) and *Silence* (1969). Unfortunately, *The Proust Screenplay*, as it is known, was never filmed, although it was successfully adapted by Pinter for staging at London's National Theatre in 2000.

Among Pinter's screen adaptations, *Betrayal* (1983) is my primary subject, so let me begin with the play itself—a filmic drama that was turned into a dramatic film. *Betrayal* concerns three middle-aged people: Jerry, a London literary agent who is married and a father; Emma, his lover for seven years, an art dealer who is married and a mother; and Robert, Emma's husband and Jerry's best friend from university days, who is a publisher. The story begins at its conclusion, in 1977, and moves backward to its beginning, in 1968. But Pinter doesn't use the reverse-chronological method slavishly, for three of the play's (and the film's) nine scenes occur temporally *after* the scene immediately preceding.

Betrayal opens when Jerry and Emma meet for a drink—again, in 1977; this is the first time they have seen each other in the two years since their affair ended (an affair that included a rented flat for the couple's afternoon meetings). Emma tells Jerry that she and Robert are separating, that they had a long talk the night before, that Robert confessed to a number of affairs and she told him about the long-finished affair with Jerry. (Thus her affair could have no real bearing on the break-up of her marriage.) As the story "progresses" backward, Jerry learns, to his astonishment, that Emma actually had told Robert about the affair four years ago. Robert had thus known about it while continuing his friendship and publishing relationship with Jerry, while remaining married to Emma, and while he had also been busy with his own dalliance (apparently much more casual than his wife's). The last scene is a party in 1968; Jerry, who had been best man at Emma and Robert's wedding, declares his love for her. And, in a long moment of quiet during which she considers the affair we know has occurred, the play ends—or begins.

For me, the chief interest of *Betrayal* is in imagining a question mark after the title. Jerry and Emma use the term "betray" in the first scene, but who is betrayed, even in the most conventional love-triangle manner? Robert knew of his wife's affair, but he did nothing about it, in part clearly because he was having affairs of his own. Jerry and Emma were faithful (or is it "faithful"?) to each other during their affair. The title *Betrayal* thus sounds oddly rigid in contrast with the play that follows it, in which extramarital affairs are practically *de rigueur* for everyone. The backward journey of the action does show us one thing, though: that the desire which precipitated an affair was bound to fade in time. And it is amoral *time* that is probably the play's true Pinteresque resonance—the poignancy of passing time, the humorous-melancholy immanence of mortality—not any suggestion that its characters are immorally betraying the very idea of marriage, honor, or self.

The film of *Betrayal*, because of the inherent flexibility of cinematic form, makes the overall temporal pattern of the play seem less of a stunt. Beyond this, Pinter found new possibilities for the play in its film adaptation (itself directed by David Jones, essentially a theater director who has done extensive television work for the BBC). This matter of genre is one of distinction, not hierarchy; the play has qualities that the movie could not have. For example, in the London-New York stage production, directed by Peter Hall and designed (scenery, lighting, *and* costumes) by John Bury, every scene began with the actors immobile in dim silhouette, with city sounds behind them, and they were brought to motion by the coming of light. Each of the London settings was done in spare line and color; the one Venice scene was executed in curves. These theatrical devices helped to distill the play's realism poetically.

Film could not accommodate those devices: they would have worked against both realism *and* poetry. The film of *Betrayal* needs rooms that are rooms, with life going on in them before and after the bits of life we see. In the theater, plaques of action were placed before us as in a three-dimensional mosaic; on screen, the camera just seems to arrive at opportune moments in these people's ongoing lives—opportune for us, that is. Growing out of such an approach, Pinter fills in material around the edges that eases the play into this second form and, without fuss, corroborates it as film. For instance, we glimpse Emma's daughter at different ages, which makes her a kind of calendar; we see Emma getting into her car after the breakup of the affair and sitting there for a moment, crying; we see her husband in his office, verified as a publisher; we even see the landlady who rents the lovers their rendezvous and, without rudeness, disbelieves everything they tell her. Pinter handles these additions so that they don't flatten suggestion into explicitness, as they would in many a movie derived from a play: here the supplements certify and expand.

Moreover, in his first feature film, David Jones makes it plain that he understands how to use a camera, how to look and choose and move. Look at the opening sequence, for one—possibly planned by Pinter but perfectly fulfilled by Jones—which takes place outside Robert and Emma's house in 1977 as they bid good-night to departing guests. The pair shut their front door—a kind of cut without actually cutting. Then the camera comes closer to the house, moving along to the kitchen window through which we see the couple conversing, not calmly. They proceed to slap each other. All this occurs in one long take, which visually certifies the essential contiguousness or inextricability of this couple's social and personal lives—in part because the camera itself begins here as a public observer, only to become a private *voyeur*.

In the next scene, focusing on Jerry and Emma in a pub the following day, Jones begins the cat-and-mouse editing technique that fills the rest of the picture, and he is greatly aided in this regard by the work of John Bloom. Jones and Bloom craft the film like jewelers, right to the finish where Jerry persuades Emma to start the affair whose end we have already witnessed. Her hand slides down the length of his phallic arm to his hand, and the two entwined hands—a pretty wryness—are the last things (*things*) we see. For all such cinematic adroitness, however, the film of *Betrayal* doesn't finally "deepen" the play, though it does deepen an element or tone that was in the original.

That tonal element can also be found in Pinter's *No Man's Land*, as well as in many of the plays of lesser English dramatists like Tom Stoppard and Simon Gray. Such works delineate a radical change in the locus of English comedy. (And make no mistake: *Betrayal*, on stage and screen if not on the page, can breathe only in the rarefied air of such comedy.) From the Elizabethan age until well into the twentieth century, that is, high comedy was virtually the exclusive preserve of wealthy, aristocratic characters. One reason was that the plots of high comedy were possible only to people with time on their hands, people who didn't have to work for a living. Another reason was that these people—I mean these people in the real world, not the characters based on them by Congreve and Sheridan and Wilde—developed comedic skill in their otherwise idle lives, qualities that distinguished them from everyone else beneath their station: of arch and elegance, of tease and (brusque) politeness, of rapier skill in the drawing-room duel of words.

Increasingly through the twentieth century and beyond, as those upper classes dwindled proportionately against an educated, reasonably affluent middle class, the talent for high comedy in life has been acquired by the middle class. Of course, the action now has to be worked around office hours and carefully planned vacations and nannies for the children, but many members of the English middle class today conduct their lives and conversations in a style as smoothly cruel and tacitly affectionate as they can make it, based on upper-class paradigms—themselves perhaps impelled by a quite English imperative to maintain poise, to keep the social backbone arched.

Harold Pinter, preeminent among his contemporaries, has perceived this social shift and writes a kind of high comedy about these middle-class people who, as far as the dailiness of their lives will permit, try to live those lives with high-comedic panache. And the tonal change in *Betrayal* from stage to screen has as much to do with the "opening up" of the play as it does with the intensification of this high-comic style in middle-class London life—partly because such "opening up," or "breaking out," permits the stylistic intensification through the situating of *haute* bourgeois existence in as realistic, even mundane, a daily context as possible.

Edmond (2005, Stuart Gordon)

Speaking of stylistic intensification, another kind is on display in the film of David Mamet's *Edmond* (2005), which I want to take up here because of this work's association with expressionism—an artistic movement that, like *Edmond*, itself began in the theater and moved into the cinema. Originally produced as a long one-act play in 1982, *Edmond* is an underrated piece, having been written between Mamet's stellar (and original) screenplay for *The Verdict* (1982, Sidney Lumet) and his best drama, *Glengarry Glen Ross* (1984; filmed 1992, James Foley), and consequently having suffered in comparison with those two highly publicized works. But *Edmond* stands on its own two feet, in part because it points up—as none of Mamet's other plays do—an aspect of his writing style that, like this particular drama itself, has been neglected. I mean the fact that Mamet's staccato or minimalist dialogue, with its occasional explosions, is essentially expressionistic, even when the plays themselves are not thoroughgoing expressionist works.

Mamet's language thus underscores the paradox of verism-cum-abstraction that inheres in all his work (but is even more apparent in his films, where verism is expected to a far greater degree than it is in the drama). The general linguistic texture is naturalistic, nearly stenographic—the broken sentences, the repetitions, the litanies of the everyday; then, suddenly, with a telegraphic word or phrase, and especially with an entire quizzical or contorted sentence, the vernacular lifts into an arch. As in, "The path of some crazed lunatic sees you as an invasion of his personal domain" (*American Buffalo*, 85). Or, "People used to say that there are numbers of such magnitude that multiplying them by two made no difference" (*Glengarry Glen Ross*, 52). And, from *Edmond*: "[God] may love the weak . . . but he protects the strong" (*Edmond*, 71). With a lesser writer, such lines might seem to be fissures in verism; but Mamet otherwise so thoroughly certifies the accuracy of his ear that in these instances we feel we are flying past the character's actual powers of expression into the thoughts in him that he isn't always able to express. In this way the real is lifted into the abstract—or what I am calling the expressionistic.

That *Edmond* appears more expressionistic than Mamet's other plays stems less from its disgorged or deracinated language, however, than from its episodic form. It's what the Germans call both a "station" drama and a *Wandlungsdrama*, a drama of transformation-cum-regeneration that is composed of a series of stations, or stages (twenty-three in *Edmond*'s case), through which a character progresses as he takes the moral, spiritual, and emotional journey of his life. (A product of European religious drama of the Middle Ages, the original station play consisted of stations that were sometimes literally Stations of the Cross.) *Edmond* has been compared to Georg Büchner's proto-expressionistic play *Woyzeck* (1836), but Mamet's drama has more in common with Georg Kaiser's lesser-known expressionistic work *From Morn to Midnight* (1912).

In this play, a bank cashier, whose humanity has been crushed beneath the social conventions, economic system, and political structure of Wilhelminian Germany, succumbs to sexual temptation and both robs his bank and leaves his wife—to embark on a pilgrimage (to a bordello for some sensual fulfillment, to a sports stadium for some passionate gambling, to the Salvation Army for some soulful religion) in search of something beyond the material, the profane, the mechanized, the quotidian. When he doesn't find what he's looking for, he kills himself rather than be imprisoned for his crime. David Mamet's own play covers more than the twelve or so hours of *From Morn to Midnight*, but it, too, is about a character in desperate search of some new intensity, truth, or meaning in his life.

Edmund Burke is a forty-seven-year-old New York stockbroker on his way home early from work after a meeting has been re-scheduled. Low on spiritual fuel, he stops to see a clairvoyant. She reads tarot cards and fatefully tells him, "You are not where you belong." (Imagined tarot cards fleck his mind thereafter, until, near the end of the play and the film, Edmond utters a line that is nearly an exact quotation from *Hamlet* (1601): "There is a destiny that shapes our ends . . . rough-hew them how we may" [*Edmund*, 100].) The result of the clairvoyant's counsel comes that evening at home when, after some clipped dialogue about a broken lamp, Edmond gets up and bluntly tells his wife he is leaving:

> WIFE. Will you bring me back some cigarettes? . . .
> EDMOND. I'm not coming back. (*Edmond*, 18)

This simple statement fractures the somnolence of his life. A quick quarrel then discloses that Edmond hasn't loved his wife for years and doesn't think she's attractive: she simply no longer interests him sexually *or* spiritually. (Mamet, who wrote this film adaptation, puts the wife in bra and panties on screen, as he did not on stage, in order to emphasize Edmond's lack of interest.) For her part, the wife (who is unnamed: more on this later) seems angered less by the bad news than by her husband's detached manner in delivering it. Edmond doesn't care: he just turns his back and walks out on her—and on his mechanical, workaday existence. *Edmond* thus takes place, as it were, after the romance of the archetypal romantic comedy is over—when, in the absence of idealized, romantic love, a desire for a different kind of union or devotion takes over.

In Edmond's case, at least initially, that desire is for sheer sex, primarily of the oral (if not oracular) kind. His first stop after leaving his wife is a bar, where he meets a gabby, suave basketball fan who infers that Edmond feels as if his "balls were cut off." The fan then casually offers some possible solutions to this problem: "money," "adventure," "pussy," "self-destruction." "Pussy" it is, so the man-in-the-bar gives Edmond a tip about a strip club where he can slake his sexual needs. When a pretty, amiable B-girl there tells him her fee for oral sex and also asks him to buy an exorbitantly priced drink, he becomes incensed. Soon Edmond's gotten himself tossed out—the start of a long round of explosive confrontations with hookers, grifters, and pimps in which he keeps heatedly complaining about the cost ("It's too much!" [*Edmond*, 43]), naïvely trying to apply bourgeois standards to an inherently corrupt underworld into which he nevertheless keeps sinking deeper and deeper.

His odyssey through New York's seedy underbelly takes Edmond to a peep show next and then to a massage parlor, before he decides to try to get his satisfaction out of a hand of three-card monte. When, however, he accuses the dealer of running a crooked game, the dealer and his shills pull him into an alley, beat him up, and steal his money. So Edmond goes to a pawnshop to trade his wedding ring for some cash—and, with no such prior plan, comes out with a knife (unlike Woyzeck, who goes to a pawnshop expressly to buy a knife with which to kill his common-law wife). Thus armed, he first threatens a woman on a subway platform, then uses the knife (and the racial epithets "jungle bunny," "nigger," and "coon," as well) on a leering, gold-toothed pimp who promises to take him to a prostitute but tries to hold him up instead—and in return gets a "knife-whipping" from Edmond that leaves this black man half dead.

Invigorated by this act of violence and experiencing the delirious liberation of living in the moment for the first time in his life, Edmond goes on a manic jag during which he is unable to keep his mouth shut as he babbles first to this stranger, then to that. One of those strangers turns out to be Glenna, a twenty-three-year-old waitress in a coffeehouse, whom he successfully propositions and whom he tells (after bedding her at her place), in a highly racialized speech, how alive beating the pimp has made him feel. An aspiring actress, Glenna—the only named character besides Edmond because, apart from him and in contrast to the generic secondary characters of expressionistic drama in general, she is the most humanized—compares his feeling of almost Dionysian ecstasy to the one she gets when she is acting. She thus fits into, shares, or even becomes a projection of Edmond's narcissistic framework, but only for a time, since Glenna proves to have a slightly different frame of reference from his. To wit: she refuses to join him in "leaving normal" and renouncing the past.

This provokes Edmond's rage and he kills her with his knife, as the fever of his quest for a higher reality, which has been burning through everything he has been doing, propels him past the rational into the hierophantic, the exalted, the truth. The truth, that is, according to Edmond Burke, but a grotesque compound of his lifelong frustrations by any other name. After he leaves Glenna's apartment, Edmond goes (like the Cashier in *From Morn to Midnight* after his bordello-visit) to a religious mission (a black Baptist one, no less) to hear a minister preach another kind of truth: that every soul can be redeemed through faith. But before he gets a chance to make his testament in front of all those assembled, Edmond is identified by the woman he accosted in the subway and is arrested—at this point, presumably only for the assault of this woman and for the attempted murder of the black pimp. (The woman's coincidental appearance here jars as it would not, or would to a much lesser degree, in the less veristic or make-believe world of the theater.) And after a short reunion with his wife, who serves him with divorce papers, he ends up in a prison cell.

A big black man is assigned to his cell, and Edmond expresses conciliatory feelings toward this African-American as well as blacks in general, musing that "when we fear something, I think we wish for it." Uninterested, his cellmate beats Edmond into granting him sexual favors. In the last scene, the two men are simply living together (perhaps for life), affectionately; and the film ends as Edmond says "good night," kisses the other man, then turns over and goes to sleep. He thus ends in an unforeseen domesticity, enforced but safe, yet a domesticity, paradoxically, through which he reaches his apotheosis—and finds the gateway to spiritual freedom, inner peace, and personal transcendence.

All of this as the prison sex slave of his hulking black cellmate, mind you, the emphasis here being not on crushing others in an outside world where every interaction, or transaction, is a struggle for power (the typical Mamet meme), but on the tender mercy of surrender in an inside or inner world of one's own willing. If Edmond's eventual contentment in captivity suggests a Jean Genet allegory, however, Mamet's hard, syncopated dialogue couldn't be less similar to Genet's flowery porno-poetry. Mamet never surrenders—or never lets his characters surrender—the armor of expressionist direct-diction, which is to say the prison-house of a kind of language that so strenuously asserts the diminished self as to seal it off insuperably in its own subjective consciousness.

Mamet's theme, then, is not that we all share Edmond Burke's particular frustrations and hungers, but that we all have them in one form or another and can be interested in a man who not only discovers his own, but does so in such a way as to set himself *apart* from us—by feeling nothing beyond his own suffering. In this he again resembles Kaiser's Cashier, who never wastes a thought on the feelings or troubles of the wife and family he abandons, the waiter he cheats, the whores he abuses, the stadium spectator whose death he engineers. Ironically, the Cashier indirectly compares himself to Christ with his last words, "Ecce homo" (the same as those uttered by Pilate, in John 19:5, immediately before Jesus's crucifixion), though *Ecce homo* was also the title of the 1888 book in which Nietzsche unfavorably contrasted Christian ideals with his own superior ideal of the *Übermensch*, or superman. A cashier, of course, is no superman, but he isn't (or hasn't behaved like) a Christian, either—which is precisely Kaiser's point in having him utter words that simultaneously call to mind the Bible and Friedrich Nietzsche.

The same goes for Edmond Burke: he's a slave by the end of *Edmond*, not a superman and not even a Christian slave, and he finds himself in a hell of his own, self-satisfied creation. (Late in his existential descent, after his visit to the Baptist mission, he can be heard openly to ask, "You think there's a hell? You think we're there?") If Edmond is a selfless martyr of a kind, moreover, he is a martyr, not for mankind, like Christ, but for men—specifically for American men of the 1980s, when the straight white male was reeling from his loss of potency at the hands of women, gays, and especially blacks in a climate of rigid political correctness as well as institutionalized affirmative action. So, after sacrificing a female waitress and an African-American pimp, Edmond sacrifices himself: to the woman who identified him as her (and the pimp's) assailant, to the wife who divorces him, and finally to the black who sodomizes him.

Mamet himself, however, has not sacrificed any of Edmond's dialogue (or any other character's, for that matter) from the play to the more visual medium of film. But he does do something that, for all the film's incisiveness—an incisiveness aided by mostly nighttime settings, which mirror its protagonist's long night of the soul—takes away from the form-conscious, almost abstract or removed, effect of the original drama. In the play of *Edmond*, that is, the twenty-three brief scenes follow one another like consecutive yet separate glimpses of a journey, a sort of mobile slide show that gives an ironclad logic to Edmond's fate, paradoxically, because of the very absence of such logic, reason, or causality from the drama's words and actions themselves. In the film, by contrast, Mamet uses connective "tissue" between the scenes or stages of Edmond's "progress," and this connectiveness takes away from the fragmented or desultory (yet nonetheless fated) quality of the play's episodes—a quality that could only be enhanced by shifting sets and characters who enter and exit from the wings, and one that is meant to mirror the fragmented or irrational perception of the protagonist himself as he manically searches out his destiny.

For example, when Edmond arrives in prison, he is dragged nude and shackled down a corridor of cells while other convicts jeer and yell at him: so we are visually told that this once prim Manhattan businessman has shed his pinstripe respectability, not so much for the prison stripes of an inmate as for the naked vulnerability of a jailhouse punk. In the *play*, Edmond's wife ends her visit to him in prison, the scene ends, and we then immediately find him in his cell with the black man: no transitional journey through a hostile cellblock here. The play is thus like a medieval morality, modernized: profane, stark, abbreviated, final. The film of *Edmond* is more of a narrative stream: equally profane but less abbreviated (even at eighty minutes or so), more explanatory if not exculpatory, and consequently both less stark and less final. After all, the camera-eye, if not the eye of God, is watching Edmond and telling his tale. The play of *Edmond*, in contradistinction, presents his drama without benefit of a guide or narrator; David Mamet may have written the words, but his presence is otherwise undetectable. Indeed, in medieval terms, he is a *deus absconditus*. And Edmond himself is what Mamet impishly-cum-impiously has left behind: naked, unaccommodated, alienated man.

Edmond was directed by Stuart Gordon, who made a name for himself in the horror-film genre by adapting several H. P. Lovecraft stories to the screen, among them *Re-Animator* (1985), *From Beyond* (1986), *Castle Freak* (1995), and *Dagon* (2001). Only one touch here, a spray of blood, belongs in a horror movie; otherwise, Gordon deals fittingly with a script that has its own horror—and, unlike most horror movies, its own alchemical reality (as opposed to science fiction)—about it. He serves *Edmond* raw, if you will, without padding (except for the aforementioned "connective tissue," which I attribute to Mamet the scenarist) and without any attempt to open the film up any more than, as a drama, it already was "open," or set in a number of different locations.

This "open" or episodic aspect of *Edmond* naturally helps it to escape the "filmed play" feeling—a feeling that, unfortunately, the movie versions of Mamet's single-set plays *Oleanna* (1992; filmed 1994, Mamet) and *Lakeboat* (1970; filmed 2000, Mamet) could not escape. Something else helps *Edmond* to escape the theatrical trap as well: Gordon's playing of Mamet's stylized dialogue against the ultra-realism of the film's horror-suspense-thriller context, as opposed to overplaying the linguistic stylization for its own incantatory sake (as Mamet-the-writer/director himself seemed to do in his film *House of Games* [1987]) and thereby drying up or (to switch metaphors) flattening out the picture.

Edmond is additionally aided, in its transition from the theater to the cinema, not only by the continuity provided courtesy of Bobby Johnston's breathy, jazz-funk trumpet on the soundtrack, but also by Denis Maloney's cinematography. I'm referring both to the film's "horror look"—its hard-edged lighting by night (making the dark "colorful") and shadow-filled imagery by day (making daylight nearly black-and-white)—and to *Edmond*'s subjective or dream-like quality, as if the whole picture, the whole world, were being seen only though Edmond's feverish eyes. This expressionistic quality in the script can be realized onstage, it's true, but only with difficulty or obtrusiveness, and only intermittently, through the use of a spotlight that "sees out" exclusively from Edmond's perspective. But the point-of-view, or first-person, shot is easy to achieve in so narrative a medium as film, and we see plenty of such camera placements in *Edmond*: most of the time we are right there with the protagonist, in the middle of things, without the "relief" of any sweeping boom shots. The editing (by Andy Horwitz) also emphasizes *Edmond*'s dreamlike or subjectively expressionist aspect: one second, for example, Edmond is looking at a tarot card, and the next he's looking down at a dinner plate—the very kind of abrupt transition that is utterly natural to the dreaming, fantasizing, or "projective" mind.

Edmond's transition from stage to screen is not aided, alas, by the performance of Mamet regular (and theater-trained) William H. Macy in the leading role. The big-eared, wattle-faced Macy is not a *bad* actor; he's a *supporting* or character actor who does his best work out of the spotlight, or in the shadow of stars. (Though I have never seen him on the stage, witness his supporting performances in such films as *Boogie Nights* [1997, Paul Thomas Anderson], *Wag the Dog* [1997, Barry Levinson], *Fargo* [1996, Joel Coen], and *House of Games*.) As the central character here, however, he is out of his depth, or, rather, we never sense any real depth of character in his Edmond. To be sure, Macy is as authentic as he can be in all the shades of the role; he never sets a foot wrong, but he never sets an especially right one, either. Thus we rarely sense the Edmond Burke in whom all these feelings—about his wife, about sex and sexuality, about race, religion, politics, and vocation—have been repressed for decades and who is now both maniacally gleeful and pitifully frightened by the bursting of his personal dam. The result is that Macy's Edmond at times appears to be an almost comic character. What the role calls for, and what Macy cannot quite provide, is the sense not of a simple robot unleashed but of a complex man who has been imprisoned for years by rote, and whose potency is only now breaking out in the only way it could at this late juncture, through physical force rather than force of character.

Macy notwithstanding, *Edmond*, like *American Buffalo* (1975)—to name only Mamet's second-best drama (also filmed: 1996, Michael Corrente)—is above all a species of incantation: profane, yes, but so desperate in its profanity as to take on spiritual overtones. Edmond may not be as vacuous as Don and Teach in *American Buffalo*, but, even as they do, he tries to create through language some sense of autonomous being. The difference is that the middle-class Edmond is reaching for a higher or more authentic being—hence the more singular and expressionistic his search as well as his speech; whereas Don and Teach (and to a lesser extent young Bobby, the third character in *American Buffalo*) are trying to create through their dialogue only some sense of their lowly—and shared—being, a verbal environment in which that being can at least subsist. *American Buffalo*, then, is solely (if superbly) an instance of dramatic naturalism. *Edmond* begins in domestic naturalism but quickly extends beyond it, into a kind of super- or supra-naturalism that I am calling expressionism. And through its very form, that of a morality or mystery play, this film invokes the spirit (if not religion itself), or the spiritual search for order, meaning, and harmony.

Thus, once again in the relatively brief history of this cinematic medium, we are indirectly reminded that the cinema began as a profane event and eventually came to include the sacred, by which it is edifyingly represented at least in part in the film of *Edmond*; while its ancient predecessor, the theater (ironically, where *Edmond* originated), began as a sacred event and eventually came to include the profane—by which it is now overwhelmingly represented on all the world's stages.

Works Cited

Hellman, Lillian. *The Little Foxes*. New York: Random House, 1939.

Mamet, David. *American Buffalo*. New York: Grove Press, 1976.

----------. *Edmond*. New York: Grove Press, 1983.

----------. *Glengarry Glen Ross*. New York: Grove Press, 1984.

Pinter, Harold. *Betrayal*. New York: Grove Press, 1979.

"Shakespeare Adapted: Films by Branagh and Others, Re-viewed"

The films discussed in the following essay are Kenneth Branagh's *Henry V* (1989) and *Love's Labour's Lost* (2000); Trevor Nunn's *Twelfth Night* (1996); Baz Luhrmann's *Romeo + Juliet* (1996); Richard Loncraine's *Richard III* (1995); Oliver Parker's *Othello* (1995); Michael Almereyda's *Hamlet* (2000); Julie Taymor's *Titus* (1999); Michael Radford's *The Merchant of Venice* (2004); and Michael Hoffman's *A Midsummer Night's Dream* (1999).

Shakespeare on Film

Every film of Shakespeare brings persistent questions about Shakespeare on film. The arts of theater and film, cognate though they are, never seem more disparate than in such an instance. The basic breach here is between a form that is classic, whatever its romantic ventures, and a form that is realistic, no matter how romantically it too ventures. Shakespeare's plays *do* flow with an unbroken and rising momentum that would seem to translate well into the sight-stream provided by the camera. But in practice it does not work out so easily or smoothly.

Indeed, the differing organisms of theater and film are never more patent than when Shakespeare is the film subject. Both arts build on texts, but Shakespeare wrote for an audience that liked to listen and films are made for people who primarily like to watch. The continuity of Shakespeare is verbal, in the poetry. The staged scenes are elliptical and fragmentary; they are crammed with hazard and action, but words, not deeds, carry the drama forward, and the real purpose of the scenes is to personify and italicize the unbroken pageant of the verse. Put another way, Shakespeare lives in his language; films are—the old term is perfect—moving pictures. The two aims blend occasionally but not consistently.

The motion picture, though it speaks, cannot be used successfully as a background for speech. It cannot stand in respectful support of a drama that moves forward without need of its special abilities. If you try to use a camera so, it begins to stutter hysterically like a propeller out of water, jumping about nervously and for no dramatic purpose, resorting to intrusive trickery in an attempt to employ itself. As a result, the timing goes so awry that climaxes misfire and behavior loses plausibility. A stage is passive—good space waiting to be filled. But a camera is a participant—selecting, arranging, juxtaposing in time and space, injecting its own comment by what it lingers on or passes over in a glance. It communicates through an ordered kaleidoscope of snapshots; that is an excellent narrative method but it is not Shakespeare's.

In a film, moreover, Shakespeare must always be condensed. Of course the texts are almost always condensed somewhat in the theater (who today would want all the verbal haberdashery that entranced the Elizabethan audience?), but film condensations are done in order to make room for cinema, so the richness of the work-as-play is bruised. (Some academics nonetheless hold that filmic elements improve Shakespeare.) What directors do is recast the narrative, filling in the visual ellipses, adding transition scenes, and throwing the narrative burden on sight, allowing the otherwise pruned verse to "explain" what we see. But Shakespeare is a miserably inefficient caption writer; he stops a camera in its tracks. The verse gets in the way of the action—and the action renders the verse superfluous. What happens is most strikingly illustrated by the soliloquies, however abbreviated. The camera cannot tolerate a man who stands and talks to himself; it is not even well served by one who paces with measured tread, which is the way men pace when they muse.

A director could, of course, photograph the replica of a stage production, holding rigidly to some satisfactory interpretation of one of the great plays. (*BBC Television Shakespeare* [1978-85] comes close to this model.) That might in fact be a valuable service, like good reproductions of great paintings, but it would not earn any artistic comment as a movie, and few directors care to be so modestly useful. Or a director could take one of the themes—as Shakespeare himself took them—and construct a movie on it entirely in terms of the screen. (*Ran* [1985, Akira Kurosawa] and *West Side Story* [1961, Robert Wise] come readily to mind.) This might work well—it *has* worked well—and the screen needs such great topics for its great technique. But the picture could not be called Shakespeare.

Much of the debate on the subject of adaptation would melt if a plain fact were recognized: a film of Shakespeare is not the original in an equivalent form; it is a different creature. This is clear enough in opera: no one, for example, mistakes the Boito-Verdi *Otello* (1887), tremendous as it is, for *Othello* (1604). The opera is a quite separate work, grown from Shakespeare and trying through its own means to equal it. Similarly, no one ought reasonably to mistake Kenneth Branagh's *Henry V* (1989), fine as it is, for the work that its author designed for the stage. I'd like to begin here by considering Branagh's *Henry V*, one of the finest of the many Shakespearean adaptations made over the last twenty-five to thirty years. Then I shall review nine other Shakespearean adaptations—including another one by Branagh—made between the years 1995 and 2004.

Henry V (1989, Kenneth Branagh)

Although I believe, with James Agee, that "the creation of new dramatic poetry is more important than the re-creation of old," and that "for such new poetry, movies offer the richest opportunity since Shakespeare's time" (Agee, 365), some remarks are nonetheless in order about a film based on the work of so "cinematic" a dramatic poet. By "cinematic" in this case, I mean not only Shakespeare's episodic form, which like film can move easily through time and space, but also his creation of poetic word-pictures that lend themselves in some measure to screen transformation—into visual images or metaphors.

Let's start with the play itself: depending on your understanding of history, *Henry V* (1599) is either Granville-Barker's sentimental appeal to patriotism fatally devoid of "some spiritually significant idea" (Granville-Barker, 146), or it is Yeats's tragically ironic treatment of an amiable egotist whose "gross vices" and "coarse nerves" (Yeats, 108) render him capable, finally, of moral evil. To most of Shakespeare's contemporaries, Henry was a great national hero whose exploits of two centuries earlier (he was King of England from 1413 until his death in 1422), depicted onstage, could only fan the patriotic fervor of a generation that had seen the defeat of the Spanish Armada.

To Laurence Olivier, directing and starring in the first film version of the play in 1944, Henry was the same national hero leading an outnumbered, underequipped army in the service of a different cause: the rallying of patriotic spirit during England's fight for survival against Nazi Germany. To Kenneth Branagh, directing and starring in the second film version (and in his first film, after much theater work in Britain) in an era of post-empire and relative anti-militarism, Henry is "someone who at times captured a certain fineness of the human spirit, and at other times was a really ruthless bastard. I wanted to get all of that. Shakespeare doesn't apologize for this man—in fact, he is quite uncompromising in the way he presents him" (Press Conference, New York premiere of *Henry V*, November 1989) at the same time as he depicts a Henry who led to victory an English army that seemingly had no chance, in a stage of despair and decay as it were, with its discipline ragged.

Branagh is right, and he includes in his film much of the unattractive side of Henry that Olivier understandably had omitted, despite an apparent attempt on Branagh's part to create a sympathetic analogy between Henry's army and the self-confessedly dispirited Britain of the late 1980s. Unlike Olivier, for example, Branagh does not dilute through comedy the early scene in which the young king seeks tortuous legal justification from two ecclesiastics for the extension of his royal power to certain French duchies and ultimately to the French crown. Olivier's Archbishop of Canterbury and Bishop of Ely are straight man and clown to Henry's good-natured, gutsy adventurer; Branagh's churchmen are astute politicians looking to protect Church monies and land from Henry's grasp, even as the King looks to carry out his dying father's advice that he "busy giddy minds / With foreign quarrels" (IV.iii.341-342, *Henry IV, Part Two*; p. 1363) so as to quiet rebellion at home. One shot epitomizes the relationship between Henry and his prelates (the kind of shot which, if somehow translated to the stage, would seem unduly forced): just before deciding to invade France, he is at the center of a tight frame, with Canterbury and Ely in profile, crowding him on either side.

Another shot shortly thereafter visually underscores the inevitability of war, the fact that nothing will get in Henry's way: as he commands that "every man now task his thought, / That this fair action may on foot be brought" (I.ii.309-310, *Henry V*; p. 1464), the King exits, followed by his lords, by walking directly at the camera. This impetuous movement carries over into Henry's next scene, during which he cunningly and somewhat pleasurably stalks and entraps—literally as well as figuratively—the three English noblemen (one of them his cousin, the Earl of Cambridge) who had taken French gold to assassinate him.

Olivier eliminates this scene (perhaps feeling that this material was inappropriate to wartime) in addition to three others included by Branagh: Henry's threats to Charles VI of France that "hungry war" will open its "vasty jaws" and leave nothing but "the widows' tears, the orphans' cries, / The dead men's blood, the pining maidens' groans" (II.iv.104-107, *Henry V*; p. 1475); the hanging of Bardolph for robbing a French church, an execution ordered by Henry (but only mentioned by Shakespeare); and Henry's vicious threats to the Governor of Harfleur to surrender or

> . . . in a moment look to see
> The blind and bloody soldier with foul hand
> Defile the locks of your shrill-shrieking daughters;
> Your fathers taken by the silver beards,

And their most reverend heads dash'd to the walls;
Your naked infants spitted upon pikes,
... (III.iii. 110-115, *Henry V*; p. 1480)

(Even Branagh, however, stops short of having Henry give his soldiers the strategic order during the Battle of Agincourt to cut their prisoners' throats—an order made all the more chilling by the fact that it *precedes* Henry's discovery of the killing of the boys [who maintain the English baggage train] by the French.)

So as to remove all taint from the character of his Henry V, Olivier goes as far as to delete the King's prayer on the eve of the decisive Battle of Agincourt (1415), in which he asks that God not make him pay this day for his father's usurpation of the crown from Richard II. (Henry's father, Bolingbroke, became King Henry IV.) But Branagh is right to keep this petition in his film, for it is key to an understanding of the play as Shakespeare wrote it and as it occupies the last slot in the cycle containing *Richard III* (1593), *Henry IV, Part One* (1597), and *Henry IV, Part Two* (1598). In these plays, Shakespeare presents a society in transition from the medieval view of the world as a great chain of being, an utterly planned cosmos, under the direction of one God, to the Renaissance and even modern view of the world as a collection of self-serving individuals under the rule of secular—and therefore mutable—law. Divine law, in the form of Richard II's divine mandate, is ruptured when Richard gets deposed by Bolingbroke, and the rebellions that follow (predicted by Richard) in both parts of *Henry IV* can be seen as a natural consequence of the break in the venerable structure of authority.

Thus *secular* law reigns at the start of *Henry V*, twisted to the new king's aggressive purposes by divine, and divinely acquisitive, hands. And despite Henry's invocation of the Lord at strategic moments in the drama, indeed, his pairing of God's will with England's destiny, it is secularism that wins the day at Agincourt and continues to do so during the troubled reign of Henry VI, "Whose state so many had the managing, / That they lost France and made his England bleed" (Epilogue, lines 11-12, *Henry V*; p. 1520). [The infant Henry VI succeeded his father, who died not long after his triumph without ever having truly consolidated his gains in France.] Branagh, in contrast to Olivier, includes these deflating lines by the Chorus at the end of his film—a chorus that has, up to this point, discharged its role as a narrative bridge in confident tones—and his aim in this as well as in his depiction of a complex Henry V could only be to capture Shakespeare's play in all its ambivalence: as a patriotic, even jingoistic paean to King and country, on the one hand, and an ironic, even bitter denunciation of moral and political disorder, on the other. That disorder pervades the three *Henry VI* plays (1591-92) together with *Richard III*, in all of which England continues to suffer retribution for Henry Bolingbroke's overthrow and murder of a rightful monarch, Richard II. In Shakespeare's wishful, providential scheme, only with the restitution of the legitimate successor at the end of *Richard III*—Henry VII, the first Tudor king—can England enjoy peace and greatness once again. There is but temporary peace at the end of *Henry V*, and the King's newfound greatness will be short-lived.

As a script, then, Branagh's version of *Henry V*—which is notably more complete than Olivier's—succeeds in capturing the essence of Shakespeare's play, of Henry's character, which is high praise for any film adaptation of a

40

literary or dramatic source and particularly of Shakespeare (where judicious cutting of dialogue is necessary to avoid the duplication of information and ideas supplied or suggested by the visuals). Indeed, the film even includes two flashbacks of tavern scenes from *Henry IV, Part Two* in order to suggest the profligacy Prince Hal-become-King Henry has left behind as well as the humanity, the fellow-feeling, he has retained from Falstaff's world. But why include these scenes and not others from that are equally important to the formation of Henry's character? I'm thinking of those scenes that depict a loveless, morbid, impudent Hotspur obsessed with the achievement of individual glory on the battlefield, a man whose boldness so attracts his enemy, Prince Hal, that the latter is moved, toward the end of *Henry IV, Part One*, to pronounce a benediction over Hotspur's dead body—a benediction that includes the following ill-omened lines:

> Ill-weav'd ambition, how much art thou shrunk!
> When that this body did contain a spirit,
> A kingdom for it was too small a bound,
> But now two paces of the vilest earth
> Is room enough. . . . (V.iv.87-91, *Henry IV, Part One*; p. 1220)

Kenneth Branagh's performance as Henry certainly could have benefited from a few more parts ruthless Hotspur and a few less parts complaisant Falstaff—Branagh tries to project the former quality, especially in moments like the speech before Harfleur, but his doughboy face and woolly voice get in his way. *Selfish* charm is what Henry should exude, yet Branagh can't quite manage that and there was no room for it in Olivier's idealized conception of the character. Patrick Doyle's nearly continuous music does help Branagh with one aspect of his character but not this one, since it emphasizes his alternatively sentimental and majestic topside, never his dark underbelly. (The near continuousness of this music, by the way, highlights a difference between Branagh's film of *Henry V* and Olivier's, where William Walton's score was good *theater* music—easily adaptable for use in a stage presentation of the play during the entrances, exits, battles, and so on.)

Kenneth Macmillan's cinematography, by contrast, simultaneously contains both sides of Henry's world: indoors, warm sepia tones over a palette mainly of browns and blacks and grays; outdoors, more or less, the same narrow range of color embraced by a softening mist, which becomes most prominent where it is most needed—at the brutal Battle of Agincourt, with its clashing swords, whistling arrows, falling horses, and flying bodies. How appropriate that in what would finally be a victory for secularism, Macmillan should keep his camera low to the ground—to the muck of earthly reality as against the pomp of imperial-celestial circumstances—and in fairly close, at a few points even agonizingly extending earthly time by shooting in slow motion.

Branagh's Agincourt is an anti-heroic, grotesque ballet fought in the rain, whereas Olivier's was a glorious, decorative pageant that took place on a sunny day, with the heavens as a backdrop. (Branagh's Agincourt thus has more in common with the mud-soaked, fragmented, gruesomely powerful Battle of Shrewsbury in Orson Welles's *Chimes a Midnight* [a.k.a. *Falstaff*, 1966] than with Olivier's shining set piece.) Toward the end of this sequence in each film (Act IV, scene viii, in Shakespeare's *Henry V*), a *Te Deum* can be heard on the soundtrack. But in Branagh's *Henry V* this choral hymn of thanksgiving, beginning with the words "We praise thee, O God," takes on a grim irony less in light of the carnage we see (in a lengthy, diagonal tracking shot, the camera follows the victorious yet stunned Henry as he carries the dead York across the battlefield, only to leave him at last and look out in long shot over an entire corpse-strewn landscape) than of the convulsion we know has taken place in the body politic and the providential design.

There are no scenes of battle-as-glory, then, in *Henry V*. War is as real as it can cinematically be made to appear in this film: savage, chaotic, claustrophobic; and what political glory may have derived from Henry's victory at Agincourt proved ultimately to be illusory. Branagh's *Henry V* is flawed, alas, but this nobly intended picture is worth seeing again and again, not least for its graphic battle sequences. Indeed, it may be the battle sequences of *Henry V* that in the end finally impress themselves most on our memories—as they never could on stage—since they alone are enough to remind us that, be the combatants English vs. French, German vs. American, or Asian vs. Caucasian, war makes equal, suffering, humble beasts of us all, no matter how glorious or ignoble the cause. For the royal Henry V, as for his plebeian men, the battlefield was ironically both the first and the last level field on which they would play. After battle, after life, would come the real judgment day—if not heaven's, then history's.

As for the besetting trouble of Shakespeare on film—the conflict between a work that lives in its language and a medium that tries to do without language as much as it can—Kenneth Branagh's *Henry V* achieves, in its essentials, that difficult double feat that André Bazin once envisaged: it respects its theatrical original while also respecting its modern film idiom, and in such a way that, at its best, Branagh's vision and Shakespeare's coincide. Unlike Olivier, who used a theater-on-film or filmed-theater approach and whose *Henry V* thus becomes a genuine mixed-media event, Branagh opts as completely for the cinematic as the work will permit. But, despite his limitations as a heroic actor (modest voice, slight build, undistinguished face), he never subverts the size and majesty of the drama by trying to "modernize" it. He concentrates on trying to render that size and majesty in film terms; and, if we allow for a few constrictions along the way when the play seems to bump up against the microphone and the camera, Branagh does as well as anyone has ever done in making Shakespeare— not Shakespearean hash—filmic. (And he does better here, in my view, than in his subsequent *Much Ado about Nothing* [1993] and *Hamlet* [1996], both of which were marred by [American] lapses in casting, and the latter of which was updated to the second half of the nineteenth century for no discernible reason.)

Let me conclude this portion of my essay with a comparison between the openings of Branagh's and Olivier's films of *Henry V*, which seem to me to epitomize the divergent ways in which drama and film proceed to their respective ends. Olivier began with a panoramic shot of Elizabethan London, after which he focused on the Globe Theatre and its bustle. Then out on stage came the costumed Chorus (Leslie Banks). Branagh's Chorus (Derek Jacobi) throws a huge electrical switch and lights up an empty film studio as he moves through it. (In the whole picture he is the only one in modern dress.) Olivier began and continued with the metaphor of theater on film. Branagh, by contrast,

42

makes us understand at once that his medium is film alone and that cinematic means, rather than transmutations of theater, will be his matter.

Olivier's own first entrance consisted of sliding his profile into place as the actor waited backstage at the Globe to go on. Branagh's first entrance is as king, not as actor. The great doors of the council chamber open, and the young monarch is revealed in silhouette against strong backlighting before he walks toward us. The camera deputizes for him, as if to suggest that in this production the camera will be king, courtiers bowing to it as it passes them. When Henry sits on his throne, we get the briefest glimpse of his face before we see the courtiers again; only then do we return for our first real look at him. This, I submit, is a purely cinematic entrance—of a singularly dramatic kind.

Love's Labour's Lost (2000, Kenneth Branagh)

I'd like now to treat another Shakespearean adaptation by Kenneth Branagh: his film of *Love's Labour's Lost*. William Hazlitt himself dismissed this 1595 play: "If we were to part with any of the author's comedies, it should be this" (Hazlitt, I: 240). But Harold Bloom has said: "I take more unmixed pleasure from this play than from any other Shakespearean play" (Bloom, 121). Branagh, if he had read this, might not agree entirely with Bloom but would certainly side with him against Hazlitt. He'd especially agree with a further Bloom comment on one of the characters: "The essence of Berowne is in that insouciant line uttered upon meeting a French lady-in-waiting in Navarre: 'Did not I dance with you in Brabant once?'" (Bloom, 124).

Lightning could have flashed in Branagh's head from Bloom's line to a way of performing Berowne to the concept of transforming the whole play into a "dance" film. *Love's Labour's Lost* did indeed become a Miramax musical-comedy film in 2000 with Branagh as adapter, as director, and as Berowne. The project was a promising possibility, not an instant sacrilege. The trouble is that the promise was not well kept.

The plot of the play, cunningly symmetrical, is so artificial—like some eighteenth-century operas (*Così fan tutte* [1790], for prime instance)—that the artificiality is part of the fun. The young King of Navarre decides to spend three years in isolated study and thought, with no women allowed into his life, and he enlists three of his courtiers, chief among them the ebullient Berowne, to immure themselves with him. When the Princess of France arrives to visit the King, she and her three ladies-in-waiting become a threat to his and his courtiers' isolation. The pastry-chef architecture of the play invites music. Surprisingly, only one operatic version has been attempted: Nicolas Nabokov composed it in 1973, with a libretto by W. H. Auden and Chester Kallman. But of musical-comedy versions, even with *Kiss Me, Kate* (1948, Cole Porter) as precedent, there are none. (Note, however, W. S. Gilbert's relevance. He didn't use Shakespeare, but he reversed the play's idea and made the men invade the women's isolation in *Princess Ida* [1884].)

Branagh saw *Love's Labour's Lost* as "a romantic musical comedy" (Press Conference, London premiere of *Love's Labour's Lost*, March 2000), and he solved the problem of the score with what must now be called the Woody Allen device, after *Everyone Says I Love You* (1996). Branagh used old favorites, songs by Cole Porter, Irving Berlin, Jerome Kern, and more. All of them are irresistible, and they are not anachronistic because he set the film in 1939. He commissioned Patrick Doyle, who had done all his previous Shakespeare music, to supply horn-rich interludes, which are like flowing gold between scenes.

The lovely songs warm us up, but they are not exactly the equivalent of Shakespeare's language—some of his most savory and delightful writing is in this play—at least two-thirds of which has been discarded. If Branagh was going to cut most of the lines to make room for the musical numbers, the numbers had to compensate us. They don't. The deficit arises less through the loss of the language, granted the idea of the project, than through two blatant producing mistakes. First, much of the casting is dull or dreadful, most notably the two leads, Alessandro Nivola as the King and Alicia Silverstone as the Princess: they are inadequate in every way. None of the principal eight is impressive except Branagh. Further, he has cast a member of the King's court with an actor who looks a good deal like the King, which is unhelpful. (There is one subtle touch in the casting: the King has one black courtier in his ensemble, the Princess one black lady-in-waiting. We expect that they are intended for each other; but they aren't.)

Second, actors who are not singers and dancers are asked to do a great deal of singing and dancing. Some of the singing may have been dubbed, but it is still uncompelling. Timothy Spall, for instance, the burly man who was so winning in some Mike Leigh films, plays Don Armado, the Spanish *poseur*, and is assigned a Cole Porter song: he merely struggles to bring it into Shakespeare. The dancing is worse. There wouldn't have been any point in improving the trite choreography; these people can just about do what they were given. What is the point in asking an audience to watch long dance numbers executed by people who are not, so far as we can see, dancers? When Peter O'Toole, as a loony lord, burst into song and dance in *The Ruling Class* (1972, Peter Medak), along with some of his townspeople, it was a bracing fracture of realism, and the pleasure was increased because none of these people were expected to be performers in the singing-dancing sense. But Branagh's actors are the cast of a musical comedy—that's what they are there for—and most of them just can't cut the mustard.

There are a few exceptions. Geraldine McEwan, who once captivated New York as Lady Teazle (in 1963) in *The School for Scandal* (1777) and who was Alice, the French lady-in-waiting, in Branagh's *Henry V*, here plays the schoolmistress Holofornia (Shakespeare's Holofornes transgendered) with her imperishable wit and charm. It is a treat to see McEwan tapping away and waving her arms as a member of the group backing up Nathan Lane in "There's No Business Like Show Business." And there's Lane himself. He has become so smirkily ubiquitous on small and large screens—was so even in 2000, when *Love's Labour's Lost* was released—that we are tempted to dislike his self-adoration. But there's no doubting that, as Costard the clown, he fulfills the Elizabethan requisite. Many of Shakespeare's clowns were written, it seems safe to say, for specific performers who could be trusted to make them funny. The roles were not intended for straight actors, however good, who were not intrinsically comic. (Remember Michael Keaton's near hernia trying to be funny as Dogberry in Branagh's film of *Much Ado about Nothing*?) Lane is funny. That's what he starts from. Then he acts.

As for Branagh the Shakespearean, there is as yet no need to despair, even though he has not acted in another Shakespearean film since *Love's Labour's Lost*. (He directed but did not perform in a film of *As You Like It* in 2006.) After the death of John Gielgud in 2000, I cited Branagh as one hope for modern yet attuned Shakespearean acting. I still think so, and am waiting for more of it from him on the screen. (On the stage, in 2002 he starred at the Crucible Theatre, Sheffield, as Richard III; in July 2013 he co-directed *Macbeth* and performed the title role at the Manchester International Festival, repeating his performance and directorial duties when the production moved to New York City's Park Avenue Armory in June 2014; and, in April 2015, Branagh announced his formation of the Kenneth Branagh Theatre Company, with which he presented a season of five shows at London's Garrick Theatre from October 2015 to November 2016, among them *The Winter's Tale* [which he directed and starred] and *Romeo and Juliet* [which he only directed].) In the patch that is left of Berowne's lines, Branagh shows that he understands exactly what he is doing in Shakespeare and can do it with assurance. Mark, however, that he and all the others pronounce "can't" and "dance" in American style, in what may be a bow to Yankee globalization.

Stanley Donen, the long-retired master director of musical films, is listed as a "presenter" of this picture. Perhaps it is the Donen presence that tickled Branagh into digging up some old Hollywood musical touches. Some examples: a swimming-pool ballet with a bunch of pretty girls; the Fred Astaire chair-tipping (while dancing, Branagh steps onto a chair, puts the other foot on the back of the chair, and tips it backward as part of the dance); the sky hooks that lift the King and his three courtiers during a number.

Shakespeare's finish for the play is a refreshing conceit. The four men and the four women do not clinch and marry for a fade-out; their unions are postponed for a year, mostly to test their loves. Berowne says of this conclusion: "Our wooing doth not end like an old play. / Jack hath not Jill" (v.ii.851-852, *Love's Labour's Lost*; pp. 798-799). Branagh evidently felt that Shakespeare's year of probation would be a tepid fade-out for a film, yet he didn't want to lose the unconventionality of Jack's not yet getting Jill. So he throws in clips of the Second World War, in black and white, with some of the characters in some of the clips. Presumably this is why he set the film in 1939—so that he could "use" the Second World War as the cause of the delay in the four marriages. But it's a somewhat grotesque choice for the finale of a spun-sugar musical. The cheeriest point to make about *Love's Labour's Lost* is that, spotty though it is (the spots are the good moments), it is not a complete collapse in Branagh's career. It doesn't signal decline, it displays mistakes—lots of them.

Twelfth Night (1996, Trevor Nunn)

There are also mistakes in the film of *Twelfth Night* (1996) as directed by Trevor Nunn, an experienced theater hand. This film is, in a way, a fair sample of the twentieth century's theater productions of Shakespeare. The guiding principle here is: transpose the play, in time or place or both, to a time or place about which it was not written. The original purpose was to heighten the play's topicality or to refresh the audience's experience of the play, but in the last few decades this motive has been somewhat smothered by another. The director doesn't want to

45

seem hidebound by tradition, so he has to do something to the play. Nunn's *Twelfth Night* is still set in Illyria, the mythical country of the original, but the time is moved ahead to the mid-nineteenth century. (When Sebastian arrives in this strange country and goes to see the sights, he carries a copy of Baedeker's *Illyria*.)

This alteration by Nunn might be called minimal. Other directors have done much more to *Twelfth Night* (1602), particularly in the sexual vein, because Viola spends most of her time in male dress and calls herself Cesario. A woman (Olivia) is smitten with her, and a man (Orsino) is strongly attracted to Cesario though the latter is "male." Add the fact that in Shakespeare's time all women's roles were played by boys, and the sexual stew really simmers. Nunn hints only slightly at this theme and restricts himself to the temporal move. But why the mid-nineteenth century? Why not the mid-eighteenth? Or mid-twenty-first?

However, having settled for minimal change, Nunn then proceeds to muck up his production. The cutting and the rearrangements of the text are not much more severe than one is braced for, but he misconstrues the play's temper jarringly. Visually the film is seen mostly in a dreary gray climate—this play that seems entirely scented with flowers. Nunn cast Sir Toby Belch with a grossly unfunny actor, Mel Smith, who suggests nothing of the minor Falstaff in his part. That otherwise excellent actor Richard E. Grant plays Sir Andrew Aguecheek, who is to Toby as *Othello*'s Roderigo is to Iago, as if Sir Andrew were on his way to becoming Hamlet. Maria, the maid who is a sort of cousin of *Henry IV*'s Doll Tearsheet, is done by Imelda Staunton without an iota of merriment.

Imogen Stubbs, as Viola, one of the most romantic roles ever written, has all the warmth and color of a popsicle. Orsino, the count whom she/he serves, is played in a muffled manner by Toby Stephens, with no poetic line. A few people in the cast suggest what they might have done with their roles in a full-bodied production. Helena Bonham Carter, as the Countess Olivia, who falls in love with the disguised Viola, moves feelingly from mourning for her dead brother to longing for the young "man." Nigel Hawthorne is a perfect Malvolio, Olivia's steward, or would be if he had not been urged by Nunn to distend his pomposities. And Ben Kingsley makes Olivia's jester, Feste, a shrewd philosopher with dignity under the motley.

A shipwreck, twins mistaken for each other, a woman posing as a man, a wise fool—all elements that Shakespeare used elsewhere—were woven by him into a lyric entity with language that is almost beyond belief. But Nunn, though modest in his alterations, has bungled the gist of the enterprise.

Romeo + Juliet (1996, Baz Luhrmann)

The Australian director Baz Luhrmann himself takes the following view of Shakespeare: he regards the mere transposition of a play in time or place as nice-nelly daring. In the case of *Romeo and Juliet* (1595), he explodes the play itself; and his explosion begins with his title. *William Shakespeare's Romeo + Juliet* (1996, Baz Luhrmann) is both a joke and a manifesto that are clear a few seconds after the film begins. The first thing we see is a TV set. A newscaster speaks the opening chorus. Then the screen erupts.

The term "music video" covers it. One visual cascade after another, one sound blast—mostly of rock—after another. The setting is South Florida, Verona

Beach, the time "today." Possibly tomorrow. The Montagues and Capulets, except for the parents, are cool cats. A racially mixed lot, they drive large convertibles and carry large pistols. (A slight disjuncture here when they talk of swords and wave pistols; but by that time, who cares?) There's a very heavy load of Catholicism: the Madonna, the crucifix, church interiors with rows and rows of candles. The Catholicism is not used in contrast with the lust and killing but as part of the texture: the lovers-haters-killers are Catholics, that's all. Of course the church is in Shakespeare, too, but the play takes place in an entirely Catholic world. Here Luhrmann has made his choice for the sake of emphasis in itself.

His first film was the garish *Strictly Ballroom* (1992), and of course he has also directed music videos in addition to making the subsequent *Moulin Rouge!* (2001) and *The Great Gatsby* (2013). His designer, Catherine Martin, who had worked with him before, here gives him bloated settings—ugly ones and overly pretty ones—by the basketful. The film devours them ravenously, burps noisily, and whirls along pyrotechnically. Amid all this splattering a few fragments of the original text remain, addressed in 1990s-style. A few members of the cast—Pete Postlethwaite as Friar Laurence, Miriam Margolyes as Juliet's nurse, John Leguizamo as Tybalt—remind us of what their roles really are. Romeo (Leonardo DiCaprio) and Juliet (Claire Danes) ought not to be better than they are or they would seem out of place. (Much of the balcony scene, for example, takes place in a swimming pool in the Capulets' garden.)

Trevor Nunn's film of *Twelfth Night* (1996), made in the same year, seems to say of Luhrmann's that it is excessive, that one can modernize Shakespeare with restraint. Luhrmann seems to be making a rude noise in response, implying that Nunn wants to swim with one foot on shore. For myself, I've never seen the need to modernize plays that don't seem out of date; but of the two approaches in these films I confess I prefer Luhrmann's. Nunn's fiddling seems mere temporal décor. Luhrmann is in effect doing a translation, almost as if he had rendered the text into Finnish or Bulgarian, with a few English wisps remaining as souvenirs of the origin. Why did Luhrmann have to fiddle with the greatest young-love story in the language? Presumably he would reply that there was no point in fiddling with anything smaller. If you want pristine *Romeo and Juliet*, he says, it's still there, it will always be there. If you want to see and hear this play soaked in a 1990s sensibility, here's the film. The result is horrifying, unsettling in its ruthlessness.

Oddly, both Nunn's *Twelfth Night* and Luhrmann's *Romeo + Juliet* do something that I've often noted about the screen versions of other, much lesser plays. The film medium is like an X-ray that enlarges flaws in plays. In *Twelfth Night* (1602) the end of the Malvolio story is always troublesome. The arrogant steward is tricked into making a fool of himself, but the result of the trickery is nasty. His story has to be finished, and Shakespeare has to interrupt the happy ending to finish it. But this rift in the concluding pleasantness is even more rude on film.

In *Romeo and Juliet* the flaw in the tragic structure is the gimmick of the poison. Friar Laurence gives Juliet a drug that will make her seem dead and keep her that way until Romeo arrives in the tomb. Romeo arrives a bit too soon, thinks she is really dead, and takes poison. She awakes to find him dead. This accident, with tragedy hanging on a few minutes one way or another, is a long way from the tragic wholeness of, say, *Macbeth* (1606) or *King Lear* (1605)—a governing wholeness, despite their own plot devices. Luhrmann, very cleverly, capitalizes on the gimmickry of the gimmick. Romeo thinks Juliet is dead and drinks the poison, but before he actually dies, she awakes and sees him dying. And he sees that she's alive. (After he expires, she finishes herself with his pistol.) This added twist underscores the patness of the original.

Richard III (1995, Richard Loncraine)

Though this is not true of *Romeo and Juliet* (1595), some works in the performing arts are interesting only if done by virtuoso performers. I wouldn't want to hear the Sibelius violin concerto again except with an absolutely dazzling soloist. The film of *Richard III* (1995, Richard Loncraine) reminds us that this play is in the same dubious state. If we penetrate the incense that surrounds the very name of the author, the play stands revealed as one of his least rewarding: in character development, moral profundity, and quality of verse. ("I had an Edward, till a Richard killed him. / I had a husband, till a Richard killed him" [IV.iv.40-41, *Richard III*; p. 144]. Etc., etc.) Only a lot of dazzle in the leading role can sustain our attention to the incessant murders and the litanies about them. And Ian McKellen is not the man for the job. Yes, he has long experience in Shakespeare. Yes, this film derives from a theater production that was successful in London and New York. Yes, McKellen is intelligent, skilled, and muscularly forceful. What he doesn't have is brilliance; and without that, both the title character and the drama sink into Victor Hugo.

Cutting the play severely, as this screen adaptation does, doesn't reduce the burden. It only makes the play less tolerable because there is less breathing space between the killings, less regard for motive and reaction. Transposing the play to the twentieth century—in this case the 1930s—only raises the question: Why? When Orson Welles did *Julius Caesar* (1599) à la Mussolini in 1937, an argument for topicality was advanced (not without strain even then). But *Richard III* (1594) set during the 1930s? In 1995? (Laurence Olivier's *Richard III*, in 1955, made no reference either to the '30s or World War II: it stuck to Shakespeare.) Are we to believe that this power-greedy homicidal malcontent was a fascist? Nonsense. He had nothing in his head except schemes for personal advancement. The apposition is facile—and reductive of the dangers of fascism.

Richard Loncraine, the director, and his colleagues labored to make the film fast and electric; but they, like McKellen with his cigarettes and pop records, only seem to be sweating with worry. "Shakespeare isn't old-fashioned and boring!" they insist and insist, thus getting in the way of whatever impact this sanguinary parade might possibly have. As a result, only one scene in the play has a kernel of intrinsic interest for me, the wooing of Lady Anne, in which Richard interrupts the funeral procession of her father-in-law—whom he killed after he killed her husband—to court Anne and propose marriage. In the film the scene is played in a morgue, over the corpse (a very different theatrical matter from a coffin), and the text is more severely sliced than the corpse.

Lady Anne is Kristin Scott Thomas, sufficiently la-de-dah. Some others do well enough with the scraps of their parts that remain: Annette Bening as Queen Elizabeth, Nigel Hawthorne as Clarence, Maggie Smith as the Duchess of York. There's a special poignancy in the case of John Wood as King Edward. He's too old for it now, but what I've seen of Wood on stage in Molière and Stoppard and Schnitzler persuades me that he must have been a scintillating Richard III when he played it in London in 1979.

The most famous line in the play, certainly, comes in the battle of Bosworth Field: "A horse, a horse, my kingdom for a horse!" (V.iv.7, 13, *Richard III*; p. 189). How does this motorized film deal with it? By putting Richard in an army vehicle that gets stuck at a crucial moment. A horse, indeed.

Othello (1995, Oliver Parker)

I know of no drama in the whole history of the art, including the Greeks and certainly including *Richard III* (1594), that surpasses *Othello* (1604) in the sense of a force launched at the start that drives unremittingly to the end, gathering speed and power as it goes. The basic trouble with the film of *Othello* (1995) is that, for what it takes to be cinematic reasons, it breaks up this direct course into fragments. Further, the adaptation by Oliver Parker, who also directed, shuns complete scenes—complete in the play at least in shape, if condensed even there. So what we get is an assemblage, a mosaic, instead of unbroken onrush.

Throughout, Parker scrabbles for "cinematizing" as constantly as Orson Welles did in his *Othello* film (1952), though not as effectively. (Welles had lately seen Sergei Eisenstein's *Ivan the Terrible* [Part I, 1944] and patently used it as a filmic model.) This leads to oddities. For instance, the scene in which Iago swears to help Othello in his quest for revenge is put by Parker in the water—on the beach at the ocean's edge. Yet when he gets the chance really to utilize film's power—to cut away for emphasis, for instance, instead of linger and deflate—he muffs it. The last scene of the play is a directorial headache in the theater. What to do with Othello while he waits for Desdemona to pray? What to do with Emilia's body after she insists on lying down to die next to her dead mistress? How to get Emilia out of the way so that, after Othello stabs himself, he can kiss his wife goodbye without a third person on hand? Parker uses none of the devices of editing to help him with these matters.

Besides the rearrangements of the text, a great deal is cut. To what is left of his role, Laurence Fishburne gives a committed try. He does well enough in dignity and manly love until the speech that ends "Othello's occupation's gone!" (III.iii.357, *Othello*; p. 119), which lacks size. His performance never regains sufficient stature. Whether or not the picture was shot in sequence, it's easy to mark this as the place where Fishburne begins to dwindle. (I must note, too, that he is not helped much by his costumes. When he arrives at Cyprus, he seems to be wearing what look like leathern Bermuda shorts.)

What was the casting principle of this film—in terms of accents? Fishburne speaks good American English. Gabriele Ferzetti (of *L'Avventura* [Michelangelo Antonioni], long ago in 1960) wrestles with English as the Duke. As for Desdemona, even if we concede that Irène Jacob is much too old for the role and concede, too, that she is insufficiently winning, why a markedly French woman? Kenneth Branagh's own speech doesn't quite fit with the others, but he makes it seem their hard luck. Branagh's Iago isn't near Christopher Plummer's magnificent performance on the stage in 1982; still, he savors neatly what text and space are granted him. The "put money in thy purse" (I.iii.337-338, *Othello*; p. 45) speech to Roderigo is a gem, delicately modeled without actorish maneuvering.

The composer, Charles Mole, had the horrible task of writing a score that, for many of us, would have to compete with Verdi's opera (1887). Mole comes off honorably, with music of lyric gravity. In a sense, his work stands alone.

Hamlet (2000, Michael Almereyda)

There is an ingenious touch in Michael Almereyda's *Hamlet* (2000), made only four years after Kenneth Branagh's own *Hamlet*. The duel scene near the finish always presents a staging problem: how to deal with the fact that Claudius doesn't stop Gertrude from drinking the poison. In the text he simply says, aside, as she drinks: "It is the poisoned cup; it is too late" (V.ii.235, *Hamlet*; p. 1753). Why is it too late? Why couldn't this clever schemer have found some way to stop her? Through the centuries, directors have tussled with this problem. But in this film Gertrude tells us, through her behavior, that she knows the cup is poisoned, and she deliberately drinks it down to save her son from drinking it. Only a slight hint beforehand suggests that she suspects Claudius of treachery, and she gets only a spot of pantomime to put the point across; still, this is a handy solution to the problem.

And it is all the more surprising here because, up to that point, this film, set in New York in 2000, hasn't been particularly concerned with the difficulties in the text. Almereyda, the adapter-director, cannot have retained more than one-third of the lines, probably fewer. (The contest here is not for the crown of Denmark but for control of the Denmark Corporation in a skyscraper.) When a difficulty arose, Almereyda simply slashed lines to get rid of it. For instance, he wanted Hamlet to show his play-within-a-play on a videotape. What, then, to do about the visiting troupe of players? Eliminate them, of course.

The rearranging of Shakespeare's *Hamlet* (1601) is hardly a new idea. The role has been played by women (Sarah Bernhardt, for one, in 1899) and by a thirteen-year-old boy (William Betty at Drury Lane in 1805); every culture has molded it to its will; the film world embraced it even before the advent of sound. Through the centuries, modern-dress versions were frequent in the theater, and now Almereyda brings it into the twenty-first century. So here we have the old idea of Shakespeare updated, in decor and behavior. Many have compared this film to Aki Kaurismäki's *Hamlet Goes Business* (1987), which I have not seen; I did see Ian McKellen's fascist *Richard III* (1995, Richard Loncraine) and Baz Luhrmann's MTV *Romeo + Juliet* (1996), but, even without them, the modernizing of Shakespeare could hardly be shockingly novel. Rather, it feels somehow cozy to see that good old avant-garde approach once more, to see (in this case) Hamlet in a mod wool cap wandering in Manhattan, to see Polonius wiring Ophelia before the "nunnery" scene so that he and Claudius can hear what she and Hamlet say and so that Hamlet's discovery of the wire is what sets him ranting.

The trouble is elsewhere: not that the director wanted to bring the play closer to the current audience but that he hasn't done so. Anyone who knows the play may get an occasional reminder of it; but anyone else will not get much hint of the depth of the characters and the magnitude of their drama. When we hear Ambroise Thomas's opera of *Hamlet* (1868), we know we are getting, not Shakespeare, but nineteenth-century Paris in all its plumpness. At Almereyda's

Hamlet, we get not Shakespeare but East Village exhibitionistic coolness. Inevitably, the acting is seen through a distorting lens because the text is so shredded and re-arranged. In any case, Ethan Hawke was the perfect choice for this *Hamlet* because his slithering, mumbling approach fits the essentially off-hand feeling of this film. The director doesn't want any touch of the theater or of classical tradition in the performances—which is why the classically trained Liev Schreiber seems out of place as Laertes—and Hawke is precisely the person to let the (condensed) role leak out of him onto the screen. "To be, or not to be" (III.i.58-90, *Hamlet*; pp. 1705-1706) by Hawke sounds just right when he mumbles (some of) it in a video shop. Julia Stiles, as Ophelia, is exactly the singles-bar girl who might go mad, which she does, at the Guggenheim Museum. Kyle MacLachlan and Diane Venora as the king and queen do what they can with their pre-shrunk roles, but it isn't even uphill all the way, it's a plateau. For those who don't know Bill Murray as a dry comic, his Polonius may seem like a last-minute substitution—as if a visitor to the set had been thrust into the part in an emergency so that they could get on with the shooting. The only person in the cast besides Schreiber who gives some sense of the size of the work that is here being battered is Sam Shepard (himself a noted playwright, of course) as the Ghost.

To level the most serious charge against this film, I dig up an old-fashioned term: beauty. Almereyda isn't interested in it. Of course, beauty is not in the postmodernist lexicon and, even without agreeing, we can understand. (I have seen elocutionary, attitudinizing, full productions of *Hamlet* that were suffocating.) But this play survives—reigns—because of its beauty, not the abstract profundity of its themes or the universality of its mysteries in themselves, but the beauty of the way in which they are expressed. *Hamlet* exists because of, and through its, language. ("Absent thee from felicity a while" [V.ii.289, *Hamlet*; p. 1755] has my vote as the loveliest line of verse in the English language.) Yes, the play is almost always condensed a bit in performance—Branagh retained too much in his film—but to rip out great chunks because they do not fit a director's design is like altering a giant's robe for a pygmy. To mash the language as an obstacle that must be cleared away for the modern audience is to cheat that audience. Only Schreiber and Shepard show some glimpse of this truth.

Watching this film is only to watch for Almereyda's gimmicks. (Much of his career has been in science fiction.) These do pop up fairly steadily: for example, Hamlet gets his invitation to the duel not from Osric but from a fax. But this sort of cleverness is self-reflexive. When in 1988 Peter Sellars put his staging of *The Marriage of Figaro* (1786, Pierre Beaumarchais) in an apartment atop the Trump Tower, he left the music alone, thus the production had some added wryness through the contextual change for Mozart—true Mozart. But Almereyda's film is only an attempt by a director to utilize *Hamlet* for personal display—at Shakespeare's expense. It has mildly entertaining moments, but that's all.

Titus (1999, Julie Taymor)

Julie Taymor, for her part, is a unique American designer: adventurous, humorous, exciting. I first saw her work in 1980, in Elizabeth Swados's theater production of *The Haggadah* (the Jewish text that sets forth the order of the Passover Seder), for which Taymor did sets, costumes, masks, and giant puppets that made the whole work epic and *gemütlich* at the same time. She is also an experienced director, in opera as well as theater, and some think that directing is her chief talent. I missed her 1994 New York production of Shakespeare's *Titus Andronicus* (1592), but I have seen some of her other work. When I heard that she was to make her first full-length film, I thought that the film world was lucky.

Not with this picture, though. *Titus* (1999) is a thesis, unproven. Taymor believes that Shakespeare's earliest tragedy (if it is entirely by him) is especially apt at this time. The story involves murder, rape, and maiming (hands lopped off) in ancient Rome, a story that she seeks to put in place as a comment on the daily data of television. To emphasize modern relevance, she begins with a modern boy in a modern kitchen who is swept back into the past as eyewitness (though he virtually disappears once he gets there), and we see modern artifacts throughout: tanks, trucks, motorcycles. But Taymor's rendering of the play is so remote and cold, so disjointed, so devoid of Shakespearean current and surge, that the result is a sequence of fragments. They don't build to unity, let alone resonate against modern brutalities.

Titus is a Roman conqueror who brings Tamora, the queen of the Goths, and her sons as captives back to Rome. Titus has one of Tamora's sons executed, thus unleashing the queen's revenge that rages through the play. It is not only difficult to follow the story in Taymor's screenplay, it is difficult to respond with either a sense of tragic fall or low-level shock. Attempts have occasionally been made by theater people and Shakespearean critics to install *Titus Andronicus* in the high Shakespearean pantheon, but nothing that happens in this film adequately counters T. S. Eliot's view that this is "one of the stupidest and most uninspired plays ever written" (Eliot, 82). [Even Gustav Cross, in the Pelican edition, begins his introduction: "*Titus Andronicus* is a ridiculous play" (Cross, 823).]

Taymor knows all this and meant to disprove it. But her best result is in distancing the gory absurdities so far that the play seems too abstract to be ridiculous. I don't understand, however, why such a superlative designer as Taymor wanted others to do the sets and costumes. Dante Ferretti and Milena Canonero are proven talents, but this production seems to be taking place in ill-lit railway terminals and football stadiums after hours. Why didn't Taymor do the designs herself? It might at least have made the film more visually engaging.

The film's main asset is Anthony Hopkins's performance as Titus; yet it can hardly be called a performance. Hopkins, magnificently equipped for the role, is so burdened with directorial maneuver that he cannot fulfill his design. Outstanding in inadequacy among the others is Jessica Lange, as the vindictive queen; regality and savagery are not within Lange's grasp. The one competent actor in the cast besides Hopkins is Harry J. Lennix, who is Aaron: Lennix is incisive, with cool diabolical pride in his evildoing. This character, by the way, is one of Shakespeare's three Moors: besides Othello, there is the Prince of Morocco in *The Merchant of Venice* (1597).

The Merchant of Venice (2004, Michael Radford)

A film of *The Merchant of Venice*, in fact, came along in 2004, inevitably raising all the old questions about Shakespearean adaptation—and more. This is Michael Radford's film, not Shakespeare's play. The screen adaptation is by Radford, with the text pared: as is often the case in Shakespearean adaptation, much of the verbal embroidery is discarded but also some of the verbal delights. This condensation has provided Radford with chances for lots of late-sixteenth-century Venetian revelry—bare-breasted wenches are plentiful—and Venetian vistas. What Radford has retained of the original, he treats warmly and intelligently, and with a few welcome surprises in the acting. But he has produced a different work, moderately successful in itself, out of materials provided by Shakespeare.

Chief among the pleasant surprises is Al Pacino's Shylock. With Pacino's past in mind, we might have expected that he would make the sulphurous most of the role's raging moments. (I remember George C. Scott in the my-ducats-and-my-daughter speech from a 1962 New York theater production: as a teenager at the time, I thought he had literally gone crazy.) Pacino, presumably with Radford's guidance, in the main does otherwise. Excellently made up and costumed, he takes the part inward and makes it tight, bitten, soul-scarred—a man rather than a collection of scenes. Lynn Collins is an admirable Portia, womanly yet commanding. Joseph Fiennes is skillful enough as Bassanio, though he doesn't have the charm that would make Portia long for his return. A particular prize is Jeremy Irons' Antonio. With his first moment, the play's first line—"In sooth, I know not why I am so sad" (I.i.1, *Merchant of Venice*; p. 1090)—he is immersed in middle-aged, virtually inexplicable melancholy. Graceful touches abound: for instance, when Shylock is preparing the bond for Antonio's signature and can't think of a forfeit, or pretends it, and finally proposes the pound of flesh, a small surprised smile crosses Antonio's face at the absurdity of the idea.

Radford pays sufficient attention to the much-bruited view of the Antonio-Bassanio friendship as homoerotic. To establish one aspect of Bassanio, we first see him frivoling with some women, but then we also see him and Antonio kiss goodbye when they part to look for money. That money is to finance Bassanio's pursuit of a wealthy wife in Belmont. The question as to why Antonio risks his life to finance his close friend's (romantic) departure is answered at the very end with a hint that Bassanio's marriage may not exclude Antonio's love.

But one prominent component of the play simply wobbles in the film. As many have noted, *The Merchant of Venice* sets the harrowing story of Shylock against the romantic comedy of Bassanio and Portia. In the theater, the contrast can be affecting. On screen those comedic elements simply look phony. The camera, cruelly veristic, turns them into papier-mâché. First, the device of the three caskets by which Portia chooses a husband, a device in which Freud found symbolic depths, seems dully mechanical when thrust at us by the camera. Second, Bassanio's failure to recognize his newly-wed wife in the courtroom just because she has put on a lawyer's gown (and here a fake moustache) is a theater convention that works with theater distances but not in film close-ups. Then there is the ring that Bassanio has promised Portia to wear forever and which he has given to the lawyer. (This ring plot also includes a parallel with a friend of his.) With this last-minute ring mix-up, Shakespeare was clearly trying to restore the key of romantic comedy to his play after the grim trial scene. It can sometimes work on stage. Here, put into our laps (so to speak), it just makes us wish for the film to end.

A much more grave problem accompanies this play, unique in the whole Shakespeare canon. Harold Bloom, the eminent Shakespearean, again puts it strongly: "One would have to be blind, deaf, and dumb not to recognize that Shakespeare's grand, equivocal comedy *The Merchant of Venice* is nevertheless a profoundly anti-Semitic work" (Bloom, 171). It took two hundred years before Shylock was played as anything other than a stock Jewish buffoon-villain. Subsequently, great actors such as Kean, Booth, and Irving portrayed him as a tragic figure—and tailored the play to fit this view. Critics, too, have tried to make this case, attempting to exculpate the author. But no amount of wishful thinking can shift this play from the social attitudes of the author's day into Shylock's tragedy. The best that can be said here in defense of the greatest writer who ever lived is that he gave his Jew a character and a rationale.

In our time, specifically the post-Holocaust era, the play has entered a changed atmosphere. John Gross, in his magisterial study *Shylock: A Legend and Its Legacy*, states the matter calmly and well: "[*The Merchant of Venice*] can never seem quite the same again. It is still a masterpiece; but there is a permanent chill in the air, even in the gardens of Belmont" (Gross, 352). Radford's film, lithe and lively though it often is, cannot quite escape that chill.

A Midsummer Night's Dream (1999, Michael Hoffman)

Speaking of a different kind of chill: in the midst of the action of a 1999 film of *A Midsummer Night's Dream*, Puck stops to urinate. And this is not even the low point of the cinematic venture. Michael Hoffman adapted the play to the screen and directed it. Hoffman's dossier includes, among other pictures, a bright modern comedy-romance, *One Fine Day* (1996), and a heavy period drama, *Restoration* (1995). Much of the time, his version of Shakespeare's *A Midsummer Night's Dream* (1595) is almost a contest between these two types. But this contest is swallowed in a larger struggle that, scene by scene, foot by foot, ensnares most films of Shakespeare, a struggle that might as well be inscribed on the screen as a supertitle: "Please, audience! We know it's Shakespeare; but see how we're trying to keep it from being dull?"

Very few Shakespeare films have been free of this subtext—most notably, Branagh's work—but Branagh's passion for the plays, and his experience with them, flowed from the stage onto the screen to produce new incarnations rather than cultural obeisance by movies to classics. And, for the most part, Branagh was supported by actors who relished the chance to do in a new form what they had always loved doing; they weren't entering a strange, intimidating obstacle race.

This particular film of *A Midsummer Night's Dream* shows no sign of the (let's call it) Branagh attitude. It seems, though of course this is supposition, that Hoffman and his producers, after deciding to film the play, surely out of love for it, faced the frightening fact—revealed in that invisible supertitle—that they were actually daring to put Shakespeare on film. Then they had to face another present-day stern injunction about Shakespeare that applies either on stage or film: to *do* something to the play, and first, obviously, to the setting. Who would care about a film set in and near ancient Athens? Even Shakespeare's Elizabethanized ancient Athens? Damned few. Where to set it, then? Among foreign countries—and it had to be abroad—which was the most "in"? No question: Italy. And which part of Italy? Again, no question: Tuscany. And what about all the references to Athens in the text? Simple: they invented a Tuscan town called Monte Athena. (Many of the exteriors were actually shot in Montepulciano, which, incidentally, was Henry James's favorite town in Tuscany.) As for the magic wood, they couldn't possibly use a real forest, because they needed room to maneuver people and cameras. Seemingly, they remembered the magic wood that Max Reinhardt had constructed for his 1937 Hollywood *Midsummer Night's Dream*, and they tried for an equivalent studio job—ponds and lakes and towering trees. Then they apparently remembered Peter Brook's 1971 theater production and gave Titania a suspended leafy bed.

Next, the costumes: modern clothes would jar the mood, yet doublet and hose and hoop skirts and perukes would distance the action from the audience. Perhaps someone remembered A. J. Antoon's fine production of *Much Ado About Nothing* (1599) in New York's Central Park in 1972 (preserved on tape), which was costumed in clothes from 1900. The turn of the century was far enough back to support romance, yet close enough so that the suits and dresses looked something like our clothes and would feel "comfortable" to us. Then there were all those cute 1900 props you could bring in—big gramophone horns, bicycles. The fleeing lovers on bicycles in the woods—oh, the possible gimmicks to divert the audience's impatience with verse! Hoffman kept grabbing at diversions, with a shrug for overall directorial design.

About his adaptation of the play, we can only sigh at the necessities. Naturally, once again many of the long speeches were condensed (even as some of them are usually condensed in the theater), and naturally anyone who knows the play will wonder why one passage was retained and another shrunk or omitted, or why some matters were added. (Chief curiosity: Nick Bottom was given a shrewish wife, whose few lines are in Italian.) But this adaptation, though a thing of shreds and patches, could have been made to work—shorn of the desperate gimmickry.

And with a different cast. Two of the actors are pleasingly secure: Rupert Everett, as Oberon, gives the fairy king otherworldly ease; Dominic West gives the lovelorn Lysander clarity and verve. Then comes a string of mediocrities. Michelle Pfeiffer, as Titania, makes the fairy queen sound like Beverly Hills in space: she is not unintelligent, but her speech is out of key. Calista Flockhart, as Helena, and Anna Friel, as her unintended rival in love, Hermia, both strive hard, and so does Christian Bale, the Demetrius, but all three give the impression that they are wrestling with Shakespeare rather than fulfilling their roles. If the director wanted a wry Puck whose arteries are beginning to harden (though why fairies should age is not explained), then Stanley Tucci was the right man. Two of the cast are disasters. David Strathairn, supposedly the mighty Theseus, looks and sounds like a bond salesman who has strayed in from a costume party. Sophie Marceau, very pretty, cannot speak English well enough to handle even the few lines that are left to Hippolyta.

But the prime catastrophe is the man who is probably the best actor in the cast. What in the name of heaven (or Avon) is Kevin Kline doing in the role of

Nick Bottom? Kline is still one of the most clever, keen, technically polished comedians on the screen or stage—therefore an actor thoroughly capable of moving us to tears as well as laughs—but what is he doing as one of the "rude mechanicals," the proles who have banded together to put on a play? Possibly Hoffman thought it would be good to have an attractive figure of a man as Titania's dream lover, even with an ass's head, but when Bottom, the alleged weaver, joins the tinker and tailor and bellows-mender in rehearsal, he looks like a slick director who has been hired to stage a labor-union show. Kline has no trace of the boisterous, big-hearted, stage-struck amateur. "Bottom is Shakespeare's Everyman," says Harold Bloom (Bloom, 150), who sees him as a predecessor of Falstaff. Kevin Kline? No Shakespearean way. (A puzzle: Bottom appears for his first scene in a spiffy three-piece suit. Two pranksters pour bottles of wine on him from above, and he accepts the act as a small annoyance. This man?)

Lastly, the music: another odd mixture. We hear Mendelssohn at the start, naturally, and later, too. But along the way we get the *brindisi* from Verdi's *La Traviata* (1853) for no relevant reason, and even more oddly we get—twice, in amorous scenes—"Casta diva" from Vincenzo Bellini's *Norma* (1831). Since the first words of the aria mean "chaste goddess" and chastity is not the mood of the moment, are we hovering on the edge of a recondite joke?

There's a very valuable stage history of *A Midsummer Night's Dream* called *Our Moonlight Revels*. The author, Gary Jay Williams, says on the first page of the book's Prologue: "My primary interest throughout this performance history has been to understand each major production in its cultural moment." (For instance, he says of Peter Brook's production, which arrived just at the end of the swinging '60s, that its "appeal lay largely in its celebration of its own youthful, aggressive contemporary engagement with Shakespeare and the possibility of *communitas*, which it promised in its curtain-call lovefest" [Williams, 233]). Trying to apply the Williams criterion to this film, I can discern only a blend of ambition and fear. Hoffman and the producers self-evidently responded to the play's enchantment, but they also self-evidently didn't quite know for whom they were making the picture, didn't sense a "cultural moment"; so, in a sort of aesthetic trepidation, they put in everything they could think of— Bottom's wife, the bicycles, etc. The result is a film that, unlike Brook's production, is constantly searching for its audience.

The worst thing about this film of *A Midsummer Night's Dream*, like the movies by Loncraine and Luhrmann, and unlike the films by Nunn, Parker, Almereyda, Taymor, and Radford, is that it takes the idea of Shakespeare on film back to where it was—before Branagh. Taymor's *The Tempest* (2010) and Almereyda's *Cymbeline* (2014) would be yet to come . . .

Works Cited

Agee, James. "Masterpiece" [review of Laurence Olivier's film of Shakespeare's *Henry V*]. 1946. In *Agee on Film: Reviews and Comments*. New York: McDowell Obolensky, 1958. 361-367.

Bazin, André. "Theater and Cinema" (1951). In Bazin's *What is Cinema?* Vol. 1. Trans. Hugh Gray. Berkeley: University of California Press, 1967. 76-124.

Bloom, Harold. *Shakespeare: The Invention of The Human*. New York: Penguin-Putnam (Riverhead Books), 1998.

Cross, Gustav. Intro. to *Titus Andronicus. Shakespeare: The Complete Works* (Pelican Shakespeare). Ed. Alfred Harbage. Baltimore: Penguin, 1969. 823-825.

Eliot, T. S. "Seneca in Elizabethan Translation" (1927). In Eliot's *Selected Essays, 1917–1932*. London: Faber and Faber, 1932. 65–105.

Granville-Barker, Harley. "From *Henry V* to *Hamlet*" (1925). *More Prefaces to Shakespeare*. Ed. Edward M. Moore. Vol. 6. Princeton, New Jersey: Princeton University Press, 1974. 135-167.

Greenblatt, Stephen, *et al.*, eds. *The Norton Shakespeare*. New York: W. W. Norton, 1997. 741-800 (*Love's Labour's Lost*); 1090-1144 (*The Merchant of Venice*); 1157-1222 (*Henry IV, Part One*); 1304-1376 (*Henry IV, Part Two*); 1454-1521 (*Henry V*); 1668-1756 (*Hamlet*).

Gross, John. *Shylock: A Legend and Its Legacy*. 1992. New York: Simon and Schuster/Touchstone Books, 1994.

Hazlitt, William. *Characters of Shakespeare's Plays* (1817). Vol. 1 of *The Selected Writings of William Hazlitt*. 9 vols. Ed. Duncan Wu. London: Pickering & Chatto, 1998.

Shakespeare, William. *Othello*. Ed. Burton Raffel. New Haven, Conn.: Yale University Press, 2005.

----------. *Richard III*. Ed. Burton Raffel. New Haven, Conn.: Yale University Press, 2008.

Williams, Gary Jay. *Our Moonlight Revels*: A Midsummer Night's Dream *in the Theatre*. Iowa City: University of Iowa Press, 1997.

Yeats, William Butler. "At Stratford-on-Avon" (1901). In Yeats's *Essays and Introductions*. New York: Collier, 1961. 96-110.

An Ideal Husband (1947, Alexander Korda) & The Fan (1949, Otto Preminger)

Oscar Wilde can still be revived—it is done successfully every few seasons, at least in England—but it is no easy task, and *An Ideal Husband* (1895) is certainly not the likeliest play for the attempt. Under anything but perfect circumstances, its morality shows threadbare and its moralizing becomes sententious. A cold piece of wit animated with paradoxes, it wants a lot of footlight warmth to keep the life in it. Probably this play should never have been tried on the screen, not even in the beguiling pastels that costume designer Cecil Beaton was able coax out of Technicolor. Alexander Korda directed it in 1947 for London Film Productions, and his—or rather Wilde's—house of cards summarily collapsed.

An Ideal Husband is the play about that most promising Member of Parliament, Sir Robert Chiltern, who committed a foolishness (i.e., sold some government information) in his youth and who is brought to book for his indiscretion by a Mrs. Cheveley from Vienna. Sir Robert's chagrin arises not from any particular feeling of remorse, but from the fact that he is married to a woman of almost superhuman rectitude. In the course of some very trying hours, however, Lady Chiltern is persuaded to take a more normal view of life, and this softening, with a few fortunate little accidents, clears up the difficulty and sends Sir Robert on the next stage of his journey to 10 Downing Street. That, at least, is the bare frame; on stage, Wilde made it sparkle.

Paulette Goddard looks the part of the beautiful Mrs. Cheveley, a tribute as much to Beaton's flair for elegance in silk as to Goddard's carriage and comeliness. But when she moves in to make Sir Robert do her bidding, and when she gives his wife a quick review of the facts to date, she tends to get tough—a mistake no Wilde character, however depraved, could ever make. Also, she speaks her lines as though she were holding a piece of cheese between her teeth. The whole cast, in fact, goes in for an extraordinary amount of dental gymnastics in quoting the wicked Mr. Wilde. Too often you lose what they're saying from watching how remarkably well they say it.

Hugh Williams as Sir Robert walks very carefully through his part and upsets no tea trays; Sir Aubrey Smith is a splendidly bushy Earl of Caversham. Michael Wilding as Viscount Goring, the scapegrace philosopher and savior of reputations more palatable than his own, and Diana Wynyard as Lady Chiltern come off best in the film. He has the showiest of Wilde's lines and seems less afraid of them than the others; she carries out her role of improbable high-mindedness with the look of rather stupid virtue the author must have had in mind.

The film moves out of the drawing room every now and then for a brisk trot through Hyde Park Corner. There is no dramatic reason for introducing this animated set, but it reminds the audience that the camera can be used for more than photographing plays if anyone has a mind to do it. The adapters have otherwise stuck close to the original, asserting themselves only to the extent of improving Wilde's craftsmanship by switching a few of his scenes around, but the spirit has gone out of the piece. (Oliver Parker did better in his 1999 adaptation of *An Ideal Husband* by slimming down the plot, keeping a great many of the epigrams that help to camouflage the arrant plottiness, and helping the story by opening it up to *varied* locations.) It has become stilted rather than brilliant; brittle rather than witty; awkward rather than mannered. Tiresome is the word Wilde would have used.

I'm not sure what word he would have used to describe the 1949 adaptation (Otto Preminger) of his four-act play *Lady Windermere's Fan* (1892). In addition to cutting one of the most allusive titles in English letters to a single, flavorless word, the producers of *The Fan* set Wilde's play within a contemporary frame and turned the brittle sentiment of his drawing-room comedy into a mawkish romance. It is a quite complete transformation, and the cold fragments of Wilde's wit stick out here like the bones of an imperfectly buried skeleton.

We are to imagine that Mrs. Erlynne (Madeleine Carroll) has returned to London after the Second World War and looked up Lord Darlington (George Sanders) to demand his assistance in identifying and claiming an old fan found in some blitz debris and now being held for auction. To gain his friendship, she must explain what really happened on that incredibly distant evening of Lady Windermere's birthday ball. But why it had to be done in this clumsy, flashback manner, heaven only knows, since Wilde made matters admirably clear within the scope of his own text, using *his* fan to string together the play's scenes, in the present, and thereby simultaneously to evoke a traditional symbol of modesty and a modern current of infidelity. Put another way, *Lady Windermere's Fan* is concerned to juxtapose the absurd and the earnest, the comic and the serious, sincerity and inauthenticity, aestheticism and activism. *The Fan* has no such concerns, amounting to little more than a strangely uninspired, nostalgic romance fitted out in nice costumes.

Martita Hunt, as that dowager dragon, the Duchess of Berwick, understands the spirit of Wilde's perverse sermonizing and brocaded dramatics. The rest of the company, including Jeanne Crain, Richard Greene, and Hugh Dempster, have been left in a state of unseemly innocence. This, at least, would have given Oscar Wilde a laugh.

Another Part of the Forest (1948, Michael Gordon)

One gets, in the play *Another Part of the Forest* (1946), a small group of authentically colorful personalities and a dialogue vastly superior to what the movies normally consider adequate for their purpose. These you get because the play was written by Lillian Hellman, once one of the most skillful, and sometimes one of the most thoughtful, of American dramatists. *Another Part of the Forest*, the forerunner in narrative chronology to *The Little Foxes* (1939), is not, however, one of her successful plays. It explains in some detail what was happening to the Hubbard family in the years before the curtain rises on the foxes in their vineyard, but by itself it states no premise and reaches no conclusion.

There is a good deal of action in *Another Part of the Forest*, but there is no drama, and that is because evil, if it is to be used as a theatrical motif, must have something besides itself to grind upon. In the persons of Marcus Hubbard, the traitor to the Confederacy, and his daughter and two sons, the play proves to the hilt that evil begets evil; the Hubbards are spawn of the devil and they prey upon one another in a feast of reciprocal cannibalism. But there is no more real conflict in a nest of vipers than in a nest of pigeons.

Despite its weakness as a play, *Another Part of the Forest* is a field day for actors, and the Universal-International production of 1948 is well cast. Fredric March, as the disdainful and unscrupulous Marcus, and Ann Blyth, as his beautiful, sharp-toothed, and amoral daughter, perhaps strike the brightest sparks. But Edmond O'Brien as the smart son and Dan Duryea as the stupid one are almost as good.

As a creative work in its own right, however, the film version of *Another Part of the Forest* does not exist. Its only contribution is to bring to the screen certain scenes and fragments of action that the play implied in dialogue. And since playwrights have shown for centuries that they were perfectly able to construct their narratives within the physical limitations of the stage, this is no contribution at all. (As Hollywood still continues to trade on Broadway, it remains immersed in the dilemma of scrupulously reproducing a play and being called unenterprising, or of departing from it and being called impertinent.)

It's true that Michael Gordon's direction gives a fluency to scenes that might easily have become static due to the profuseness of the dialogue, and that there is hardly a shot which does not set up visual tension against the script's lashing, steel-spring dialogue. But Gordon is no William Wyler, who was the director of the 1941 film adaptation of *The Little Foxes* as well as the 1962 movie version of Hellman's *The Children's Hour* (1934), and who remains the master of the dramatized stage play. (Even when Wyler's camera ceases its roving to remain still, it invariably matches the pace and tension of the scene being played before it, and the precision of his shot-to-shot relationships is still unexcelled by any other director.)

Another Part of the Forest, though, is still worth seeing for the excellence of its individual performances and perhaps as a memorable example of the poison that can be distilled from the Southern vernacular.

Cyrano de Bergerac (1950, Michael Gordon)

There are still many film critics who maintain stoutly that movies never should and never can effectively be made from stage plays. The two media, they insist, are not only completely different but completely opposed to each other. Oddly enough, one play that was adapted with outstanding success to the screen was just the one that would seem to pose the knottiest cinematic problems—Edmond Rostand's ultra-romantic, ultra-poetic drama *Cyrano de Bergerac* (1897).

Almost no critic, when speaking officially, has a good word to say about Rostand's *Cyrano*. It is grossly improbable and emotionally absurd, a play for the groundlings that reeks of grease paint, stale dust, and mice in the upholstery. But just because of that sharp, exciting aroma, no one with a love for the theater can resist a capable performance of *Cyrano de Bergerac*; it is still the most completely theatrical play in the standard repertory, and addicts return year after year to gorge themselves on its staginess, with or without a star in the main role.

That said, those who remember (if there still are such people and such performers) great stage Cyranos will be quite unprepared for the drive, the tempo, the movement of this 1950 screen version. For on the stage *Cyrano de Bergerac* moved chiefly through the power of its language. There was action with the famous "rhyming duel," but for the rest physical action was largely a matter of events described by words. Carl Foreman's screenplay, built from the familiar Brian Hooker translation, skillfully supplies images for those words, and even more skillfully supplements words with action that somehow never obscures the text.

I would suggest that Foreman here has succeeded in doing what Laurence Olivier always wanted to do in his three Shakespearean movies, *Henry V* (1944), *Hamlet* (1948), and *Richard III* (1955). Pruning speeches, translating descriptive passages into pictures, using language richly where it describes personality (Cyrano's "No, thank you" speech) and sparsely where it might repeat what our eyes have already told us, he has fully developed Rostand's poetic drama into film terms. No doubt the fact that he was working with unhallowed Rostand rather than revered Shakespeare facilitated the process. There are not so many Rostand purists to insist upon the inclusion of every speech—and fewer speeches whose absence or manipulation could be objected to.

Whatever the reason, Foreman has prepared a script that starts with action and moves smoothly from high point to high point in the Rostand play. As Michael Gordon's camera (cinematographer: Franz Planer) wanders through seventeenth-century Paris or out to the battlefield, there is no sense of switching locales simply to supply some fresher visual interest. Foreman has, rather, drawn from the play its full screen potential of duels, battles, and romance and staged those scenes against their appropriate backgrounds, freed from the limitations that the theater would impose.

But *Cyrano de Bergerac* is still essentially the performer's tour de force. Written as such for the French actor Benoît-Constant Coquelin, it was later added to the repertory of the Briton Richard Mansfield, and became virtually the repertory of the American Walter Hampden. Then, in the mid-twentieth century, the Puerto Rican José Ferrer surrounded the part, first on stage and next on film, and made it completely his own. Ferrer's *Cyrano* is virile, a sword-flashing braggart whose poetry is second to his prowess. Throughout, he moves with the agility of a Douglas Fairbanks, fighting, leaping, and gesticulating with the same fine freedom. But Ferrer also has a voice that he can use magnificently, snarling his insults, roaring his defiance, edging his sarcasms, and breathing the fires of romantic love so softly, so affectingly that Rostand's old fustian becomes momentarily and magically real.

It may be frivolous or ungrateful to say so at this point, but I thought that Ferrer's nose was too large. The screen is a more intimate, though less immediate, medium than the stage, and details are easily overstated. Cyrano's nose was certainly a misfortune, but only he suggested that it was a promontory, and the proboscis that Ferrer wears is so alarmingly unstable that it distracts attention from Cyrano's personality and dwarfs the humanity that he must at times convey. I would have had it about five centimeters shorter. On the other hand, I would not spare a foot of the swordplay; it is virtuoso fencing, deft, witty and seemingly dangerous.

Finally, there is the sheer wonder of this film, nose or no nose. The utter skill of its adaptation, the magnetic shadings of Ferrer's bravura, gas-lit performance, overcome all disbelief. We can dismiss the play's improbabilities— Christian, the lover who can only see in Cyrano a helper, not a rival; Roxanne, who can believe that the voice that won her belonged to another man; even Cyrano, who prolongs the masquerade and misery through some romantic, half-baked notions of honor. We almost welcome them, because it is these very improbabilities that make possible the luscious poetry of the garden scene and our tears at Roxanne's final awakening to the truth.

This is a magic that may fade as soon as we leave the theater, but what is wrong with that? For in *Cyrano de Bergerac*, the viewer has—and can have again—what is, to my mind, one of the first really successful translations of a stage play to the screen. How such a "faithful" picture will appeal to an audience raised on movies and with no theater memories to fall back on, I cannot say; such observers may find it tame and miss the excitements of Steve Martin in the adaptation known as *Roxanne* (1987, Fred Schepisi), or, maybe, of Gérard Depardieu in the *Cyrano* of 1990 (Jean-Paul Rappeneau). Pity them.

The Glass Menagerie (1950, Irving Rapper) & *A Streetcar Named Desire* (1951, Elia Kazan)

To mention the most obvious point first, first, Warner Brothers' 1950 transcription of *The Glass Menagerie* is patently a stage play with screen appendages. It is not necessary to have seen the Tennessee Williams 1944 original to detect where his framework stops and the movie superstructure is tacked on. Amanda, driven frantic by her dream-bound daughter and her feckless son, recalls a moment of romantic glory, and we are carried back thirty years to a heady, carefree plantation ball; there are scenes in a shoe factory, in a business school, in a dance hall, at the zoo, on a ship at sea. They are woven rather skillfully into the original fabric (Williams assisted at the work), and they get around the obvious fact that no movie can spend an hour and a half photographing what goes on in one small room and hope to survive as entertainment. But dramatically these film asides have no more function than the chrome on a 1950 Buick, and, as usually happens, a tight, economical piece of stage construction now appears on the screen distended and sagging with superfluities.

Aside from this almost inevitable weakness, the quality of the performance was disappointing. The content of Williams' little tragedy is almost as fragile as its title, and the acting struck me as coarse-grained for the occasion. It was as though all the characters had been italicized to make sure that the least perceptive moviegoer would grasp them. Gertrude Lawrence came as close to ranting as so accomplished an actress can; Jane Wyman, apparently typed forever as a mooncalf, was asked to do almost nothing except appear moist in closeups; Kirk Douglas was brash to the point of insupportability; and Arthur Kennedy expressed himself mainly by punching his hat and flinging his coat to the floor in the manner made famous by his namesake, the late Edgar Kennedy.

To be sure, Williams did not create very subtle people in the first place, but under Irving Rapper's direction they carry labels around their necks. Paradoxically, the screen is both more impersonal and more intimate than the theater, and actors working for the camera should be encouraged to interpret their roles less broadly than would be appropriate on the stage. Yet it often happens that a screen cast does just the opposite: conscious that it will be compared to a beloved flesh-and-blood stage company, it presses hard for emotional impact. What results is less a facsimile than a parody of the original. *The Glass Menagerie* may in the end be a respectable translation and a good many people may weep contentedly at it, though you can't in good conscience say that the film is very interesting.

When a play is as successful, as esteemed, as beribboned with special awards as Williams' *A Streetcar Named Desire* (1947) itself finally arrives on the screen—as it did in 1951, one year after *The Glass Menagerie*—its intellectual and artistic mettle has been so thoroughly assayed that the film critic, then or now, is not expected to proceed farther along those lines. It is enough if he comments on the faithfulness of the adaptation, compares the dramatic merits of the two productions, and informs the mass market that it may sample (if it has not already done so) what had the New York audience by the ears seventy-five years before.

63

This restriction of function may be frustrating, but in the present instance I am glad of it. The theatrical merits of *A Streetcar Named Desire* are so obvious and its dramatic defects, if not subtle, would take so many words to make entirely clear, that I willingly forego the demonstration this late in the day. Very briefly, it seems to me that Williams' great powers of observation are not matched by equivalent insights; that what happens to his characters is insufficiently reflected in what they do as a consequence; that, although the play abounds in lines that are not only striking but acute, they do not combine into a compelling statement, point of view, or philosophy; that, therefore, and despite its evident claim to be taken seriously, *Streetcar* is less a tragedy than a depressant.

As a movie translation of a great Broadway hit, however, *A Streetcar Named Desire* is successful—with some reservations. It is directed, acted, staged, and produced at a level Hollywood still infrequently attains, and for these merits alone it is decidedly worth seeing—or re-seeing. The film's quality is less surprising than gratifying: Elia Kazan directed on the screen as on the stage and the principals, except for Vivien Leigh in the Blanche DuBois role that made Jessica Tandy famous in the theater, are the same: Marlon Brando, Karl Malden, Kim Hunter. Charles K. Feldman, the producer, deserves credit for having given his visitors every technical assistance that Hollywood could provide. The New Orleans set itself is squalid without being grotesque, the pace of the picture is fast without being hurried, and scene after scene is striking without becoming self-conscious. In a word, screen translations from the more inventive arts can be no better than this.

Tremendous, prime, even better than I remembered, is Marlon Brando's performance as Stanley Kowalski. The role is altered slightly from the original play; still, this is his performance. The screenplay, by Tennessee Williams himself, gives Brando a different "entrance" from the play. The play begins with Stanley coming in and tossing a package of meat to his wife. By the time the film was made, the stage Brando had become the Brando of popular imagination, and his entrance was delayed. The film opens with Blanche arriving in New Orleans, then finding her sister, Stella, with her husband, Stanley, in a bowling alley near their apartment. Blanche and Stella greet each other while Stanley roughhouses with some men in the distance. We are thus teased for a moment before the bomb explodes. A basic image of the play is of a wave of latter-day immigration (personified by the Polish-descended Kowalski) rolling right over domestic Anglo-French gentility; and here came that raw new power, rolling tidally.

Vivien Leigh's performance as Blanche Dubois doesn't have equal conviction. Leigh had played the role previously on the London stage, directed by Laurence Olivier, and she brings to the screen a real knowledge of Blanche and of the means to realize it. But—perhaps because she played Blanche first for a director quite different from the director of the film, Kazan—she never seems absolutely at ease. She is always working at the part, with great skill and of course with affecting beauty, but she is ever reaching for the pathetic. What's missing is the blank, frenzied evisceration, the cloak of true-false poetry that (to judge by the contemporary reviews) Jessica Tandy had in the New York production. When Leigh leaves at the end, it's a pathetically deranged woman being taken to a hospital. With Tandy, it was the netting of a butterfly-tarantula, a victim who assisted in her own victimization.

Kazan's film-directing style, for its part, is a little heavy. All through the first sequences in the apartment, the lighting is almost a parody of 1920s German expressionism, with street signs flickering on the faces of people within. Throughout, in that small apartment, Kazan concentrates on actors' movement, rather than on camera movement. Possibly he believed this more "honest" or possibly he wanted to re-create theater on film. But often the film looks as if it's being performed in a submarine. And Kazan uses off-screen sounds more blatantly than they would be used in the theater, especially the Mexican vendor selling *flores para los Muertos* ("flowers for the dead"; Williams, 149).

But the most upsetting element in the film of *A Streetcar Named Desire* is the screenplay. Under censorship pressure, Tennessee Williams was willing to tamper with his play significantly. This isn't without precedent. (Ibsen gave *A Doll's House* [1879] a happy ending for the German production. O'Neill altered *Desire Under the Elms* [1924], hoping for a Hollywood sale.) But precedent doesn't really help. A few scenes are so condensed that they almost sound like synopses (when Warner Brothers re-released *Streetcar* in 1993, some of this footage was restored), but those aren't the worst matters. Williams made two huge injurious changes. First, Blanche's long speech to Mitch—in which she reveals how she discovered her husband's homosexuality and caused his suicide—is made nonsense. She says in the film that she discovered that her husband was "weak." Not only is the sanitized speech silly, it destroys the complex of sexual relations that leads from the suicide to her promiscuities and on to Stanley, a figure exactly the opposite of her husband.

Second, the ending is changed. Stella punishes Stanley for his rape of Blanche by leaving him. In the play Stella tells a friend that, if she believed Blanche's account of the rape, she couldn't go on living with Stanley. Clearly, for her own reasons, Stella has convinced herself that Blanche's story is a fantasy of the unbalanced. In the film Stella apparently believes Blanche (to underline her story, Kazan has given us a shot of Stanley advancing on Blanche melodramatically), even though there's a quick line later to disavow that the rape ever took place. The film finishes with Stella's noble, head-high departure. This is not merely a sop to simplistic morality: it contravenes the torrential flow of the work. The play ends with Stella outside, sobbing after Blanche is taken away, and with Stanley going to her and embracing her. "He kneels beside her," says the stage direction, "and his fingers find the opening of her blouse" (Williams, 179). That is, the play ends in its glandular habitat. The film ends as a tract.

Ought *A Streetcar Named Desire* to be remade more faithfully for the big screen? (It was redone for American television in 1984 and 1995.) Eventually, it will happen, I suppose, and it may be done well, but I can wait. Maimed though Williams' art is in the 1951 movie version, Brando's art is monumental. That's enough.

Work Cited

Williams, Tennessee. *A Streetcar Named Desire*. New York: New Directions, 2004.

Death of a Salesman (1951, Laszlo Benedek)

One reason why Arthur Miller's *Death of a Salesman* (1949) was so popular in its day in New York, Chicago, and other centers of business enterprise was that it permitted living salesmen—and that included many men in those days—to shiver pleasantly at their own narrow escapes. The 1951 screen version of the play, more explicit as to character and motive than the stage original, makes clear how those salesmen were able to ignore the warning, or escape the fate, of Willy Loman and why as a tragedy the play is dubious.

The Greek prerequisites for a tragic hero are certainly not rigidly observed anymore, just as they weren't in 1949, but it is still true that if the protagonist is to move us, if in any degree he is to arouse fear and wonder in the spectator, he must have some soul, some strength, some beauty. A lunatic is not tragic, he is merely depressing, and from any moral viewpoint Willy Loman is a lunatic, perhaps just a fool. He is an abstract—and rather superficial—embodiment of salesmanship, completely dishonest, completely craven; in a proper tragedy, he would be lucky to be found as one of the furies tearing at the flesh of the hero.

To wit: Is Willy Loman a man shattered by business failure and by disappointment in his sons, as businessmen? Then why, when is he is younger and at least making a living, when he is proud of his sons and they of him, does he lie about his earnings to Linda and then have to correct himself? Why, at the peak of what is otherwise a molehill of a life, does he undercut his own four-flushing to tell his wife that people just pass him by and take no notice of him? The figure that comes through this play, in fact, is not of a man brought down by various failures but of a mentally unstable man in whom the fissures have only increased. Willy is thus shown to be at least as much a victim of psychopathy as of the bitch-goddess Success. When was he ever rational or dependable? Is this really a tragedy of belief in the American romance, or is it merely the end of a clinical case?

Let's assume for the sake of argument that Willy is *not* a psychopath, that he was a relatively whole man now crushed by the American juggernaut. To take up *Death of a Salesman*'s theme, what then is its attitude toward that capitalistic juggernaut, toward business ideals, or did Miller have nothing more than muzzy anti-business, anti-technology impulses in mind as he wrote the play? I ask such a question because there is no *anagnorisis* for Willy that would suggest the play's attitude, no moment of recognition for him, let alone a great downfall: he dies believing in money. Indeed, he kills himself for it, to give his son Biff the insurance benefit as a stake for more business, and because he confuses materialistic success with a worthiness to be loved. (Yet, while re-seeing the 1951 film of *Salesman*, which makes the play's environment more vivid—unlike Dustin Hoffman's 1985 television film of the theatrical production in which he had starred on Broadway—I could not help wondering why Willy had money worries. To wit: he had almost paid off the mortgage on his house, which was a piece of real estate in an increasingly valuable and desirable section, to judge by the building going on all around it.)

What we are left with in this play, then, is neither a critique of the business world nor an adult vision of something different and better, but the story of a man (granting he was sane) who failed, as salesman and father—or who failed to live up to his own unrealistic dreams of what salesmanship and fatherhood constitute—and who made things worse by refusing to the end to admit those failures, which he knew were true. The *pathos* of such a salesman lies in the fact that, unlike a genuine tragic hero, he has neither sufficient (let alone complete) freedom of action nor demonstrable public significance. Actually, he just is one of many just like himself, and, unlike classical or neoclassical dramatic protagonists, appears to have been conditioned passively, even gladly, to accept the very conditions of life that will lead to his own annihilation. This may in the end be sad, but it does not arouse the same kind of feeling as the classic tragedies.

As a matter of fact, newly titled as *Death of a Hero*, the play could have a real hero in the person of Willy's wife, Linda Loman. It is not entirely because Mildred Dunnock is a strong and evocative actress that she made the part spring forward both on the stage and on the screen. Linda is the true focus of the play-as-written (as is, secondarily, her elder son, Biff, who achieves some form of recognition, about himself and about his father, by the end of the drama), and it is only by strained force that our attention is kept on Willy.

That strain is personified by the performance of Fredric March in the film's title role. He plays Willy with his wings flapping and his feathers awry, behaving as though he had watched Lee J. Cobb's stage work in the original production and determined to go him one better at every turn. More exhausted at the start, more phony in the flashbacks, more insane in the present, March melodramatizes the emptiness of the role. As Biff Loman, Kevin McCarthy turns in the performance next best to Dunnock's. He works intelligently with his material and the confusion in the part is not of his making. It arises from the fact that Miller provided two different reasons for Biff's degeneration, and it is thus impossible to decide whether he is to be played as a youth suffering from the corrosion of fake ideals or the trauma of finding his father shacked up with another woman.

The film of *Death of a Salesman* is nonetheless well staged in a tone of dreary respectability—a tone more appropriate than the chic squalor of the play's stage set. The picture has also been directed with efficient if mechanical competence by Laszlo Benedek. Some people may think that by virtue of its flashback structure, between the immediate postwar period (late 1940s) and the time of the Great Depression (early 1930s), *Salesman* in fact makes a better film—with its dissolves, cross-fading, and minutely detailed realism as opposed to the modified, simplified, or theatricalized kind—than a play. Yet, in the case of Arthur Miller's play, the theater has a superior ability to suggest both the childishness of Willy's sons (by having the adult actors of Biff and Happy "unrealistically" play their boyhood selves onstage) and the momentousness of Willy's adultery (by having it occur, not "on location" in Boston, but on the forestage—right in the Lomans' living room, as it were). The problem here is not the medium but the messenger: Miller himself.

Saint Joan (1957, Otto Preminger) & Joan of Arc (1948, Victor Fleming)

By 1957, the history and legend of Joan of Arc obviously had long been in the public domain, so it was a waste of money to pay George Bernard Shaw's estate for permission to make a film about her unless you planned to use his script. The Otto Preminger production features a screenplay by Graham Greene, "based" on Shaw's *St. Joan* (1923), but there isn't enough Shaw in it to warrant the royalty. The old man's name is magic, however, and that probably is what Preminger was buying.

Shaw's play is about the mortal struggle between the divinity of kings and the God-given right of the individual to follow her own conscience. It was not the church but the state that was threatened by Joan's voices, and Shaw's heroine died less because she was a heretic than because she was a revolutionist. She was a mystic, but she was also very much a sturdy, rough-tongued feminist in the English style; I wonder sometimes how much of their saint the French recognize in Shaw's Joan.

Preminger's movie is about a nice peasant girl who has a knack (never demonstrated) for making soldiers, generals, and troops alike follow her suggestions. Her precocious grasp of logistics goes a little to her head, and she is burned at the stake for being stubborn in the face of her ecclesiastical advisors. Warwick is skulking about, it is true, but you would never guess why if you didn't know; and the various state and church dignitaries who keep assuring one another that the execution will have grave consequences sound merely ponderous or pontifical out of Shaw's context.

Not knowing any actresses who could play Joan, Preminger hired Jean Seberg, a high-school girl who had never acted before. She could not possibly have played Shaw's Joan, but Graham Greene has thoughtfully omitted from his text everything that might exceed her grasp. What is left is a rather dim and dolorous girl who makes foolish boasts and is a general nuisance around the French departments of state. She deserves, and gets, a harsh dressing down from the Archbishop of Rheims (Finlay Currie), but the stake is drastic discipline for uppity school girls. There is, in other words, no point to the role as Seberg has been taught to play it; and there is no more point to Richard Widmark's portrayal of the Dauphin as a halfwit boy from the Middle West. John Gielgud, deprived of any cogent reason for pulling strings at Rouen, makes something mean and fancy of Warwick.

The movies had proved before this that Joan of Arc is a suitable heroine for melodrama (see below). I'm not much interested in that interpretation of her legend, but it is more acceptable than this denatured and dramatically static version of a great play. Shaw was alive, and so alive, for so long that, in 1957, it must have been hard to believe he was dead. But dead he must have been, or they would never have dared this travesty.

The American playwright Maxwell Anderson permitted another such travesty in 1948. Indeed, he participated in the travesty himself. Anderson adapted his 1946 play *Joan of Lorraine* for the screen in a production titled *Joan of Arc*. The play is about a company of actors who stage a dramatization of the story of Joan of Arc, and the effect that the story has on them (the real interest in the drama). The film is no such play-within-a-play: it is a straightforward recounting of the life of the French heroine. Anderson retains the play's dialogue and adds scenes involving historical characters who do not appear in the original play. Ingrid Bergman is the star of *Joan of Arc*, just as she was the star of the original New York theatrical production of *Joan of Lorraine*, playing both Joan and the fictional actress who portrays her in the play-with-a-play.

Now, by 1948, let alone 1957, the legend of Joan of Arc was so well known, down to its details, that a valid presentation of it had to offer something new either of dramatic intensity or spiritual insight. The film of *Joan of Arc* brings neither. Victor Fleming's picture, as produced by Walter Wanger, is a religious rodeo, a western in armor. It provides bedazzlement in preference to invention; it displays actors in box-office profusion but does not require them to act; it rejects plausibility in favor of commercial acceptability; it is contemptuous of its audience. For all its Technicolor lavishness, *Joan of Arc* is as black and white a picture as ever came off a sound stage. The good people are radiant; the evil ones drool and leer like a convention of lascivious mortgage foreclosers. No strain is placed on the fragile understanding of a public that might be confused by conflicting motives or divided loyalties. The instructions are so simple a child could follow them—which is the idea.

Admittedly, there is no objection to telling the life of a saint in childlike terms. Folk heroes steer wide of complications. But if the chronicle of the Maid of Orleans is to be shown as a simple morality, it must be fashioned in a spirit of exaltation and innocence. *Joan of Arc*, for its part, is as down-to-earth, as uninspired a chronicle as could well be made of saints and kings and princes of the church wrestling for the possession of a nation. It is too shrewdly designed to be innocent, too aware of the titillation of a girl in boy's clothing, of the snob interest in wealth and position, of the pleasures of vicarious bloodletting (particularly in Technicolor). The film is simple only in the sense that it is emotionally threadbare; it is uplifted only by apocalyptic lighting and portentous music and the flaunted symbols of church and state. Nobility is spread on the screen like an ointment.

Ingrid Bergman, the star, does not have a strikingly ethereal personality; she is too healthy and sensible for morbid wool-gathering. Still, something might have been done to raise the pressure of her dedication. As it is, she lectures her heavenly counsellors like a nice little girl disciplining her dolls; and when Bergman rallies the demoralized French army beneath the walls of Orleans, she seems, for all her aluminum armor, like a Junior League slummer in a mission hall. "There will be no gambling and no blaspheming and none of *those* women in my army," she says in what seems a strangely hard-shell speech for a Catholic saint. She is Miss Arc, a competent and entirely worthy young lady; she is not the God-ridden Saint Joan.

In the trial scenes, Bergman fares better, for there is something inevitably appealing about a young girl being bullied by a bunch of grown men. But here the producers have gathered such an outrageous gang of sadistic assassins that the film almost lowers itself to the burlesque of a road-show *Uncle Tom's Cabin* (1852, Harriet Beecher Stowe). When it develops that Joan's jailer has an amorous interest in witches, the farce begins to show all around the edges and the bonfire is lighted just in time. The stake is a splendid thing in this picture, much more elaborate than you would expect for just one martyr. An executioner suffers a severe but belated attack of remorse and, as Bergman begins to perspire gently, someone remarks that now she belongs to posterity. The film has signally failed to show why that should be true.

José Ferrer makes his screen debut in *Joan of Arc*. He is the Dauphin whose weakness and venality betray the Maid to her English enemies, and he deserves to be mentioned separately because he has almost no share in the general foolishness. Ferrer is not a subtle actor (he excels in such diversely extravagant parts as Iago and Lord Fancourt Babberley/Charley's aunt) but he is intelligent and hard-working. He plays the wastrel kingling with a style and a restless invention that knock the other performers off the screen.

In sum, *Joan of Arc* is a pretentious and false picture that makes its appeal through sensation and sentimentality, but because it goes through the motions of a martyrdom and because it makes a great show of the crucifix in the closing moments, it will probably be called moving and deeply religious. As the Maid and the cross are a part of my faith, I am indignant at this debasement of their symbolism. If Maxwell Anderson was not, I pity him. Bernard Shaw was still alive when this film first appeared, and I wonder what he would have thought of it. Probably nothing.

Long Day's Journey into Night (1962, Sidney Lumet)

For all its faults, Eugene O'Neill's autobiographical *Long Day's Journey into Night* (1941) made memorable theater. Through three stolid, talkative, repetitive acts, the play slowly generated a charge of electricity that, in the fourth act, crackled all over the stage like chain lightning. Each new encounter of the tortured, loving, hating Tyrones bit deeper into the nerves, hearts, and minds of the audience; and suddenly it became clear that the overwhelming effectiveness of this shattering finale lay in the slow accretion of detail in those lumbering preliminary acts. One has to know as much, and care as much, about the Tyrones as they do themselves to participate in their anguish, to be wrenched by their tragedy. O'Neill, intent upon total revelation, prepared the way by peeling off layer after layer of each of his characters until, as midnight settled upon the ugly house, they were raw, bleeding, and ready for the final plunge into the abyss.

Obviously, this is unlikely stuff for the movies, in which it is preferable, in Herbert Gold's phrase, to have "happy people with happy problems" (Gold, 4, 78). Even more obviously, movie audiences—and American movie audiences particularly—are rarely willing to accept a gradual unfolding and involvement. They want to be grabbed, then hustled through their hero's predicaments. None of this happens in the 1962 film of *Long Day's Journey into Night*. Both the O'Neill play and the O'Neill method have been preserved, line by line and scene by scene. Ely Landau has produced it with a sense of dedicated integrity. He and his director, Sidney Lumet, assembled a truly remarkable cast (all of whom worked, I have learned, for minimum pay), then hewed to the original play with a fidelity both praiseworthy and self-defeating.

Films have a tendency to telescope, you see. They can tell a great deal in relatively little time, for the eye drinks in more detail and the ear listens more acutely at a movie than at a play. (After all, both sights and sounds are magnified a hundredfold by the camera and the microphone, while the screen sharply delimits the playing area at the same time as the sound recordist has eliminated all but the essential voice-and-effects tracks.) But O'Neill's technique, with its repeated lines and recapitulated situations, is the very antithesis of this. As a result, the early acts, sluggish enough on the stage, are often unbearably turgid on film—a situation hardly enhanced by Lumet's direction of the camera, in which brilliant flashes alternate with shots that are awkwardly composed and clumsily put together.

Where Lumet excels, however, is in the handling of his cast. Katharine Hepburn caps her distinguished career in the role of the pitiful, dope-addicted mother, groping back to the past for dimly remembered moments of happiness. Her transformations are extraordinary as, in recollection, she suffuses her tense and aging face with a coquettish youthfulness or, in the larger scheme of the play, changes from a nervous, ailing, but loving mother into a half-demented harridan. Her final scene, which contains some of O'Neill's most beautiful writing, is in every way masterful (including Lumet's daring cut from a long pull-back to a huge close-up).

No less impressive is Jason Robards, Jr., as the dissipated, ironic elder son, perhaps the most complex of all the Tyrones. With his magnificent voice and lean, lived-in face, he immediately becomes the film's most winning character—until he turns Jamie inside out to reveal the rottenness beneath the charm. Ralph

Richardson, the senior Tyrone and Dean Stockwell, as young Edmund (the youthful O'Neill himself), seem to do most of the listening, though each has moments of eloquence.

What is most extraordinary about the film of *Long Day's Journey into Night* is the way it builds. Shot in progression, the actors come to the peak of their powers just as the script rises to its climax. Together, they provide a final half-hour of sustained intensity the like of which has seldom been seen in the cinema. This may not be justification enough for an approach that pointedly ignores the potentialities of the film medium, but no one who has ever demanded serious, mature entertainment on the screen could afford to miss this picture at the time of its making—and can afford to miss it now.

Work Cited

Gold, Herbert. *The Age of Happy Problems*. 1962. New Brunswick, N.J.: Transaction Publishers, 2002.

Who's Afraid of Virginia Woolf? (1966, Mike Nichols)

Edward Albee's *Who's Afraid of Virginia Woolf?* (1962), the best American play of the 1960s and a violently candid one, was brought to the screen without pussyfooting. This in itself makes it a notable event in American film history. About the 1966 film as such, there is more to be said.

First things first. The most pressing question, since we already know a great deal about the play and the two stars, is the direction. Mike Nichols, after a brilliant and too brief career as a satirist, proved to be a brilliant theatrical director of comedy. This is his début as a film director, and it is a successful Houdini feat. Houdini, you remember, was the magician who was chained hand and foot, bound in a sack, dumped into a river, and then appeared some minutes later on the surface. You do not expect Olympic swimming form in a Houdini; the triumph is just to come out alive. Which Nichols has done. He was given two world-shaking stars, the play of the decade, and the auspices of a large, looming studio. What more inhibiting conditions could be imagined for a first film, even if the director is a man of talent? But Nichols at least survived. The form is not Olympic, but he lives.

Any transference of a good play to film is a battle. (That is why the best film directors rarely deal with good plays.) The better the play, the harder it struggles against leaving its natural habitat, and Albee's extraordinary comedy-drama has put up a stiff fight. Ernest Lehman, the screen adapter, has broken the play out of its one living-room setting into various rooms in the house and onto the lawn, which the play accepts well enough. He has also placed one scene in a roadhouse, which is a patently forced move for visual variety. These changes and some minor cuts, including a little inconsequential blue-penciling, are about the sum of his efforts. The real job of "filmizing" was left to the director.

With no possible chance to cut loose cinematically (as, for example, Richard Lester did in his 1965 film of the stage comedy *The Knack* [1962, Ann Jellicoe]), Nichols made the most of two elements that were left to him: intimacy and acting. He has gone to school to several film masters (Akira Kurosawa among them, I would guess) in the skills of keeping the camera close, indecently prying; giving us a sense of his characters' very breath, bad breath, held breath; tracking a face in the rhythm of the scene as the actor moves, to take us to other faces; punctuating with sudden withdrawals to give us a brief, almost dispassionate respite; then plunging us in close again to one or two faces, for lots of pores and bile.

There is not much that is original in Nichols' camerawork (cinematographer: Haskell Wexler), no sense of the personality that we once got in his stage direction. In fact, the direction is weakest when he gets a bit arty: electric signs flashing behind heads or tilted shots from below to show passion and abandon (both of them hallmarks of the college-cinema virtuoso). But he has minimized the "stage" feeling, and he has given the film an insistent presence, good phrasing, and a nervous drive. *Who's Afraid of Virginia Woolf?* sags toward the end, but this is because the third act of the play sags.

As for the acting, Nichols had Richard Burton as George. To refresh us all, George is a fortyish history professor, married to Martha, the daughter of the president of a New England college. They return home from a party at 1:30 A.M., slightly sozzled, drenched in their twenty-year-old marital love/hate ambivalence. A young faculty couple come over for drinks, and the party winds viciously on until dawn. In the course of it, Martha sleeps with the young man as an act of vengeance on George. The play ends with George's retribution: the destruction of their myth about a son they never had.

Burton was part of the star package with which this film began, but—a big but—Burton is also an actor. He had become by this time a kind of specialist in sensitive self-disgust, as witness the latter scenes of *Cleopatra* (1963, Joseph L. Mankiewicz) and all of *The Spy Who Came In From the Cold* (1965, Martin Ritt), and he does it well. He is not in his person the George we might imagine, but he is utterly convincing as a man with a great lake of nausea in him, on which he sails with regret and compulsive amusement. On past evidence, Nichols had relatively little work to do with Burton.

On past evidence, he had a good deal to do with Elizabeth Taylor, playing Martha. She had shown previously, in some roles, that she could respond to the right director and could at least flagellate herself into an emotional state (as in *Suddenly, Last Summer* [1959, Joseph L. Mankiewicz]). Here, with a director who knows how to get an actor's confidence and knows what to do with it after he gets it, she did the best work of her career, sustained and urgent. Of course, Taylor has an initial advantage: her acceptance of gray hair and her use of profanity make her seem to be acting (figuratively) even before she begins. ("Gee, she let them show her looking old! Wow, she just said 'Son of a bitch'! A star!") It is not the first time an American star has gotten mileage out of that sort of daring. Taylor does not have qualities that, for instance, Uta Hagen had in the Broadway version, no suggestion of endlessly coiled involutions. Her venom is nearer the surface. But, under Nichols' hand, she gets vocal variety, never relapses out of the role, and charges it with the utmost of her powers, which is an achievement for any actress, great or little.

As the younger man, George Segal gives his usual good-terrier performance, lithe and snapping, with nice bafflement at the complexities of what he thought was simply a bad marriage. As his bland wife, Sandy Dennis is credibly bland, which is all that she need be.

Albee's play looks both better and a little worse under the camera's magnification. A chief virtue for me is that it is not an onion-skin play—*Who's Afraid of Virginia Woolf?* does not merely strip off layers, beginning at the surface with trifles and digging deeper as it proceeds. Of course, we learn more about the characters as we go, and almost all of it is fascinating; but, like its giant forebear, August Strindberg's *Dance of Death* (1900), the play begins in hell, and all the revelations and reactions take place within that landscape.

What does not wear well in the generally superb dialogue is the heavy lacing of vaudeville cross-talk, particularly facile *non sequiturs*. (Also, in Lehman's version, so much shouting and slamming takes place on the front lawn at four in the morning that we keep wondering why a neighbor doesn't wake up and complain.) More serious is the heightened impression that the myth of the son is irrelevant to the play. It seems a device that the author tacked on to conclude matters as the slash and counter-slash grew tired—a device that he then went back and planted earlier. Else why would Martha have told the other woman the secret of the son so glibly, not when she was angry or drunk, if she knew she was breaching an old and sacred compact with her husband? Her "confession" obtrudes as an arbitrary action to justify the ending.

The really relevant unseen character is not the son; it is Martha's father, the president of the college. It is he whom she idolizes and measures her husband against; it is his presence George has to contend with in and out of bed. It is Daddy's power, symbolic in Martha, that keeps the visiting couple from leaving, despite circumstances that would soon have driven them out of any other house, let alone George and Martha's. Awareness of this truth about Daddy, of multiple other truths about themselves and their world, is the theme of this play: not the necessity of narcotic illusion about the son, but naked, peeled awareness. Under the vituperation and violence, under Martha's aggressive and self-punishing infidelities, this is the drama of a marriage flooded with more consciousness than the human psyche at mid-century was able to bear.

George and Martha's world is too much with them, their selves are much too clear. This is the price to be paid for living in a cosmos of increasing clarity—which includes a clearer view of inevitable futilities. And, fundamentally, it is this desperation as articulated in a childless, broken-hearted, demonically loving marriage that Albee crystallized in his flawed but fine play. And in its forthright dealing with the play, *Who's Afraid of Virginia Woolf?* becomes one of the most scathingly honest American films ever made. Its advertisements at the time said that "No one under 18 will be admitted unless accompanied by his parent." This may have safeguarded the children; the parents had to take their chances.

Inadmissible Evidence (1968, Anthony Page)

If there was one thing that John Osborne could do, it was write dialogue. This is a handy knack in playwrights and not to be taken for granted, even among famous ones. Osborne's 1964 play *Inadmissible Evidence* has faults, but one of them certainly is not pallid, clumsy, incredible, or trite dialogue. In speech, at least, he is proof that in England, in the mid-1960s, the line of John Marston was not yet dead. Osborne's particular brand of acid-torch rhetoric is the body of this play. He creates characters, sprinkles humor, and tells something of a story, but it is in the very texture of his language that the true drama resides. It is in the words, sword-slashing through the air, that he fixes the modern England that he would like with all his soul to loathe, if only he could.

I've seen *Inadmissible Evidence* twice on the stage and each time was struck strongly by several matters. Here are some of them. The nightmare prologue, which is virtually a long monologue for Maitland, the solicitor hero, is really the play in capsule. It could be played separately and would give us the essence of Maitland and of Osborne's views on most of what follows; mainly, the rest of the play is varyingly successful articulation of what is compressed in the capsule. The mind of Maitland is really the arena of the play; everything else exists there or else is significantly excluded. The character of Maitland—embittered, self-hating, viciously funny, lecherous, lost, agonizingly self-aware—is a plateau, not a cumulative growth.

The exposition of that character goes on too long, but the wonder is that Osborne can find as much variety and nuance in it as he does. There is some tension or change going on between Maitland and almost every other character, yet the sense we get is not of dramatic progress but of dissection. The short scenes in which the clients appear and tell their troubles are excellent—lives not merely summarized but distilled. The very existence of the play itself is a statement of social relevance: it is only eight years from *Look Back in Anger* (1956) to *Inadmissible Evidence*, and Osborne has shifted in subject from the outsider looking in to the insider looking wistfully out.

Whatever it lacks in cumulation and growth, the play of *Inadmissible Evidence* is committed to its language and to its theater-form. This commitment is what is lacking in the film. Where the play had courage of conviction in its form, the screenplay by Osborne settles for imitating the form of many other films. The opening monologue is drastically condensed and partially replaced by (dream) sequences of Maitland en route to the dock, as we are shown his home and his commuting. We also see him frisking on the beach with his secretary; we see Maples the homosexual being arrested in the subway lavatory; and so on. All this seems to me meek subservience to clichés of what makes films "visual." Osborne would simply have snorted if anyone had tried to impose equivalent formulas on him in the theater.

The play need not merely have been reproduced on celluloid (although Peter Brook's 1967 film *Marat/Sade* showed that this—or nearly this—can be cinematically practical). But most of the cuts in the play weaken the 1968 film, and most of the expeditions simply state prosaically what had been vividly suggested. Two "improvements" are particularly poor: the walks along ugly streets with ugly faces, to show how debased modern life has become, are an unhelpful bow to early Tony Richardson; and yet again the strip-club scene.

(Britain should by this point have banned movie scenes in strip-clubs to symbolize failed depravity.) What is left of the play is often very pleasantly vitriolic and sometimes quite moving. Anthony Page, who directed both play and film, has again done well by his actors; but his camerawork (cinematographer: Ken Hodges) lacks the immediate sense of self-assurance, of confident individuality, that his stage work had.

Nicol Williamson presents here a large portion of his original Maitland, surely one of the prodigious acting performances of the decade. (But the film diminishes him in a sense, besides condensing the role. In the theater he earned the audience's added admiration for a marathon sustained effort; here we know it was all done in bits and pieces.) Isobel Dean as a divorcing woman is beautiful in her brief scene, but the script omits her character's fantasy reappearances that, in the play, bore out the opening fantasy mode. Eileen Atkins is fine as the disgusted mistress-secretary. There is one advantage in the perambulating film script: it gives us more of a chance to see Jill Bennett, the "permanent" mistress. She is strong but also warm and tender, just the kind of mistress that any right-thinking (!) man would want and that a wry-thinking man like Maitland desperately needs.

Osborne and Page missed a chance in this film, I think. The original *Inadmissible Evidence* was too long for what it had to say; the evidence was rather too admissible but it had its own sense of being, which is here badly cracked. A play that was conceived as an increasingly bad dream has been made into a grittily detailed, naturalistic film. The energy that went into making the picture "visual" would have been much better spent on developing the dream concept, rather than on photographing pavements. The central image of the play—Maitland trapped in his office, sinking in a swirling sea, sucking for life at the end of a telephone—is thereby lost.

Henry IV (1984, Marco Bellocchio)

> Pirandello's importance seems to me of an intellectual and moral nature, i.e., a cultural rather than an artistic one: he sought to introduce into popular culture the "dialectic" of modern philosophy, in contrast to the Aristotelian-Catholic mode of conceiving "the objectivity of reality." (Gramsci, 30)

Thus Antonio Gramsci, who was a theater critic for four years in his late twenties. (Later, in his *Letters from Prison* [1947], he said that he had written enough about Luigi Pirandello in those years to make a book.) I venture to agree with Gramsci on the locus of Pirandello's importance, most clearly in *Henry IV* (1922). Many commentators compare that play with *Hamlet* (1601), a comparison that, for me, only underscores Gramsci's view. The lasting worth of *Henry IV* is not in its intrinsic artistic vitality but in its exploration of reality. No such choice is possible with *Hamlet*.

An Italian film of *Henry IV* in 1984 brought the subject up. It starred Marcello Mastroianni and was directed by Marco Bellocchio, who made the adaptation with Tonino Guerra, celebrated for his work with Michelangelo Antonioni. The names bristle with promise, but it is not kept. And after all the film's faults are noted, the central broken promise is Pirandello's.

To remind you: the time is today, in a castle. Twenty years earlier, a wealthy man (never named) was dressed for a carnival as Henry IV, the Holy Roman Emperor, when he fell from his horse and hit his head. Apparently this man then became deluded that he *was* Henry IV and, with the support of his family, has been living in eleventh-century dress, attended by appropriately dressed servants. The present action of the play includes the woman he once loved in vain; her nineteen-year-old daughter, who is her youthful image; the woman's lover, who may have pricked Henry's horse on that fateful day; and a psychiatrist who, along with these people, visits Henry. The doctor's intent is to stage a shock that may bring Henry to his senses, but the result is that Henry—who has not always been as deluded as he seemed and who has partly taken refuge in his "affliction"—stabs the lover in a frenzy, and is now sealed into his delusion.

The oddity of the film is that it does something of what I think the play needs, and still it doesn't succeed. In my minority view, the last act of the play is the only material of genuine interest. A two-minute choric prologue could easily replace the previous two acts of tortuous exposition and padding. The screenplay, made originally for Italian television, though it doesn't follow this prescription, greatly condenses the acts leading to the climax; yet the work isn't saved. It remains a demonstration of views of reality, not a gripping drama.

Mastroianni struggles with the role of Henry—rather, he keeps struggling to struggle. Throughout the film he seems to be reaching for substance to engage him and test him, substance that he can probe and crack open. All he seems able to find is a series of attitudes, admittedly somewhat more interesting than in several lesser films of his where he had been tempted to loaf. He isn't loafing here, but neither does his performance create the ark of mysteries that he and Pirandello wanted.

Bellocchio began his career smashingly with such strong films as *Fists in the Pocket* (1965), *China Is Near* (1967), and *In the Name of the Father* (1972). Subsequently he lapsed into ambiguous vacuities like *Leap into the Void* (1980) and *The Eyes, the Mouth* (1982). Pirandello hasn't helped him. The film adaptation puts in a couple of subtle touches to help the play-acting theme: when Henry falls from his horse (in flashback), he doesn't really strike his head hard; after he stabs his old rival and the wounded man is taken out, we see that Henry has used a trick, collapsible sword. But Bellocchio doesn't significantly use this "performance": his direction fragments into unwieldy bits. Any overview he may have of the work is never realized.

Is such directing thematically in keeping with the nature of *Henry IV* itself? Pirandello might have said yes, but I do not think that critics and audiences would agree. They'd want to know more about Henry.

Work Cited

Gramsci, Antonio. "The Theater of Pirandello." Trans. Naomi Greene. *Praxis*, 3 (1950): 30-37.

A Doll's House (1973, Patrick Garland)

With *A Doll's House* (1973) we are back with questions raised, hardly for the first time, by the contemporaneous Soviet film of *Uncle Vanya* (1970, Andrei Konchalovsky). Is there such a thing as a good film of a major play? Allowing for arguable exceptions like the films of *Henry V* (1944, Laurence Olivier) and *Pygmalion* (1938, Anthony Asquith), I think the answer was still no in 1973, as it is today in 2022. The better the play, the less alterable the form. What we get here are some swatches of Ibsen, scissored apart, with some gussets of transition and transposition inserted, and the whole renovation stitched together again. And, as is the way with film adaptations, although stuff is inserted, the whole altered thing is smaller than the original. This film runs only about 100 minutes—yet seems much longer.

It was made for two reasons: first, the topicality of the theme; second, the success that Claire Bloom, the star, had as Nora on the New York stage (as directed by Patrick Garland) and then on the London one. (Another film of *A Doll's House* [Joseph Losey], with Jane Fonda as Nora, came in the same year: 1973.)   As to the first reason, it's dubious. I think the play is as much a struggle against nineteenth-century dramaturgy as against nineteenth-century marriage, but it does have some size; and that size is reduced by harping on topicality.

Others have pointed out, rightly, that *A Doll's House* could have been about either Nora or Torvald; it is really about marriage, not the oppression of women. Indeed, five years after Henrik Ibsen wrote the play in 1879, the first great writer to discuss it, August Strindberg, argued vigorously that Ibsen had proved the direct opposite of what he intended to prove. (See the preface to Strindberg's collection of stories titled *Getting Married* [1884/1886], translated by Mary Sandbach and published by Viking, also in 1973.) Even granting Strindberg's biases, his argument delivers a jolt. In any event the play still creaks and cranks along, driven through its mechanics only by the great mind that knew all along how it would end.

Claire Bloom (born 1930) proves again here that she is a much better actress on screen than on stage: to put it properly, she is good on film and weak on stage. I saw her in this play and several other ones, I once even went to a solo poetry recital of hers, and never did she have a trace of *command*, let alone of conviction. Her voice and person simply were not able to cope with space. On film, with a compressed environment, with an opportunity to work almost completely for "interiorness," Bloom is truthful and at ease. On film she looks a bit old for Nora, which she didn't on stage; but here, insofar as the shredded script permits, she can more clearly paint in the character's substructure: her concept of Nora as consciously playing her little squirrel tricks, debasing herself deliberately to play the itsy-bitsy wifey-pifey for Torvald, so that when she changes, we can see her throw off a role rather than suddenly alter character.

Anthony Hopkins bulges forcefully as Torvald and cracks credibly. Denholm Elliott, who was a fine Judge Brack in Ibsen's *Hedda Gabler* (1890) at the Royal Court during the 1972-73 season, is an equally fine Krogstad here. Anna Massey is a reedily affecting Mrs. Linde, while Ralph Richardson delights as Dr. Rank.

Christopher Hampton derived the screenplay from his own reasonably limber 1972 stage version. Patrick Garland, like Claire Bloom, gains from the move to film. His direction of *A Doll House* on stage was like a Schubert operetta, warmed-over. He is much better off with less space to live in, moment by moment, and with enforced control of the audience's eyes. Sadly, this was Garland's first and only feature film; he made no others, though he continued to direct for the theater.

The Dresser (1983, Peter Yates)

I saw Ronald Harwood's play *The Dresser* in London in 1980 and wasn't greatly taken by it. I saw it again on Broadway a year later, hoping that a major cast change would help. It did, but not enough. I went to the film (1983, Peter Yates) more in duty than hope and was nicely surprised. The script is essentially what it was, a theatrical *tour de force* about the theater with more *tour* than *force*, but in 1983 there was Albert Finney. His performance not only enriches the role he took over, it improves the balance of the piece. Finney can't rid the work of its fundamental vanity, but he certainly gives it more life along the way, and he does it in a style with a particular reward for anyone interested in acting.

During the 1950s Harwood spent seven years in the theatrical company of Donald Wolfit, as actor but part of the time as Wolfit's dresser, and out of that experience Harwood wrote both a biography of Wolfit (1971) and this play. Americans know Wolfit chiefly through his substantial supporting roles in films—such as the girl's tycoon father in *Room at the Top* (1959, Jack Clayton)—but in the British theater he was a star who headed his own touring company, specializing in Shakespeare.

In *The Dresser* Harwood drew on his Wolfit experience for character and atmosphere only; it's not strictly factual. For instance, the play/film takes place in wartime Britain, January 1942, in a small town before, during, and after a performance of *King Lear* (1605) by the knighted star, on what turns out to be the last day of his life. He is supposed to have played Lear hundreds of times before. But Wolfit didn't play his first Lear until six months after the date in the play, wasn't knighted until 1957, and died (in a hospital) in 1968. These differences deliberately keep the script from being taken too biographically, but nothing can—or is meant to—keep it from conveying the flavor of the man and his theater.

The basic structural twist is familiar: a shift of the spotlight from the expected protagonist to a peripheral figure. Some previous examples: Arthur Caesar's play *Napoleon's Barber* (1922; filmed by John Ford in 1928) and Tom Stoppard's drama *Rosencrantz and Guildenstern Are Dead* (1966; filmed by Stoppard in 1990). Harwood has taken the hero-valet combination and, if he doesn't concentrate exclusively on the valet, at least he shows how important the latter is to the hero. Harwood draws both these characters with intimacy and skill, and he sketches in the others adroitly—the star's wife, the quietly adoring spinster stage manager, the differently pathetic members of the company. The dialogue is neatly turned. The trouble is that, despite the script's various virtues, it comes at last to only one more *agon* about the Agony of It All—the strain of being a star performer on whom the vampiric public feeds. I know of few subjects more tedious.

The protagonist in past films on this theme has moved from actor (*A Star Is Born*, 1937, 1954, 1976, and 2018) to rock singer (*The Rose*, 1979). Those films are always telling us how the public uses up the star cruelly, but whatever the specific subject, the idea is vain. It may be true, even for the best artists, but it's no more true than for many doctors or teachers or social workers or any professionals on whom many others depend greedily, even selfishly. These other professions don't in themselves provide media for self-glorification, as the performer's profession does. To me, the strain is part of the game. A star's sufferings move me just about as much as a President's complaint about overwork after years of campaigning to get the job.

Harwood had an instinct about the defect in the theme and has tried to buffer it by setting the play in wartime. The star thus can wave the banner of duty: he is fighting the barbarians with his own means, by taking Shakespeare to every corner of the embattled island; and his effort to pull his racked self together and perform can thus be seen—through his own eyes anyway—as something more than "the show must go on." But it's just wartime camouflage for perennial histrionism. The last day of an actor who summons himself to give what may have been his best performance before dying in his dressing room is, at the end, nothing more than that. It has no reach or resonance; it's just an exercise in self-pity before a backstage mirror

Finney, however, embellishes the texture. In London in 1980 the star was played by Freddie Jones, who supplied little more than the plummy vocal quality. In New York in 1981 a much better actor, Paul Rogers, gave the part greater range but, within the structure, he couldn't enlarge the play sufficiently. In the screen adaptation Harwood has given the star more "space," and Finney fills it. Filling it, he alters the balance to the film's benefit. Besides, Finney does something that neither Jones nor Rogers did: he models his performance of the star on Donald Wolfit himself.

I never saw Wolfit on stage, but I don't think experience of Wolfit is a prerequisite to appreciating what Finney does here. It's clear that he's not giving us Finney, as he had done engagingly in many films and as he did less engagingly in *Hamlet* on the London stage in 1975: he is creating, out of himself, someone distinct from himself. Wolfit subscribed whole-souledly to what he called the "unfashionable theater," with a large-scale style that is too often glibly confused with hamminess. If Finney has a fault in this film, it's that confusion: the segments of his Lear that we see are somewhat hammily broadened. But as the actor himself, the offstage man who goes onstage to speak those lines, Finney does a work of imaginative transformation, with the perception that an actor who spends his time in great roles, often regal ones, sometimes loses sight of where the stage ends and the so-called real world begins.

Tom Courtenay plays Norman, the dresser, as he did in London and New York, and it's a flawlessly turned performance. But that's what it was at the start. Courtenay is as rhythmically tidy, touchingly effeminate, understandably vindictive, and fiercely loyal as he was in 1980-81. In the film, however, because of the extension of the "Wolfit" role and Finney's power in it, Courtenay has to bear less of the weight, which helps. This is no reflection on Courtenay. If the soul's turmoil of an actor pulling himself together for a performance is less generally fascinating than theater people think, the travails of his dresser in maneuvering him are even less so. Courtenay is better off here for sharing the burden.

Another pleasant surprise is the direction of Peter Yates. Most of what I had seen of his work up to this point, from *Bullitt* (1968) to *Eyewitness* (1981), was consecrated to the ideal of flash, of dazzle. Here he simply places his film, which is about acting, at the service of his actors. There's no trickery, no egotistical director's attention-grabbing. He puts his camera at every moment where it will be of most use to the moment and to us. He keeps it close much of the time, not for immense close-ups but because the faces are what the film is about. If a director hasn't developed a style through which a film can move to its truth, and Yates never did, his best course is to be invisible, which is what Yates does effectively here. And which is why, in the best sense, I can still "see" him.

Plenty (1985, Fred Schepisi)

In 1985, the exceptionally gifted David Hare made a screen adaptation of his 1978 play *Plenty*, and quite evidently began with decisions about form. To understand those decisions, a glance first at the play. It deals with an Englishwoman named Susan Traherne: her exaltation during her underground war service as a late teenager in France, 1943-44; her anticipation of splendid change in the postwar world; her growing disappointments; her various jobs; her various grabs at personal fulfillment, including a rocky marriage; her decline into mental shakiness and a threat of utter dissolution. It ends with a retrospective glimpse of her in France, August 1944, exultant at victory.

The play's power (despite some faults discussed later) lay not only in its concise dialogue and sharp characterizations but in its very shape. In a postscript to the published play Hare wrote: "I planned a play in twelve scenes, in which there would be twelve dramatic actions" (Hare, 87). Part of his plan was to breach chronological order at the start. The play begins in 1962, then goes back to 1943 so that we see the young committed Susan only after we have had a hint of her postwar fate. Another effect of Hare's plan is that the very shapes of the twelve scenes are mimetic of the dialogue, tense and astringent. The play is, so to speak, shaped the way it sounds.

I see no intrinsic reason why the play could not have been filmed pretty much in that form or cluster of forms, allowing for some cinematic easements at the joins. This was done well (to choose two examples) with Pinter's *The Caretaker* (film, 1963; Clive Donner) and *The Homecoming* (film, 1973; Peter Hall). I can easily see the commercial reasons for converting the play into a more "producible" item. I don't mean explicit betrayal of ideas: I'm speaking only of form, though of course form is aesthetically connected with those ideas. The story is now lined up in strict chronology, except for the closing flashback; this takes care of any worries about confusing a film audience, but it seriously diminishes that first wartime scene.

Almost everything implicit in the play is now spelled out in the film. When Susan gets her first postwar job, utterly prosaic, we see the dingy office. When she's working in advertising and quits in the middle of a dog-food commercial, we are given the inanities in detail as if we needed proof that Susan is superior to them. When her husband, a foreign-service officer, is posted to the Middle East, we go there. (Said to be Jordan but shot in Tunisia. The producers weren't going to miss *that* visual chance, irrelevant though it is.) The argument for such adaptation of a play—not arbitrarily true—is that to confine the action to a few rooms, more or less, is uncinematic. Another argument, incontrovertibly true, is that one can't get many production values out of a film confined to a few rooms. And everyone concerned with *Plenty* wanted to transform it into a big picture for a big star.

The basic problems of Hare's extraordinary play persist, even grow, in the film. It's hard to believe that a person of Susan's mind could have been so deluded by the excitements of war as to forget history: to forget that no war has ever been followed by the complete realization of the aims for which it was fought, or nominally fought. We know that war experience often proves to be the high point of many people's lives, but that's quite a different matter. Further, *Plenty* strikes me as a political work with the political credo omitted. Hare, alone or in collaboration, has written plays with radical political views. Here he criticizes strongly a self-gratifying society and a stodgy government but does so almost peripherally. And now, the revised, bloated structure of the film only emphasizes the play's flaws. Susan seems even more ethically and intellectually slothful, a woman waiting for the good *not* to happen so that she can take refuge first in bitterness, then in recurrent "mental" episodes. She looks down disdainfully from unearned elevation. (Her war experiences were brave but scarcely unique.)

This makes the film sentimental, where the play, though flawed, was not. Hare underscores that sentimentality in two ways particularly. In the first wartime scene Susan meets a British agent who tells her that his chief gave him a pair of cuff links for good luck. This is in the play. In the film we go back with them to her room in the French village, where the pair sleep together. When he has to rush off suddenly on a mission, he leaves the cuff links as a memento. From then on, she keeps the cuff links in her pocketbook, and they become a visual leitmotiv as she recurrently looks at them through the years. In the penultimate scene in 1962, she and that agent are reunited in a shabby room in an English seaside hotel. When she zonks out on marijuana, he goes, but not before he sees the cuff links in her open bag. (All that's missing is a "links" theme in the score.)

And there's a small but significant change in the final scene, the flashback to the end of the war that is in both play and film. In the film it's on a lovely French hillside overlooking a village where victory is about to be celebrated—Susan and a lovable old French farmer and his lovable old horse. There's some wistful conversation, then he invites her home to have some soup with his wife and himself. In the play, before that invitation, the farmer says he's not going down to join the celebration. "Myself, I work. A farmer. Like any other day. The Frenchman works or starves. He is the piss. The shit. The lowest of the low" (Hare, 85). Susan completely disregards him and ends with her joyous last line, "There will be days and days and days like this" (Hare, 86). The film, too, ends with that line, but the softening of the farmer's dialogue eliminates the play's clear signal at the (chronological) start of her story that the war has made little change in many people's lives and that she is incapable of seeing it. The cuff links and the sweetened farmer are among the alterations that slacken tensions around and within Susan.

The Susan is Meryl Streep. I've been fervent about her since her drama school days, but I think her performance here—excepting *Still of the Night* (1982, Robert Benton), which was just a blip on the screen for all concerned—is her least successful film work to date. This is a relative statement, relative to Streep's gifts, which easily embrace the emotional range of this role. But her voice sounds limited, uninflected, insufficiently interesting. Vocal richness has long been a problem for her, I think; and here she is surrounded by English actors brought up in a tradition where the voice is not just a means of making words audible but is the instrument with which acting begins. That tradition is not one of hammy scooping and gliding but of belief in the magic of the word itself and of the finest shades of inflection.

Streep has several big scenes to play with John Gielgud, the emperor of this tradition; one long scene with Ian McKellen, who is very adept in it; and a great deal to play with Charles Dance, who is decently competent in it. All of them, merely by using their techniques truthfully, make Streep sound vocally lackluster. Even Tracey Ullman, a young woman of limited experience, has, simply by virtue of an ear conditioned to England's English, more color than Streep. Unlike Streep's work with accents in *Sophie's Choice* (1982, Alan J. Pakula) and *Silkwood* (1983, Mike Nichols) and *The Seduction of Joe Tynan* (1979, Jerry Schatzberg), her work here makes her seem so concerned about merely sounding English that it absorbs much of her imaginative energy. (Her English role in *The French Lieutenant's Woman* [1981, Karel Reisz] was in a quite different vein—lush romance.)

Gielgud, as an arrogant but honorable ambassador, is a high-comedy delight. McKellen, in his one long scene as a lofty foreign-service official, embodies the dictum he pronounces: "Behavior is all." Dance, in the largest male role, is perfectly cast: he is winning enough to persuade us that Susan could feel fondly for him yet mild enough to let us understand that she might tire. As a cockney whom Susan selects to father a child in one of her attempts to replenish her life—an attempt that doesn't click biologically—Sting (Gordon Matthew Sumner) has aggressive sensitivity. Ullman, button-eyed and pert, is lively as Susan's chum, but her part is condensed to mute its counterpoint. In the original, this scattery young woman blunders her way up from bohemianism to give her life some purpose. This aspect of the play is present but dimmed in the film. Sam Neill, first widely visible in the Australian *My Brilliant Career* (1979, Gillian Armstrong), is adequately taciturn as the secret-agent lover.

Fred Schepisi, also Australian, who directed the haunting *The Chant of Jimmie Blacksmith* (1978), has a touch of David Lean: he suggests intimacy in the large scenes and sizable power in the intimate ones. Richard MacDonald's sets are first-class. He uses fireplaces as totems of change in Susan's life. In her first postwar flat, there's a small gas heater; in a later home, there's a mod fireplace set above floor level in a plaster wall; later, in her married home, there's a huge ornate hearth and mantel. Ian Baker, Schepisi's constant colleague, is one of three or four Australian cinematographers who have lately established themselves as peers of the best. Every moment of *Plenty* looks lovely without being beautiful.

In that postscript to *Plenty*, Hare said: "It's a common criticism of my work that I write about women whom I find admirable, but whom the audience dislikes," and he explains that what he's aiming at is ambiguity. He wants the audience to make the decision. My complaint about *Wetherby* (1985), the fascinating film he wrote *and* directed, was that I couldn't determine that he found his heroine admirable or anything else and that I didn't like or dislike her. What I felt was incompletion, not ambiguity. As for *Plenty*, in the original play there was never any doubt about liking Susan, by Hare or us, but the ambiguities of theme seemed to be more in Hare than in the work. The film discloses fewer ambiguities in him, more (questionable) clarity of purpose. Without actually traducing his ideas, he has somewhat smoothed out his fractious play for a star, according to the film world's needs.

Work Cited

Hare, David. *Plenty*. New York: Penguin/New American Library, 1985.

The Madness of King George (1994, Nicholas Hytner)

Scarlet begins it. British officers swirl into an ante-chamber of Windsor in 1788, their scarlet uniforms declarative of pomp and glory, the dresses of the ladies around them glittering in complement. Thus Nicholas Hytner opens *The Madness of King George* (1994), establishing the visual drama of court life as an element, not mere background, in the political and personal conflicts shortly to follow.

The film is adapted by Alan Bennett from his 1991 play *The Madness of George III*. (The title was altered slightly so that we movie mutts won't think this is the second sequel to a first film about George.) Hytner directed the play's premiere for the (London) National Theatre, and this production was brought to New York. For those who, like myself, were disappointed in the play, the film contains pleasant surprises, all of them resulting from differences between the two arts.

The story starts just before the onset of King George's first bout of madness, then follows his treatment by several physicians, his recovery, and his resumption of power. Wound into this account, itself harrowing and pathetic by turns, are all the strands dependent on the king's condition. Political balance varies from day to day according to the color of the royal urine, which is supposedly an index to his recovery. The opposing leaders in the House of Commons, William Pitt the Younger and Charles James Fox, jockey to keep or get control, and they vie to maneuver the Prince of Wales, whose hopes rise and fall as his father's health falls and rises. (Some digs about royal-family behavior continue to have present-day sting.)

All of the above, as material for drama, may sound remote and moldy to modern viewers. Shakespeare can grip us with stories of English kings, but even he had occasional troubles. (Take another look at *King John* [1596].) Lesser dramatists, which all other dramatists are, have crammed theaters and libraries with plays about royal hugger-mugger that are torpid. There are usually two troubles with them. Only a really vitalizing art can make us empathize today with royal lives; and history isn't artistic—it insists on *longueurs*, and it doesn't always provide climaxes.

On the first score, Bennett's play does better than most. The fear and fascination of madness link kings and commoners. And Bennett's dialogue can glisten. He writes in chewy morsels that render period speech with a modern edge. Says the Prince of Wales: "To be heir to the throne is not a position; it is a predicament" (Bennett, 55). Or the king to a doctor who had previously been a clergyman:

> KING. You have quitted a profession I have always loved, and embraced
>   one I heartily detest.
> WILLIS. Our Saviour went about healing the sick.
> KING. Yes, but he had not 700 pounds a year for it. (Bennett, 41)

Bennett can also be nicely wry. In one episode Dr. Francis Willis orders the king to read aloud, as therapy presumably, a scene from Shakespeare, and they light on the recognition scene from *King Lear* (1605), in which the mad Lear recovers. (Bennett would have gotten more from this episode if he had told us that this was possibly the last time these words were spoken in George's lifetime.

When his madness subsequently returned, Shakespeare's text was banned from the stage; only a prettified version was performed until George's death in 1820.)

But on the second score, even Bennett's clever style on stage didn't triumph over an integral burden of fact. Madness was not a play but a chronicle. There was no climax. Some things happened; then they stopped happening. Bennett tried to compensate by inserting, just before the finish, a flash-forward, which told us that the madness was going to recur and that the twentieth century would discover that the trouble was physiological, not psychological. But the flash-forward didn't make us forget that we had spent a long evening only to return to the situation where it all started.

Thus the play. Bennett's film adaptation omits the last-minute warning of more trouble ahead—along with other trimming—yet it's much stronger than the play. True, the film audience will now believe at the end that the king was permanently cured; so, in script terms, the film is even more of a chronicle than the play. Yet, paradoxically, it is more gripping than the play. The simple explanation: it is a film. As film, *The Madness of King George* is strong proof that the immediacy of the human countenance, the almost palpable verities of costume and place, the ranges of vista, the enforcements of rhythm—all of them film prerogatives—can fuse and create genuine dramatic sustenance. It happened, for example, in Roberto Rossellini's *The Rise to Power of Louis XIV* (1966), and it happens again here.

I suggest no superiority of film art over theater art: I'm describing a difference. (To note one contrary instance of the theater's power: no film, however great, has done for me precisely what Ariane Mnouchkine's *Les Atrides* [1990] did.) A central beauty of the theater is that it can suggest physicalities, though it often fulfills them; a central beauty of film is that it can fulfill physicalities, though it often suggests them. In the case of *The Madness of King George*, helped marvelously by the deployment of Handel on the soundtrack, film fulfills.

Nigel Hawthorne, who was George in the National Theatre production, plays him again here. He was scintillating on stage, and he's even better here—because it's film. Skilled and vivid though his theater performance was, it impressed most in its marathon effect: Hawthorne did the whole long demanding role right there before us in one evening. On film, obviously, that effect disappears, and his acting supervenes. Here it scintillates even more brightly: shrewd, vain, pathetic, regal. And film brings us a Hawthorne quality that escaped me in the theater: his resemblance, in face, voice, speech, and flavor, to Ralph Richardson. Wonderful. Film could certainly use such an actor, and did: Hawthorne subsequently performed in *Richard III* (1995, Richard Loncraine), *Twelfth Night* (1996, Trevor Nunn), and *The Winslow Boy* (1999, David Mamet) before passing away in 2001.

Most helpful among the others are Julian Wadham as Pitt, Jim Carter as Fox, Rupert Everett as the Prince (though he's not as fat as his father keeps complaining), and John Wood as the cobra Edward Thurlow. Ian Holm is not his most incisive self as Dr. Willis. Helen Mirren, who plays Queen Charlotte, doesn't convince as the mother of fifteen children, nor does she consistently sound German, which Charlotte was. The costume designer, Mark Thompson, has seen the entire company ingeniously, as figures out of the painters Johan Zoffany and Thomas Rowlandson and Angelica Kauffmann. Andrew Dunn, the impressive cinematographer, serves both the director and the designer with perceptible relish.

A comparative study, international, immense, could be done of directors who have worked in both theater and film. Some broad categories are apparent. First, directors whose style is essentially unchanged in both arts—Elia Kazan and Mike Nichols, for instance. Second, those whose theater and film works are markedly different. A towering instance is Ingmar Bergman: to judge by the three theater pieces of his that I've seen, his films allow him to shed gimmicks and concentrate on intensity. Hytner, much lower in the scale, is also in this second group, a director whose film work is distinct from his theater approach.

In 1993-94, in New York, I saw two of Hytner's theater productions, *The Madness of George III* and *Carousel* (from the 1945 musical by Rodgers and Hammerstein), and thought that, contradictorily, *Carousel* had less musical-comedy fluency than *Madness*. But the film of *Madness* displays new resources in Hytner—freedoms offered and exploited, motion understood as something other than action and speed, a comprehension of texture itself as a form of dynamics. In *Hamlet* (1601) Claudius says, "Madness in great ones must not unwatched go" (III.i.202, *Hamlet*; p. 135). Hytner, Bennett, Hawthorne, and their colleagues ensure that George will be watched.

Works Cited

Bennett, Alan. *The Madness of George III*. London: Faber & Faber, 1992.

Shakespeare, William. *Hamlet*. 1992. New York: New Folger Shakespeare Library, 2012.

Oleanna (1994, David Mamet) & *American Buffalo* (1996, Michael Corrente)

David Mamet dazzles. Here are a few selections from his crowded career (and, in 1994, he was not yet fifty). Film: *House of Games* (1987), which he wrote and directed; the screenplays of *The Verdict* (1982) and *Hoffa* (1992). Theater: *The Water Engine* (1976), *American Buffalo* (1975), *Glengarry Glen Ross* (1983), *The Shawl* (1985), *Speed-the-Plow* (1988), a version of *Uncle Vanya* (filmed as *Vanya on 42nd Street* [1994, Louis Malle]). He has published books of essays, and his first novel, *The Village*, appeared in 1994. He has also taught acting in several universities.

Mamet's plays and his original screenplays differ in style and intent, but most of them, up to *Oleanna*, share some characteristics: a sense of life as tangle, of truth as prismatic and mercurial, of secrecy and deception as contemporary dynamics. Then a change arrived. His most hotly discussed play—subsequently filmed by him—has almost none of these qualities. A two-character work about a fortyish university professor and a female student, *Oleanna* (1992) tackles the subject of male attitudes toward women, of women's changing attitudes toward themselves. It is much leaner, more two-dimensional, more argumentative than most of Mamet. Possibly this was inevitable because *Oleanna* attempts to deal with concrete social ideas. Perhaps, too, that's why he stripped his characters of the mysterious or quasi-mythical qualities that often attend his people. But if Mamet did indeed tell himself that he had to put aside his characteristic art in order to do this job, he paid a price for the choice.

I saw *Oleanna* on stage in its Cambridge premiere and much admired Mamet's courage in confronting this thorny issue—one that's complicated both by oppressive tradition and bumptious innovation. But the play left me uncertain, distanced. I hadn't expected a "solution," but I had expected to be more greatly involved. A year later the film medium did ruthlessly to *Oleanna* what it often has done to other plays. This film, directed by Mamet himself, exposes what was ungainly in the play.

Let's look first at the writing, and we might as well begin with the title. As epigraph, Mamet quotes a traditional folk song in which Oleanna is a place where the singer would rather be than "be bound in Norway / And drag the chains of slavery" (Silber, 47). I dare to question the title's relevance. It's no more relevant than *Speed-the-Plow* is to a play about the pyrotechnics of Hollywood deal-making. Unlike in the earlier play, however, this fancy title is the only non-prosy element in *Oleanna*.

At the start, the student, Carol, comes to the office of John, a professor of education. She has read his book, which is the text of his course, but she can't understand what is happening in class, and she thinks she is failing. He is the one with power; she is the suppliant. The play's action, over several days, brings about a reversal of positions: at the end John needs Carol's help. Her persistence in her feminist views, as a base for her relations with this professor, her corkscrewing into his code of male acceptances, her newly realized insights about the (sometimes unconscious) harassing and patronizing of women, eventually unsettle John drastically—a man who had thought he was decently behaved and who finds that the social territory in which he has lived is slipping under his feet.

This is a highly promising subject for a play. But from the start Mamet loads his characters with broken dialogue that does nothing but impede character and thematic development. It seems an attempt to give these people familiar Mamet verism but without the inner counterpoints that so often take his dialogue past stenography into revelation. From the opening scene of *Oleanna*:

> JOHN. Don't you think ... ?
> CAROL. . . . don't I think ... ?
> JOHN. Mmm?
> CAROL. . . . did I ... ?
> JOHN. . . . what?
> CAROL. Did ... did I ... did I say something wr ... (*Oleanna*, 3)

Now, since this kind of writing seems inflicted on the characters, rather than internally generated by them (i.e., John hasn't interrupted Carol, yet there are interruptions), we're made to feel that Mamet is uneasy in this new territory, that he must "Mametize" what otherwise might have been pungent straight dialogue. Thus, from the very beginning, the dialogue itself suggests that the author is ill at ease.

Oleanna suffers, too, from distention. Mamet had here the material of a substantial one-act play in three scenes, but he wanted more bulk to provide more sense of the passage of time and possibly for practical reasons of theater production. (A long one-act play is, pragmatically, a white elephant.) So throughout the play, he braided long telephone conversations for John with his wife and his lawyer about the possible purchase of a house to celebrate his expected promotion to tenure. The telephone has long been suspect as a dramaturgical device, and it rarely has been used so blatantly to pad and to vary.

The prospective purchase of that house and the real estate agent's pressure might have made a good accompaniment to the onstage action if Mamet hadn't used them so baldly. (Worse, at the one moment in the play when Carol reaches a point of self-revelation—"I have never told anyone this" (*Oleanna*, 38)—the phone interrupts her, and John goes into still another long phone aria. Her story is never resumed, which makes us think that Mamet is teasing: he didn't really know what Carol was going to say.)

There are other bothersome matters. Early in the play John quotes a wisecrack about copulation so obviously out of character that it seems thumpingly planted for Carol's later accusation of abuse. Later, when she is about to leave, John grabs her by the shoulders and forces her to sit, an action that is extremely hard for us to believe—again a plant for later citation. And John's closing explosion, which finishes the story and him, comes after another phone talk with his wife in which he calls her "baby" a couple of times. When he hangs up, Carol tells him not to call his wife baby. This ignites him. I could believe her noting to John that he had used the word but not her ordering him to stop it. It's another contrived provocation. Add further that Carol, who in the early scenes had to ask for definitions of some common words, becomes competently articulate when Mamet needs her to be so.

Several commentators have said that *Oleanna* forces us to take sides. Exception, please. I felt tugs of sympathy for both characters from time to time, but the blunt mechanics of the work intruded between me and conviction either way. *Oleanna* seems to me a chunk of ore that needed greater refinement. Mamet, I'd say, needed to live longer with this idea before he began to write.

His direction of the film (1994) gives it some suppleness of movement without egregiously "opening up" a theater work. Debra Eisenstadt has more color as Carol than Rebecca Pidgeon had in the 1992 New York stage production. W. H. Macy repeats his theater performance as John. Mamet is devoted to Macy and often has used him in plays and films. This devotion may be understandable as friendship but not otherwise. Macy is a modestly adequate actor without distinction of face or voice or presence. He seems born for secondary roles at best and is out of place in larger ones—especially when he is half the cast. Pidgeon, who is Mamet's wife, did not act here but wrote some old-timey songs for the soundtrack, and Mamet supplied old-timey school-song lyrics. Their intended satire on the action before us is only mildly helpful.

Obviously the one-set play with very few characters, like *Oleanna*, is not suitable for filming—except that, like so many obvious wisdoms, it's untrue. Precepts bend to talent. Before *Oleanna*, *Stevie* (1978, Robert Enders) and *The Caretaker* (1963, Clive Donner) and *My Dinner with André* (1981, Louis Malle) were made from small-scale theater works, and all three are valuable films. Mamet's *American Buffalo* (1996, Michael Corrente) is another one.

David Mamet made the screen adaptation of his play and has done only a little physical "opening up": most of the film takes place where the play does, in Don's Resale, a junk shop crammed with all kinds of odds and ends. One of the play's fascinations is that it seems to put that shop under a microscope. A minuscule speck of the world is hugely enlarged, like the eye of a fly in magnifying photography; so, paradoxically, the shop becomes massive in veristic detail at the same time that it becomes an abstraction.

In the film this paradox is heightened with a simple device. The streets outside are always empty, whether we glimpse them through the windows or occasionally go out there. Once in a long while, a car drives by. Not one other person is seen, other than a few partially glimpsed faces in a poker game right at the start. Thus this intensely realistic shop is simultaneously anywhere and nowhere. It's in a dingy part of whatever city it is. Opposite Don's place is a vacant movie theater, for rent. Diagonally across the way is the coffee shop that figures in the dialogue, but the doorway there is not exactly busy. Sometimes it rains, heavily, and, as heavy rain will do, this increases the sense of enclosure.

Two men are the center of the piece: Don, who owns the shop, and Teach, of no known occupation except burglaries now and then. They gab and fret and discuss and pass the time until, almost obliquely, a plan for a burglary is broached by Don. There's a third character, a young go-fer called Bob, a sort of apprentice to Don, who is also involved in the burglary plan. The title refers to an American buffalo nickel that a customer bought in Don's shop a week or so earlier. Don suspects, though he's not sure, that the coin is worth more than he got for it and that the customer has other rarities. Don decides to rob the customer's house, and it's around this scheme that the play simmers and boils.

The burglary scheme is inchoate—very loose indeed if these are experienced burglars—but the play's emphasis is not on the burglary itself; it's on the dialogue around it, the verbal volleyball that the two principals keep playing. In Samuel Beckett's *Endgame* (1957), Clov asks, "What is there to keep me here?" Hamm replies, "The dialogue" (Beckett, 58). Beckett's pair are inside an empty sphere scraping its top; Mamet's pair are also inside, scraping the bottom. Both pairs live and breathe through interchange.

American Buffalo is full of opportunities for the eager symbolic interpreter. The junk shop as the detritus of an errant, wasteful society; Teach (which is only his nickname) as an instructor who can't instruct; and (bingo!) the quest for the coin whose true value isn't known, plus the fumbling of that quest—all this is fodder for exegetes. For me, however, the play is a species of incantation, profane and desperate, by vacuous men trying to create through their "dialogue" some sense of being, some environment for that being.

The producer of this film was Gregory Mosher, long experienced in the theater, who directed the world theatrical premiere of *American Buffalo* in Chicago in 1975. The director was Michael Corrente, who had written and directed one previous film, *Federal Hill* (1994). Corrente was trained for the theater and once worked there, including a production of *American Buffalo*. Presumably aided by Mosher and certainly aided by the editor, Kate Sanford, he keeps the film moving without jostling it. Corrente never seems worried about the one-room venue, and his freedom is even clearer in those few scenes where we go outside—they never seem frantic attempts to escape four walls. The film just takes place, naturally and energetically, where it takes place.

About the performances themselves, some question. Dustin Hoffman is Teach, long-haired and scruffy, loping around like a man who has nowhere to go and is, from moment to moment, inventing a dynamic for his life. Hoffman was implicitly up against tough competition in this part. Some of us have seen Robert Duvall and Al Pacino as Teach in the theater (1977 and 1981, respectively), and each was, in his own temper, superb. Hoffman, ultimately, is not. He has all the technique, the vigor of address, the experienced actor's ravening of actor's chances, but sometimes these attributes become apparent. A gesture is too clearly enjoyed, an intonation slips upward from this mucky world; and we become aware of Hoffman, the star, slumming. Remembering his Ratso Rizzo in *Midnight Cowboy* (1969, John Schlesinger) twenty-seven years before this film, in some measure an antecedent of Teach, I hoped to see Ratso much more full and complex. But in those twenty-seven years Hoffman became so stellar that he couldn't keep every wisp of his success out of this performance.

Don is played by Dennis Franz, once known for his running role on television in "NYPD Blue" (1993-2005). Here his performance exemplifies the freeze that TV acting can inflict. I saw that show a few times during its long run and saw how Franz presented his bulky presence, his taciturnity, his knowingness week after week in episodes that were in part tailored to keep him turning out the Franz product. He keeps doing it in *American Buffalo*. Franz certainly has some substance but only to the degree that his predetermined persona allows. He renders the same brusque authority, and, as on TV, his expression scarcely alters throughout the picture. "This is what you bought," he seems to say, "and this is what you'll get."

Bob is done by a teenaged black actor, Sean Nelson. He is completely competent, but Nelson adds another element to the mix apart from his race. Bob has usually been played by someone in his early twenties. The use of Nelson in the part puts Don and Teach in the position of contributing to the delinquency of a minor. Two further notes. When, toward the end, Teach trashes the shop, it's done much more violently than I've ever seen; this takes Don's passivity past the credible. And Thomas Newman's music is incomprehensibly harsh at the start and finish.

At any rate, in 1996 *American Buffalo* became available on film, in a lucid version. Whatever that version's flaws, Mamet's linguistic incantation works again: outside the theater, on the big screen. Which is saying something for a single-set play—like *Oleanna* before it.

Works Cited

Beckett, Samuel. *Endgame* and *Act Without Words I*. New York: Grove Press, 1981.

Mamet, David. *American Buffalo*. New York: Grove Press, 1976.

----------. *Oleanna*. New York: Pantheon, 1992.

Silber, Fred, & Irwin Silber, eds. *Folksinger's Wordbook*. 1973. London: Oak Publications, 2014.

Introduction: Fiction into Film

As many commentators have noted, film is closer in form to fiction than to theater. Like fiction, film can move easily through time and space. Novelists may enlist our collaboration by assuming that readers, taken by the manner of the telling, will themselves supply any additional magic required, but the cinema doesn't need such collaboration. (As previously noted, however, all movies themselves are massive collaborations between artists, artisans, and technicians, while most novels are almost all solo efforts.) Film is the very home of ascendancy over the literal, the earthbound. Changes of place and century, in an instant, offer no problem whatsoever and need no kind of collaboration from the audience. Many decades of movie miracles have left us, in a sense, imaginatively slothful because we need not lift a figurative finger. Fantasy on screen demands less. It is "normal".

Also like fiction, film employs narration—sometimes in the first person, through subjective camera and voiceover; rarely in the third person, through the anonymous commentaries that accompany certain documentaries; and most often and most naturally in the omniscient mode, which enables a filmmaker to cut from a subjective point-of-view shot to a variety of objective shots, from a single reaction in close-up to the simultaneous reactions of several characters in medium or full shot. (Every picture may tell a story, but every moving picture is "told"—by a narrator called the camera.)

Unlike fiction, or I should say in a more powerful way than fiction, film can go inside human beings to explore interiority. It does this through the voice and the voiceover, through the close-up, and through the ability to present multiple states of consciousness, as Federico Fellini does in *8½* (1963): present awareness, memory, dream, and daydream. A novel could do all this, of course, but its words wouldn't have the immediacy and effect of film, the power of the image and its accompanying sound. (Movies are, after all, primarily visual, while novels are verbal.) To be fair to the novel, the Russian filmmaker and theorist Sergei Eisenstein showed, in his 1944 essay "Dickens, Griffith, and the Film Today", how such cinematic innovations as fades, dissolves, and parallel editing were in fact taken directly from the pages of Charles Dickens. And to praise the novel, it has learned from film, as has poetry: a number of critics have remarked upon the cinematic qualities of much twentieth-century fiction and poetry, including James Joyce's *Ulysses* (1922) and T. S. Eliot's "Love Song of J. Alfred Prufrock" (1915).

As for the adaptation of fiction into film, the chief problem for the adapter is that of narration, or how to transmute narrated prose into cinema. As I suggested earlier, omniscient narration is almost inevitable in film: each time the director moves his camera—either within a shot or between shots—we are offered a new point of view from which to evaluate the action. Many films employ first-person narrative techniques, but only sporadically, because in order to produce continuous first-person narration on film, the camera would have to record all the action "subjectively", through the eyes of a narrator. The problem with such a subjective point of view is that it creates frustration in the viewer, who wants to *see* the hero. In fiction, we get to know the first-person narrator through his words, through the judgments and values he expresses through those words. But in movies, we get to know a character by seeing how he reacts to people and events, and unless the director breaks the first-person camera convention, we can never see the hero—we can only see what he sees. So the solution for the adapter of a first-person novel is to include just enough first-person narration—usually in the form of voiceover—to remind us from whose point of view the story was originally told.

More than one writer, it must be said—more than one critic, more than one filmmaker even—has challenged the aesthetic justification for the adaptation of fiction to the screen; however, there are few examples of those who take actual exception to this practice, of artists who refuse to sell their books, to adapt other people's books, or to direct them when a producer comes along with the right blandishments. So their theoretical argument doesn't seem altogether justified. In general, they make claims about the specificity or distinctness of every authentic literary work. A novel, for example, is a unique synthesis whose molecular equilibrium is automatically affected when you tamper with its form. Essentially, no detail in the narrative can be considered as secondary; all syntactic characteristics, then, are in fact expressions of the psychological, moral, or metaphysical content of the work. All it takes, though, is for the filmmakers to have enough visual imagination to create the cinematic equivalent of the style of the original, and for the critic to have the eyes to see it.

My intention here is not to defend the indefensible. For most of the films that are based on novels (to speak only of them for now) merely usurp their title, even though a good lawyer could probably prove that these movies have an indirect value, since it has been shown that the sale of a book always increases after it has been adapted to the screen. And the original work can only profit from such an exposure. Although *The Idiot* (1951, Akira Kurosawa), for instance, is very frustrating on the screen, it is undeniable that many potential readers of Dostoevsky found in the film's oversimplified psychology and action a kind of preliminary trimming that has given them easier access to an otherwise difficult novel. The process is somewhat similar to that of the authors of "abridged" classics for schools in the nineteenth century. In any event, I won't comment further on this, for it has more to do with pedagogy than with art. I'd much prefer to deal with a rather modern notion for which the critics are in large part responsible: that of the untouchability of the work of art.

The nineteenth century, more than any other, firmly established an idolatry of form, mainly literary, that is still with us and that has made us relegate what has in fact always been essential for narrative composition to the back of our critical consciousness: the invention of character and situation. I grant that the protagonists and events of a novel achieve their aesthetic existence only through the form that expresses them and that somehow brings them to life in our mind. But this precedence is as vain as that which is regularly conveyed to college students when they are asked to write an essay on the precedence of language over thought. It is interesting to note that the novelists who defend so fiercely the stylistic or formal integrity of their texts are also the ones who sooner or later overwhelm us with confessions about the tyrannical demands of their characters. According to these writers, their protagonists are *enfants terribles* who completely escape from their control once they have been conceived. The novelist is totally subjected to their whims, he is the instrument of their wills. I'm not doubting this for a minute, but then writers must recognize that the true aesthetic reality of a psychological or social novel lies in the characters or their environment rather than in what they call the "style."

The style is in the service of the narrative: it is a reflection of it, so to speak, the body but not the soul. And it is not impossible for the artistic soul to manifest itself through another incarnation. This assumption, that the style is in the service of the narrative, appears vain and sacrilegious only if one refuses to see the many examples of it that the history of the arts gives to us, and if one therefore indulges in the biased condemnation of cinematic adaptation. With time, we do see the ghosts of famous characters rise far above the great novels from which they emanate. (Think only of Don Quixote and Madame Bovary.) Insofar as the style of the original has managed to create a character and impose him or her on the public consciousness, that character acquires a greater autonomy, which might in certain cases lead as far as quasi-transcendence of the work itself.

The ferocious defense of literary works is, to a certain extent, aesthetically justified; but we must also be aware that it rests on a rather recent, individualistic conception of the "author" and of the "work," a conception that was far from being ethically rigorous in the seventeenth century and that started to become legally defined only at the end of the eighteenth. In the Middle Ages, there were only a few themes, and they were common to all the arts. That of Adam and Eve, for instance, is to be found in the mystery plays, painting, sculpture, and stained-glass windows, none of which were ever challenged for transferring this theme from one art form to another. The reason is that the work of art was not an end in itself; the only important criteria were its content and the effectiveness of its message. But the balance between the public's needs and the requirements for creation was such in those days that all the conditions existed to guarantee the excellence of the arts.

You may perhaps observe that those days are over and that it would be aesthetic nonsense to want to anachronistically reverse the evolution of the relationship among the creator, the public, and the work of art. To this I would respond that, on the contrary, it is possible that artists and critics remain blind to the birth of the new, aesthetic Middle Ages, whose origin is to be found in the accession of the masses to power (or at least their participation in it) and in the emergence of an artistic form to complement that accession: the cinema. But even if this thesis is a rather risky one that would require additional arguments in its support, it remains true that the relatively new art of cinema (feature films, after all, are only a little over 100 years old) is obliged to retrace the entire evolution of art on its own, at an extraordinarily quickened pace, just as a fetus somehow retraces the evolution of mankind in a few months. The only difference is that the paradoxical evolution of cinema is contemporaneous with the deep-seated decadence of literature, which today seems designed for an audience of individualist elites.

The aesthetic Middle Ages of the cinema finds its fictions wherever it can: close at hand, in the literatures of the nineteenth and twentieth centuries. (It can also create its own fictions, and has not failed to do so, particularly in comic films, western epics, and gangster pictures.) The cinema borrows from fiction a certain number of well-wrought, well-rounded, or well-developed characters, all of whom have been polished by twenty centuries of literary culture. It adopts them and brings them into play; according to the talents of the screenwriter and the director, the characters are integrated as much as possible into their new aesthetic context. If they are not so integrated, we naturally get these mediocre films that one is right to condemn, provided one doesn't confuse this mediocrity with the very principle of cinematic adaptation, whose aim is to simplify and condense, or digest, a work from which it basically wishes to retain only the main characters and situations. If the novelist is not happy with the adaptation of his work, I, of course, grant him the right to defend the original (although he sold it, and thus is guilty of an act of prostitution that deprives him of many of his privileges as the creator of the work). I grant him this right only because no one has yet found anyone better than parents to defend the rights of children until they come of age. One should not identify this natural right with an *a priori* infallibility, however.

In sum, adaptation is aesthetically justified, independent of its pedagogical and social value, because the adapted work to a certain extent exists apart from what is wrongly called its "style," in a confusion of this term with the word "form." Furthermore, the standard differentiation among the arts in the nineteenth century and the relatively recent, subjectivist notion of the author as identified with the work no longer fit in with an aesthetic sociology of the masses, in which the cinema runs a relay race with drama and the novel and doesn't eliminate them, but rather reinforces them. The true aesthetic differentiations, in fact, are not to be made among the arts but within genres themselves: between the psychological novel and the novel of manners, for example, rather than between the psychological novel and the film that one would have made from it. Of course, adaptation for the public is inseparable from adaptation for the cinema, insofar as the cinema is more "public" than the novel.

Even the very word "digest," which I use above and which sounds at first contemptible, can have a positive meaning. If the word indicates a literature that has been previously digested, one could also understand it as a literature that has been made more accessible through cinematic adaptation, not so much because of the oversimplification that such adaptation entails but rather because of the mode of expression itself, as if the aesthetic fat, differently emulsified, were better tolerated by the consumer's mind. Indeed, as far as I'm concerned, the difficulty of audience assimilation is not an *a priori* criterion for cultural value.

All things considered, it's possible to imagine that we are moving toward a reign of the mixed medium, or the adaptation, in which the notion of the unity of the work of art, if not the very notion of the author himself, will be destroyed. In the case of the films made of Steinbeck's *Of Mice and Men* (1937), for instance, the interdisciplinary critic of the year 2050 would find not a novella out of which a play and at least two movies had been made, but rather a single work reflected through three art forms, an artistic pyramid with three sides, as it were, all of them equal in the eyes of the critic. The "work" would then be only an ideal point at the top of this figure, which itself is an ideal construct. And the chronological precedence of one part over another would not be an aesthetic criterion any more than the chronological precedence of one twin over the other is a genealogical one.

I'd like to close here, again, not by arguing for the overall superiority of fiction or film as an art form—each is superior in some ways, inferior in others. What I would like to say, however, is that film was certainly *the* art form of the twentieth century and, despite its current troubles (finance, distribution, piracy, pandemic), dominates the twenty-first century as well. That's because it's the one technology that is—or at least can be—absolutely humanistic in its outcome. The cinema can still put many of the technological impulses, cravings, and interests of our age at the service, not merely of the machinery of sensation, diversion, and profit, but of the mystery of the human spirit as well. I'm speaking about film at its best, of course. Why it often isn't at its best is a subject complicated by the commerce of the world, and one better left for another day.

"Literature Become Cinema: Eight Transmutations, 1965-1997"

This essay treats the venerable (but paradoxically—in the age of the computer, the Internet, social media, iPhones, and YouTube, let alone DVDs and cable TV— not yet tired) subject of literature versus film through an examination of the screen adaptation, over some thirty years, of novels by eight notable Euro-American writers: Joseph Conrad's *Lord Jim* (1900), D. H. Lawrence's *Women in Love* (1920) and *The Virgin and the Gypsy* (1930), Henry Miller's *Tropic of Cancer* (1934), Milan Kundera's *Unbearable Lightness of Being* (1984), E. M. Forster's *Where Angels Fear to Tread* (1905) as well as *A Room with a View* (1908), Edith Wharton's *Age of Innocence* (1920), Henry James's *Portrait of a Lady* (1881), and Stendhal's *The Red and the Black* (1930). Though none of the transmutations of these fictions is a superior work of art unto itself, I analyze them in this piece because in-depth analysis discloses not only a lot about the nature of the novel (and shorter forms of fiction), as well as the cinema. It also uncovers, in depth, what can only be called these films' state of aesthetic limbo.

Lord Jim (1965, Richard Brooks)

Richard Brooks's 1965 version of *Lord Jim* (1900) raises the question of whether one likes films, in addition to whether one likes Conrad. Much of the picture is extraordinarily well made, and Peter O'Toole's performance in the title role is touched with the poetic; but the revisions, deletions, and additions to the original have the effect of changing the subject under discussion. I am thinking only of those who know the book when I say that they may find this film enjoyable as such. Is the phrase "as such" tenable? The point seems worth exploring when a novel is an accepted classic and the film that has been derived from it has certain virtues of its own.

It seems to me hypocritically naïve to go to a film version of such a book expecting or hoping that no changes at all have been made and being shocked at discovering otherwise. All of us know that the times when the novel has not been altered or wrenched out of shape are rare. (*David Copperfield* [1935, George Cukor]? *Great Expectations* [1946, David Lean]? *Wuthering Heights* [1939, William Wyler]? It would require a fresh look to make sure.) But beyond sad experience, there is the fundamental fact that, even in understanding hands, adaptation cannot mean mere reproduction. To belabor the obvious, there is the sheer matter of time: a film that included all the dialogue in an average novel would run perhaps twenty or twenty-five hours. But there is the even more fundamental fact that a novel exists in its prose; to put it into pictures—to substitute actual places and persons for places and persons that are meant to be suggested inside one's head by the author's words—is to put Conrad largely out of the question and to make demands on another aesthetic. Even to take the synopsized plot—intact, without rearrangement—is not really to be faithful: it is merely to extract a skeleton, which turns to rubber when it is extracted and which can be hardened into bone again only if the new, cinematic flesh that is put on it is molded by that new aesthetic.

It is purely academic to argue from the above that adaptation ought not to be attempted. The history of film is the history of adaptation, usually from novels. It is true that the best films—with rare exceptions like Vsevolod

Pudovkin's 1926 version of Gorky's novel *Mother* (1906)—are original works or are liberal adaptations from inferior fiction that could only be improved by adaptation. But the amount of useful original material written for the screen has never been enough to fill it, and the attraction of certain novels has been understandably strong. As in this case. (I wonder only why *Lord Jim* has been relatively neglected; the one previous version I know of was made by Victor Fleming in 1925, in the silent days.) Besides, there is the added value of a famous title. So it is mock heroics to play Canute to the sea of adaptations.

Still, the paradox remains: one enjoys much in this film *at the same time* that one is disconcerted by the changes. But if it is fruitless to complain of changes as such or of the very practice of adaptation, how can the dissatisfaction be resolved? (Not merely by staying away if, like me, you often get various kinds of pleasure along with the dissatisfaction.) One helpful method, when a good or great book is involved, might be the recognition of a Third Force: one that is neither the original novel nor an original film. In music there is an ancient tradition of variations on other composers' themes, and no one complains because Brahms and Rachmaninoff have, each in his own way, been "unfaithful" to Paganini. Robert Lowell showed in *Imitations* (1960) that a related process is possible in poetry. Not to equate Brooks with these gentlemen, but perhaps the same attitude could apply to this kind of film. In the most rigorously artistic view, the cinema has demands to be filled in faithfulness to itself; it needs to be as self-centered as any other art. Anything else leads to adaptations petrified with reverence (the 1960 film of Lawrence's *Sons and Lovers* [1913], for example). From this point of view, there seems to me a place for "variation" films: to be judged by standards analogous to variations in music and poetry. To wit: has the adapter exploited the original material satisfactorily? Does he justify his alterations?

One obvious objection to this approach is that Brahms's variations are in the same medium and are not intended to produce the same effect as the original work; Brooks's variations, in a different medium, *are* so intended. But unless we are going to dismiss automatically as rape every film of every worthy novel, then we need some way of appreciating them as what they are: since they cannot, in the nature of the case, be the novels themselves. The work of the adapter *judged as possible contribution*, rather than being arbitrarily dismissed as vandalism, seems one viable approach. Let us shelve the literary-purist view that the film's success must be judged by degree of fidelity, and instead judge whether the changes help the film, as film, to arrive at the same general effect; further, whether the changes show virtuosity in the new medium and thus actually add artistic values that were not possible in the first medium. (This, of course, in addition to those original elements that are retained and simply translated.)

By these standards, some of the changes in the script of *Lord Jim* are understandable: the untangling of the time-skein, for instance. But many are incomprehensible. Why, for instance, is the ship *Patna* in the midst of a storm when she strikes the obstacle? Surely it is less pictorially trite and dramatically much more conducive to Jim's later shame if, as in Conrad, the officers panic *before* the squall breaks. A large addition in the script is more understandable but less excusable: a character called The General has been invented, a dictator who tyrannizes the fictional country of Patusan and against whom Jim leads a revolution. I would guess that this whole episode is the producers' back-formation. They realized that the film would have to be shot partially in some Oriental location (Cambodia, as it turned out) as well as in studios; that to follow the synopsized Conrad story, as is, would give them a film of perhaps 100 or 110 minutes; that they needed a longer picture to justify the high prices they would have to charge even if it were shorter. Therefore they had to put in more story; and Brooks has supplied an extensive action-packed episode, with heavy implications about the People and Freedom. The General himself is one more try at the new-style philosophizing torturer, two of whose better incarnations can be found in tow novels: Arthur Koestler's *Darkness at Noon* (1940) and Bridget Boland's *The Prisoner* (1954). Eli Wallach plays him equally derivatively, with no suggestion of the necessary force.

Other changes—regrettable even by "variation" standards—are too many to detail, but two must be noted. By building the General (out of the character of Sherif Ali from *Lawrence of Arabia* [1962, David Lean]?), Brooks has diminished Doramin, thus making Jim's last action less inevitable. Second, the pervasive tone of the script misses the important Conradian irony. It is all written as straight tragedy of honor—neo-Elizabethan style—without the ambience of the modern view that Conrad uses to keep his fiction from being stiffly absolutist. As a "variation" film, then, *Lord Jim* shows expansion without inner justification; change of key to its detriment; italicizing of theme to disproportion. What John Osborne's script for *Tom Jones* (1963, Tony Richardson) is supposed by some (not by me) to have accomplished, will hardly be claimed for Brooks's script here. It is different but not equal.

But Brooks also directed, much more successfully than he adapted; and it is in this area that the cinematic values, as such, begin to appear. The montage section of Jim's marine training is swiftly and engagingly done, and the battles are clear, spacious, convincing. Some scenes that depart from Conrad—like Jim's last moments—are in themselves good film episodes. Of course Brooks had the help of one of the best film editors, Alan Osbiston. It may be true, as some believe, that critics overestimate the editor's contribution. I note, however, that this is by far the best direction that Brooks had done up to this point and that J. Lee Thompson—whose taut *Guns of Navarone* (1961) was made with Osbiston's help—did not made a bearable film after he changed editors. As for cinematography, Brooks had the asset of Freddie Young, the superb cinematographer of Lean's *Lawrence of Arabia*.

In the large cast Paul Lukas, as Stein, is outstanding, displaying a magical power to move us. Daliah Lavi, as Jewel, is also outstanding because she is so bad. She is duskily lovely, but when she opens her mouth, she becomes a lump. And there is O'Toole as Jim. His work is the premier example in this picture of the benefits that a "variation" film can add. Obviously, the character is, as written here, a simplified version, without much of the original's humor or conscious self-dramatization. But the Conradian quintessence is there, a man torn in an agony that would not bother all men, although many might wish that they were capable of it. Peter O'Toole's person, voice, and performance heighten this romantic truth, making a somewhat different character from the original but nonetheless a fascinating and affecting one.

There are certainly resemblances between O'Toole's Jim and his T. E. Lawrence; but besides the fact that his King in *Becket* (1964, Peter Glenville) showed that he is not limited to this kind of part, there are subtle and lovely differences in Jim: the sheer sunny happiness of the early scenes, the hushed shock at discovering what he is capable of doing. (Much of the later portion is played in daring gradations of *piano*.) His last glance at the sky before he dies is that of the man who "goes away from a living woman to celebrate his pitiless wedding with a shadowy ideal of conduct" (Conrad, 372). All in all, this variation on the character of Conrad's Jim—simplified by Brooks but enriched by O'Toole—is as good a justification as the whole matter of adaptation is likely to get.

Women in Love (1969, Ken Russell) & *The Virgin and the Gypsy* (1970, Christopher Miles)

The number of times that fine fiction has been made into good film can almost be counted on your fingers; and you won't need another finger for the 1969 picture of D. H. Lawrence's *Women in Love* (1920). Still, some of the cinematic elements are remarkable.

The screenplay is, inevitably, the least successful of those elements. It was written by the producer, Larry Kramer, and it sniffs out the "action" the way those French pigs are supposed to sniff out truffles. There are snatches of discussion left in the script, but the balance is in favor of dancing and lovemaking and swimming and sledding. Certainly all those things are in the book and certainly a film lives by motion, but the balance is quite different in the book, where the action exists for the sake of self-discovery and thought. The crucial chapter in the book, the conversation when Ursula goes alone to Rupert Birkin's house for tea, is reduced to a snippet, yet Kramer retains—unexplained—nutty old Mrs. Crich and her dogs. We get a syllabus tour of the novel until we arrive at the last section, in Switzerland, where a whole new picture seems to start and to go on at length, because the transformations in Gerald Crich and in Gudrun are even more difficult for Kramer than they were for Lawrence.

Gerald is played by Oliver Reed, one of the film's best choices. The character is an unsatisfying one, to begin with. Lawrence modelled this turbulent, idealistic, unconsciously homophile man at least partly on J. Middleton Murry (ironic because Lawrence presumably didn't know that Murry was having an affair with Mrs. L.), but the model was insufficient. Reed works hard and well to realize the part. He is growing as an actor in this picture. He carries himself with increasing seriousness, without the oily, smug sexiness of his first films, with an interest in inner complexities and a growing ability to substantiate them. But Alan Bates, as Rupert Birkin, is once again Alan Bates. The film's best chance for success lay in the casting of this role. The actor of Birkin might have supplied some complexity to compensate for the thinning of the original material in the script. Bates is a smooth, silky actor with some schoolboy honesty and mild intelligence but no mystery and no conviction of pain. There is just one moment when he touches Birkin depths—at the *al fresco* luncheon where he eats a fresh fig and discourses about sexual parallels. Otherwise, just a pleasant young leading man.

Jennie Linden plays Ursula with wit and passion, and her film début once again demonstrates the English miracle of producing young actresses in command of style. Glenda Jackson plays Gudrun, originally the younger sister, though that relation is not credible here. Jackson is a very fine actress, but she will probably never be a box-office star because she is not interested in star "sympathy", either in the parts she chooses or the way she plays them. She is not an actress in order to be loved but in order to act. Her Gudrun catches the buried wildness, the appetite for self, of this New Woman.

The costumes by Shirley Russell are wonderful, just sufficiently dramatic. The settings by Luciana Arrighi insist just sufficiently on their presence. And the color photography by Billy Williams is lush. Overly lush, I think, in wheat fields and woods. The director, Ken Russell, was evidently out to make Nature "perform." The wheat fields are so golden, the pine-woods so healthy, that there are uncomfortable, Beautiful reminders of *Elvira Madigan* (1967, Bo Widerberg). Russell is also nervous about "cinematizing": he throws in fancy, superfluous dissolves, mirror shots, a sideways sequence, and other evidences of insecurity. A pity, because when he faces his material straight on, he shows talent for human revelation and for the camera motion dictated by it. The dance sequences—spoofed Russian ballet and Dalcroze—are nicely handled, and the nude wrestling scene between Rupert Birkin and Gerald Crich is done with tact, stated but not exploited, so that it supplies the homophile element that disturbs, in differing ways, all four principals.

Lawrence's novel—whole-souled, often beautiful, sorely imperfect—is his largest inquiry into the opportunities and burdens of new freedom, with its men and women trying to understand more about love and sex and affinity. But it depends, for its continuing validity, on its moment in social and artistic history. It depends on its *form*, as a novel published in 1920, for that validity. It is as a 1920 novel that the freshness of it, such as it is, remains fresh. Restated fifty years later (during the sexual revolution of the 1960s), in someone else's new medium, the themes seem somewhat dated (and seem even more so in the 2020s, during the era of transsexuality and gender fluidity)—even if it were possible to make a good film of a novel whose life is in its thought.

Unlike the film adaptation of *Women in Love*, the one of *The Virgin and the Gypsy* (1970) is fairly faithful to Lawrence's original novella, from 1930, and is therefore fairly silly. This posthumous short novel, unrevised by the author, simplifies foolishly some of the themes used better in, among others, *Lady Chatterley's Lover* (1928) and *Women in Love*. Ken Russell's 1969 film of the latter, as noted above, was unsuccessful but at least it had some complexities to dally with.

Here Lawrence uses the same opposition of warm blood and cold climate, the "poetic" urge battering at the cabbage-and-potato proprieties that still pertained in England after the First World War: but with what baldness and mechanics! And, as filmed, *The Virgin and the Gypsy*, directed by Christopher Miles, is a color-me-passionate primer, full of italicized symbols: the fumed-oak rectory imprisoning the repressed clergyman's daughter, the black stallion on which the handsome gypsy rides the countryside, the girl's first view of the dam as a crack in it is being repaired, the bursting of the dam that floods the virgin into the gypsy's arms, and so ludicrously on.

Still, putting the symbols aside, if that were possible, this faded story of life-hungry revolt might have made a tolerable period piece if the heroine had been well played. Joanna Shimkus, however, is an Anglo-French Candice Bergen: a pretty girl who, by trying to act and failing, makes herself unpretty. Shimkus pouts, or doesn't pout, and has a thin, vapid voice that disintegrates if she has two consecutive sentences to speak. (And some of the things she has to say are horrendous. To a friend: "It's as you were saying the other day—life can be very difficult.") Franco Nero, the gypsy, has the asinine job of being the Male Principle incarnate; he tries earnestly, but sinks into repeated ruts.

In London in 1963 a half-hour film was made called *The Six-Sided Triangle* (1963), directed by Miles with his sister Sarah in a leading role—six comic versions of a love story, an old revue idea and not very well done. Christopher Miles was then being highly touted as a new talent; yet it took six years for Americans to get his second feature (*Up Jumped a Swagman* [1965], unseen by me, was his first). *The Virgin and the Gypsy* has all the latest cinema lingo: lush color (as photographed by Bob Huke), dream and reverie sequences in slow motion without sound, exaggerated lyricism (why was the brief trip across the lake *so* dazzling?), the lopping off of scenes before they actually end to hurry things along. As was by 1970 customary with directors of British films set in the country—particularly in the past—Miles gets the most out of stone bridges and old artifacts (a wooden coal scuttle, for instance), and their beauty went a long way to gain him credit for making a beautiful picture, which it is not.

Young American directors had developed their own anonymous, interchangeable filmic patter; young British directors were developing their equivalent, equally interchangeable among them. In both countries they represented the most deplorable aspects of the, at the time, new film consciousness: linguistic cleverness and novelty as a substitute for flavor and commitment. "How can you say I'm not an artist when I've just shown you this ingenious shot in the bedroom mirror?"

At the end the ex-virgin goes off with a free-living lady named Mrs. Fawcett and the latter's lover, which the girl does not do in the novella, thus cheering up Lawrence's tale of Anglican doom. In the film Mrs. Fawcett is not Jewish, which omits not only Lawrence's persistent anti-Semitism (he refers to her throughout the book as "the little Jewess") but his fascination with her as the outsider who can better afford to Dare. "Dare" this movie adaptation of *The Virgin and the Gypsy* did, as did the film of *Women in Love*, but both left me asking the same rhetorical question: How *dare* you?

Tropic of Cancer (1970, Joseph Strick)

The first thing we see is a fountain, spurting; the next is a bidet, spurting; and away we go on Joseph Strick's 1970 film tour of *Tropic of Cancer* (1934). These two shots symbolize the whole picture. The world of Paris and what Henry Miller called the world of fuck are all that Strick's film is concerned with. Heaven knows (if that's the right reference) that those elements are prominent in Miller's novel. But Strick has used the same principle here that he used in his abortion of Joyce's *Ulysses* (1922; filmed 1967): he has picked a famous and respected novel with lots of sex in it and has been chiefly faithful to the sex. The damage in this case is much less than with *Ulysses* because Miller's novel is very much smaller than Joyce's in every sense, so there simply is less to omit, but the formula is the same: find a critically celebrated, sexy book, and under the guise of homage, exploit the sex.

Consequently, we see a parade of breasts and of female pubic hair, and we hear—often—all of Miller's four-letter words, plus one particularly vivid six-letter one ("squish"). All the material has been taken from the novel. So, too, are a few passages of non-sexual ruminative prose including the book's conclusion. But the sum is a long way from representing the novel, because Strick has left out Miller. There is no hint in this film of the two most important elements in the book, from which everything else proceeds. First, the hero—Miller—is a writer. Strick gives us not the slightest hint of this. Second, he has come to Paris to write, as an escape from America, which he loathes. He loathes a lot about Europe, too, but Paris is freedom, America is prison, here is where he can fulfil himself as artist and man; and his sexual gallivanting is part of his declaration of artistic and environmental release, after almost forty years of slavery and constriction. All the film shows us is an amiable fellow, drifting around Paris, mooching on his friends, laying girls.

This leads to another defect. As he did with *Ulysses*, Strick has updated *Tropic of Cancer* to the present. Not credible. First, the group of American expatriates do not seem like contemporary men, in manner or thought; they have a Hemingway-Fitzgerald air to them. Second, the sexual liberation of France vis-à-vis the United States was very much less marked in 1970 than in 1930, both in life and literature. The tone of the present has a cracked ring.

Some credit does go to Strick and to the co-author of the script, Betty Botley, because they have not tried to impose a formal story on Miller's rhapsody of flow. They have rearranged and reassigned some material but have tried to keep a sense of ease and happenstance. And, admittedly, the film does get some humor from time to time by reason of the glandular pitch at which it operates. But when Strick gives us the nonsexual passages on the soundtrack, he resorts to obvious Terry Southern touches by showing us shots of tanks and soldiers and parades—shots that considerably straiten Miller's larger intent in his remarks about the hollowness and dissatisfaction of life. And, of course, Strick uses by-now platitudinous modern editing: jump-cuts *à la* Godard in the middle of sequences, plus glimpses of events past or to come.

We even get a quick look at old Henry Miller himself in one montage; the young Miller is played by Rip Torn, with some of the appealing goofiness that he showed in Milton Moses Ginsberg's 1969 film *Coming Apart*. (Those two pictures must have made Torn, at the time, Filmland's champion copulation-simulator.) But the best performance is by James Callahan as Fillmore, the American who cracks up and has to go home.

The presence of lots of girls who have lots of everything clarifies something about the novel that is even clearer in the picture. The sexual viewpoint is pure male-chauvinist; the girls are, or might as well be, faceless. To Miller, Paris is a harem, and he is a newly crowned sultan sweating to make up for lost tail. This view of woman-as-utensil is much more apparent now, long after the female revolution, and it is underscored by Strick's lavish, impersonal display of women's liberated fronts.

The Unbearable Lightness of Being (1988, Philip Kaufman)

Milan Kundera's *The Unbearable Lightness of Being* (1984), according to some, is a great novel. Maybe. Of greatness, tomorrow's critics are better judges than today's. But one point is sure: Kundera is the greatest café companion imaginable. To be seated across a small table from him with drinks or coffee cups between us, which is where his books seem to put me, certifies the sometimes dubious existence of civilization, even though Kundera's discourse wryly turns civilization over to show its underside.

What wit, what tacit grief, what quiet terror, what fresh insight into received ideas, what poignant interplay between eroticism and the political climate in which various lovers go to bed. And what nonchalance about traditional novelistic structure—a blitheness tolerable only in a writer with diamond-cutter's control. Reviewing an earlier Kundera novel, *The Book of Laughter and Forgetting* (1979), Robert M. Adams wrote:

> A constant interweaving of fantasy and realism, surreal metaphor and prosaic literalness, is characteristic of Kundera's technique. He intervenes frequently to address his readers directly, question his characters, recite his own experiences, or account for his authorial proceedings. He is particularly careful to leave undefined the relations between episodes of his novel; it is the reader's business to make of these relations what he can. Again and again in this artfully artless book an act or gesture turns imperceptibly into its exact opposite. . . . These subtle transformations and unemphasized points of correspondence are the special privileges of a meticulously crafted fiction. (Jones, 207)

Word for word these comments apply also to *The Unbearable Lightness of Being*. I would add only, in small dissent, that Kundera's intent to charm, and the knowing pathos of that charm because it comes from an exile writing about a country in bondage, is ultimately a bit theatrical.

Still, I've quoted Adams at length because he cites the important aspects of Kundera's work, and it is precisely those aspects that are missing from Philip Kaufman's 1988 film of *The Unbearable Lightness of Being*. Only a director with gifts analogous to Kundera's might have approximated the book's "artfully artless" qualities—say, a Godard or Makavejev at his best. Otherwise we were bound to get more or less what we got: plot elements extracted, connected, expanded, contracted. The depth and sparkle and shadow of Kundera's novel depend on the different glimpses of his story he gives us as he talks all around it. Without that context, the story itself is rather banal, disjointed, arbitrarily maneuvered; and without that context, the film has only a tenuous relation to the book.

Does knowledge of the book prejudice a prospective viewer of the film? Well, it made this prospective viewer hopeful. I hoped at the time that Philip Kaufman, the director and co-author of the screenplay, would expand the capabilities he had suggested in the past. (*The Right Stuff*, from 1983, and a remake of *Invasion of the Body Snatchers*, from 1978, are his two best previous films, both of them competently done.) I hoped that Jean-Claude Carrière, the co-author, who had often worked with Buñuel, among others, would help to liberate the screenplay from convention. But the collaborators chose to make a film of a book that Kundera expressly did not write, a traditional, continuous, mostly present-tense novel.

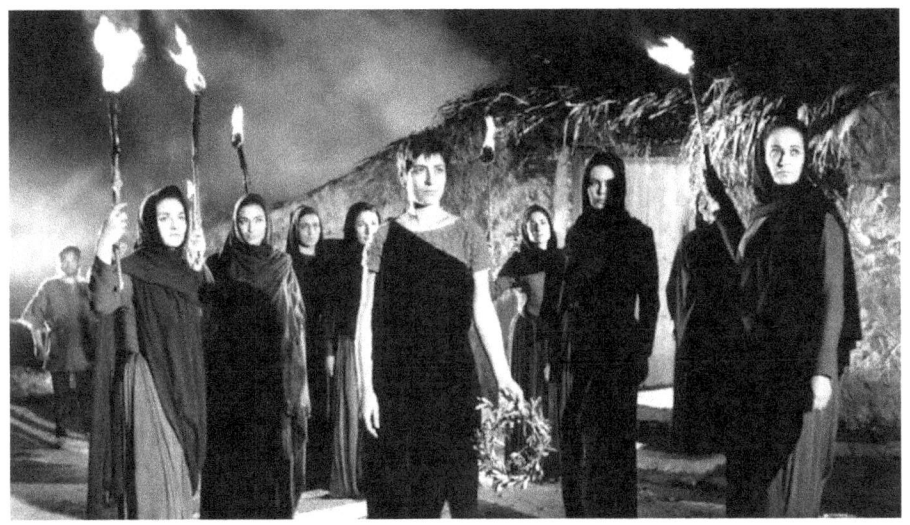

1.   *Electra*

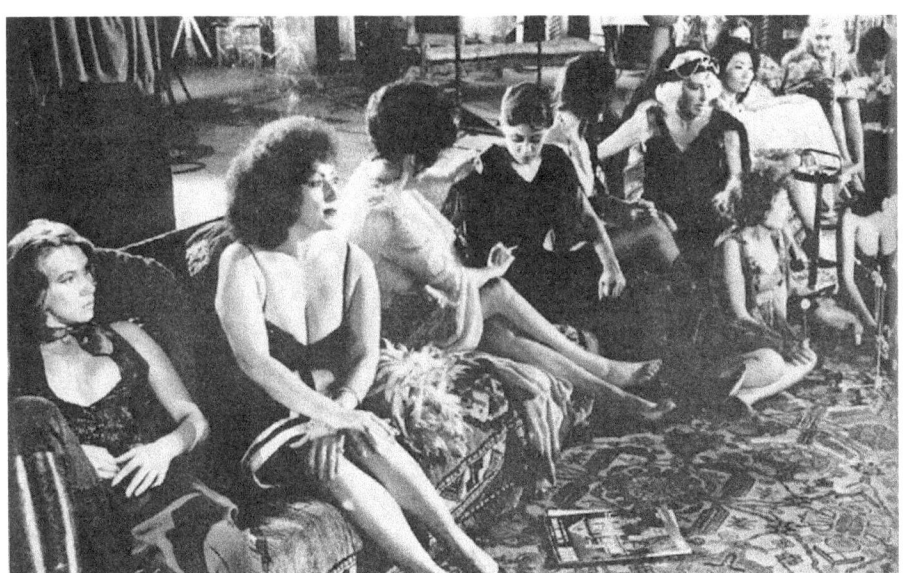

2.   *The Balcony*

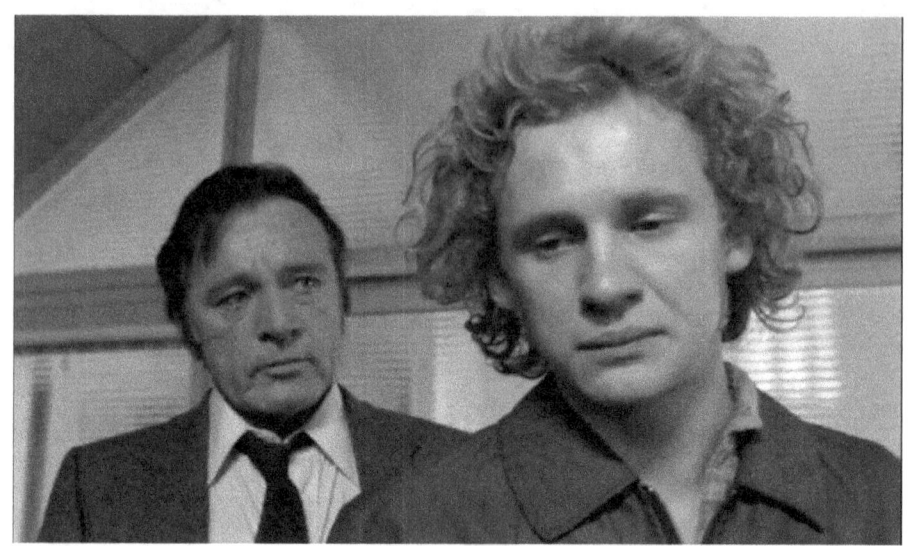

3.   *Equus*

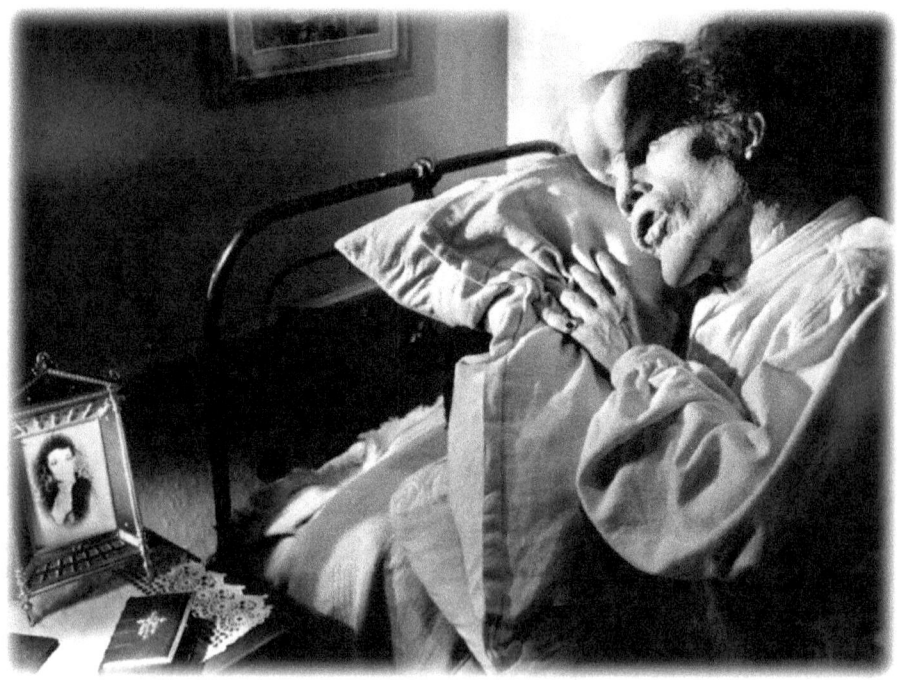

4.   *The Elephant Man*

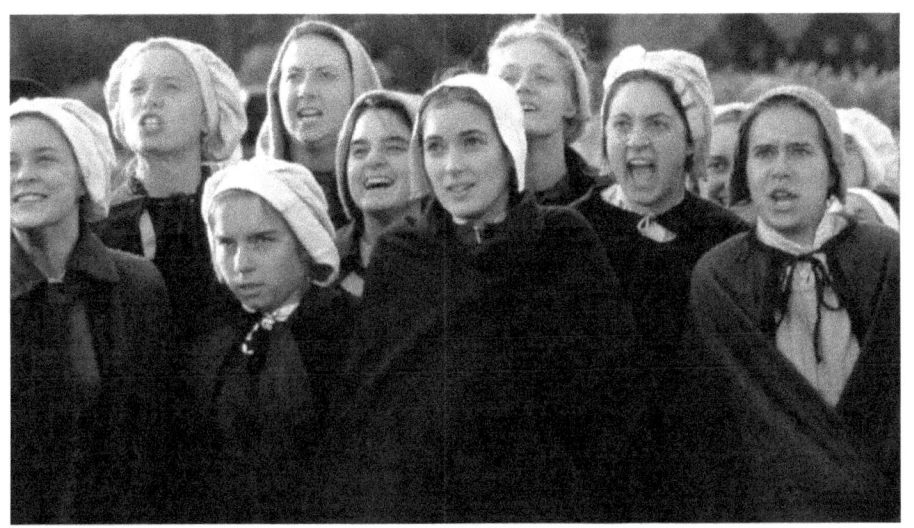

5. *The Crucible*

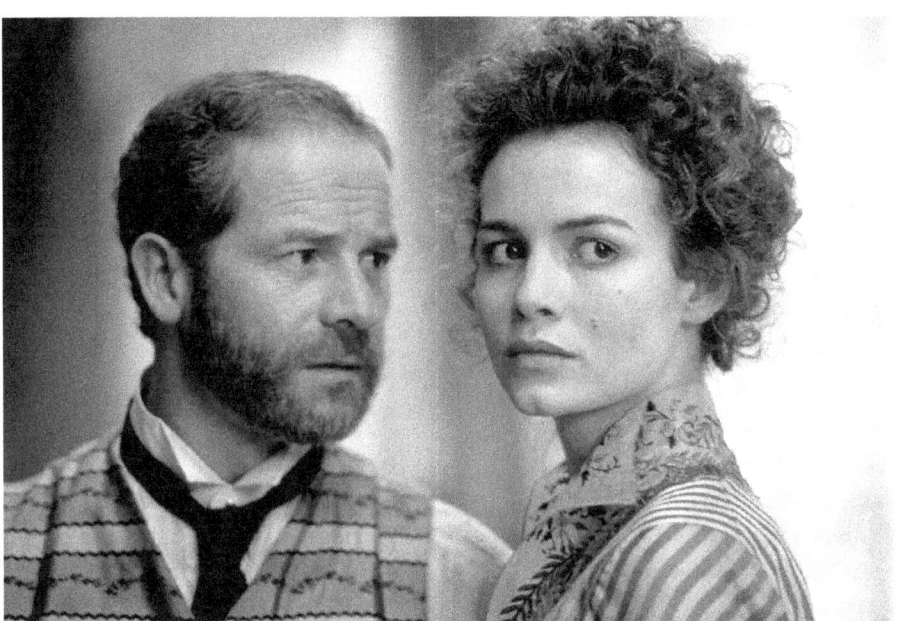

6. *Miss Julie*

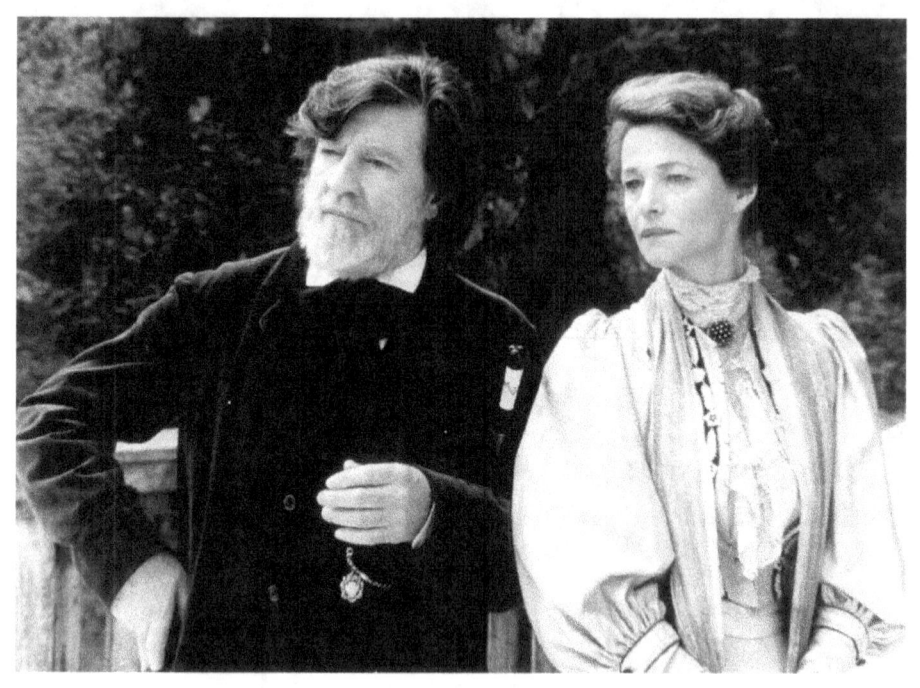

7.   *The Cherry Orchard*

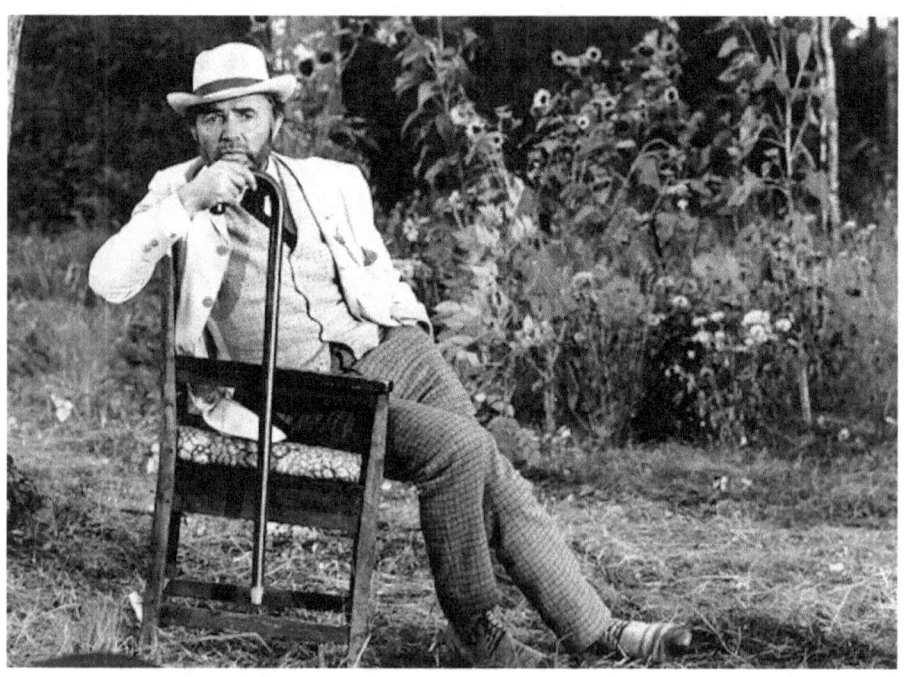

8.   *The Sea Gull*

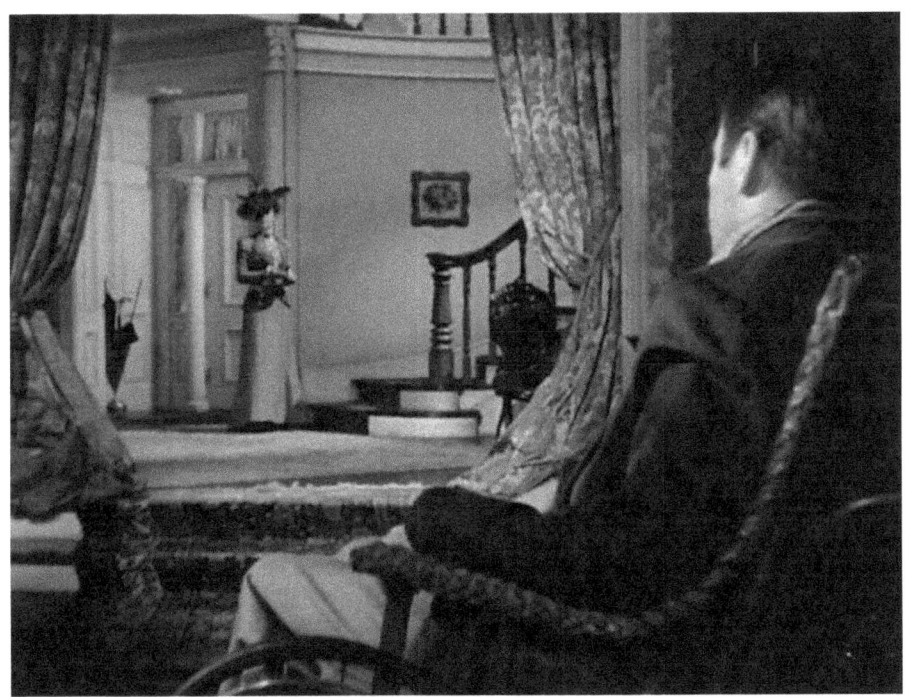

9.　　　*The Little Foxes*

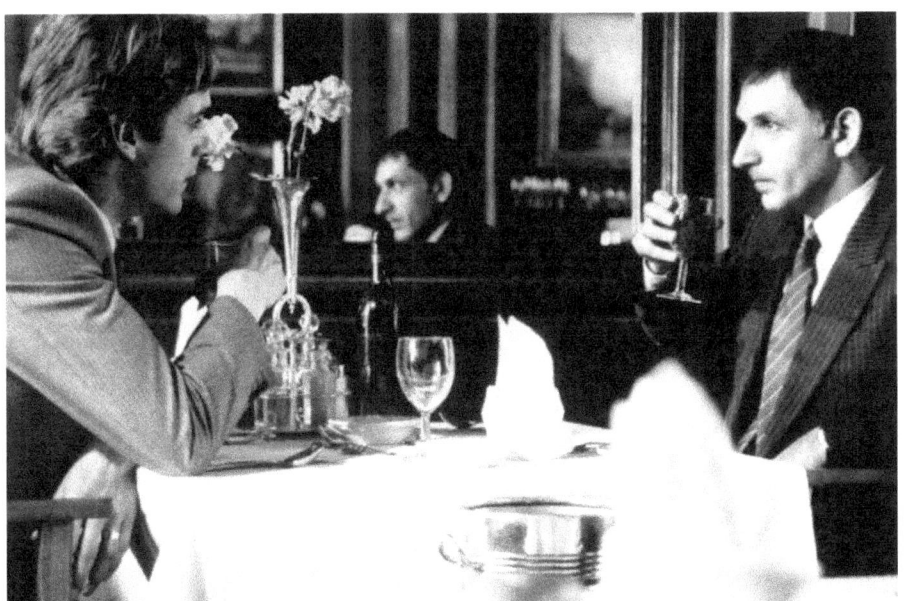

10.　　　*Betrayal*

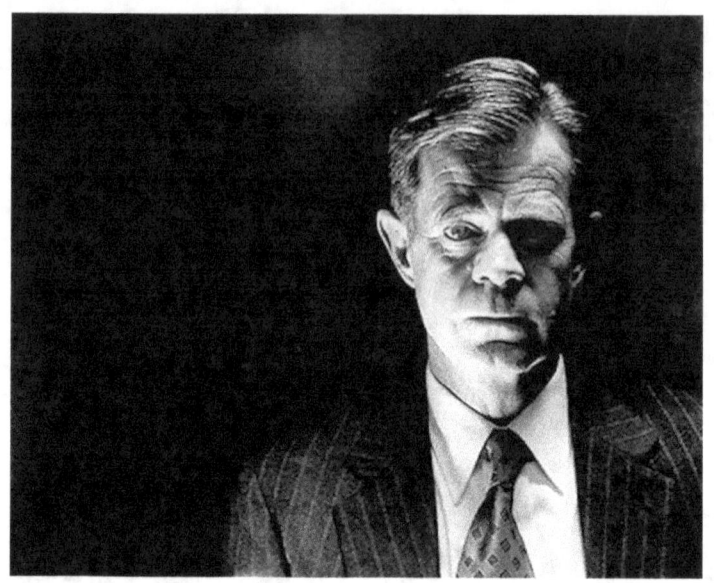

11.   *Edmond*

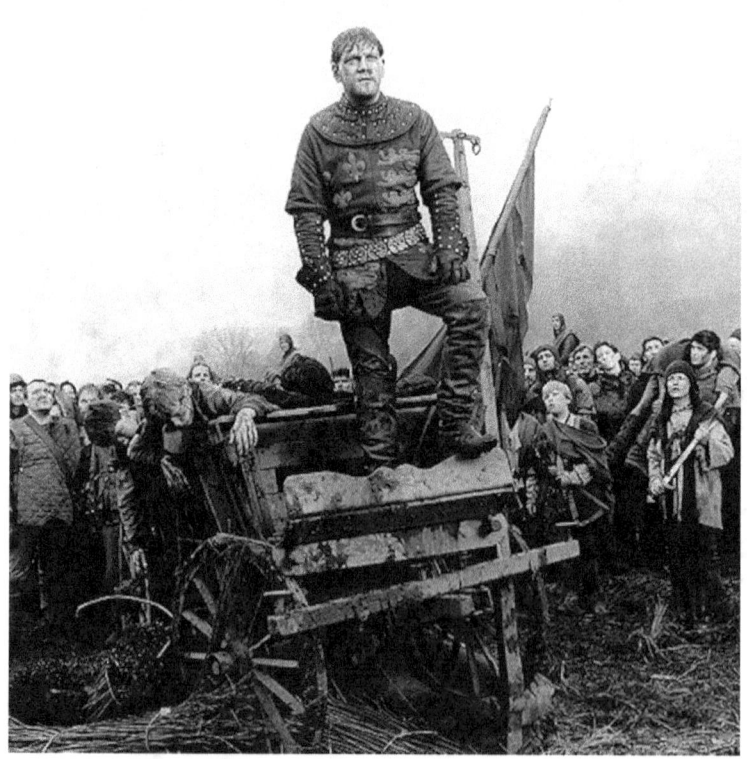

12.   *Henry V*

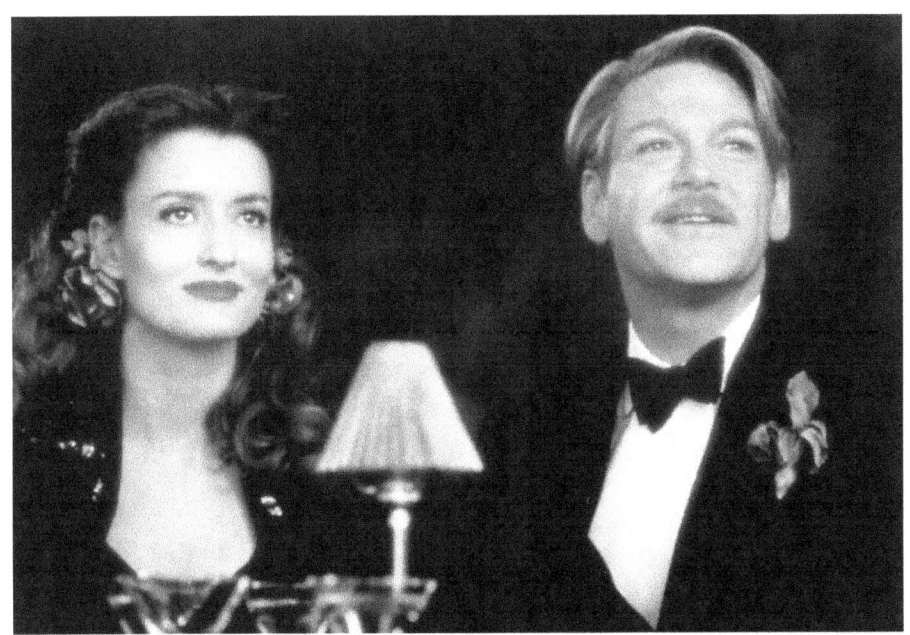

13.   *Love's Labour's Lost*

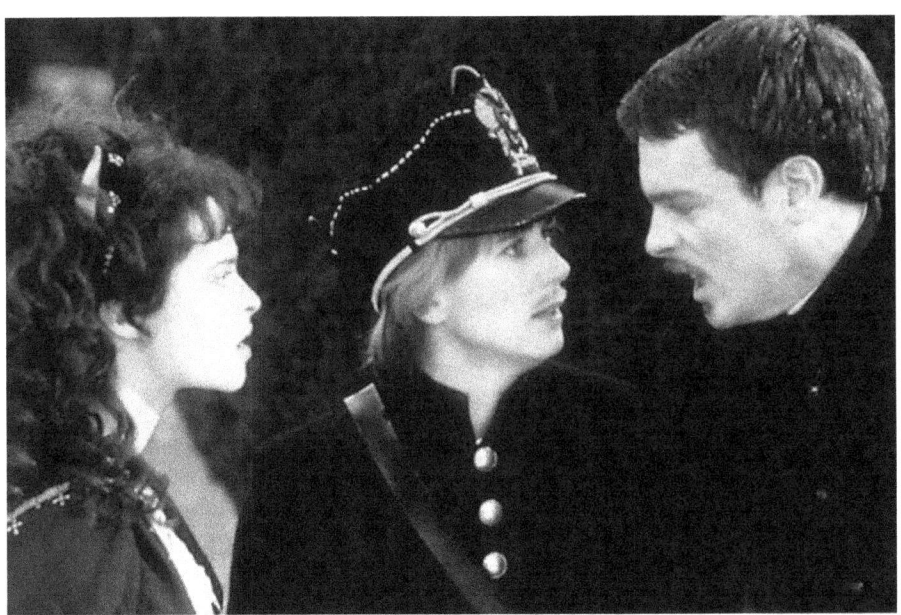

14.   *Twelfth Night*

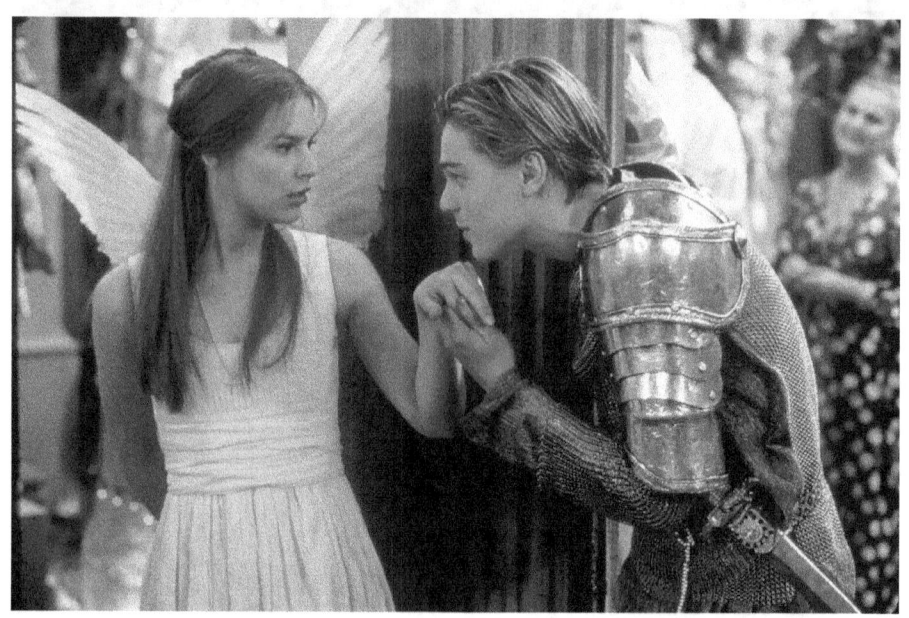

15.   *Romeo + Juliet*

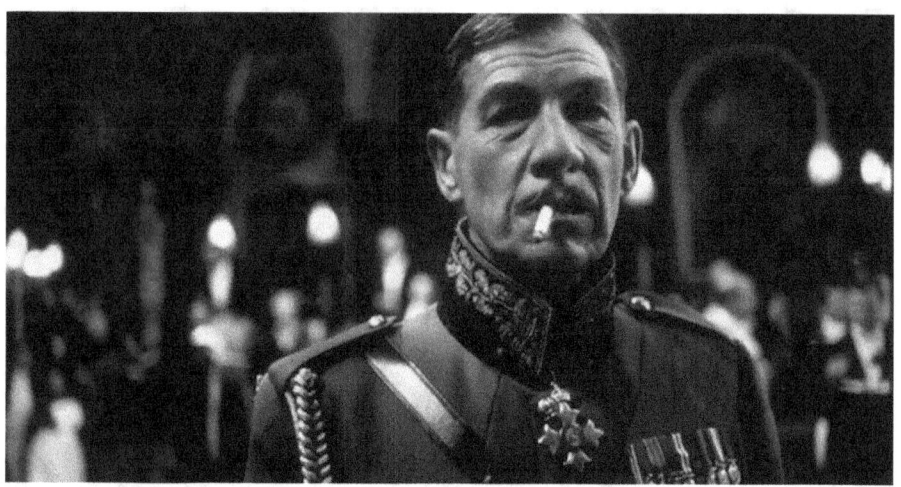

16.   *Richard III*

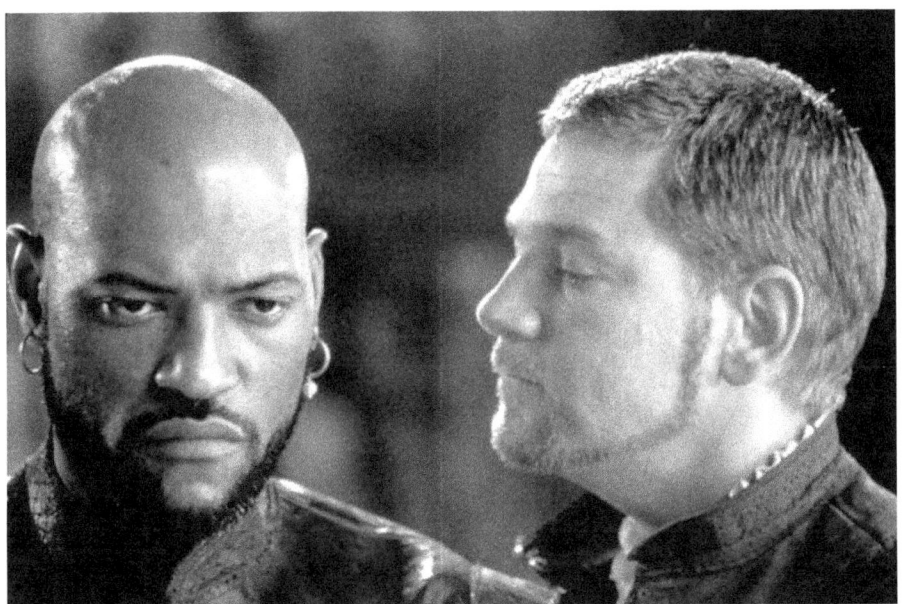

17.   *Othello*

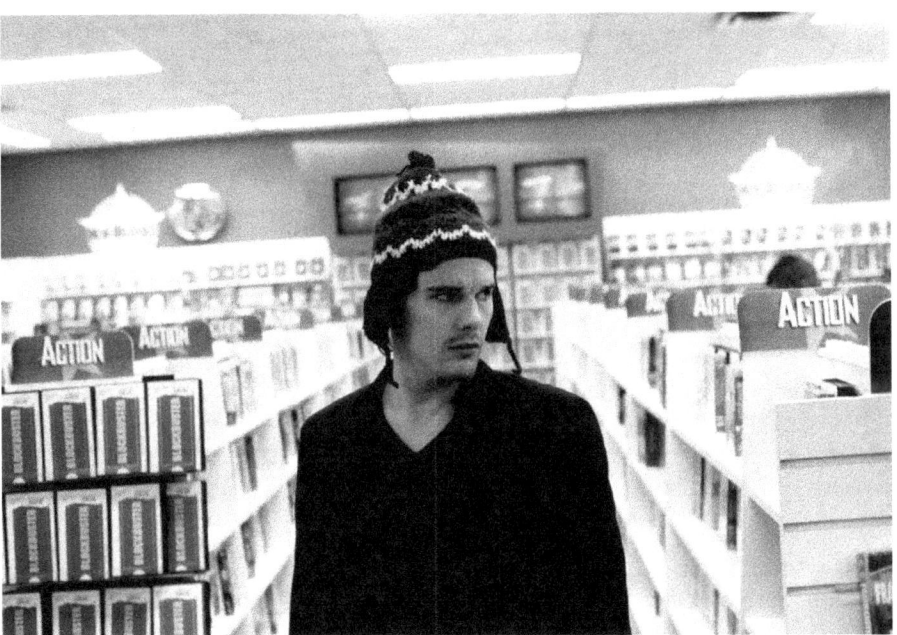

18.   *Hamlet*

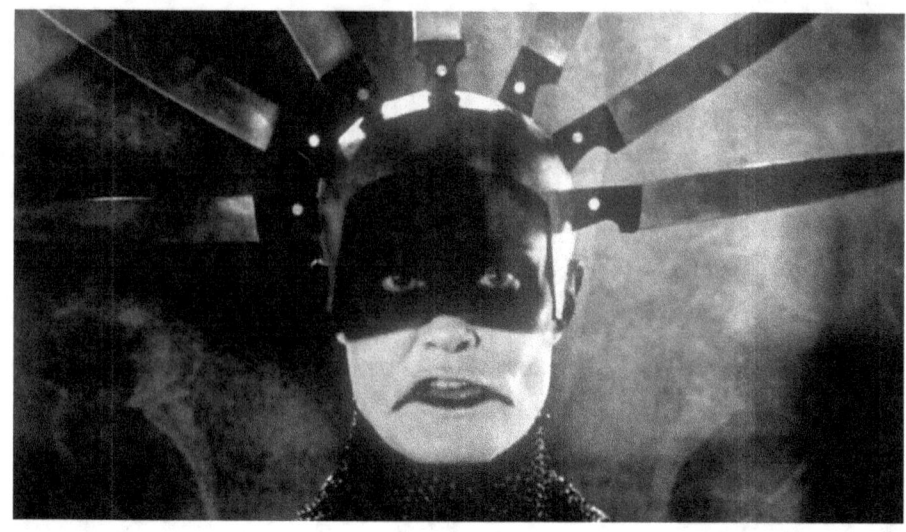

19.   *Titus*

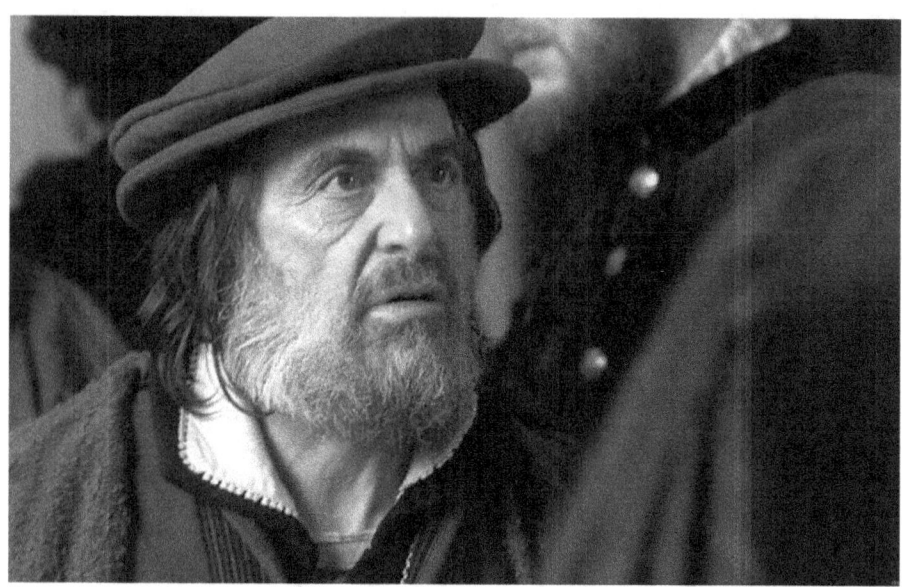

20.   *The Merchant of Venice*

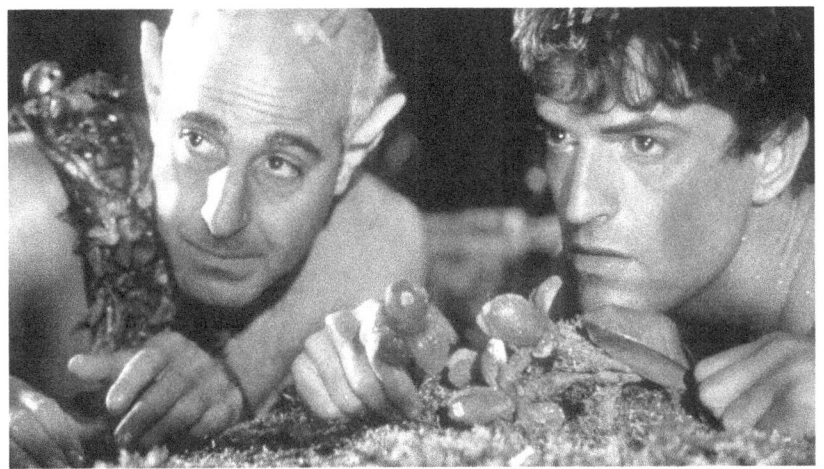

21. *A Midsummer Night's Dream*

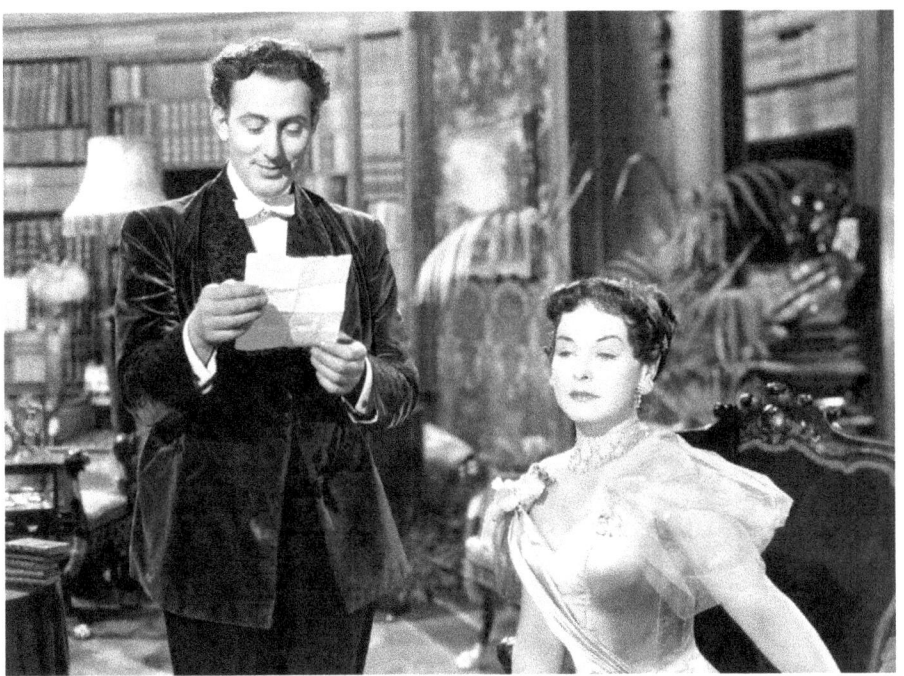

22. *An Ideal Husband*

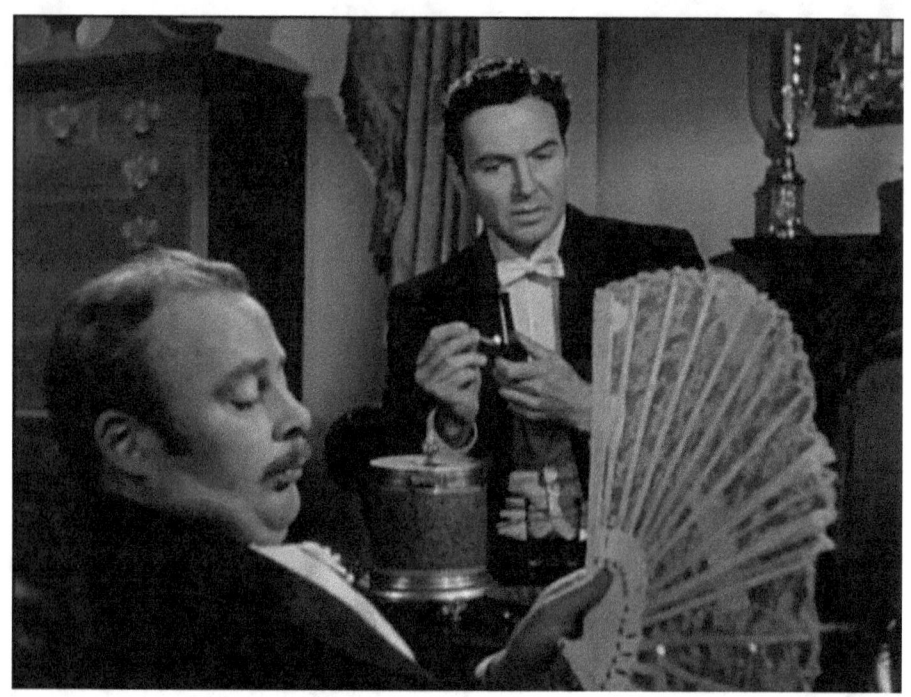

23.   *The Fan*

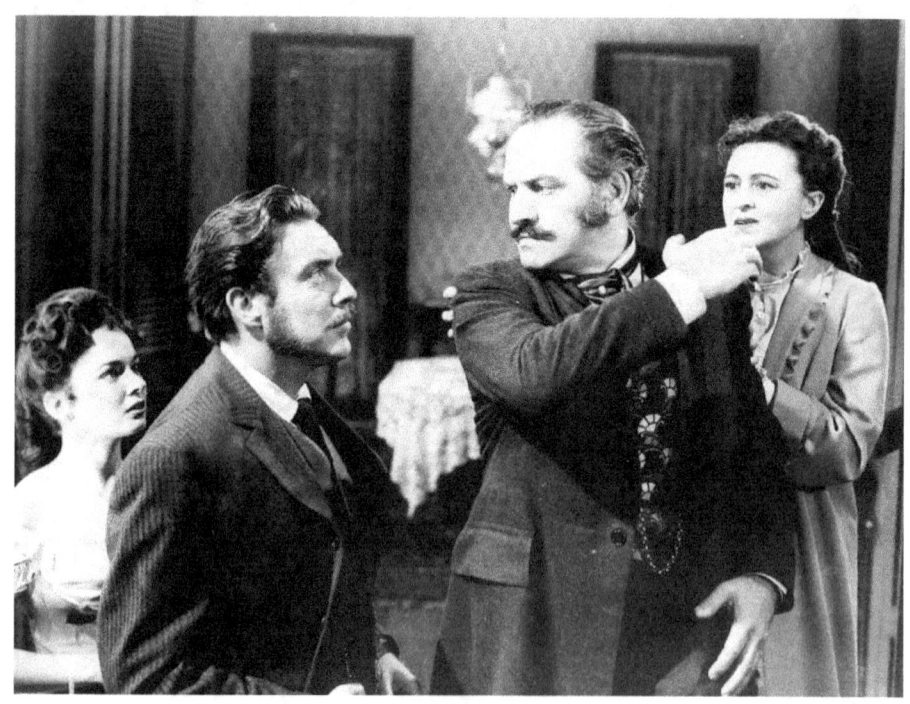

24.   *Another Part of the Forest*

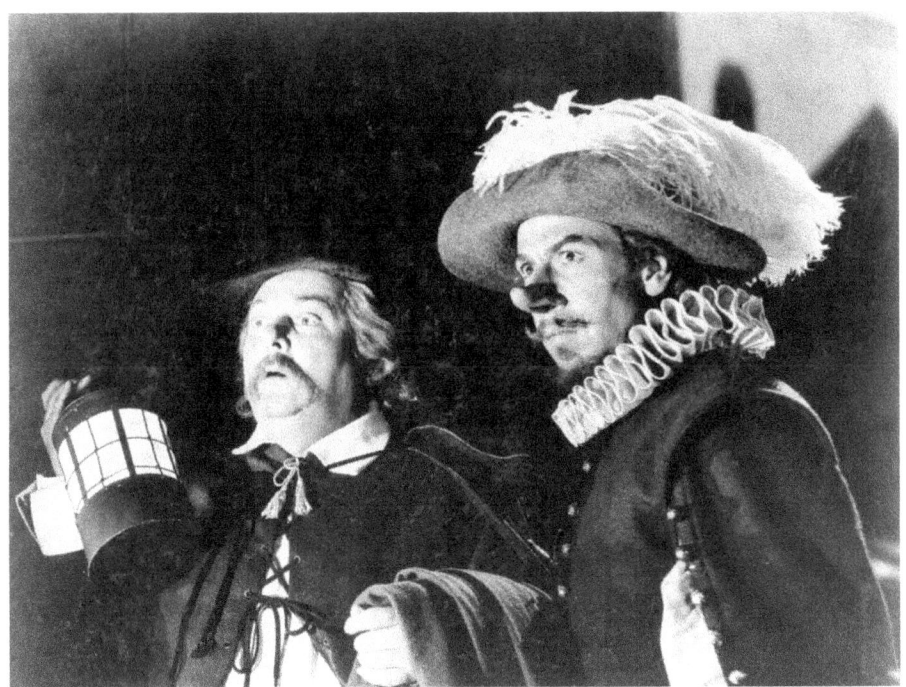

25.　　*Cyrano de Bergerac*

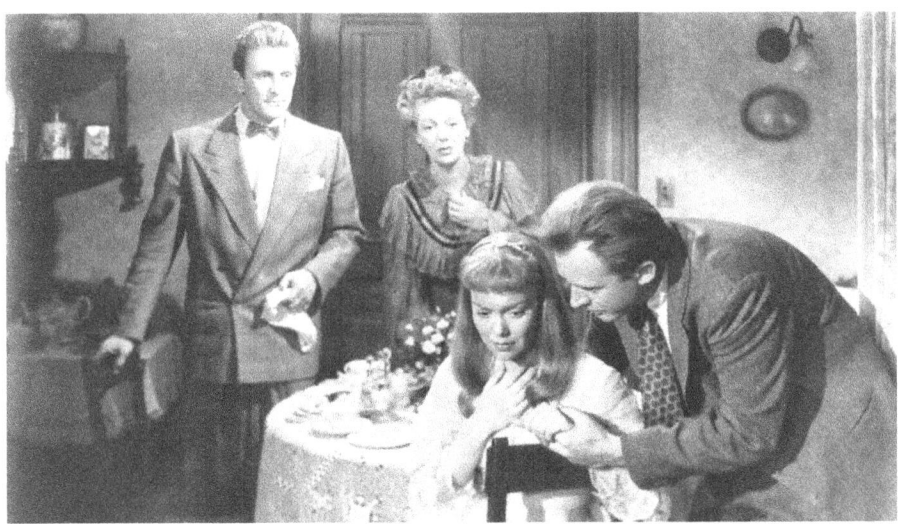

26.　　*The Glass Menagerie*

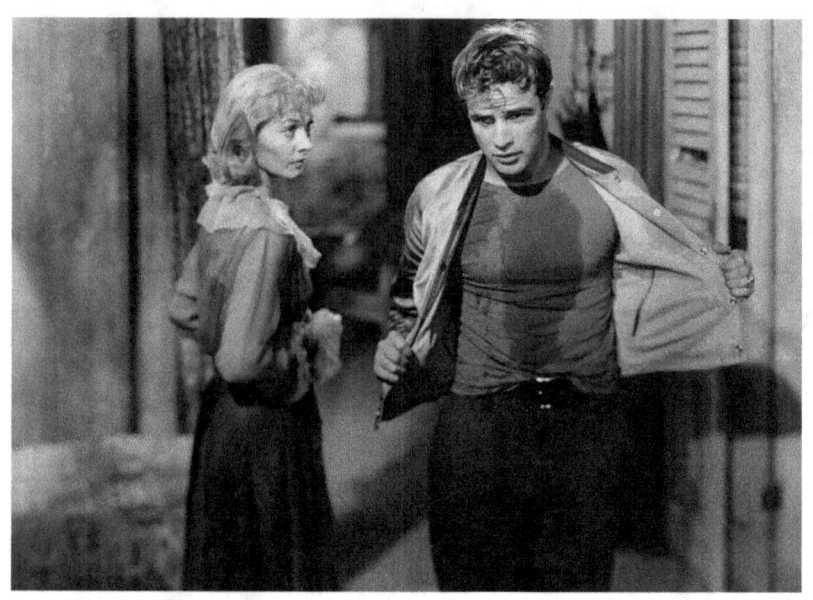

27.   *A Streetcar Named Desire*

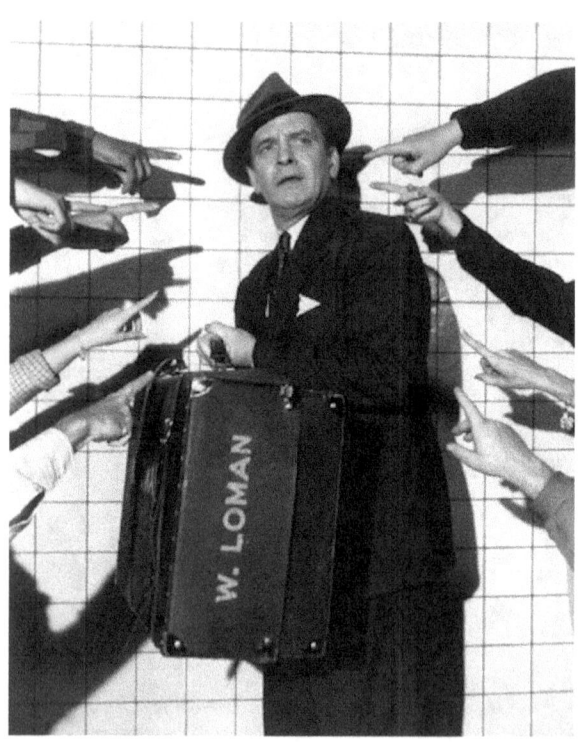

28.   *Death of a Salesman*

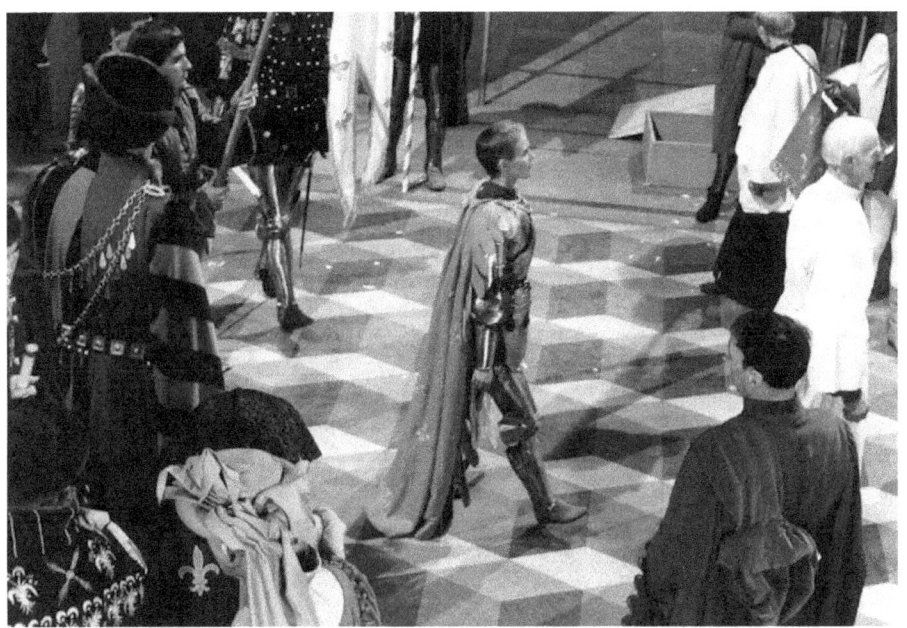

29.   *Saint Joan*

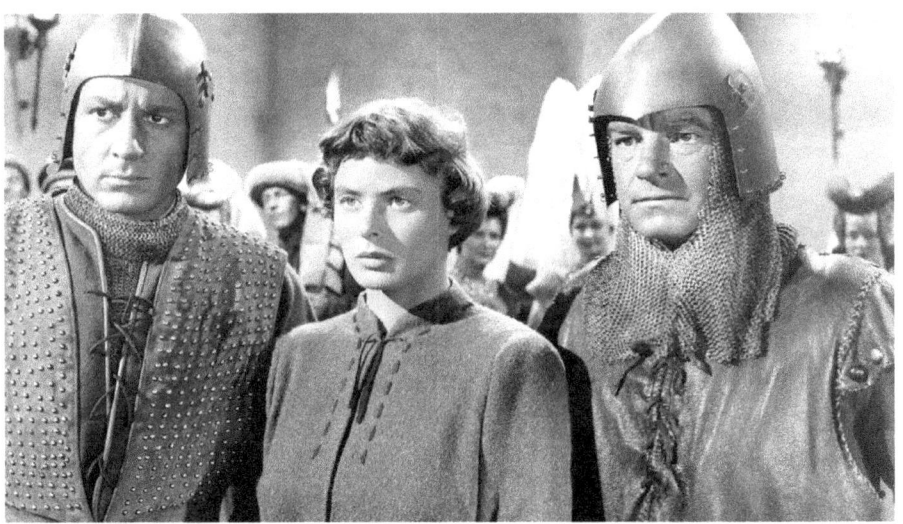

30.   *Joan of Arc*

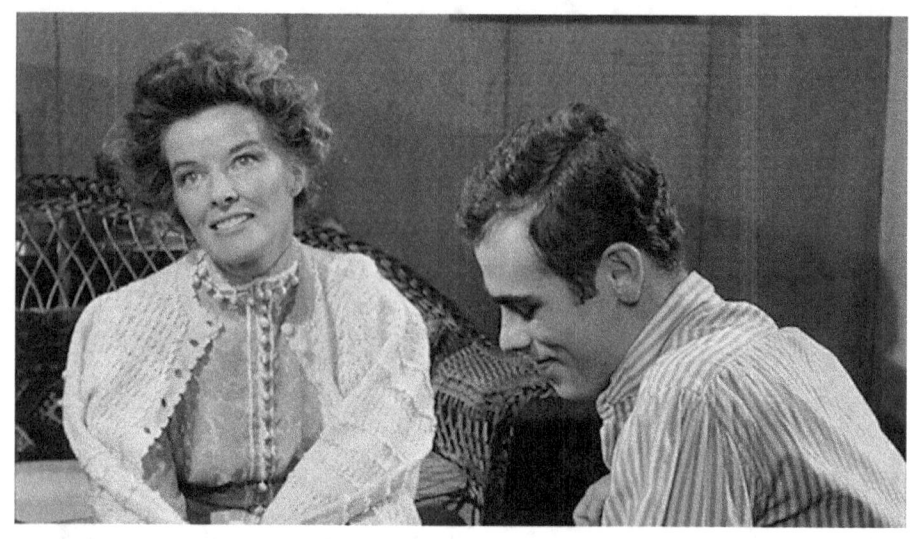

31.   *Long Day's Journey into Night*

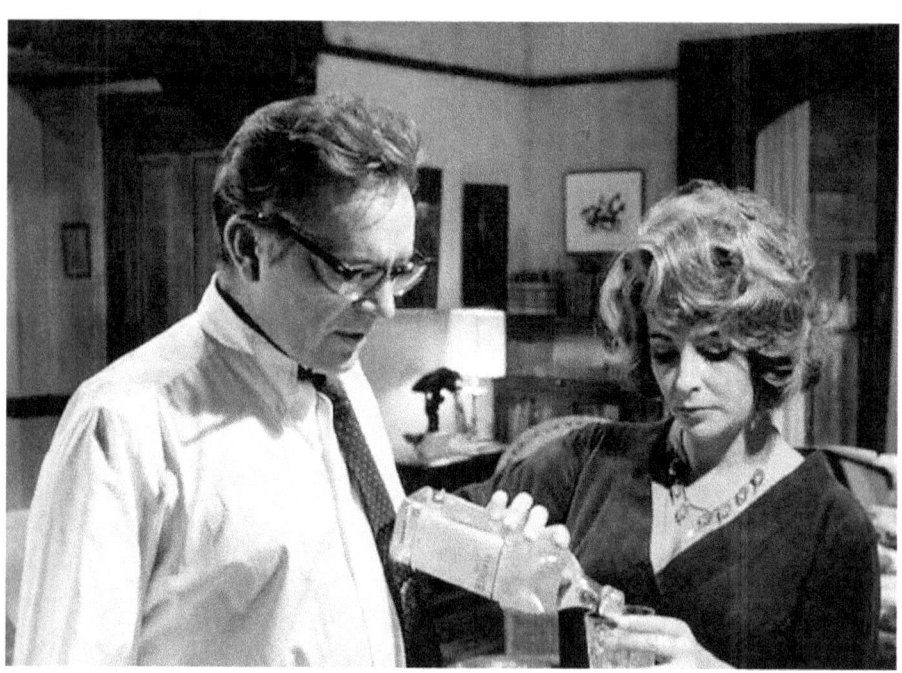

32.   *Who's Afraid of Virginia Woolf?*

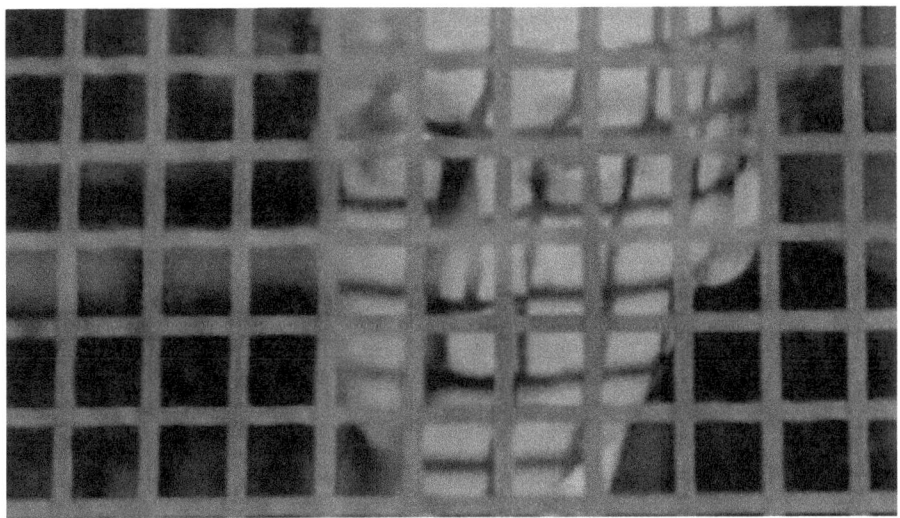

33. *Inadmissible Evidence*

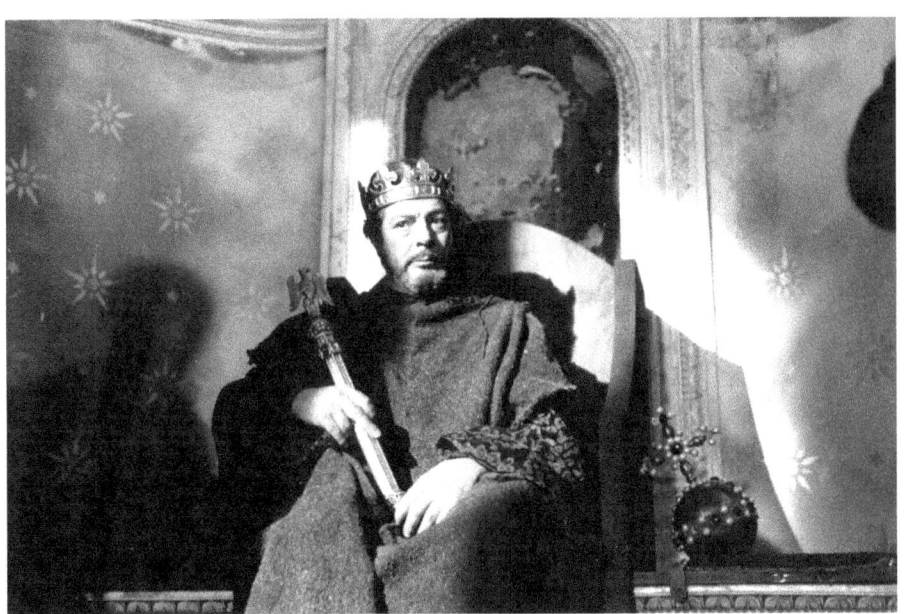

34. *Henry IV*

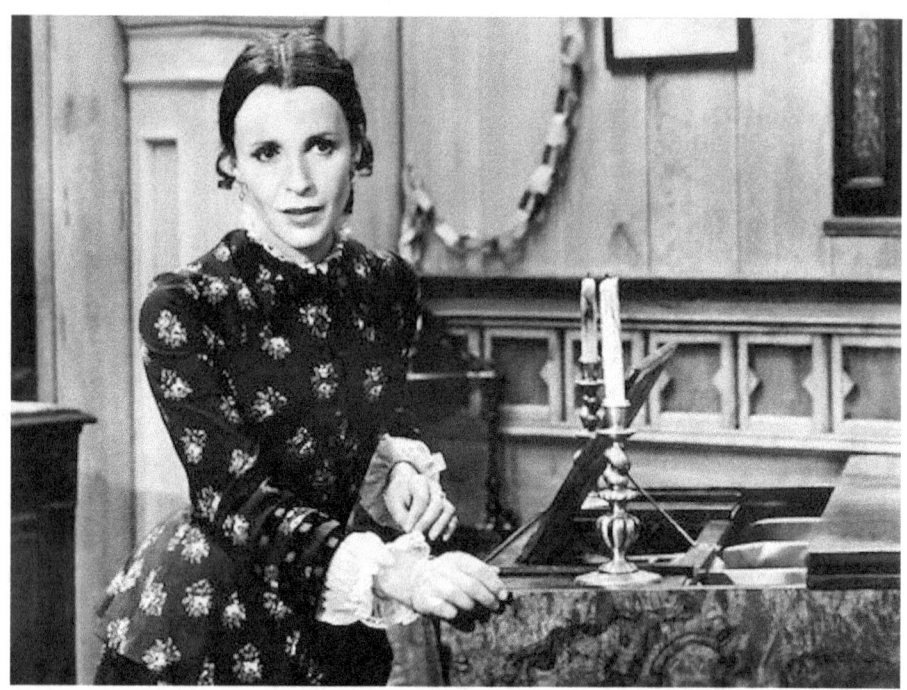

35. *A Doll's House*

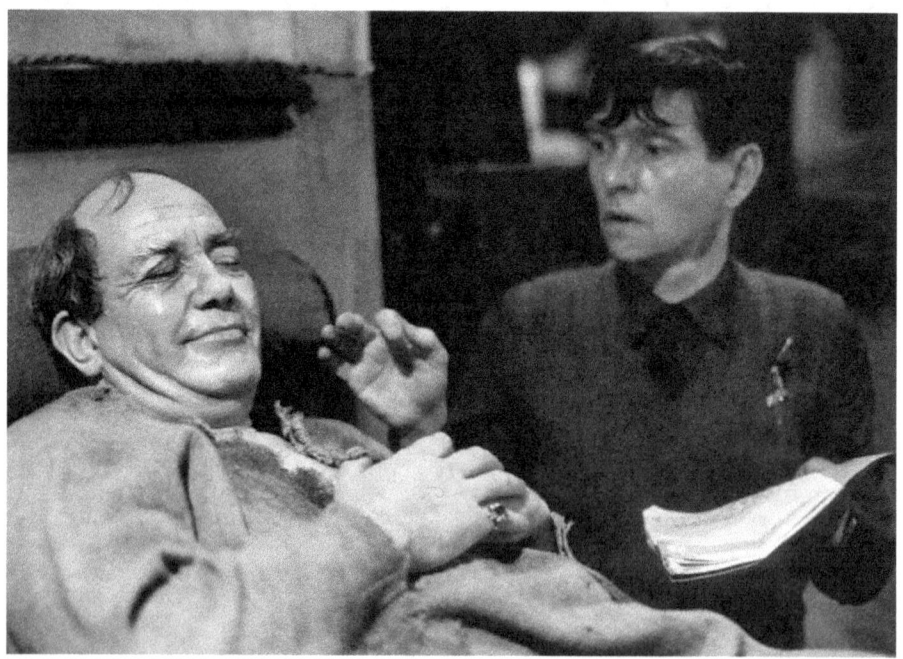

36. *The Dresser*

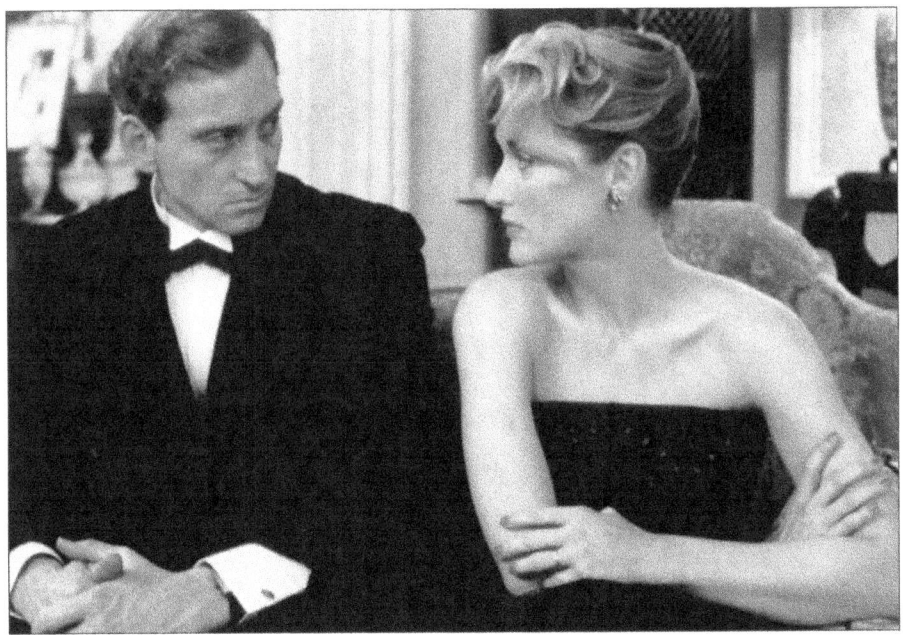

37.   *Plenty*

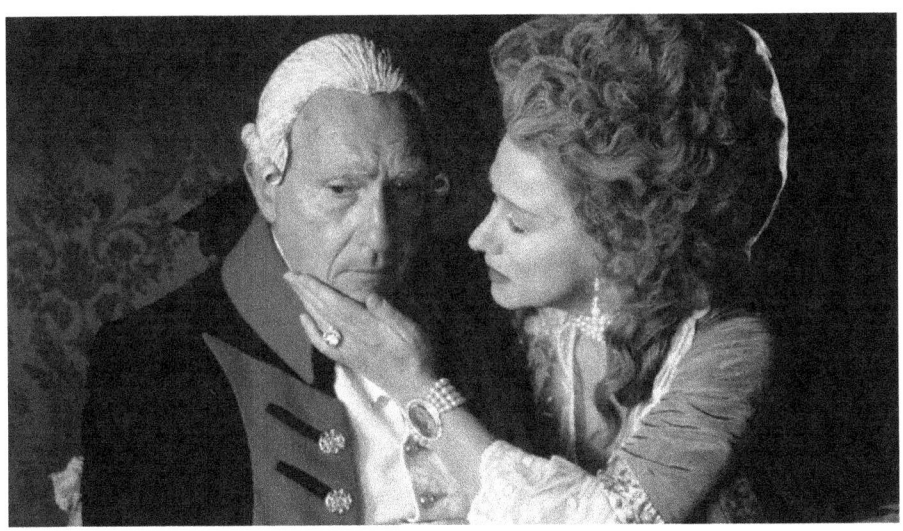

38.   *The Madness of King George*

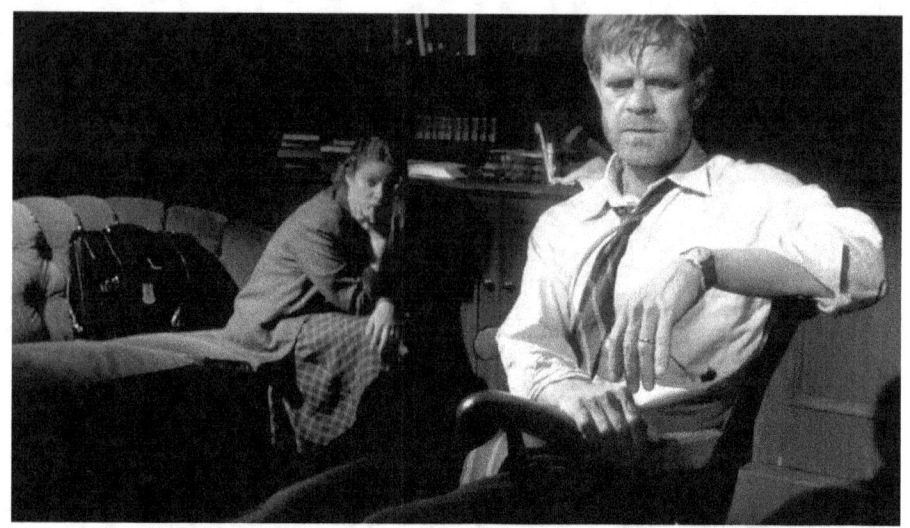

39. *Oleanna*

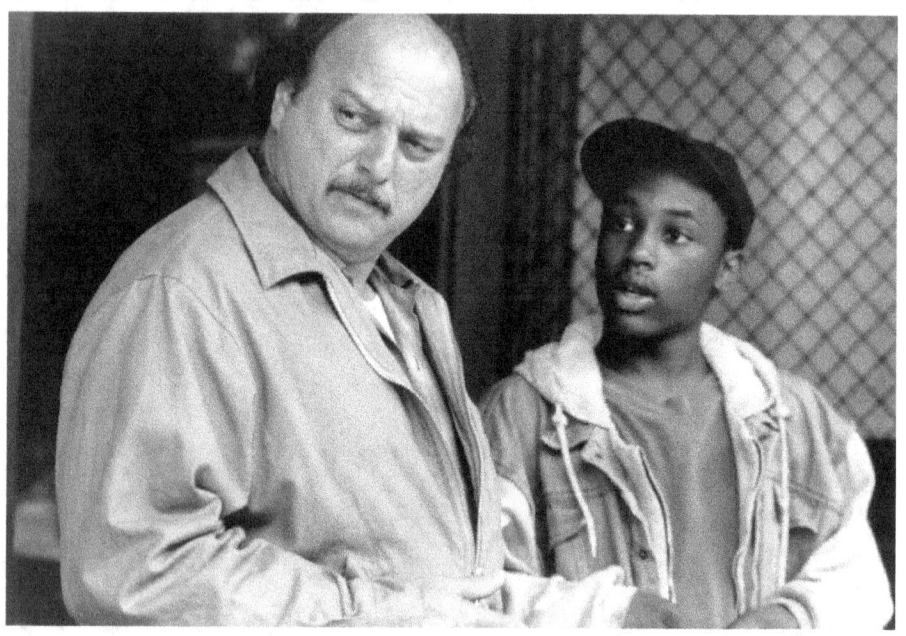

40. *American Buffalo*

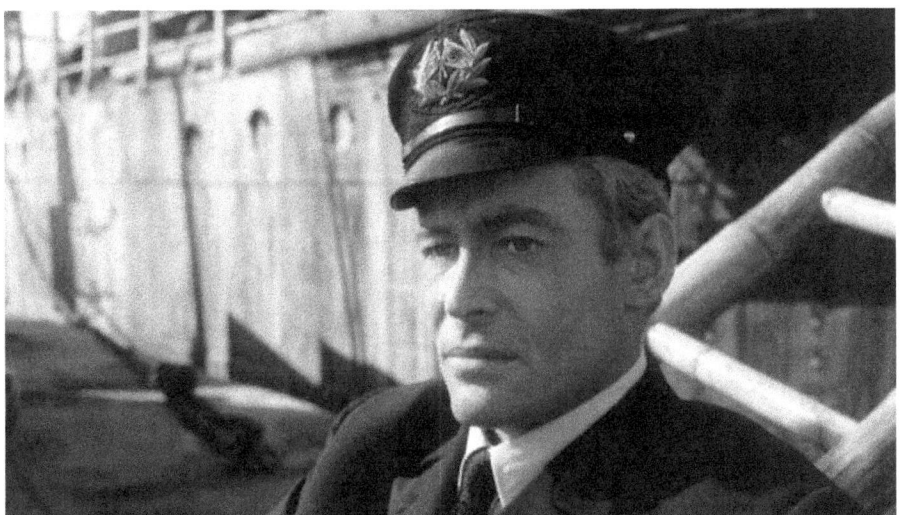

41.   *Lord Jim*

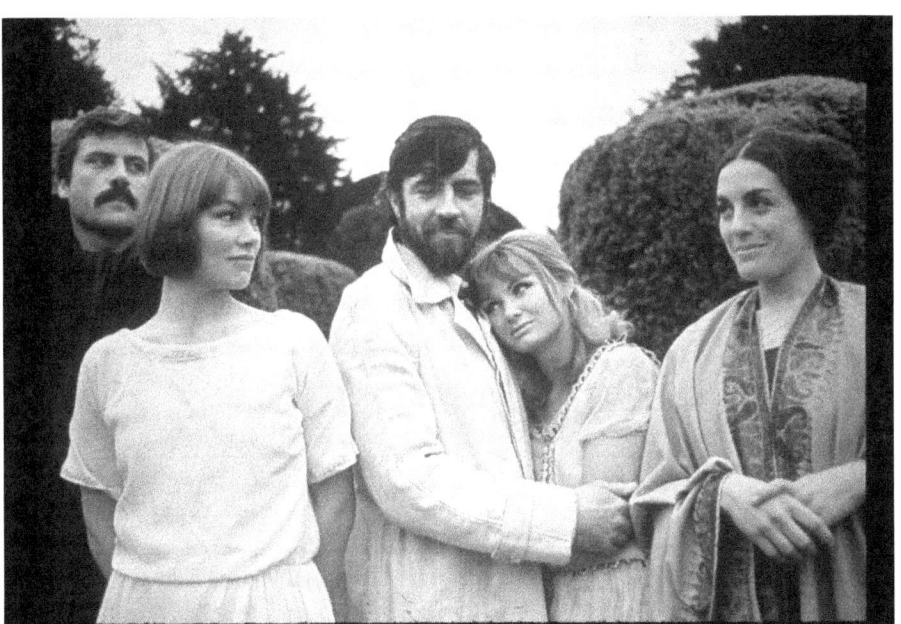

42.   *Women in Love*

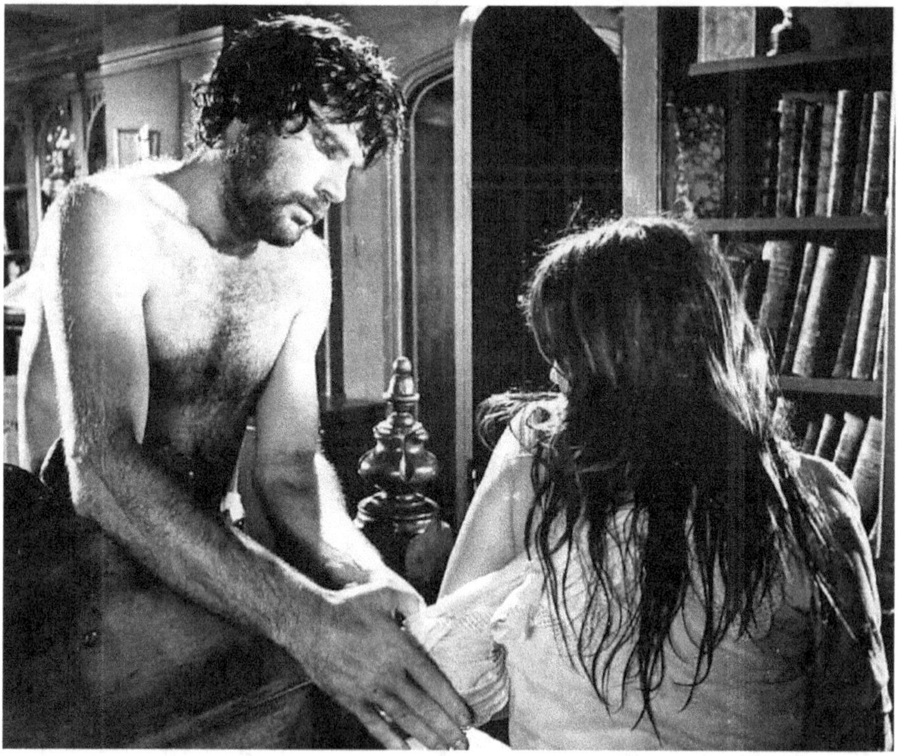

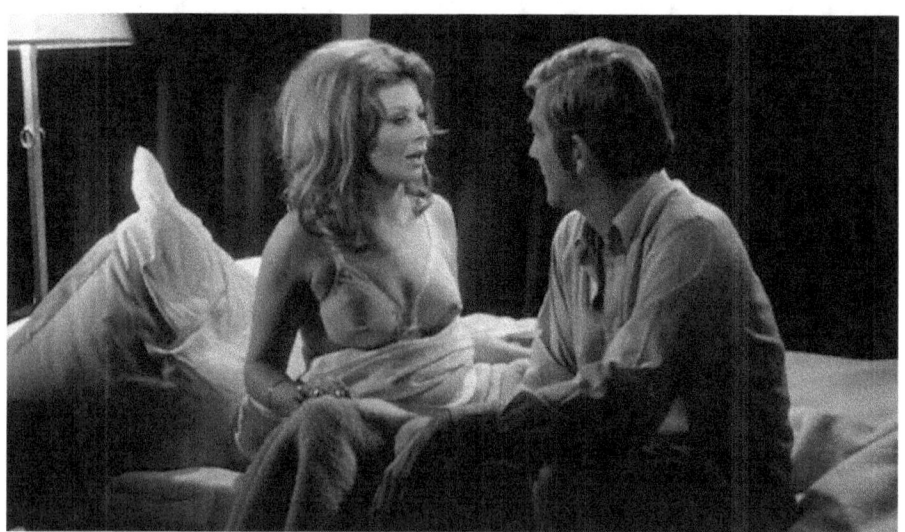

43.   *The Virgin and the Gypsy*

44.   *Tropic of Cancer*

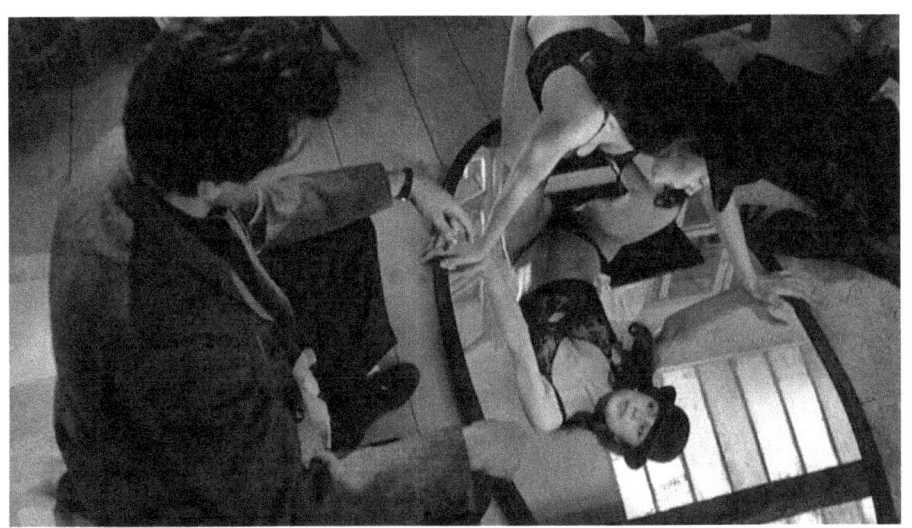

45.   *The Unbearable Lightness of Being*

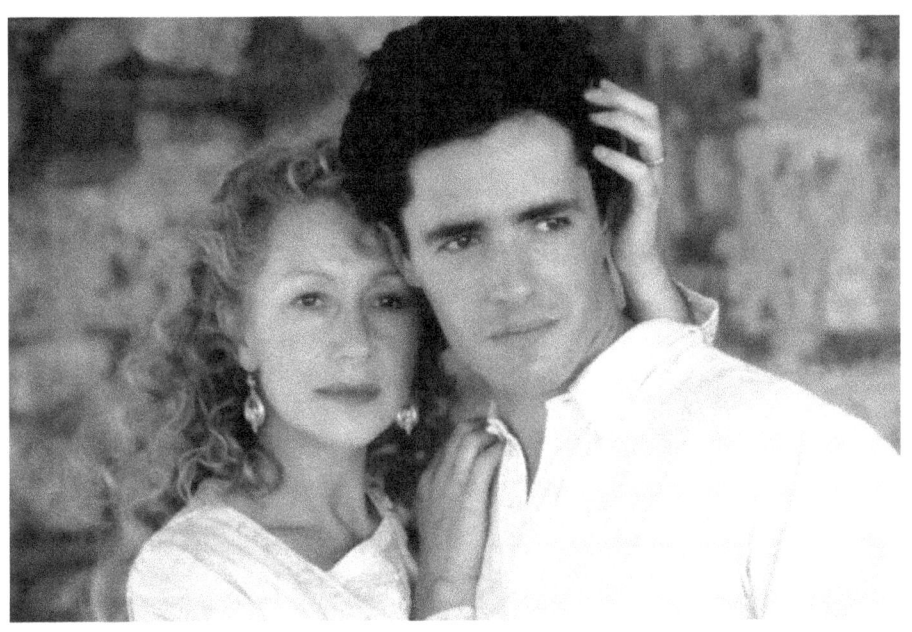

46.   *Where Angels Fear to Tread*

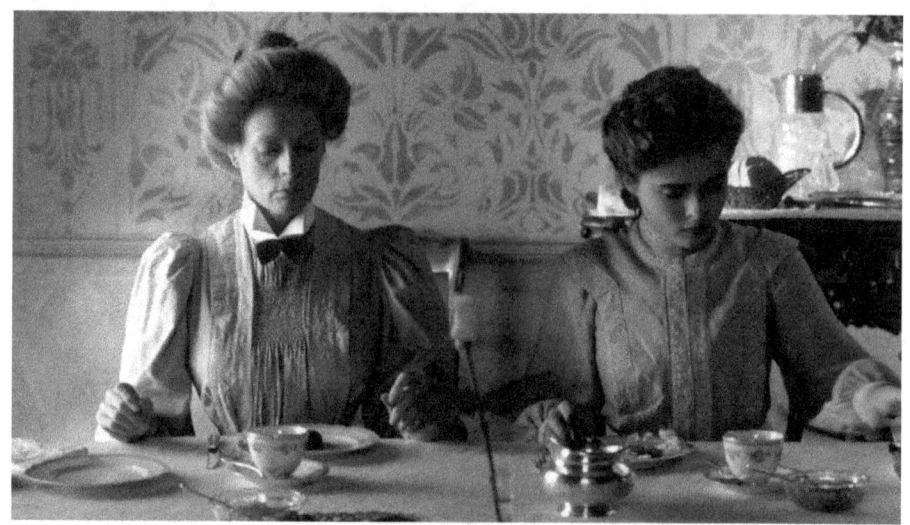

47.   *A Room with a View*

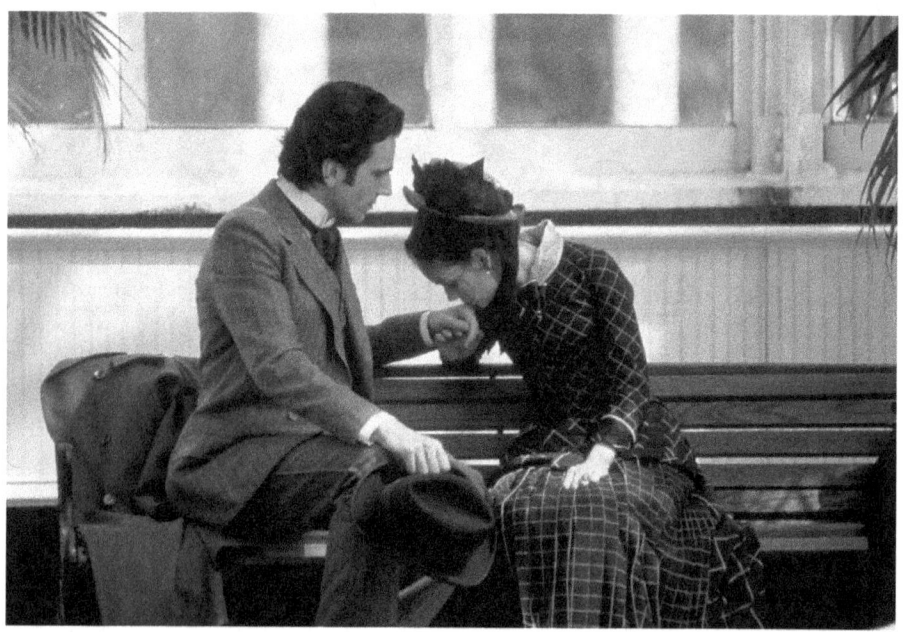

48.   *The Age of Innocence*

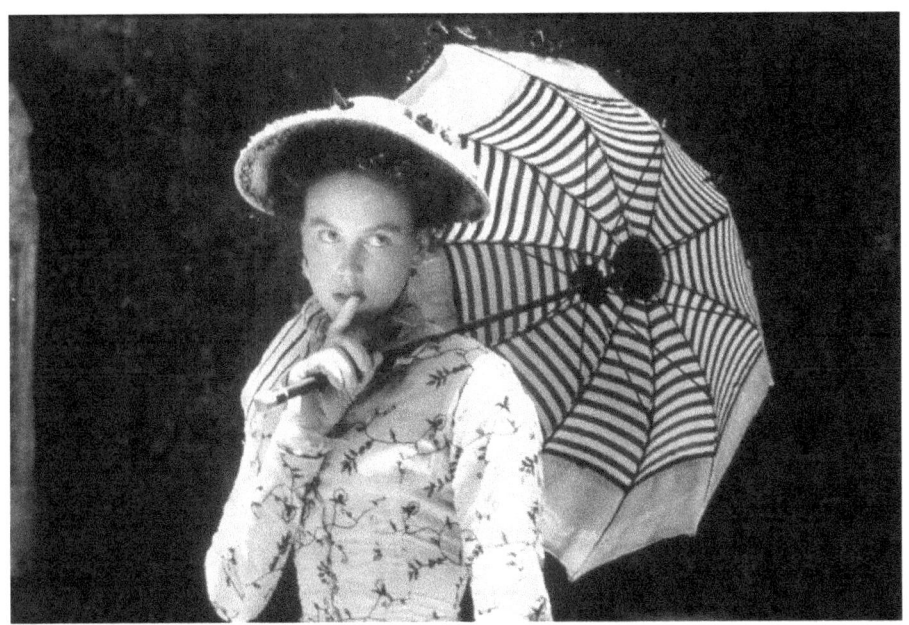

49.   *The Portrait of a Lady*

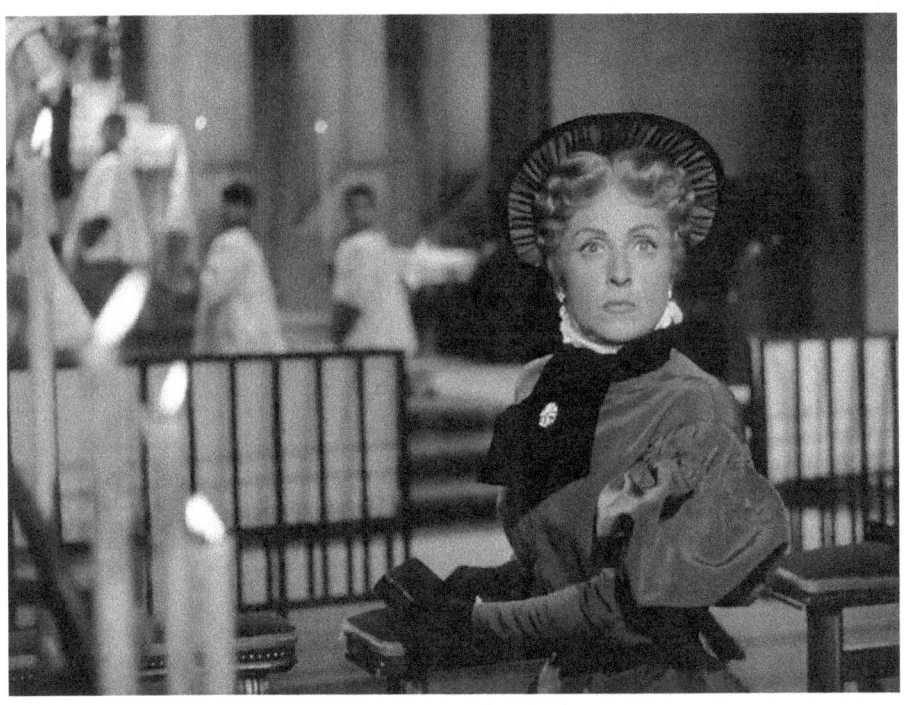

50.   *The Red and the Black*

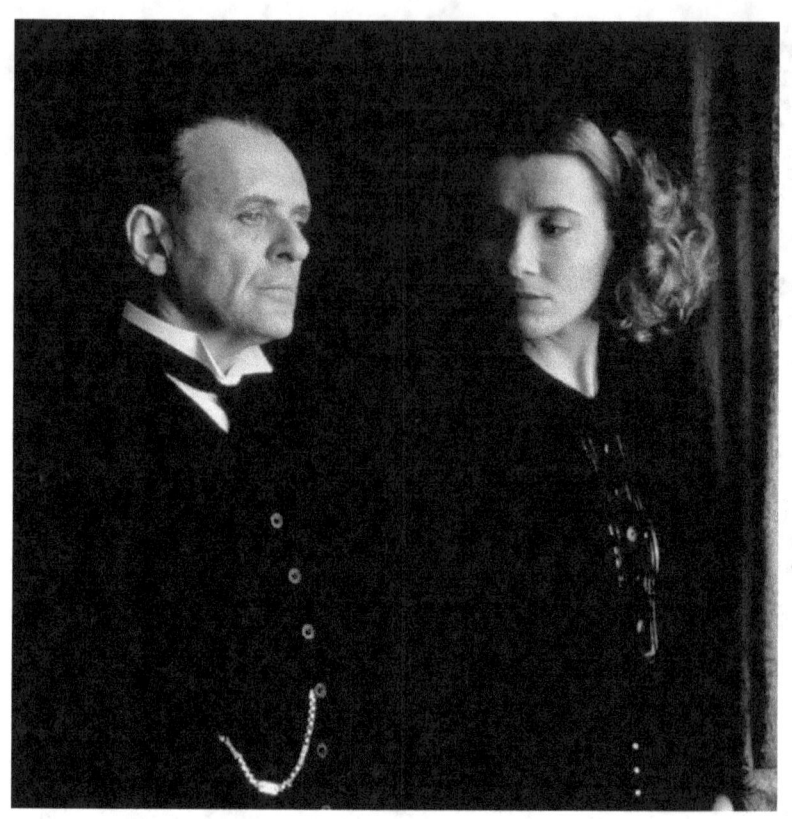

51.   *The Remains of the Day*

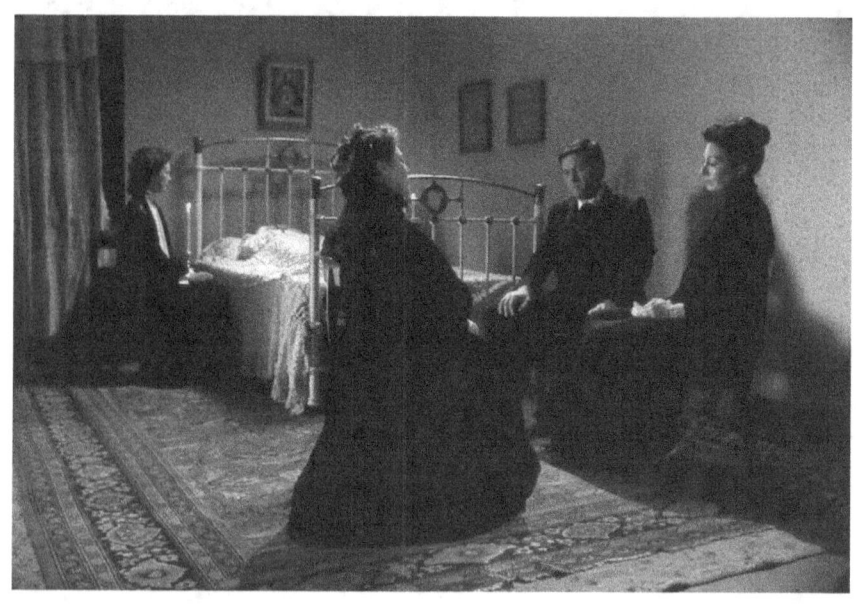

52.   *The Dead*

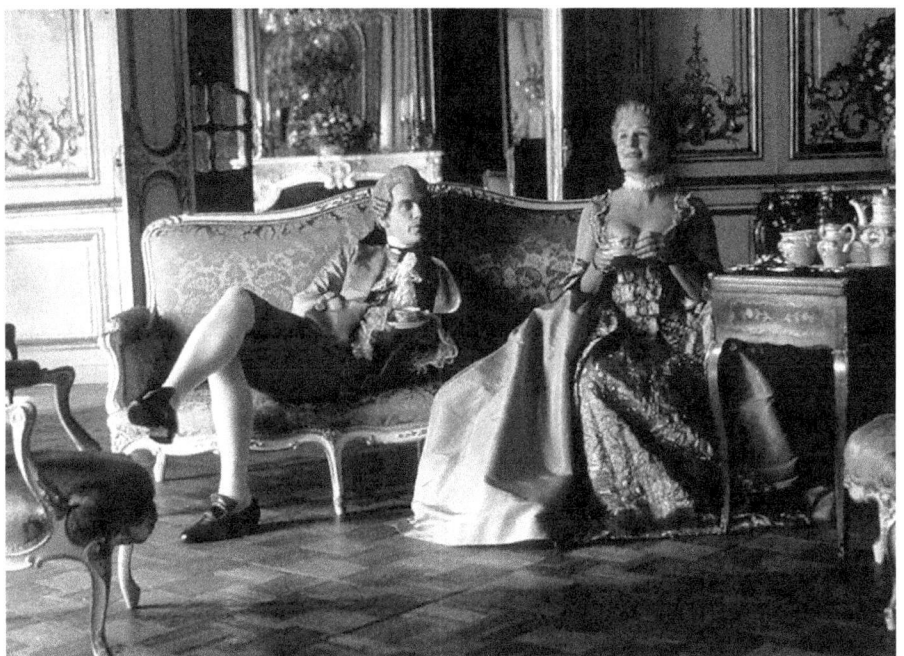

53.	*Dangerous Liaisons*

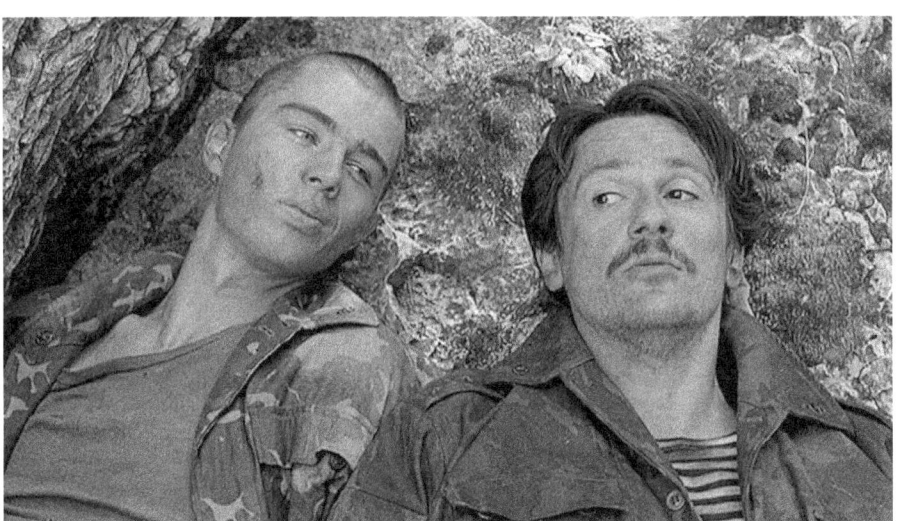

54.	*Prisoner of the Mountains*

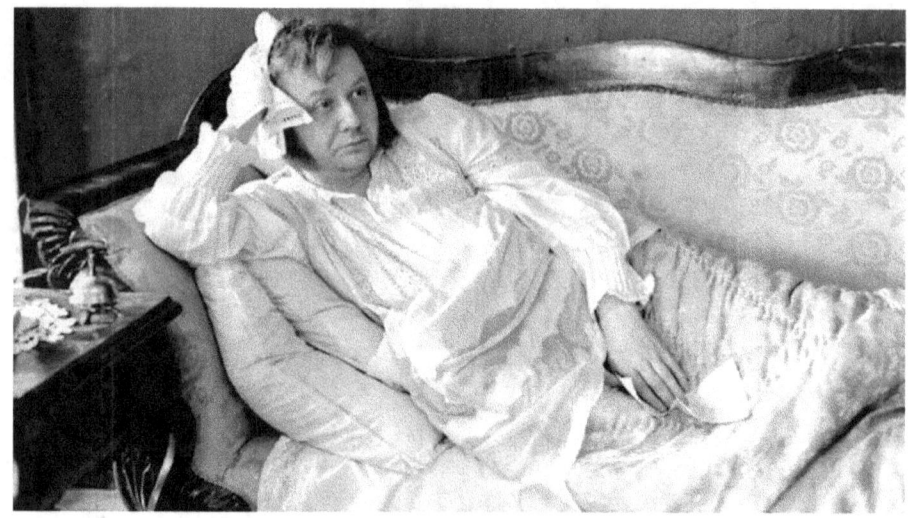

55.   *Oblomov*

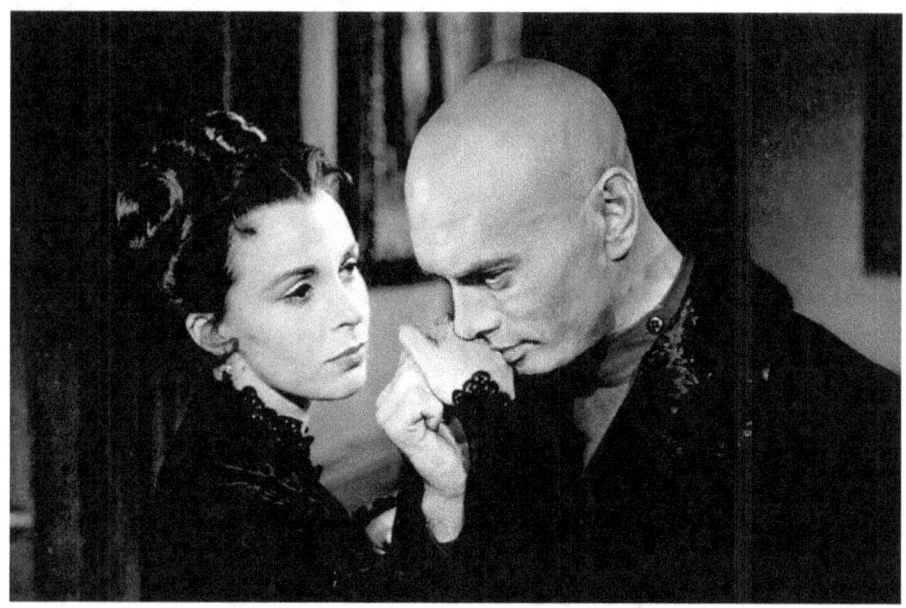

56.   *The Brothers Karamazov*

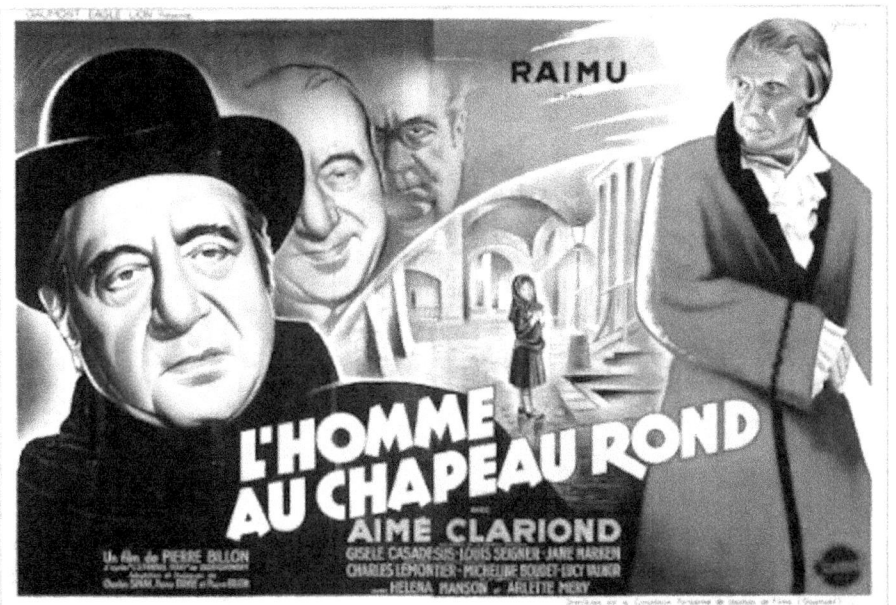

57.   *The Eternal Husband*

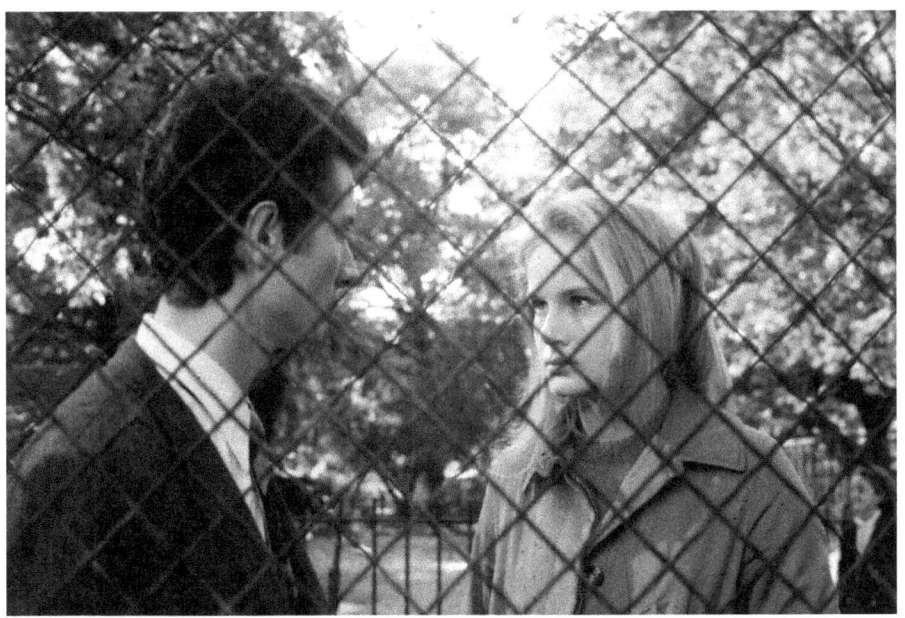

58.   *A Gentle Creature*

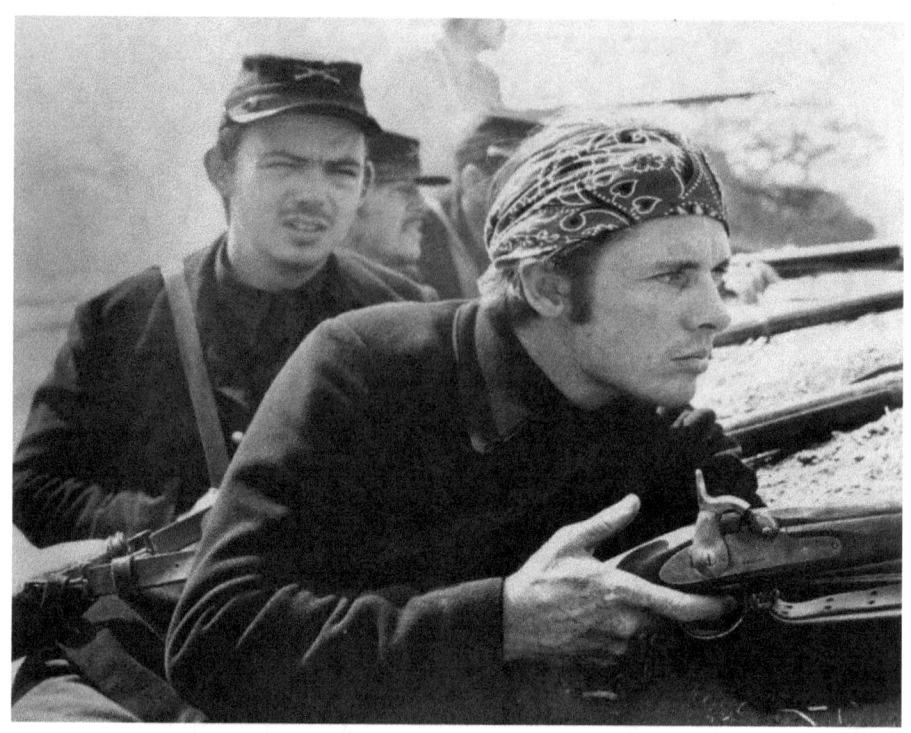

59.   *The Red Badge of Courage*

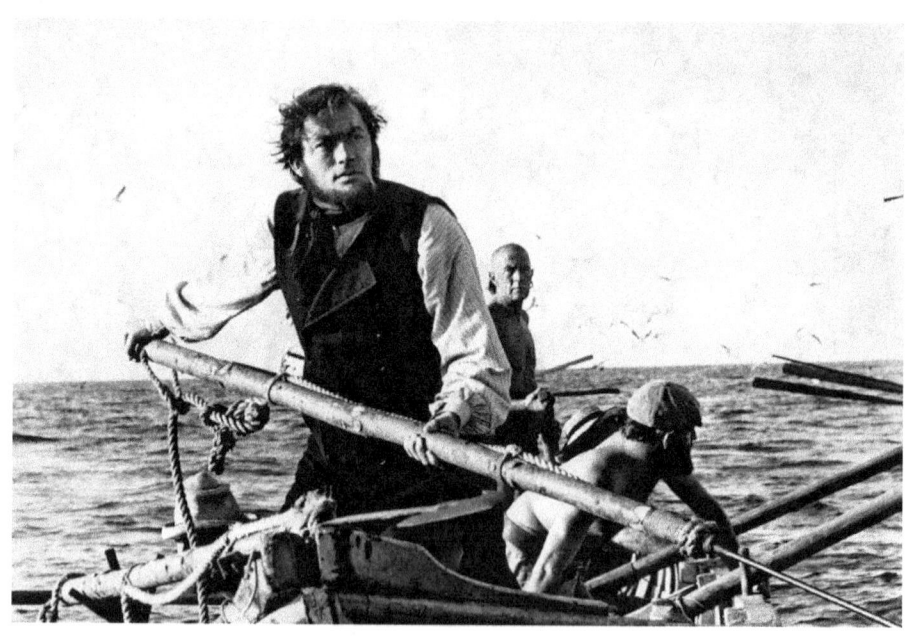

60.   *Moby Dick*

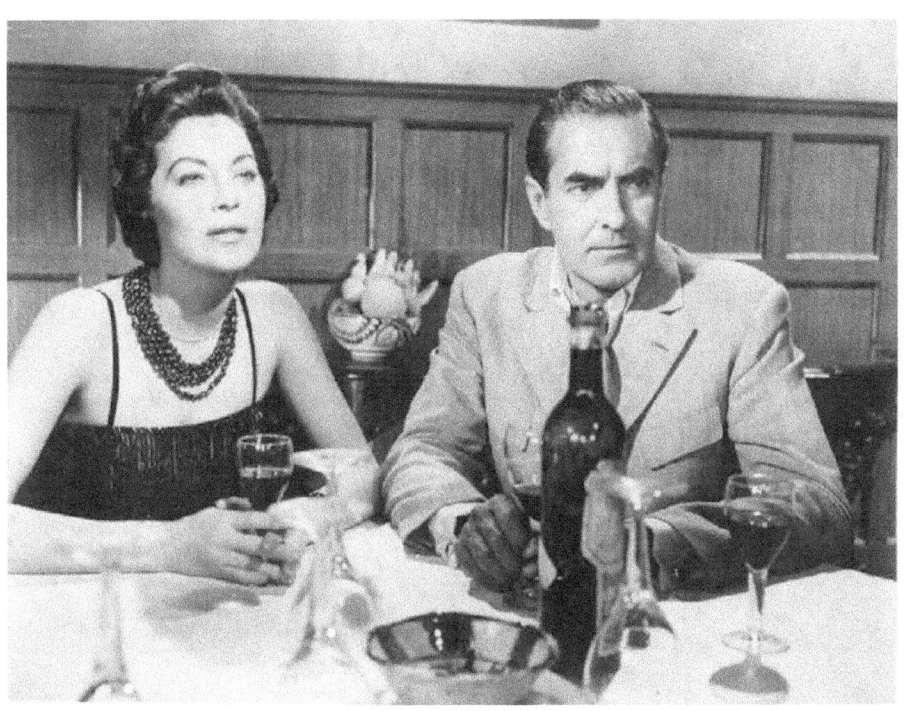

61.   *The Sun Also Rises*

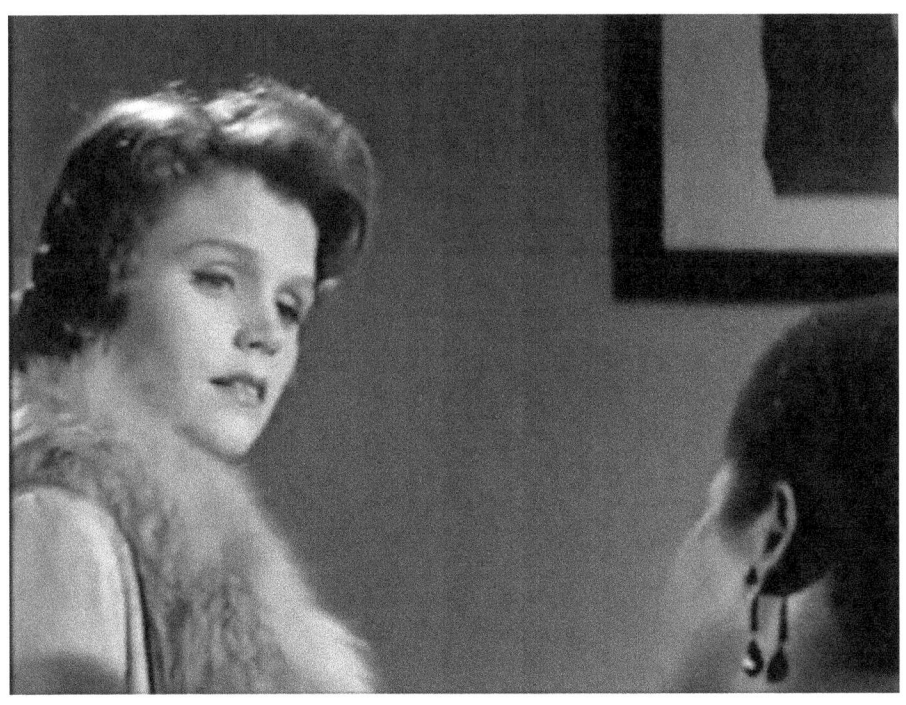

62.   *Sanctuary*

139

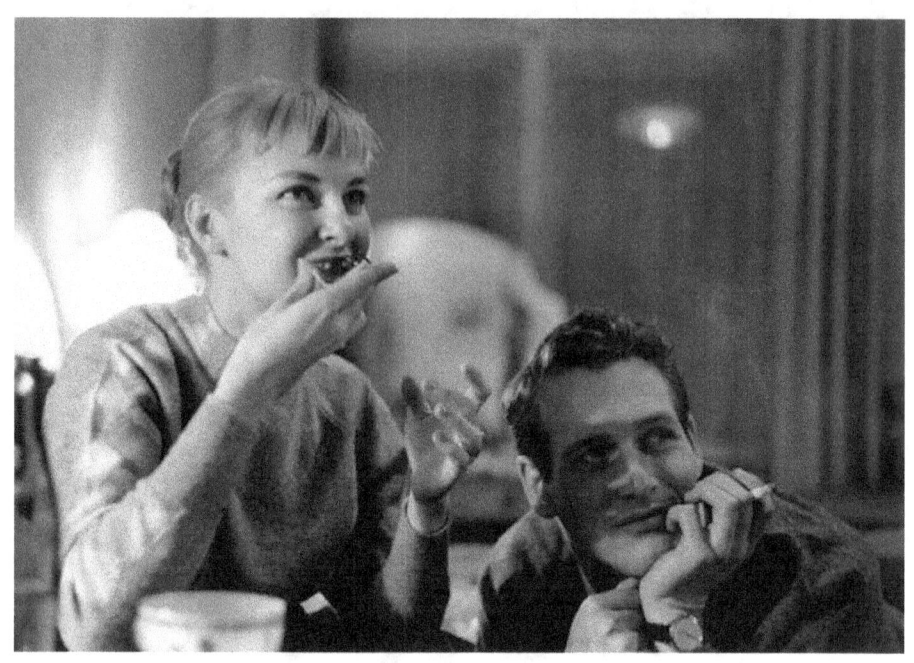

63. *The Long, Hot Summer*

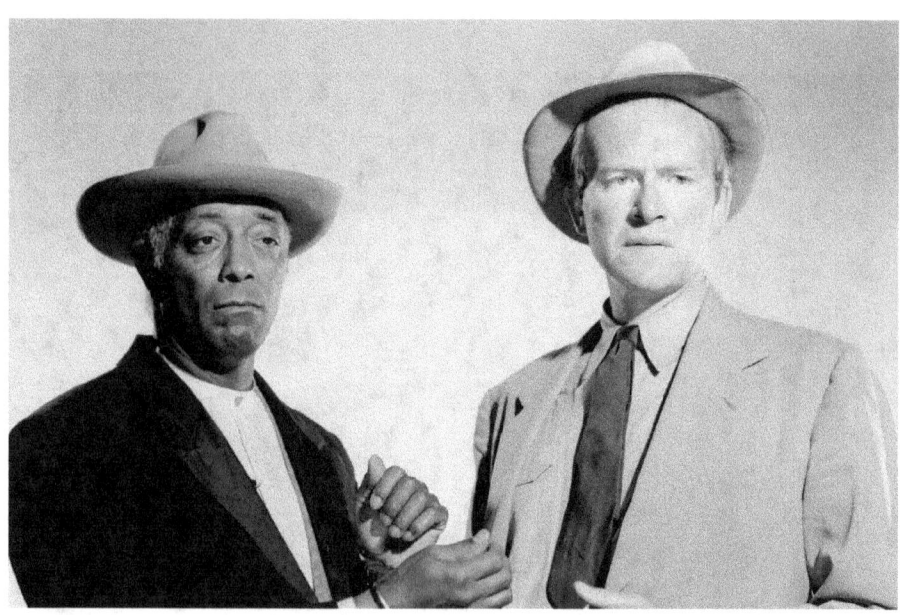

64. *Intruder in the Dust*

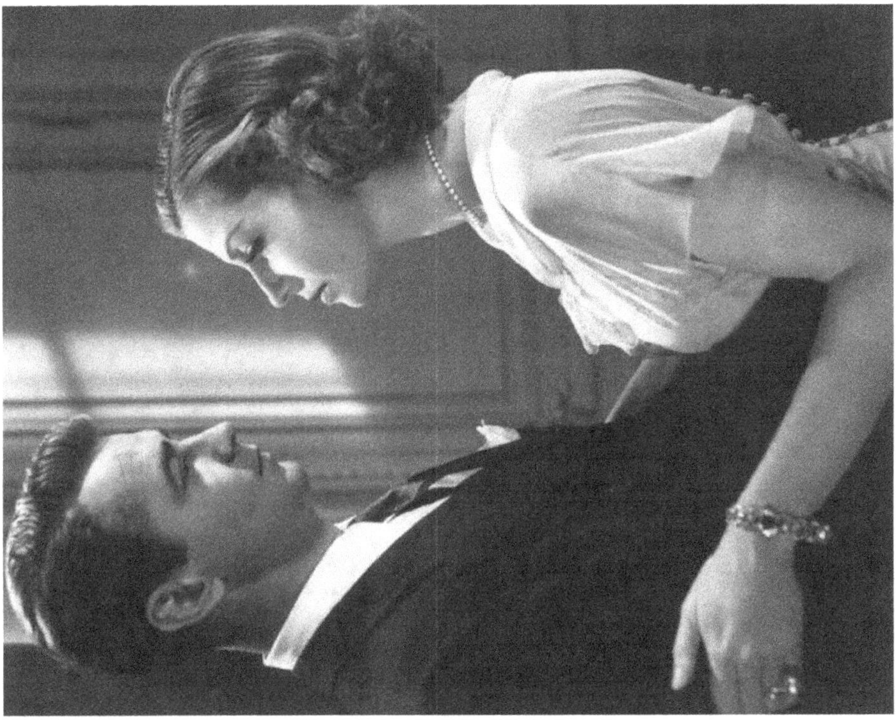

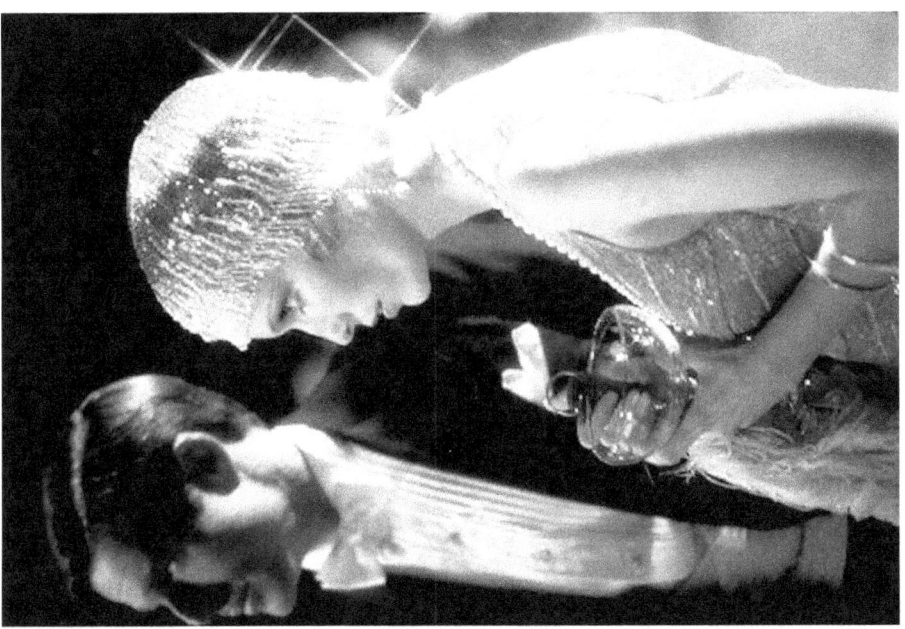

65.   *The Great Gatsby*

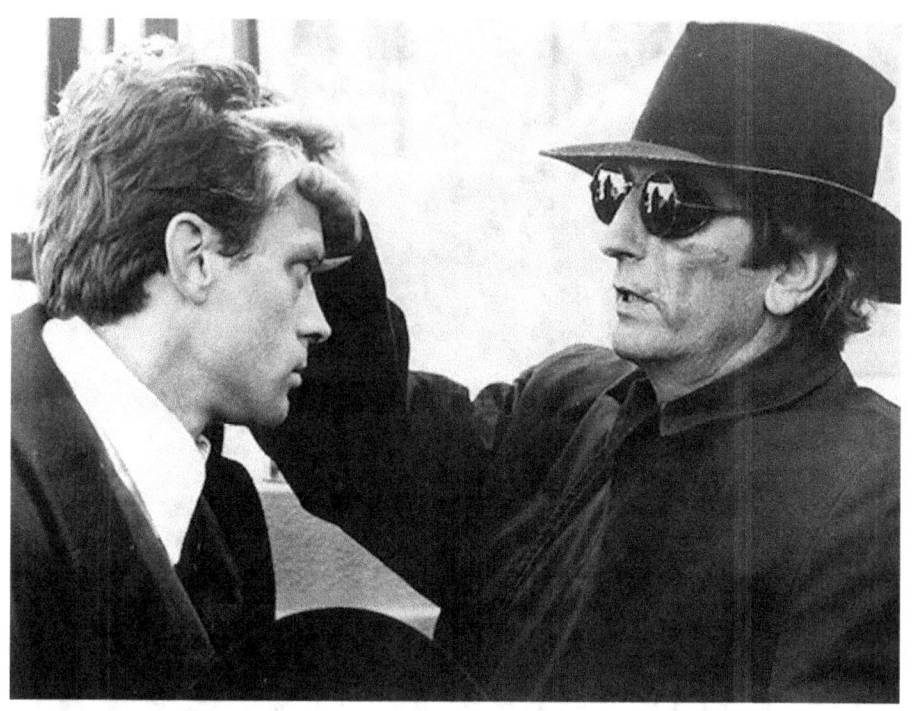

66.   *Wise Blood*

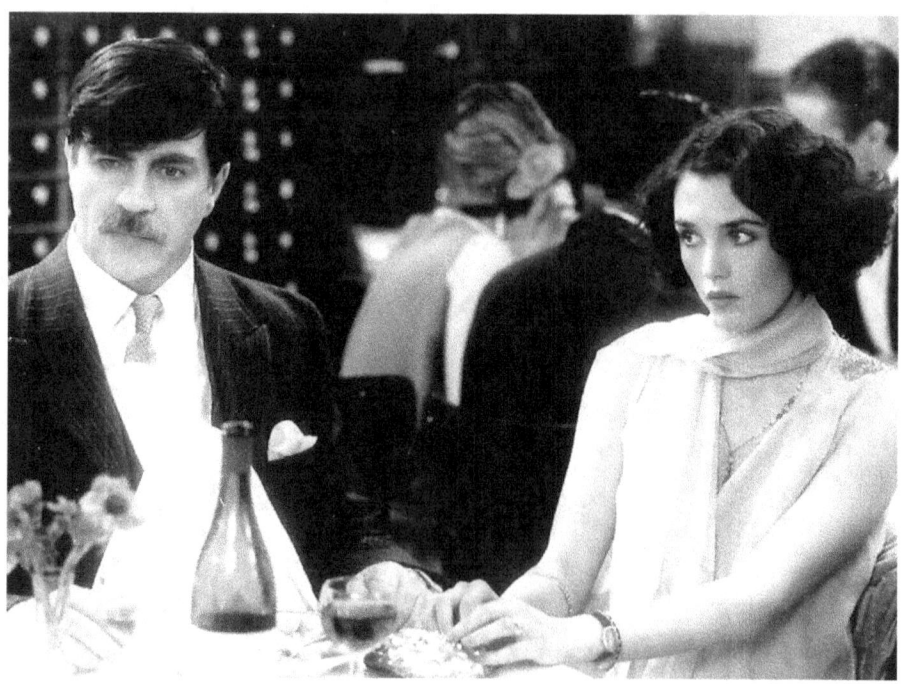

67.   *Quartet*

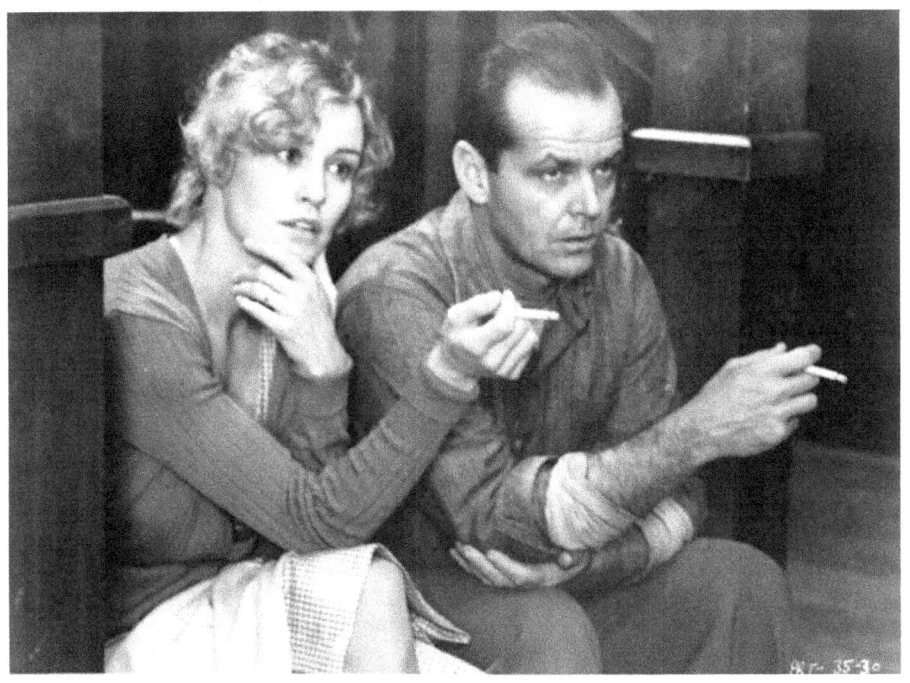

68.   *The Postman Always Rings Twice*

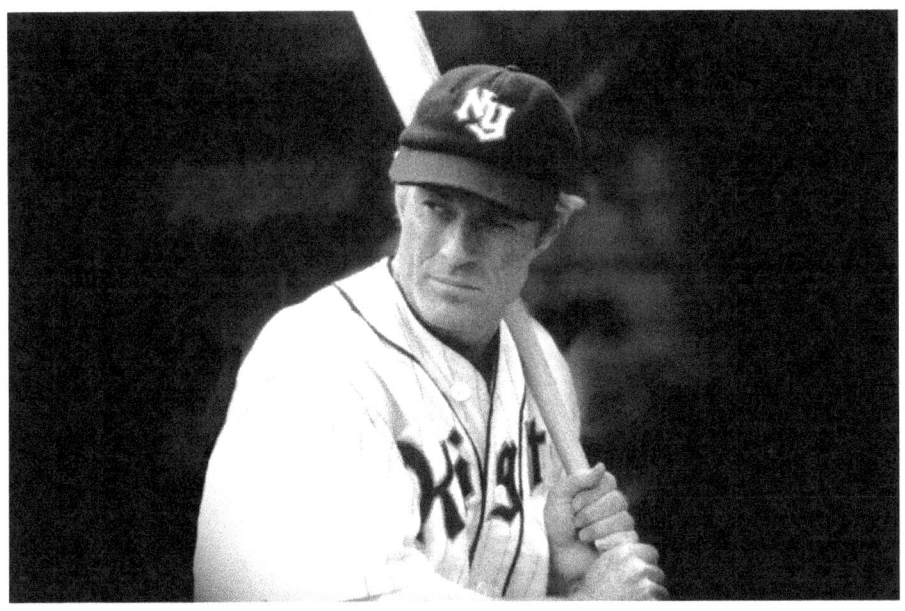

69.   *The Natural*

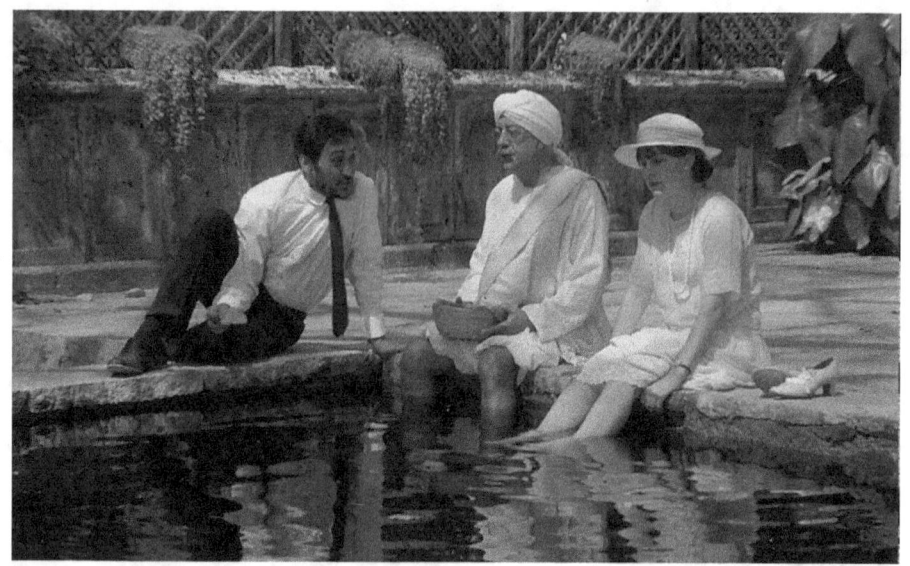

70.   *A Passage to India*

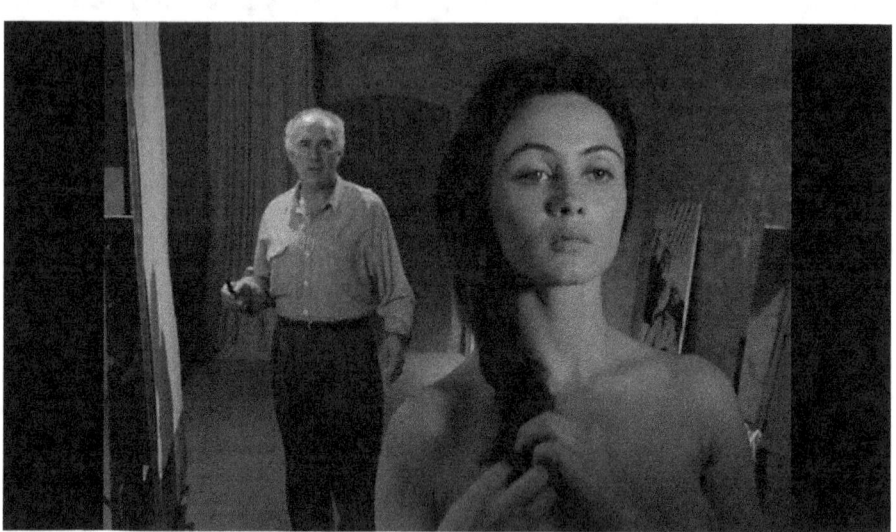

71.   *La Belle noiseuse*

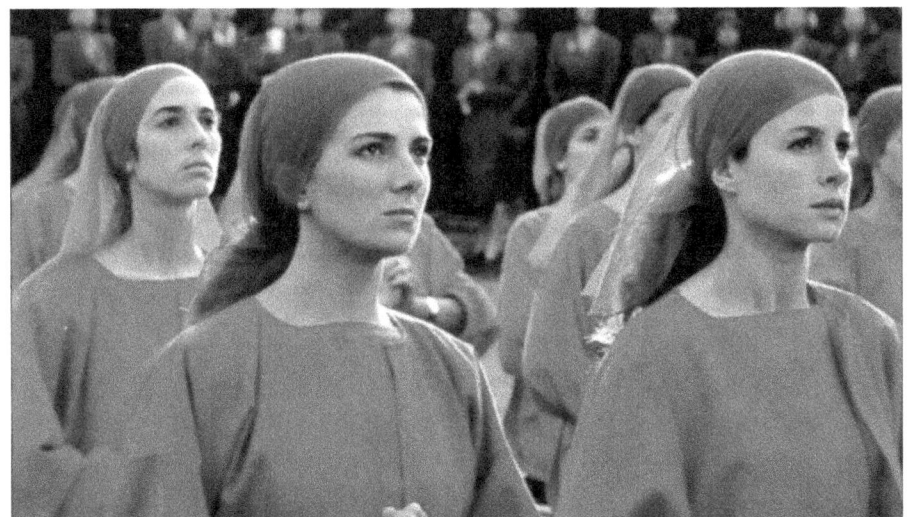

72.   *The Handmaid's Tale*

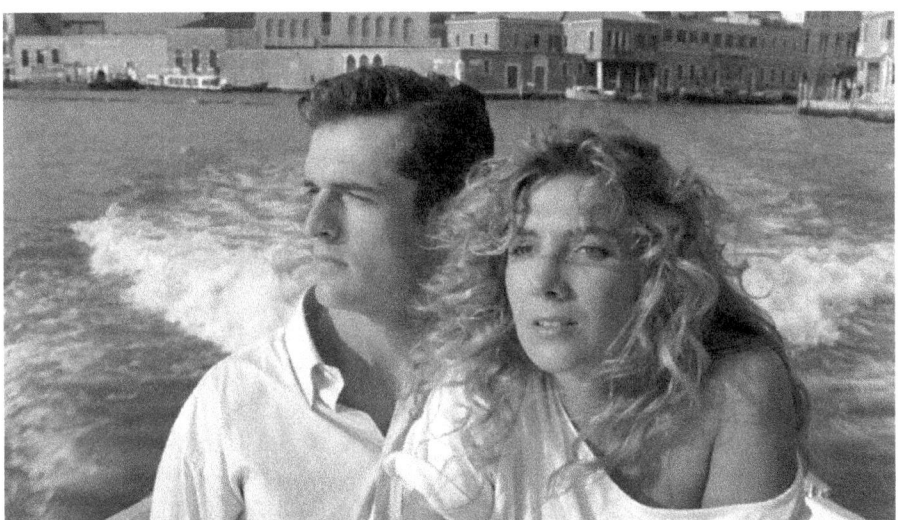

73.   *The Comfort of Strangers*

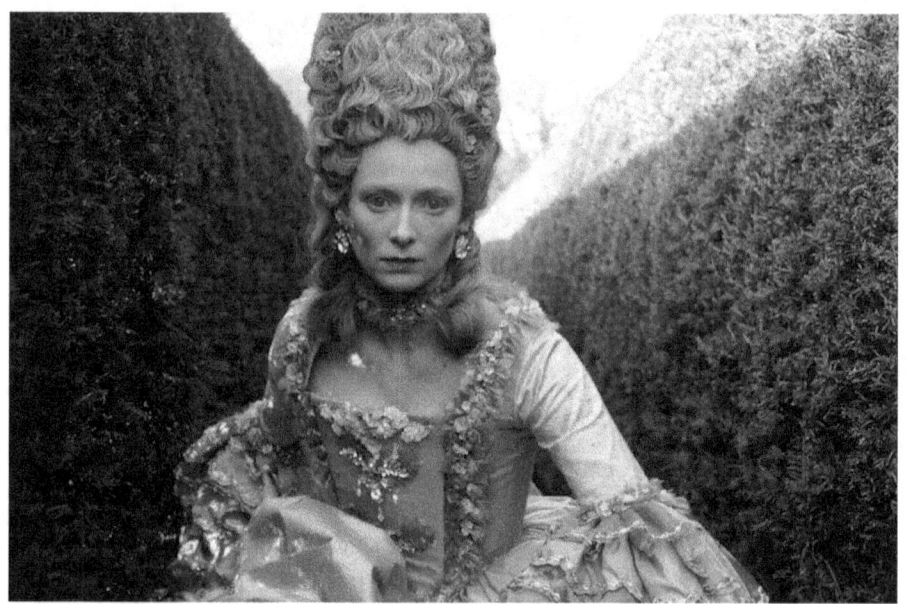

74.   Orlando

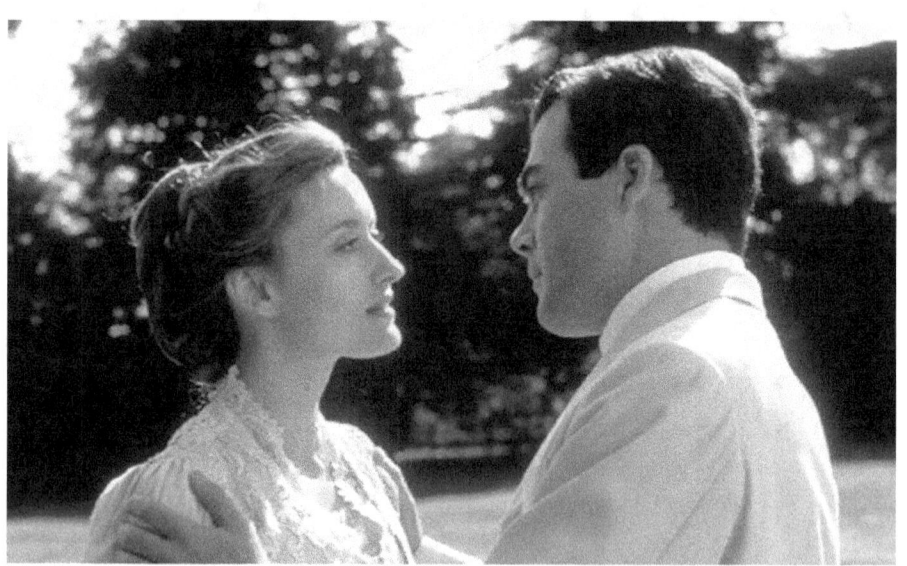

75.   Mrs. Dalloway

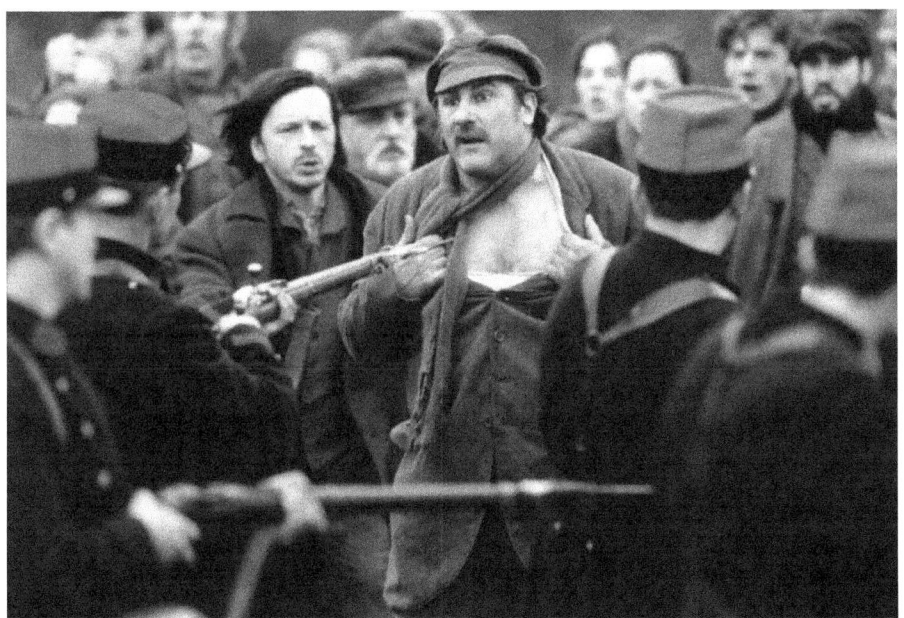

76.   *Germinal*

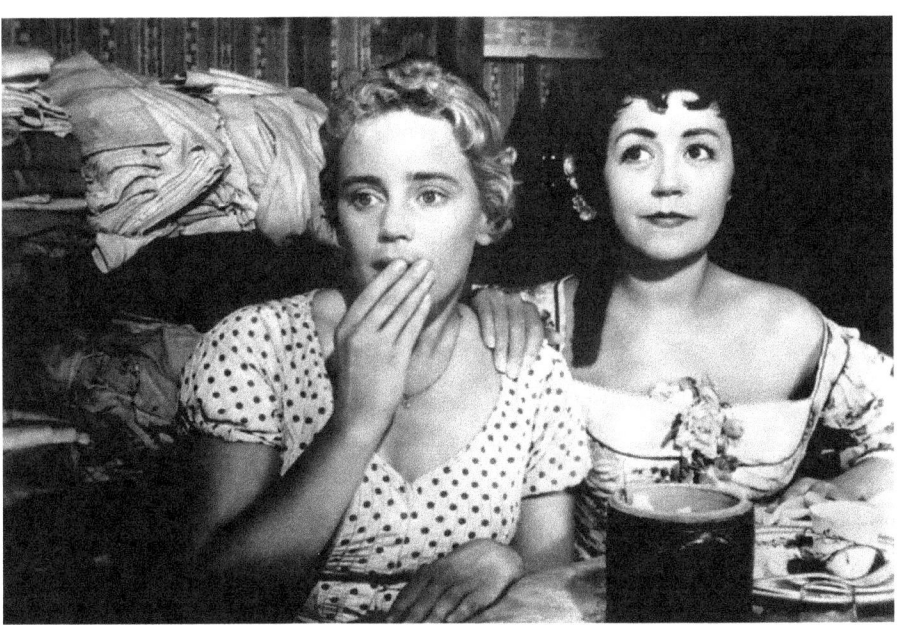

77.   *Gervaise*

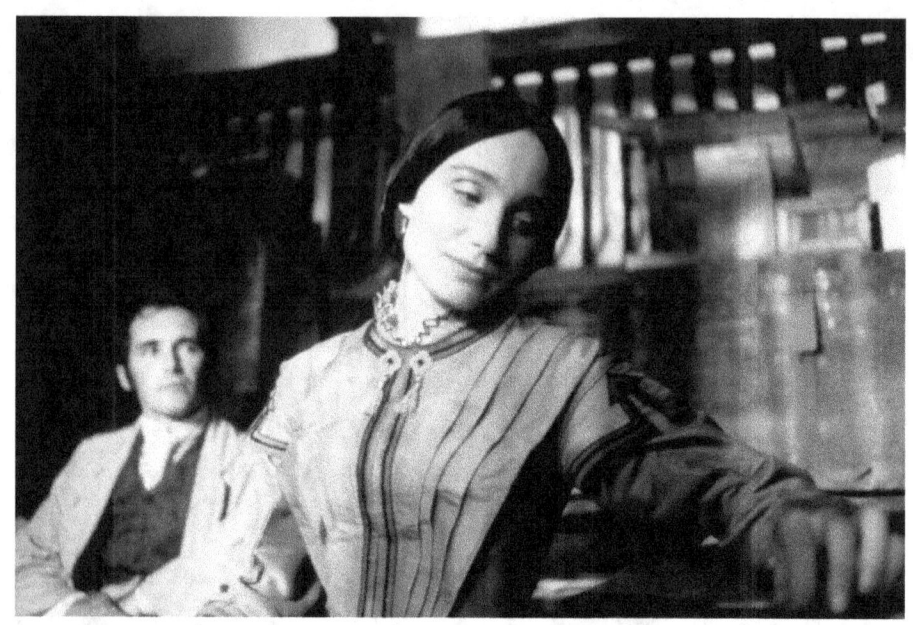

78. *Angels and Insects*

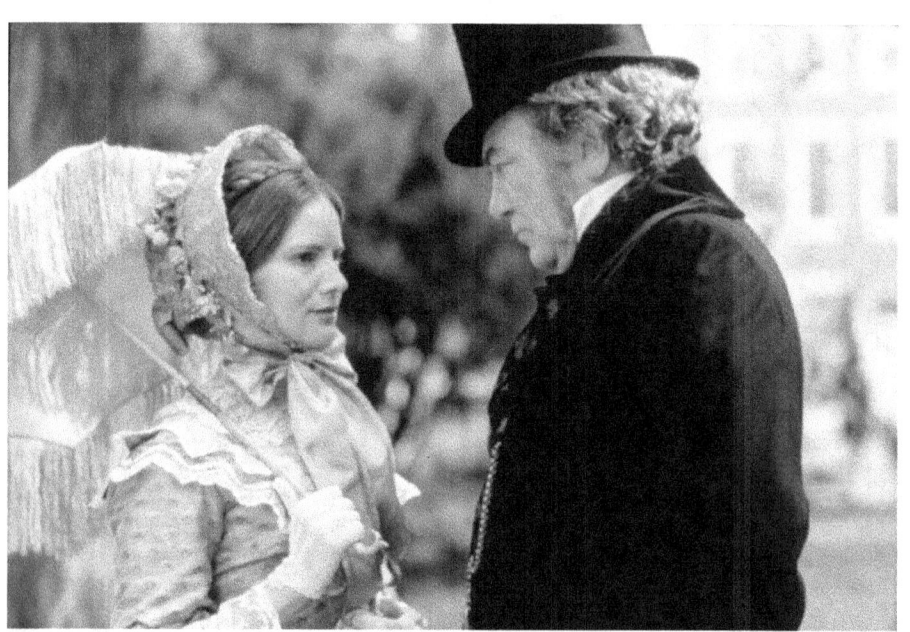

79. *Washington Square*

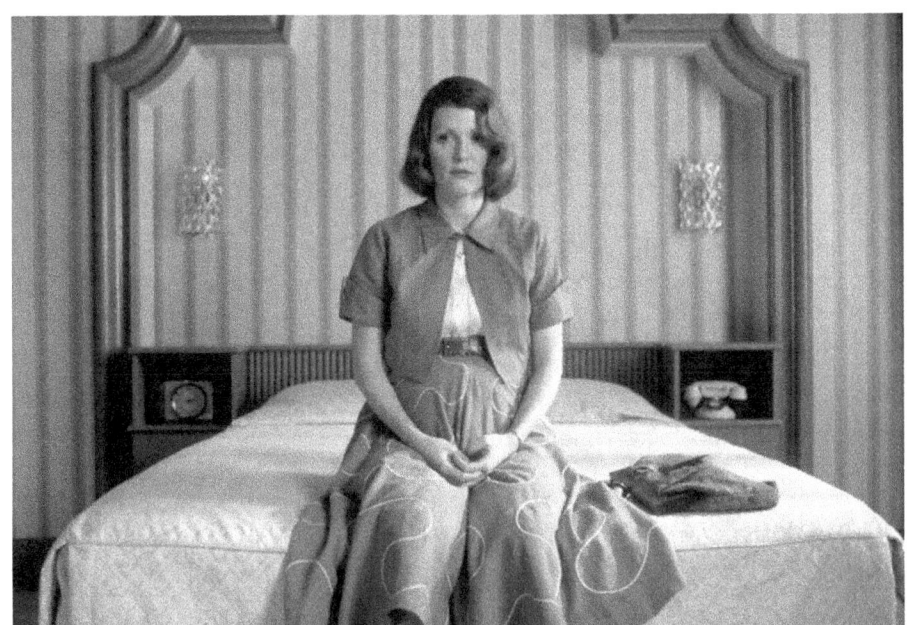

80.   *The Hours*

Not only are the characters shorn of the Kundera context, they are shorn of characteristics so that they can slip more neatly into regular film slots. Of course the book had to be compressed—the picture runs almost three hours anyway—but Kaufman and Carrière have done their compressing less with an eye to condensing the original than to transforming it into a well-behaved film with good, conventional narrative manners. Tomas, the central figure, is shorn of a previous marriage and of the son who grows to manhood and a life contrapuntal to his father's. The three other chief characters—Tereza, Tomas's wife; Sabina, his most recurrent mistress; and Franz, Sabina's principal other lover—are also shorn. Sabina comes off best for a negative reason: there's less of her background in the book to shear away.

Virtually none of the themes that Kundera weaves through his novel, that give the novel *its* character, is broached: compassion, cyclical repetition, Beethoven, the theological implications of shit, and others—many others. As for the theme in the title, it's mentioned once. (I don't know what the title can mean to those who haven't read the book.) So is kitsch, which is one of Kundera's major motifs. The Oedipus theme is mentioned in the film, only to be mangled. What we are left with is just a story—not particularly enthralling by itself—in which, in the Prague of 1968, lives and works an attractive, philandering young brain surgeon named Tomas. The movie opens in a hospital, where a nurse strips for him behind clouded glass while other doctors watch; even their patient sits up to look. This beginning made me expectant. Had they made the book into a comedy? This would emphasize only one of its tones; still, it might make a lively picture. Soon, however, the pace slowed to a plod, relieved—frequently—by passionate couplings.

Tomas's meeting with Tereza, his falling in love, their marriage, their flight to Geneva after the Soviet invasion, their return, the results of Tomas's one overt political action, the Sabina episodes with and without Tomas—all these are stitched into sequence, but the more we see, the thinner the film becomes. Even (or especially) when incidents are expanded from the novel, they are thinned. The marriage, which is one sentence in the book, is spun out into a heavily comic "big" scene. The nude photographing of Sabina by Tereza and vice versa is much expanded and is given a homoerotic suggestion. (The book treats the scene as a teasing frolic between two members of Tomas's harem.) These scenes are typical of Kaufman and Carrière's predictable choices, which eat up screen time that might have been used to Kundera's advantage.

There are good touches. Early in the film Tomas goes to a hospital in a spa to perform brain surgery. Outside, a band is playing a waltz; Tomas hums along as he saws his patient's skull. The Soviet invasion of Prague is excellently done—Sven Nykvist is the cinematographer—blending newsreels with shots that include Tomas and Tereza. (Still, riots may not be so difficult: the best part of Spielberg's attenuated *Empire of the Sun* [1983] is the rioting in Shanghai.) And the screenplay does honor one point in the book: Kundera's insistence that we know in advance about the fate of Tomas and Tereza. The film, like the book, ends with ironic happiness—their finish just ahead of them.

The film's best investment is in the cast, and Kaufman's best achievement is what he does with his actors. Juliette Binoche, the French actress who was in *Rouge Baiser* (*Red Kiss*; 1985, Véra Belmont), gives Tereza the right vulnerability and sweetness and desperate strength. The Sabina is Lena Olin, the

Swedish actress who was the young woman in Ingmar Bergman's *After the Rehearsal* (1984). How Olin has grown in spirit, guile, variety! She creates, to use an old-fashioned noun, a true bohemian. The Dutch actor Derek de Lint is appealing in what is left of Franz's character. (Because of the international cast, I'd better note that the film is in English—not Czech.)

Daniel Day-Lewis, who was the cockney gay in *My Beautiful Laundrette* (1985, Stephen Frears) and the Edwardian prig in *A Room With a View* (1985, James Ivory), comes on like a house afire as Tomas. (His hair darkened, he looks like a more supple Maximilian Schell.) But Day-Lewis's role is so sparely written, its dialogue so bald and trite, that the director seems to have relied on him to fill it out with acting. Day-Lewis tries his best. For instance, every time someone opens a door and finds him on the threshold, he goes through a little facial ballet to suggest complexities around the skimpy lines he is given to speak. It's clear that if the part had really been written, instead of being sketched at length, Day-Lewis could have carried it.

Where Angels Fear to Tread (1991, Charles Sturridge) & *A Room with a View* (1985, James Ivory)

To some nineteenth-century Anglophone writers, the romantic land of passion and trial was Italy. Nathaniel Hawthorne, Robert Browning, and Henry James are among those who thought that the social mores and emotional depths of their own cultures were put to the test in Italy. For us, Italy may have become the source of Armani and high cuisine, but, for them, it was a furnace where primal flame burned through figurative and sometimes literal corsets. No twentieth-century writer more fully subscribed to that view than E. M. Forster, a fact emphasized by the 1991 film made from *Where Angels Fear To Tread* (1905). This novel, Forster's first, is almost diagrammatic in its contrastings of England and Italy, of upper-middle-class English decorum and indecorous, unbuttoned Italiana; and the screenplay, by Tim Sullivan, Derek Granger, Charles Sturridge (who also directed), is faithful to this scheme.

But once again, in the adapting of novels to films, fidelity is not necessarily helpful. The basic trouble here, to put it elementarily, is that a film is not a novel. The quintessence of Forster's method is that his story progresses from propriety to melodrama—ending in a baby-stealing episode that is right out of mid-Victorian theatre—and that he tells it all in a calm, wry, shrewdly observant manner. The tone contrasts comically and sometimes poignantly with the tale. It's as if the contrast between Italy and England within the story were mirrored in the contrast between the story and the voice of the narrator.

Now this contrast, between story and narrative tone, is precisely what the film does not capture—probably no film could. Sturridge directed *A Handful of Dust* (1988) and came respectably near the Waugh texture, but this was in some degree easier because the tone of Evelyn Waugh's dialogue is fairly close to the tone of the book as a whole. If the actors merely speak Waugh's lines, they achieve at least something of the flavor of Waugh's novel. This is not true of Forster's book. Forster doesn't envy his characters, as Waugh does: he reveals them. Plucked from their context, they leave the novel far behind, especially that essential contrast between them and their prose environment.

151

Sturridge makes it worse. The story's initial situation is complicated, and the screenplay doesn't clarify it quickly. Lilia (played by Helen Mirren) is a widow, close to her ex-mother-in-law, Mrs. Herriton (Barbara Jefford), and the surviving Herriton children, Philip and Harriet (Rupert Graves and Judy Davis). Lilia, leaving her own small daughter with Mrs. Herriton, visits Italy with a friend, Caroline (Helena Bonham Carter). It takes too long to understand Lilia's relationship to the Herritons, and the film never clarifies who Caroline is. More: some of the dialogue is spoken incomprehensibly—Sturridge knows it so well that he hasn't always been able to tell when it is mumbled—so this picture has its share of murk. Michael Coulter's camera seems commissioned to underscore the murk with a dark palette, in England and abroad.

When Lilia sends word of her engagement to a young Italian in the Tuscan town where she is staying, Mrs. Herriton dispatches her son (and Lilia's brother-in-law) to rescue the woman from Italian wiles. Too late. Lilia is already married. Subsequently, after Lilia dies in childbirth, Mrs. Herriton sends both son and daughter to get the child and bring it back for a proper English upbringing—something Caroline also wants to do. The climax, an unhappy accident, is treated by Forster with tact and by Sturridge with clumsiness.

That excellent actress Judy Davis unwittingly highlights the difficulty of filming this book. Her role, the frustrated, frightened, imperious Harriet Herriton, is written full out by Forster. "Screamed", "violent", "snarling" (Forster, 5, 17, 100) are some of the terms he uses about Harriet, and Davis fulfils them. But that's exactly what's wrong. In the novel Harriet's screaming is contained within its Forsterian ambience; in the film, without the ambience, the screaming seems out of scale. It's not Davis's fault: she is doing what Forster says. But he didn't write Harriet's words to be spoken aloud, bereft of their prose context.

Graves, who was in *A Handful of Dust*, does much better as her brother, conveying the melting of adenoidal northern stuffiness by Italian warmth, but the role of Philip Herriton is much more congenially transportable from page to screen. Bonham Carter is chiefly successful at defining the class to which Caroline belongs and which means so much to her. Giovanni Guidelli, as Lilia's husband, hardly seems the best choice among young Italian actors to suggest a blend of charm, sex, innocence, and guile.

Further Forsterian contrastings of England and Italy on film: in *A Room with a View*, made six years before *Where Angels Fear to Tread*.

Up to 1985, the director James Ivory, the producer Ismail Merchant, and the screenwriter Ruth Prawer Jhabvala had been collaborating since 1963. They had made over ten films, all of which were unmistakably serious and most of which were nagged by dullness; the hallmark of their work consisted of good intentions. Over a ten-year period, along with other films, they turned to famous novels, beginning with Henry James. *The Europeans* (1979) was sluggish in every way. *The Bostonians* (1984) was much better in nearly every way and had Vanessa Redgrave's sterling portrayal of Olive Chancellor. In 1985 the trio presented another adaptation, *A Room with a View*. It's easily the best of their adaptations up to this point, but at the risk of sounding mean-spirited, I think it's the best because E. M. Forster's book is in all dimensions less demanding than James.

A Room with a View (1908) is, with reason, considered the weakest of the five major Forster works. It shows us English people in Florence and in

Surrey, and, among other matters, it shows them looking at Italy with English eyes, then at England with eyes quickened by Italy. It's the story of young Lucy Honeychurch—well-bred and chaperoned in Florence by her aunt, Miss Bartlett—who nonetheless is kissed by young George Emerson in a Tuscan meadow; who bears this secret, with her aunt, through her return home and her engagement to Cecil Vyse. Then she re-meets George, who by coincidence (a coincidence that is like a bone in the book's throat) rents a house nearby with his father; is kissed again by George; breaks off her engagement to Cecil; and after the requisite inner turmoil, marries George. The shape of the story is so patently formal that, if it weren't for the exquisitely perceptive writing, the book would be only a broad satire of romantic novels (like one such novel that is written by a novelist *in* the book). And to ensure that the reader realizes that the author knows what he is doing, Forster gives each chapter a slightly mocking title—even if he only follows the numeral 4 with the words "Fourth Chapter."

Clearly the filmmakers chose a book that in no way, except that it's a period piece, approaches James. It approaches someone else. One doesn't need to read Forster's 1924 essay on Jane Austen ("I am a Jane Austenite. . . . She is my favourite author!" [Sarker, 321]) to recognize that *A Room with a View* was written under her influence. The mode is social comedy. The style is built on engaging rhythms, ticked with tiny surprises. (Lucy's first kiss is interrupted by the sudden arrival of her aunt: "The silence of life had been broken by Miss Bartlett, who stood brown against the view" [Forster, 89].) The book reads as if Forster, allowing for a century's passage, had set himself an Austen exercise with, I'd say, *Emma* (1815) in mind. But Forster's book quite lacks the quality much noted in Austen, the darkness below the politesse, the ruthlessness. "She is never for one moment soft in any way" (Heath, 52), says the English literary critic and novelist Walter Allen. *A Room with a View* is often soft in many ways; and this, despite its charms, is what dates the book, while Austen remains timeless. It is this lesser dimension, smaller than Austen—and James—that makes Forster's book more accessible to these filmmakers.

Jhabvala retains as much as possible of the book, which means that she gives as much as possible to the camera without losing sight or sound of Forster. There was no need to transmute any of this novel into cinematic equivalents, as David Lean was forced to do with his 1984 film of Forster's incomparably more complex *A Passage to India* (1924). Jhabvala has quarried out her script neatly and, by including many of the chapter titles on prettily decorated title cards, has helped to "place" the film. Tony Pierce-Roberts, whose previous work includes the dissimilar and inferior *Moonlighting* (1982, Jerzy Skolimowski) and *A Private Function* (1984, Malcolm Mowbray), photographed as if to match Forster's mocking titles in motion, but with no hint of the precious. Those superlative costume designers Jenny Beavan and John Bright, who did *The Bostonians*, delight us again with the harmonies and easy richness of the clothes. A particular triumph is the dressing of Cecil, which touches caricature without losing touch with reality.

Ivory and Merchant cast the film as well as *The Bostonians* and with the same major flaw. Denholm Elliott is screen-filling as the elder Emerson, who has slightly absurd but quite moving concern for his son George's happiness. Maggie Smith, the Miss Bartlett, who is always dexterous, enters a new phase of her career here as she begins to take on roles without sexual lives of their own. The local vicar is Simon Callow, quite jolly as the roast beef of Old England, clerical style. And the two young men, Julian Sands as the heated George, Daniel Day-Lewis as the Edwardian aesthete Cecil, could not be improved on. (Prior to seeing *A Room with a View* for the first time, I had just seen Day-Lewis, son of the poet Cecil Day-Lewis, as a mod homosexual London crook, in a picture called *My Beautiful Laundrette* [1985, Stephen Frears].) But, as in *The Bostonians*, the leading female role is poorly cast.

Helena Bonham Carter is better as Lucy than she was in *Lady Jane* (1986, Trevor Nunn) chiefly because the role is much better for her—less demanding in some aspects, more varied in others. As in the previous film, Bonham Carter has the initial advantage of the right quality, the (unavoidable term) class that the role needs. Most of the time she is passable, the exceptions being the big dramatic moments where, hand-wagging and all, she looks amateurish. But to be passable is not enough in a role that is pivotal in an elaborate *gavotte*. Bonham Carter is a remote presence, her remoteness underscored by her face. The trouble is not that she's not conventionally pretty, but that her round, undefined face with its inordinately heavy eyebrows is simply not a good actor's mask, as it used to be called. Her face is a barrier; we have to convince ourselves that she means what she says despite the way she looks—and sounds. Bonham Carter is like an undergraduate in a university production who seems rather good considering that her performance is only an intelligent diversion while she prepares herself for a career in another field.

Whatever Bonham Carter does achieve must be credited in some measure to Ivory, just as he must have contributed to the very good work of the others. Ivory makes the whole film move fluently enough; the lack of excitement must, in this instance, be charged as much to Forster as to him. Like Forster, he has opted for style rather than passion. To put it otherwise: we know it was an option with Forster; and Forster's choice fit Ivory's abilities. All the more mystery, then, why he chose to use a lush Puccini aria under the beginning and end of the film—"*O mio babbino caro*" (Oh My Beloved Father), which in fact comes from an opera (*Gianni Schicchi*, 1918) that was written ten years after Forster's novel was published. It's Italian, yes, but so are three or four thousand other airs that might have better fit the film's temper.

Possibly Ivory was trying to underline a conflict recurrent in the book, between decorum and passion, as evidenced in the demure Lucy's fierce playing of Beethoven or the murder that she finds herself witnessing in the Piazza Signoria. In that case, Jhabvala and Ivory chose an ironic ending, not Forster's, that puts Lucy's passion in some doubt. She and George are back in the Florentine pension where they met, sitting in the window overlooking the Arno River—the room with a view that marriage now permits them to share. As he kisses her cheek and neck, she reads a letter from her brother over his shoulder. As he kisses her bosom, she continues to read. Is this a comment on their marital life ahead? If so, why? There's no ground for it in anything earlier.

Pass it off to buttoned-up English decorum in indecorous, unbuttoned Italy—in *A Room with a View* as well as *Where Angels Fear to Tread*.

The Age of Innocence (1993, Martin Scorsese)

The basic trouble with Martin Scorsese's 1993 film of *The Age of Innocence* (1920) is Edith Wharton's novel. Looking back fifty years in 1920, Wharton conceived a tale of love versus honor set in the New York high society of that past era, and she embodied it in a full-dress novel. But her material would have served only as a short story, at most a novella, for Tolstoy or Chekhov. What helps to sustain Wharton's more extended treatment is the attractive prose in which she wraps her narrative. Her writing has so much wit and perception, such a taking blend of satire-cum-nostalgia, that the book holds us though the story is slender. (I still feel that the ending short-changes us. I want to know what Ellen Olenska said to Newland Archer's son in her Paris apartment, what the youth thought when she ordered the shutters closed against his father, how he later reported the meeting to his father.)

In the film, without its garment of text, the denuded story is thin. It's worse than that—because the film tries to be the novel. Attempting to reproduce the text's quality, very nearly page for page, Scorsese even uses considerable prose excerpts on the soundtrack (read flatly by Joanne Woodward). He and his co-adapter, Jay Cocks, have been zealously faithful to the original, but, ironically, all that this fidelity does is make the picture seem slow. Film can't cloak, can't justify, as Wharton's prose does, the linearity of the story.

It's even worse—because (to close the novel's trap) Scorsese and Cocks had no choice: the picture has to run as long as it does. The adapters understood that there was absolutely no point in the enterprise if the decorum of drawing room and dining room, the rustle of silk and the spruceness of *boutonnières*, were slighted. Etiquette, at its most stately, is the theatre of this drama. Among some critics at the time, there was advance worry about this; could Scorsese, the director from Little Italy, cope with the Four Hundred? That worry always seemed unnecessary to me. A director of his gifts, flanked with brigades of various period experts, aided mightily by the camera of Michael Ballhaus, would delight in the nooks and crannies of the period—and he does. But it's a bitter triumph. Scorsese had to include all the glitter and elegance; yet it doesn't sustain the story as Wharton's writing does.

Not for lack of cinematic imagination. Martin Scorsese is still one of the two or three best American directors at work, and his talent is quickly evident here in the way the camera searches out every wisp of possible action in a scene, the way that characters move up to and past the camera to suggest that the theatre in which we are sitting is part of the room on screen, the way the camera often nestles in to people as if to hear secrets. In a moment that might have been static for another director, when Newland Archer gets an important telegram from his fiancée, May Welland, Scorsese has May speak it in front of an immense bank of flowers as the camera comes close, charging the moment with perfume and intimacy. When twenty-six years elapse, after Ellen takes herself out of Newland Archer's life and returns to Europe, a time-lapse that Wharton can handle with a simple chapter break, Scorsese shuns the banality of fade-out on the young Archer and fade-in on the middle-aged man. He concentrates instead on Archer's library, "in which most of the real things of his life had happened" (Wharton, 271). He circles the room slowly, showing us moments in the Archer family chronicle during those years.

And music! The most Scorsesean touch in Wharton's book is that it begins at the opera. (Remember the Intermezzo from Pietro Mascagni's *Cavalleria Rusticana* [1890] under the opening of *Raging Bull* [1980].) Red meat to Scorsese, as it was to Visconti in *Senso* (1954). Onward from this opening, Scorsese uses lively music to spank sequences into life—often, at balls and parties, with music that comes from within the scene or else with Elmer Bernstein's felicitous score.

But—a heavy but—Scorsese has made serious mistakes with his principal actors. The biggest disappointment is in the crucial part, Daniel Day-Lewis as Newland Archer. Archer is the protagonist, happily affianced to May Welland, who then falls in love with the newly arrived Ellen Olenska. The central drama is his. (Ellen's *agon* is no less, but she isn't placed at the center.) On the basis of Day-Lewis's past work, forceful and graphic in *A Room With a View* (1985, James Ivory), *My Beautiful Laundrette* (1985, Stephen Frears), and *My Left Foot* (1989, Jim Sheridan), he seemed very likely to inhabit the role, to vitalize it. He doesn't. He merely moves through it. There's never a spark to sting us: he leaves us cold, observant. Perhaps Scorsese was counting on his personality to grip us, a resident power such as Fredric March or James Mason had. Day-Lewis doesn't have it. He needed to act (which Mason or March would have done, too!), but he doesn't. He skates through. It's surprising that Scorsese didn't remedy this.

Michelle Pfeiffer is a somewhat more complicated case. As Ellen Olenska, the American who returns to New York after a broken European marriage, Pfeiffer tries hard but fails. It's sad. She was living as intelligent a life as possible for an American film star in the 1990s: seeking variety, taking chances, addressing every role with all the resources she could command. She just didn't command enough—in fire or depth or resonance. The result in film after film was a somewhat washed-out version of the woman she was playing, like a painting that had faded. Her Ellen here is perceptible but pallid. What helps Pfeiffer most is the fact that, though she is exceptionally pretty, she patently doesn't rely on her prettiness: she wants to act. But, with her Ellen, though we know what she means from moment to moment, we simply don't feel it.

Winona Ryder is disastrously miscast as May Welland, Archer's utterly conventional fiancée and eventual wife, who turns out to have been more perceptive than her husband knew. Ryder is wrong, first, physically. Wharton describes May as being "tall, round-bosomed, and willowy" (Wharton, 274) with a "goddess-like build" (Wharton, 255), and comments frequently on her features. Clearly Wharton means May's physical being to help explain why Archer wanted her. Here Archer has chosen a moderately pleasant, quite unremarkable girl. As for Ryder's acting, the one smile for me in this film—which is and must be socially hyperconscious—occurred when Ryder remarks to Archer that a man she has just met seems common. To put it gently, her social superiority is unconvincing.

Robert Sean Leonard, who trivialized Claudio in the contemporaneous *Much Ado About Nothing* (1993, Kenneth Branagh), has less chance here to do damage in the small role of Archer's son. But most of the supporting actors in the lustrous New York social parade are neatly cast, and two of them do the best acting in the film. Alec McCowen, as Sillerton Jackson, the aging socialite, has the gravity of a man to whom protocol is his reason for being. Miriam Margolyes, as the obese and ultra-rich Mrs. Mingott, curls the surrounding air with dry disdain and hierarchical rigor.

The Age of Innocence was dramatized on Broadway in 1928 (Margaret Ayer Barnes), and was filmed in Hollywood in 1924 (Wesley Ruggles) as well as 1934 (Philip Moeller). I don't know any of those versions, and I wonder how (which means I doubt that) they avoided the snare that Wharton unwittingly set for her adapters—the snare that, for all his gifts, caught Scorsese.

The Portrait of a Lady (1996, Jane Campion)

Once more unto the breach, dear friends—the breach between a distinguished piece of fiction and a film made from it. This time it is Henry James's 1881 novel *The Portrait of a Lady*. Jane Campion's 1996 film summons, once more, a wild fancy: this would be an even better picture than we can imagine if the novel didn't exist.

Concede at once that condensation—of James's fifty-five chapters, of his deep explorations of character—was inevitable if we were going to survive the film, which runs 144 minutes as it is. Viewing, contrary to popular assumption, is harder than reading: we have all read for more than 144 minutes many times, but film is more draining per second than reading, more unrelenting in its command of our collaboration. Besides, there is the subconscious imperative of theatrical shape that nags at the back of our brains while viewing, which doesn't occur while reading. Whether the actors are live or photographed, an acted story has temporal obligations.

The screenplay by Laura Jones, who has written for and with Campion in the past, nonetheless tries to frame the events—more important, the moral adventure—in some kind of Jamesian proportion. In 1872, Isabel Archer, a young American woman, is in England at the estate of relatives when she gets a marriage proposal from the highly eligible Lord Warburton. She declines: certainly because she doesn't love him, but certainly, too, because she is hungry for experience, of a kind she can't specify. Another man proposes, too, while—so to speak—she is observed by her cousin, Ralph Touchett, a gentle soul ill with consumption. After she declines the second man, Ralph persuades his rich, dying father to leave Isabel a large legacy to empower her quest for who knows what. "The conception of a certain young woman affronting her destiny" (James, 8) was how James conceived the novel; and Isabel heads for the continent to do her affronting.

In Florence, she meets a fortyish American who lives there, Gilbert Osmond, an aesthete with "an odd mixture of the detached and the involved" (James, 223). He, too, proposes. Isabel takes three years to make up her mind, traveling the while; then, following her destiny, she marries Osmond. Her destiny darkens. The couple has a baby that dies, and they develop an enmity that lives. Previous suitors reappear. For these and other reasons, Osmond becomes even angrier at Isabel. She, for her part, learns disturbing facts about Osmond's past. When Ralph Touchett, back in England, begins to die, Osmond forbids Isabel to go to him. She disobeys. With her lovingly at his side, Ralph dies. The novel ends with her return to Italy, though not necessarily to her marriage. The film leaves us wondering whether she will indeed return to Italy. In either case, there is more destiny to affront.

It is a critical commonplace that Isabel in some ways resembles James himself. She comes from Albany, New York, where James spent some of his childhood. Like James, she is of an era in which the gaining of experience for young Americans of her class meant going to Europe, being seasoned there. Whether or not James would have adapted, to himself and Isabel, Flaubert's "Madame Bovary, c'est moi" (Heath, 34, 91, 154), Campion has colored her film as if he had that empathy. To her, James was not only concerned with "a certain young woman", he was a pioneer in feminist issues as such.

Some of Campion's embroidery is strange, some heavy. The sequence before and under the credits shows us contemporary young women of different races, all in airy gowns in a woodland glade, all circling and beseeching the camera. Perhaps this is to suggest that, even today, the persistent image of young women is that of available nymphs. Interludes in the film take James's implication into the explicit. We see Isabel's frustrated sexual hunger in a dream scene in which she rolls on a bed with her suitors. Her travels in Mediterranean countries are synopsized in a heated fantasy that presents her naked. (Did James ever see a naked woman?)

These additions, and others, seem more than an attempt to assure us that James is up to date; they also seem an attack on Jane Austen's acceptances. Contemporaneous Austen films (*Sense and Sensibility* [1995, Ang Lee]; *Emma* [1996, Douglas McGrath]; *Persuasion* [1995, Roger Michell]) italicized that her young women have no options in life but to hunt for rich husbands. Isabel is aware of other options (her friend Henrietta Stackpole is a journalist), but, even within the marriage game, she has more nuance, more suggestion of secret shadow; she chafes more at social boundaries. Campion apparently wanted to dramatize this difference from the Austen pattern.

Cinematically, too, Campion is sometimes intrusive. A number of sequences begin with a tilted establishing shot, for no reason except that she wants to remind us that she's at the helm. The cuts between scenes, intended to be elliptical, are sometimes merely jerky. And Campion leans a lot on great close-ups, which get a bit repetitious even when she keeps the heads off-center. But, with the exquisite camera work of Stuart Dryburgh, she gives us an inviting view of every scene, sometimes a touch tricky (past statuary), sometimes a touch too picturesque (with huge trees), but on the whole with an eye that searches and perceives.

And crowning Campion's work are her accomplishments with her cast— except Shelley Winters as Mrs. Touchett and Shelley Duvall as Countess Gemini. The two Shelleys could have been left wherever they were. Nicole Kidman, for her part, may not be the Isabel Archer of our imagination, but neither is she the Nicole Kidman of our past acquaintance. In the bizarre *To Die For* (1995, Gus Van Sant), she was surprisingly colorful, and here Campion has induced her to mine herself further. Kidman comes up with tones of hurt and resolve and poise and warmth that she has never shown before.

John Malkovich, not always easy to admire, is perfectly cast here, which is itself a rarity. His moodiness and almost disinterested viciousness fit Gilbert Osmond. He gives a performance that, without grotesquerie, makes us scent from the start that there is unpleasantly more to him than Isabel suspects. The most adroit casting is of Barbara Hershey as Madame Merle. Hershey is light-years away from her beginnings in film as a Barbie doll with a voice (*The Baby Maker*

[1970, James Bridges]; *Boxcar Bertha* [1972, Martin Scorsese]).Through her several decades of film, she has grown and grown, with insufficient praise for her continuing development. Playing the mature American-born woman who has long lived in Europe and has learned from it, Hershey immediately and perfectly suggests complexity.

Martin Donovan, known for his quite different work with Hal Hartley, is touching yet manly as the afflicted Ralph. John Gielgud is his father, a small part but, naturally, unforgettable. (Odd thought: How does a ninety-two-year-old actor feel about playing a deathbed scene?) And a note of gratitude, as well, to the film's Polish composer, Wojciech Kilar. Kilar's music, relying on meditative strings, helps to carry the film along. Campion's choice of Kilar is one more sign that the woman who made *An Angel at My Table* (1990) had emerged from the preciousness of *The Piano* (1993) to resume an interesting career.

The Red and the Black (1954, Claude Autant-Lara)

In 1954, admirable taste and eloquent acting made a charming picture of the novel *The Red and the Black* (1830). If the adjective seems odd, it is nonetheless just. Jean Aurenche and Pierre Bost, once two of France's most deft screenwriters, and Claude Autant-Lara, a director of ingenuity and wit, conspired in the middle of the twentieth century to make a lovely, lively, and yearning romance of Stendhal's savage classic in two volumes. The book's full title, *The Red and the Black: A Chronicle of the 19th Century*, indicates its twofold literary purpose as both a psychological portrait of the romantic protagonist, Julien Sorel, and a sociological satire of the French social order under the Bourbon Restoration (1814–30) following the disruptions of the French Revolution and the reign of Napoleon Bonaparte.

The shift of the novel to the screen was the easier because Stendhal's irony is cloaked in velvet; the filmmakers have removed the steel and shown just the sensuous fabric. This happens even though, as the producers could point out, many key statements and key situations are brought over from the novel. Much, of course, has been left behind—particularly the ecclesiastical maneuverings of which Sorel was both the beneficiary and the victim. The picture thus evades the anti-clericalism that was one prong of Stendhal's attack. This in itself greatly lightens the tone, and also lends an unmeant air of mystery to Sorel's rapid displacements of fortune. But Sorel's hypocrisy, his peasant strategy, and his cold estimate of what he owes himself as a hero born too late for Bonaparte's legions—these are all explicitly stated.

The statements don't "take," however, because the environment of the film won't support them. Stendhal says of the Faubourg Saint-Germain townhouse owned by the Marquis de la Mole, for instance, that it was "as depressing as it was magnificent . . . the native heath of boredom and dreary argument" (Stendhal, 22). What the film shows is a décor of quiet, happy, excellently cultivated luxury. The marquis's home enchanted Sorel, and it could be explained that the picture reflects that enchantment. But Julien was not enchanted by the seminary at Besançon, yet its chambers might have been designed by Matisse. The eye, it seems, will not accept rancor in such settings.

And so with the acting. Everyone commented at the time on how well Gérard Philipe gratifies one's mental image of Julien Sorel. So he does, but the resemblance is one of person, not of manner or motive. Philipe is an actor of uncommon gifts, but they are gifts for passion, grace, and wit. He can look whimsical, he relishes persiflage, he can behave like a heedless romantic, but he cannot—or at least he does not—look calculating or gauche. Even when he says "now I calculate" in the film, the viewer knows that the dear boy is merely in a transport of amorous adventure.

Antonella Lauldi as Mathilde is in much the same situation. Here is no forced bloom of aristocracy, heated by the constrictions of her life into an illness of chivalric romance. She looks and acts like a girl who seizes the chance of love with the strength of her roistering ancestors; indeed, there is something familiarly American about her behavior. Moreover, she is spared that terrible consummation of neuroticism at the end of the book when Mathilde carries the severed head of her lover to its mountain grave. Danielle Darrieux herself may come some closer to Stendhal's Madame de Reval, though again the grasp on love, however unrealistic, seems healthier than the book intended.

Finally, the film of *The Red and the Black*—in scene and character—is overwhelmingly good-looking; it exhales a joy in life that quite sweeps aside the implications of action and characterization. Thus it is a great pleasure to watch. This sort of travesty usually makes me angry; in this instance it didn't because, I guess, the filmmakers did their work with such zest. I'm not really satisfied, but it would seem prudish to be petulant in the face of so much skill and style.

As for substance: in its describing of the feelings and thoughts of its characters (through first-person, interior monologue, for example, as opposed to straight dialogue framed by objective narration), *The Red and the Black* is considered a work ahead of its time, a psychological novel more realistic than romantic and thus attuned more to readers of the twentieth than the nineteenth century. In the twenty-first century, we are still waiting for a feature-film adaptation to supersede Autant-Lara's and catch up with—or go back to—Stendhal.

Works Cited

Adams, Robert M. "The Cold Comedian: *The Book of Laughter and Forgetting*, by Milan Kundera." *New York Review of Books*. Feb. 5, 1981: 22-23.

Conrad, Joseph. *Lord Jim*. Ed. Cedric Watts. Peterborough, Can.: Broadview Press, 2001.

Eisenstein, Sergei. "Dickens, Griffith, and the Film Today" (1944). *Film Form: Essays in Film Theory*. Trans. & ed. Jay Leyda. 1949. New York: Harcourt, 1977. 195-255.

Forster, E. M. *A Room with a View*. New York: Penguin, 1990.

----------. *Where Angels Fear to Tread*. New York: Vintage, 1992.

Heath, Stephen. *Flaubert: Madame Bovary*. Cambridge, U.K.: Cambridge University Press, 1992.

Heath, William. *Discussions of Jane Austen*. Boston: D. C. Heath, 1961.

James, Henry. *The Portrait of a Lady*. Ed. Lionel Kelly. Hertfordshire, U.K.: Wordsworth Editions, 1996.

Jones, Daniel, ed. "Milan Kundera." *Contemporary Authors*. Vol. 74. Detroit: Gale, 1999. 199-208.

Sarker, Sunil Kumar. *A Companion to E. M. Forster*. Vol. 1. New Delhi: Atlantic, 2007.

Stendhal (a.k.a. Marie-Henri Beyle). *The Red and the Black*. Trans. C. K. Scott Moncrieff. New York: Modern Library, 1949.

Wharton, Edith. *The Age of Innocence*. Ed. Paul Lauter. New York: Houghton Mifflin, 2000.

"Literature Become Cinema: Notes on Three Emblematic Adaptations: *The Remains of the Day, The Dead,* and *Dangerous Liaisons*"

The films discussed in the following essay are James Ivory's *The Remains of the Day* (1993), from the 1989 novel by Kazuo Ishiguro; John Huston's *The Dead* (1987), from the 1914 short story by James Joyce; and Stephen Frears's *Dangerous Liaisons* (1988), from the 1782 novel by Choderlos de Laclos.

The Remains of the Day (1993, James Ivory)

If I may quote from my own preface to this volume, "In movies, we get to know a character by seeing how he reacts to people and events, and unless the director [and adapter of a first-person novel] breaks the first-person camera convention, we can never see the hero—we can only see what he sees. So the solution for the adapter of a first-person novel is to include just enough first-person narration—usually in the form of voiceover—to remind us from whose point of view the story was originally told."

This is what James Ivory and Ruth Prawer Jhabvala attempt to do in their 1993 film of the novel *The Remains of the Day*, whose subject is the life of an emotionally and sexually repressed butler as it dovetails with that of his employer, a well-meaning but wrongheaded aristo-twit who, in the mid-1930s, secretly works to appease Hitler, avoid war, and preserve England's rigid social hierarchy. In other words, this is a work dealing chiefly with issues of politics, class, and sexuality. The novel (1989) was written by Ishiguro, who was born Japanese but bred English; it was supposed to have been adapted to the screen by Harold Pinter, but Ivory discarded Pinter's script in favor of Jhabvala's.

Pinter has proved himself adept at adapting novels with first-person narrators (e.g., *The Go-Between* [1970, Joseph Losey], *The Proust Screenplay* [1977], and *The Heat of the Day* [1989, Christopher Morahan]), something that is made difficult by the natural omniscience of the camera eye. The solution is obviously not to use a first-person camera throughout, to show only what the narrator can see and never the narrator himself, nor to employ large chunks of first-person voiceover narration; what the camera eye must do as much as possible is *see as the narrator in the book does*, see selectively that is, as if it were using the narrator's eyes. This is a neat trick, a kind of imaginative leap, and it can be made only by a screenwriter who is genuinely creative in her own right yet spiritually faithful to her source. Ruth Prawer Jhabvala, alas, is not such a scenarist, though she isn't without a certain skill.

The story of her screenplay begins in 1958, shortly after Lord Darlington's death and the sale of his palatial manor, Darlington Hall, to a solitary, rich American. Stevens, the butler, is staying on to work for the new owner, Mr. Lewis, but with a staff reduced from twenty-eight at the climax of the British empire to four during its present decline. Stevens is thinking of adding to that staff one Miss Kenton, the former (superbly efficient) housekeeper of Darlington Hall, who has recently sent him a letter (parts of which she reads in voiceover, and to which Stevens responds with his own letter read in voiceover) implying that she would like to return to her old position. So, having been given a week's vacation by his new employer, together with the use of the American's car (a Daimler, not the novel's Ford), he sets out from Oxfordshire on a journey to the West Country to meet Miss Kenton. She's been Mrs. Benn for the past twenty years, during which time Stevens has not seen her, and by now has a grown daughter, but her marriage is in trouble. Miss Kenton seems to be searching for something, then, to be reaching out, and so does Stevens. As he rides through the countryside to his appointment with her, he flashes back to their relationship—or non-relationship—in the past, as well as to his role as master servant in a house once brimful of statesmen and ambassadors.

It was Stevens' role as servant, as server of Lord Darlington rather than fulfiller of himself, that got in the way of any personal relationship he might have had with Miss Kenton. A love seemed to evolve between these two household workers who never so much as call each other by their first names, but it remained unacknowledged and unexpressed—at least on Stevens' part. There is no real acknowledgement of its existence by Miss Kenton either, but there is some expression of feeling, which unexpectedly gets underscored in the film. Indeed, even Stevens' feeling gets expressed in the movie version, which recasts Ishiguro's exquisitely balanced tale more as doomed romance than as political allegory.

This is a direction Pinter, with his latter-day political engagement, may have reversed, and a direction the normally reticent Ivory has apparently chosen to take in the condescending belief that the lower orders of society are more given to venting their emotions. For example, during one of their nightly meetings to discuss the management of the house, Miss Kenton responds to Stevens' question "Are you with me?" with the excuse that she is very tired. She is tired, of course—tired of meeting with him under these circumstances, solely to discuss work—but this meaning of "tired" remains subtextual in the novel. In the film, Miss Kenton directly expresses the sentiment that she wants to *be* with Stevens, not merely to talk with him about the discharge of their servants' duties.

The next day, her day off, she has a date in a pub with Tom Benn, a former butler who wants to marry her and open his own boarding house in Clevedon-by-the-sea. There is no such scene in the book; it fractures the first-person perspective of Stevens; and it's almost immediately followed by another insertion, Miss Kenton's desperate revelation to Stevens of her impending engagement, to which he reacts by hastily leaving the room. Later, after she becomes formally engaged, he impatiently offers her his "warmest congratulations," for "there are matters of global significance taking place upstairs and [he] must return to [his] post" (Ishiguro, 219). Then, in the process of fetching drinks for Lord Darlington's guests, Stevens drops a fine bottle of port—one more "emotional" event that does not occur in Ishiguro's novel—peremptorily replaces it with another, and proceeds to deliver it.

But he must pass Miss Kenton's room in order to do so, and here again the film tellingly diverges from its source. This is what the author understatedly writes, in the first-person voice of Stevens:

> As I approached Miss Kenton's door, I saw from the light seeping around its edges that she was still within. And . . . that moment as I paused in the dimness of the corridor, the tray in my hands, an ever-growing conviction [mounted] within me that just a few yards away, on the other side of that door, Miss Kenton was at that moment crying. As I recall, there was no real evidence to account for this conviction—I had

certainly not heard any sounds of crying—and yet I remember being quite certain that were I to knock and enter, I would discover her in tears. (Ishiguro, 226-227)

In Ivory's film, as you might guess, the door does get opened and Stevens discovers Miss Kenton in tears, only to advise her that some household article wants dusting! Further, after the butler departs, the camera remains on Miss Kenton, regarding her heartbroken face in a way that Stevens could never bring himself to do.

The camera does this once more near the end of *The Remains of the Day*. Stevens and Miss Kenton have had their meeting and character-history has proved to be human destiny: the aging butler will return to his butlering without ever having brought up the subject of their dormant love, and the now matronly housekeeper will go back to her marriage and the promise of a grandchild from her expectant daughter. As he puts Miss Kenton on a bus in the novel, Stevens notices that she is crying and comforts her with some pleasantries—nothing more. As he puts her on that same bus in the film, Miss Kenton is not yet in tears. For heightened effect, we see her crying through the window of the departing bus as Stevens does; then, after he leaves the frame, we get another shot of her face receding in tears. From whose point of view? The omniscient camera-as-narrator, or Ivory-cum-Jhabvala as italicizers of emotion.

This team even manages to inject heat into the novel's politics, or to put its heart where Ishiguro's head has prevailed. Before departing for the West Country, for example, Stevens is sent by Ivory and Jhabvala on business to the local general store, where he denies ever having known Lord Darlington, whom the clerk has decried as a Nazi sympathizer. No such scene occurs in the novel, and its effect is to change Stevens from an obtusely loyal, blindly trustful servant to a shifty timeserver masquerading as a man of conscience. En route to Clevedon, Stevens has a similar encounter—embellished by the filmmakers—with a doctor at an inn, where customers mistake the butler for a gentleman on account of his proper diction and dignified bearing. Dignity is the mark of a true gentleman, several villagers agree in the book, but one farmer argues that "Dignity's something every man and woman in this country can *strive for* and get. . . . Dignity's not just something for gentlemen" (Ishiguro, 186; emphasis mine). On screen, this gets reduced to "every Englishman has the *right* to be called a gentleman."

The high-born doctor arrives, senses Stevens' working-class origins beneath his superficial dignity and acquired speech, and gets him to admit, in the film, that he is "in service" at a great house in Oxfordshire. Inevitably, their cinematic conversation comes around to Lord Darlington of Oxfordshire, whom the doctor pillories for his virtual collaboration with the Nazis, and with whom Stevens once again disavows any acquaintance. Then he relents and tells the truth: he was proud to have served Lord Darlington but his job was just that, *to serve*, not to agree or disagree with his employer's political views. He goes on to say that, in attempting to accommodate Hitler, Darlington made a mistake for which he later sincerely repented; whereas he, Stevens, once made a mistake too—but one that he can correct rather than lament. The teasing implication, of course, is that his mistake was a matter of the heart rather than politics: to have repressed his love for Miss Kenton, which he will shortly express to her in Clevedon.

Stevens' words here are a complete reversal of what he says in the novel, *two days after* Miss Kenton's departure by bus, to a man sitting next to him on a pier in Weymouth:

> Lord Darlington wasn't a bad man. He wasn't a bad man at all. And at least he had the privilege of being able to say at the end of his life that he made his own mistakes. His lordship was a courageous man. He chose a certain path in life, it proved to be a misguided one, but there, he chose it, he can say that at least. As for myself, I cannot even claim that. You see, I *trusted*. I trusted in his lordship's wisdom. All those years I served him, I trusted I was doing something worthwhile. I can't even say I made my own mistakes. Really—one has to ask oneself—what dignity is there in that? (Ishiguro, 243)

Stevens appears less politically correct in this speech, since he calls Darlington courageous if misguided; but he also appears more emotionally honest because he speaks of his own mistakes as irremediable in addition to undignifying, as inherent in his character as the narrative has established it. And they are *mistakes*, not one mistake, the use of the plural serving to conflate Stevens' relationship to Lord Darlington with his relationship to Miss Kenton. For the two relationships, and the butler's mistakes in them, are indeed related, as is Stevens' first-person perspective to the novel's thematic intent.

Ironically, Stevens gets to speak for himself in Ishiguro's tale, whereas in the past he had always allowed Lord Darlington to speak for him or at least to speak in his place. But in speaking for himself, he only reveals the tragicomic extent of his political capitulation and emotional barrenness, his substitution of a life of peripheral protocol for one of direct involvement. Being a butler, for Stevens, has been an act of selfless fealty toward a lord, not a mere profession or business—moreover, toward a lord engaged in great undertakings designed to secure England's future. He has allowed nothing to come between him and his duty to Darlington, not even the love of Miss Kenton (for which he unconsciously substitutes the reading of sentimental romances), so satisfactory has his relationship with his master been. And Lord Darlington, for his part, has allowed nothing to come between him and his duty to his country, not even the love of a wife, so satisfactory has his life of (behind-the-scenes) public service been. As a member of the household staff at Darlington Hall, Miss Kenton serves Stevens even as he serves his lord and his lord serves the state. The problem with this hierarchy of faithful service, however, is that it permits no room for second-guessing, and second-guessing is what the actions of both master and butler so desperately require. When Miss Kenton tries to question the actions of her "betters"—particularly in the dismissal of the Jewish maids—she is rebuffed.

Ishiguro means, I think, to make Stevens' blindness—both to Darlington's political naïveté and Miss Kenton's emotional warmth—stand as a metaphor for England's blindness to its own national character and destiny. Just as Stevens trusted in Lord Darlington, Darlington trusted in his, and his country's, ability to broker a lasting peace with the Germans where no one else had been able to do so. That is, he and his associates—who recall the members of the notorious if somewhat mythologized "Cliveden Set" (a 1930s aristocratic, Germanophile social network was not only in favor of the appeasement of Adolf Hitler but also in favor of friendly relations with Nazi Germany)—placed their trust in the cachet of British empire and aristocracy, as did Prime Minister Neville Chamberlain after them. They were mistaken to do so because, as Hitler clearly saw, the empire and its royalty were headed for extinction. Stevens thought he was serving the empire by denying himself, but all that he really did was *deny himself*, deny the love that could have given his life some dimension. He unquestioningly accepted the class system and his insulated place in it, and his reward, like that of many of his countrymen high and low, was a life of lovelessness if not brutality, of coldness if not desolation, of constriction if not misery.

Stevens' singular detachment or self-enclosure is well conveyed by the novel's first-person perspective, which naturally permits no other points of view to interject themselves, least of all the omniscience of the author; and which furthermore allows Stevens to create his character, as well as its social significance, by indirection, without resort to psychologizing on the one hand or historicizing on the other. One of the problems with Ivory's film, as I've indicated, is that the omniscient camera *does* intervene and perhaps had no choice but to intervene. In doing so, however, it sacrifices Stevens' integral tunnel vision without providing any compensatory light.

If it is ironic that Stevens finally gets to speak for himself in the novel of *The Remains of the Day*, it is doubly ironic that a butler is made to serve as England's national symbol. Or perhaps it is appropriate in the postwar period, if only the butler were not so proudly subservient as this one. For the postwar period in Britain was a time, if not for the dismantling of the class system, then for a definite questioning of its premises—a questioning brought on by the very war the Tory Darlington had tried to avoid, which gave new experiences, freedoms, and responsibilities to proletarian soldiers that they weren't so willing to relinquish upon their return from the fighting abroad. Instead of serving in the war, Stevens served his lord at home, where, he tells Mr. Lewis, over the years the world—in the form of Darlington's political confreres and social peers—had always come to his door. Lewis responds that his butler should now get out and see the world for himself; and Stevens does so, even if that world is limited to the beautiful English countryside through which he drives on his way to the West Country.

The year of his trip to Clevedon-by-the-sea is 1956 in the book, July 1956 to be exact, which the filmmakers have changed to 1958 in keeping with their recasting of the narrative more as doomed romance than as political allegory. The "Suez Crisis" occurred in 1956 as a result of Egypt's nationalization of the Canal in July and expulsion of British oil executives together with embassy officials from the country in August. Great Britain sent an invasion force to retake the Suez Canal in October, but this final attempt to reassert its traditional imperial influence ended with a whimper when English troops were forced to leave Egypt under the threat of United Nations sanctions. For Stevens the end of empire does not seem imminent, which is one reason he doesn't mention the unfolding crisis over the Canal in his story. But the title of Ishiguro's novel refers both to the remains of Stevens' own day—to the quiet evenings following his daily yeoman's service as well as to the lonely retirement that awaits him—and to the twilight of British imperialism. And the onset of that twilight is signaled by the year 1956. Why change it to 1958, especially when the filmmakers have gone out of their way in another instance—the changing of Stevens' West-Country destination from Compton to Clevedon in order to echo Cliveden—to literalize the book's political suggestiveness?

The twilight of British imperialism tends in general to get moved back to its heyday or sunshine in Ivory's film, partly because of Tony Pierce-Roberts' cinematography, which appears celebratory instead of elegiac, lush rather than weathered; partly because of the movie's ending, which instead of finding Stevens sitting alone on a seaside bench in the evening (as the novel does), shows him back at Darlington Hall the next morning going about his duties, which happen to include the cliché of releasing a trapped pigeon into the verdant beauty of the surrounding countryside; and partly because of the film's documentary-like sequences.

These sequences show, even glory in, how a great manor is run, from the butler's ironing of the morning paper page-by-page to the scullery maid's cleaning of the cutlery, from the elaborate preparation of meals to the equally elaborate accommodation of numerous important guests. The camera remains somewhat removed through all of this, yet one can't help thinking that the preoccupied Stevens would never take the time to scan the place and process of his work in such loving detail. Nor, as I've already pointed out, would he regard Miss Kenton in the way the camera does: lingeringly and lovingly. In the novel, she's a figure of imagination, cretaed by words, a player in Stevens' internal drama whose face we never see. In the film, Miss Kenton takes on a life of her own, and that life with *its* drama detracts a bit from Stevens' own.

The Dead (1987, John Huston)

Next I'd like to consider the adaptation of a short story written in the third person: John Huston's last film, *The Dead* (1987), based on the last short story in James Joyce's collection *Dubliners* (1914) and the last story Joyce ever wrote. Nearly all of Huston's films are based on novels, plays, or short stories, and James Agee was right to conjecture in 1950, when Huston was shooting *The Red Badge of Courage,* that the director "lacks that deepest kind of creative impulse and that intense self-critical skepticism without which the stature of a great artist is rarely achieved. A brilliant adapter, he has yet to do a Huston 'original,' barring the war documentaries" (Agee, 331).

Agee added that the better the original material, the better Huston functioned as an artist. This is because Huston was a faithful adapter, not a loose one. He didn't seek to put his own stamp on source material; he tried to be as faithful as possible to the original, to re-create the literature in filmic terms. The loose adapter *does* seek to put his own stamp on original material, to interpret it independently, and consequently he often works with lesser literary sources—sources, that is, that leave room for improvement, for expansion or refocusing. For the most part, Huston stayed away from these, as the following sampling of his films will attest: the aforementioned *Red Badge of Courage* (1951), *Moby Dick* (1956), *The Bible* (1966), *Wise Blood* (1979), *Under the Volcano* (1984), and finally *The Dead.*

The problem for the faithful adapter, of course, is that sometimes filmic equivalents for the literary can't be found. If prose could easily be translated into film, then it would lose some of its distinctiveness as prose. The following example from Joyce's story makes my point:

> A light fringe of snow lay like a cape on the shoulders of his overcoat and like toecaps on the toes of his galoshes; and, as the buttons of his overcoat slipped with a squeaking noise through the snow-stiffened frieze, a cold fragrant air from out-of-doors escaped from crevices and folds. (Joyce, 128)

Gabriel Conroy and his wife, Gretta, have just entered the Dublin home of Gabriel's two aunts, Kate and Julia Morkan, for their annual dinner party-dance on the Feast of the Epiphany. We get none of Joyce's effect here in the film in part because *we see Gabriel himself*, all of him, and he is what captures our attention; in the story the words quoted above create a picture, and Gabriel's physical distinctiveness is missing from that picture. Joyce's emphasis is on the snow, which plays an important role in the story and is introduced at this moment.

Aside from the fact that cold, fragrant air escaping from crevices and folds can't be filmed, to have cut to the fringe of snow on the shoulders of Gabriel's overcoat and on the toes of his galoshes would have been to italicize that snow in a way that the prose does not do. Joyce's prose is a *description* that, in the course of the story, gains symbolic importance. Huston's cutting to the snow, had he done so, would have been to give it symbolic portent immediately, to direct us forcibly to its significance, and this would have been too much. With a choice between too much and too little, Huston wisely chooses too little: we see *Gabriel*, the shoulders of whose overcoat and the toes of whose galoshes are in fact covered, in turn, with a fringe of snow. But too little is not enough, and "enough" could only be contained in prose.

Huston faced another problem in filming Joyce's "The Dead" that was solvable but that he nonetheless did not solve. Joyce wrote in the third person— a non-participating narrator tells the story from the point of view of Gabriel's consciousness, as in the following:

> Gabriel felt humiliated . . . by the evocation of this figure from the dead, a boy in the gasworks. While he had been full of memories of their secret life together, full of tenderness and joy and desire, she had been comparing him in her mind with another. A shameful consciousness of his own person assailed him. He saw himself as a ludicrous figure, acting as a pennyboy for his aunts, a nervous well-meaning sentimentalist, orating to vulgarians and idealising his own clownish lusts, the pitiable fatuous fellow he had caught a glimpse of in the mirror. (Joyce, 158)

Few fiction films employ a third-person narrator, and those that do don't employ much of one, because the more we hear him, the more we feel we might as well be reading the story or novel itself (third-person narration is most often found in documentaries). Third-person narration is usually translated into the more immediate interior monologue and we hear it in voiceover as we see the character; again, though, we can't hear too much of it or else our visual experience will be thwarted.

Now Joyce wrote "The Dead" in the third person for a reason, best described by Allen Tate:

> The author suppresses himself but does not allow the hero to tell his own story, for the reason that "psychic distance" is necessary to the end in view. This end is the *sudden* revelation to Gabriel of his egoistic relation to his wife and, through that revelation, of his inadequate response to his entire experience. Thus Joyce must establish his central intelligence through Gabriel's eyes, but a little above and outside him at the same time ... (Tate, 10)

Perhaps Huston thought that Joyce's "psychic distance" would be destroyed by translating third-person narration into the interior monologue of Gabriel Conroy, for we hear Gabriel speak in voiceover only toward the end of the film, after Gretta has fallen asleep in their hotel room. Huston was wrong, however, if he did think this, because film, through the very device of framing the action, is ideally suited to maintaining the "psychic distance" of third-person narration at the same time that it periodically translates the third-person narration of fiction into interior monologue on a soundtrack.

Huston keeps his camera back for the most part in *The Dead*, using it to objectively frame the action rather than to subjectively enter it, but he fatally damages his film by not allowing us, through voiceover, to enter Gabriel's consciousness at significant moments. We cannot know, from Huston's film and from the performance of Donal McCann—and we should *not* be presumed to know the story—that Gabriel regards his aunts as only two ignorant old women, that he considers his fellow party guests vulgarians, that he pities his wife the loss of her youthful beauty when she feels no such pity for herself. The *narrator* tells us these things in the story because we must know them if we are to appreciate both the size of Gabriel's ego and the extent of his "recognition" at the end, his movement outside himself into an expansiveness that includes "all the living and the dead" (Joyce, 160), that includes the room in which he's staying as well as all of Ireland and even the universe, throughout which he imagines snow softly falling.

These criticisms made, I must say that *The Dead* is a delight to look at and to hear, in music and in the music of Irish accents. Alex North, who did the score for Huston's *Under the Volcano* and is best known for the scores of *A Streetcar Named Desire* (on screen; 1951, Elia Kazan) and *Death of a Salesman* (on stage and on screen; 1951, Laszlo Benedek), has composed delicately and evocatively. North has captured in his music the double nature of Joyce's story as a lament for Gabriel and a hymn to him, to the gentle, moving epiphany he achieves at the end. Fred Murphy's cinematographic world is filled not so much with color as with light—lamplight or night light. Murphy's palette consists largely of browns, grays, and blacks, and it is his intimate lighting during the party scenes that makes these colors mingle and dance, while it is his cold lighting during Gabriel and Gretta's coach ride back to the hotel and in the hotel room itself that makes these colors congeal and recede, to be surrounded by the whiteness of snow's blanket.

I cannot be as positive about the performances of Donal McCann as Gabriel and Anjelica Huston as Gretta, but, as is often the case in film, this has less to do with the performances themselves than with the film of which they are a part. Gretta is too prominent at the dinner party and dance, as she is not in the story—Huston cuts back and forth a number of times between her and her husband when she is dancing and he is not, and when she, unlike him, is unsettled by the recitation of a poem called "Broken Vows" (not part of Joyce's story). Huston does this to try to convey possessiveness and insecurity on Gabriel's part, but in the process he diminishes the effect of Gabriel's reversal at the end. Joyce's point is that, up to the moments of reversal and recognition, Gabriel is completely wrapped up in himself and in his role as his aunts' favored guest. The result of Huston's distortion of the story is that his daughter injects into Gretta a preciosity or self-consciousness that isn't part of her character and a remoteness that shouldn't be part of her character until much later, when she hears the tenor Bartell D'Arcy (a guest at the party) sing "The Lass of Aughrim" and is reminded thereby of Michael Furey, a boy who had once been in love with her in Galway and who used to sing the same song. Michael died at seventeen and, Gretta later says to Gabriel, " I think he died for me" (Joyce, 158).

Donal McCann is hindered, as I have pointed out, by the absence of his interior monologue on the soundtrack until the end of the film, and he simply doesn't have it in himself to tell us physically—facially and gesturally—what Joyce does in words. Add to this the fact that McCann's eyes aren't expressive, whereas Gabriel's are "delicate and restless," and that he's not helped by the omission of the character's "glimmering gilt-rimmed eyeglasses," and you have an actor hamstrung less by his own shortcomings than by his director's shortsightedness. Before his death, John Huston did his part in the unsuccessful campaign against the "colorizing" of black-and-white movies. I wish that he had been as faithful to Joyce's "The Dead" as he wanted Ted Turner to be to his *Maltese Falcon* (1941).

Dangerous Liaisons (1988, Stephen Frears)

Lastly, I'd like to treat what I call an omnibus adaptation—of fiction to drama to film—and the case in point is *Dangerous Liaisons*: a novel by Choderlos de Laclos (1782), from which Christopher Hampton took his play of the same title (1985), and from which Hampton then derived his screenplay for Stephen Frears's motion picture called, appropriately enough, *Dangerous Liaisons* (1988). Laclos's novel *Les Liaisons dangereuses*, for its part, is a product of its age in two senses: it is in epistolary form, a dominant narrative mode of the eighteenth century, and it embodies the conflicting philosophical and political impulses of this, the so-called age of reason.

On the one hand, the French *comédie larmoyante* and *drama bourgeois*, as well as the English sentimental comedy, sentimental tragedy, and sentimental novel, were arguing along with Rousseau that man was by nature good and could remain so by following his instincts—that is, the promptings of his heart; evil persons, on their side, might be reclaimed (at the same time they might be punished) if their hearts could be touched, if the callus of their vice could be penetrated to reveal the soft skin of their virtue. On the other hand, the Marquis de Sade was arguing that the "promptings of the heart" were in fact the product of reason, of teaching and socialization, not of instinct, which modeled itself after the chaos of the world and obeyed the laws of desire.

Sentimental literature was designed, of course, to appeal to the growing middle-class audience, to assist that audience in developing its own, self-congratulatory moral code and social ethic. Anti-sentimental literature—in the form of the libertine novel of eighteenth-century France and the British Restoration comedy of manners before it—was designed, by contrast, to confirm the shrinking upper classes in their unsentimental self-knowledge as well as in their ability to use their superior intelligence to outwit others and *liberate* themselves: from repressive moral codes, from political domination, from social subservience of any kind. Sexual intrigue and indulgence play such a great role in this literature partly because, for the idle and wealthy, gaming is the natural pastime, and sexual gaming is the most natural pastime of all.

Christopher Hampton's screenplay for *Dangerous Liaisons* happens, happily, to be faithful to the time period as well as the setting of the original. There are seven major correspondents in Laclos's *Les Liaisons dangereuses*, moreover, and all of them appear as characters in Frears's *Dangerous Liaisons* as well—characters who remind us of their origins in epistolary, or multiple first-person, fiction by periodically exchanging letters with one another during the film. (The very first shot is of someone's hands holding a letter, which itself bears the title of the film.) The chief characters are the Marquise de Merteuil, a young widow and arch manipulator of men; the Vicomte de Valmont, her former lover and an inveterate womanizer; and the Présidente de Tourvel, the young and pious wife of a magistrate (a Présidente, or presiding judge) away on business in Burgundy, and the closest we shall come to a bourgeoise.

Then come Cécile de Volanges, the young and innocent daughter of Madame de Volanges, who has recently arranged the girl's marriage to the Comte de Gercourt, a former lover of Merteuil's; Madame de Volanges, confidante to Merteuil (her cousin), the Présidente de Tourvel, and Rosemonde, and one of Valmont's many previous sexual conquests; the Chevalier Danceny, a young music tutor and suitor for Cécile's hand as well as the eventual lover of Merteuil; and Madame de Rosemonde, Valmont's eighty-year-old aunt, who is the Présidente de Tourvel's close friend and the owner of a country estate between which location and Paris the action alternates.

The plot—and what a plot, given its seven "narrators"—hinges on Merteuil's desire for revenge against Gercourt for his engagement to Cécile, and on Valmont's desire for yet another night in bed with Merteuil. As part of her plan, Valmont agrees to seduce the fifteen-year-old, convent-brad Cécile, but regards this as such an easy task that he won't accept Merteuil's renewed favors unless he is also able to bed Tourvel, whose religion and virtue present with a real challenge. Valmont succeeds easily with the young virgin, as he predicted, but must work so assiduously at seducing Tourvel that after he finally does, he realizes that he is as passionately in love with her as she is with him. Merteuil realizes this, too, and refuses Valmont his night in bed on the ground that he has breached the rules of their game: to achieve purely sexual consummations that are then rapidly and dispassionately severed.

Valmont severs his relationship with Tourvel but Merteuil still refuses him his prize, so jealous is she of his love; Valmont counters by arranging the first sexual liaison between Cécile and Danceny, Merteuil's own most recent conquest; and Merteuil retaliates by telling Danceny of Valmont's affair with Cécile. Danceny kills Valmont in a duel, but before dying the vicomte hands over his letters from Merteuil and Tourvel to the young man, thereby exposing the marquise's machinations and causing her public humiliation. Tourvel has retired to a convent, where she lapses into madness and dies; Cécile, who miscarried Valmont's child, will eventually enter a nunnery as a postulant; and the remorseful Danceny will opt for a life of celibacy as well by joining the Knights of Malta.

In Laclos's novel, Merteuil soon contracts smallpox, becomes so disfigured that she loses an eye, then loses a lawsuit and with it her fortune, whereupon she flees Paris for Holland. In Hampton's dramatic adaptation as in the film version, we see none of this. We last view Merteuil on stage playing a game of cards (just as we saw her at the start of the drama) as the shadow of a guillotine falls on the rear wall of the theater—a somewhat heavy premonition of the French Revolution and the beginning of the end of the aristocratic class. Hampton's film ending is lighter in touch than both his stage ending and the ending of the novel, and it fills in the "sentiments" that Laclos had only outlined.

The last shot of *Dangerous Liaisons* is a close-up of Merteuil in front of her dressing-table mirror, removing her make-up after her humiliation at the opera, where her former friends booed her as she stood alone in her box; the film had begun with a shot of her face in that same mirror she was preparing to make herself up. The implication is that there are two Merteuils: the heartless, egotistical one "made up" in the mirror, and the real woman beneath with a heart and with love to give rather than desire to slake. After Merteuil removes the last of the make-up from her pale face, she stares blankly—at herself—and tears begin to fall as the screen slowly fades to black. She cries at her own ruin, her own folly, but also at the death of Valmont, for whom she had begun to have genuine feelings.

Valmont, for his part, tearfully declares before his death both his love for Tourvel and his sorrow for the licentious life he has led: "Her love is the only real happiness I have ever known"; "[Danceny] had good cause [to slay me]; I don't think that is anything anyone has ever been able to say about me." Ironically, it is Valmont's love for Tourvel that gets him killed in Hampton and Frears's interpretation. As he duels with Danceny, Valmont flashes back to his lovemaking with Tourvel even as the film cross-cuts to the scene of her being bled with leeches in the convent; their deaths thus become visually intertwined with their love, or their love becomes a kind of death. Tourvel dies of her love, and Valmont dies of his: clearly the superior swordsman, he lets his guard down at one point as his memories of Tourvel overtake him, and Danceny takes the opportunity to run him through. Our final look at Valmont is from on high, along with, by implication, a judgmental God: in a stunning high-angle shot, we see him lying on his back in pure white snow, his servant and Danceny hanging over him and a long, thick trail of blood leading randomly away from his body.

Like sexual gangsters, Merteuil and Valmont have had their way, up to a point, and like dutiful spectators, we have thrilled to their exploits, up to a point—the one where moral duty intervenes and we assent, with God, to their penitence and punishment. Religion triumphs at the end of the filmic *Dangerous Liaisons* more than revolution, sentiment more than slaughter, conversion more than conquest. The greater truth of Hampton's movie ending, as opposed to his stage ending, is that the bourgeoisie assimilated, rather than assassinated, the aristocracy (even as the twentieth-century cinema did to the nineteenth-century theater, and that theater itself did to the eighteenth-century novel); that the sentimental view of life outflanked, rather than outmatched, the anti-sentimental one.

Sentimentalism acknowledged that good souls like Tourvel could be tempted to commit evil precisely because they were so good and trusting; and that even souls as evil as Merteuil could be made to see the error of their ways, precisely because their evil had finally consumed them together with their victims. If Sade's "instinct" obeyed the dictates of universal chaos, then sentimentalism's "heart" obeyed the dictates of providential design, and that design is adumbrated more by the omniscience of film form than by the discontinuous first-person narration of the epistolary novel, let alone the absence of narration in the drama.

In *Dangerous Liaisons*, we see events as they happen from the point of view of an omniscient camera/narrator not bound by time, space, or self-interest; we get Laclos's fragmented and disordered fiction, told by several people who don't know the whole story, converted into a complete and ordered film, told by someone who knows all. At the same time, Stephen Frears does his best to preserve the immediacy, intimacy, and secrecy, even solipsism, of the letter-form by shooting much of *Dangerous Liaisons* in close-up, going so far as to rack focus—to alter the plane within a shot—in order to isolate a character in medium close-up in the foreground of the image while turning the background (of which Frears has given us a compensatory glimpse) into a blur.

The "epistolary" close-up alternates with Frears's omniscient, and highly skillful, cutting among scenes to give us what Laclos's novel really cannot—as no other novel could, either—and what Hampton's stage adaptation could only awkwardly attempt to convey (particularly without resort to simultaneous staging): the paradoxical sense that we share in the immediacy of the confidences exchanged at the same time as we are in the hands of a silent divinity who overhears, and oversees, everything. *We* put together the pieces Laclos gives us when we read the 175 letters of the novel, or as we watch the eighteen scenes of Hampton's theatrical version; as we see the film, someone else is putting the pieces together, for us as well as for the characters.

Works Cited

Agee, James. "Undirectable Director" [John Huston]. 1950. In *Agee on Film: Reviews and Comments*. New York: McDowell Obolensky, 1958. 320-331.

Hampton, Christopher. *Dangerous Liaisons*. London: Faber & Faber, 1985.

Ishiguro, Kazuo. *The Remains of the Day*. New York: Viking, 1989.

Joyce, James. "The Dead." In Joyce's *Dubliners*. Hertfordshire, U.K.: Wordsworth, 1993. 127-160.

Laclos, Pierre Choderlos de. *Les Liaisons dangereuses*. 4 vols. Paris: Durand Neveu, 1782.

----------. *Dangerous Liaisons*. Trans. P. W. K. Stone. Harmondsworth, U.K.: Penguin, 1961.

Tate, Allen. "Three Commentaries: Poe, James, and Joyce." *The Sewanee Review*, 58 (Winter 1950): 1-15.

"Masterpiece Theater, or Four Film Adaptations from Classic Russian Literature: Tolstoy's 'Prisoner of the Caucasus'; Goncharov's *Oblomov*; Dostoevsky's *The Brothers Karamazov, The Eternal Husband*, and *A Gentle Creature*"

The films discussed in the following essay are Sergei Bodrov's *Prisoner of the Mountains*, from the 1870 short story by Leo Tolstoy; Nikita Mikhalkov's *Oblomov* (1980), from the 1859 novel by Ivan Goncharov; Richard Brooks's *The Brothers Karamazov* (1958), from the 1879 novel by Fyodor Dostoevsky; Pierre Billon's *The Eternal Husband* (1946), from the 1870 novella by Dostoevsky; and Robert Bresson's *A Gentle Creature* (1969), from the 1876 novella by Dostoevsky.

Prisoner of the Mountains (1996, Sergei Bodrov)

Prisoner of the Mountains (1996), by the Russian director Sergei Bodrov, is about cultural clash and the moral enlightenment as well as emotional awakening that, under the right circumstances, can come of it. Ironically, the "right circumstances," in this instance, are those of war and captivity. This was not exactly a new subject when the film was released in 1996—the attempt to reveal a human bond between characters who are otherwise military enemies, political opponents, religious rivals, or racial opposites—but it need *not* have been in the hands of a sensitive writer-director like Bodrov, interested in something other than sentimentality, hyperbole, and oversimplification.

Indeed, in Bodrov's case, he is a better *auteur* than the original author of the story on which *Prisoner of the Mountains* is based: Leo Tolstoy, the action of whose "Prisoner of the Caucasus" (1870) the Russian director, along with his co-scenarists Arif Aliyev and Boris Giller, transposed from the Chechnya of some 140 years before (where and when Tolstoy did a portion of his military service) to the same general area today, on the northern slopes of the Caucasus mountains. In this area the Russian army is simultaneously governing and fighting the Muslim population—prior to that army's withdrawal in August 1996 as the result of a treaty signed between Chechnyan rebels and the Russian government, which had ordered a full-scale invasion of the former republic in December 1994.

The real-life Russian encounter with the Muslim world over the past thirty years, let alone the last century-and-a-half, has often been characterized by the violence of war rather than by attempts at understanding: in addition to the Chechnyan struggle (which erupted into war again in 2000) and a number of smaller engagements along the former Soviet border, there was the Afghan war of the early 1980s. Despite these conflicts, the Caucasus region has long fascinated Russians as the nearest manifestation of the inscrutable Orient, and nineteenth-century literature abounds with encounters between young Russians—frequently army officers—and this Muslim portion of their empire. To wit: the Russian title of Bodrov's film, whose literal translation is *Prisoner of the Caucasus*, was used not only in the short story by Tolstoy, but also in poems by Alexander Pushkin (1822) and Mikhail Lermontov (1828) as well as in an 1883 opera by César Cui based on Pushkin's poem.

Moreover, *Prisoner of the Mountains* is not the first Russian movie to feature the Caucasus in the wake of the Chechnyan wars. Vladimir Khotinenko's

The Muslim (1995) told the tale of a young Russian soldier who returns to his native village after having embraced the Islamic faith during his stint as a prisoner of war, only to be met by family and friends with incomprehension and violence; while Aleksei Balabanov's *Brother* (1997) followed Bodrov's film with the story of a Chechnyan war veteran who turns into a Petersburg killer. Subsequent to *Prisoner of the Mountains*, as well—and a bit like it—Alexander Rogozhkin's *The Checkpoint* (1999) offered a sympathetic portrayal of a group of Russian soldiers manning an isolated outpost, who nonetheless remain alien occupiers in the strange, nearly incomprehensible region of the Caucasus, despised by the locals and exploited by their own commanders for personal prestige and gain; while Alexander Sokurov's anti-war film *Alexandra* (2007) told the tale of a grandmother visiting her son on the front-line during the Second Chechnyan War

    Prisoner of the Mountains is distinctive, however, in being entirely set among the Muslim rebels, many of them played by local people who had never acted before. (Such a setting can also be found in Russian films like Andrei Konchalovsky's *House of Fools* [2002] and Mariya Saakyan's *The Lighthouse* [2006], each of which takes place in Chechnya and foregrounds Chechnyan characters.) Yet from these locals Sergei Bodrov coaxed natural, unforced performances, even as he had done from non-professional actors in three of his six features prior to *Prisoner of the Mountains*: *Non-Professionals* (1986), *Freedom Is Paradise* (1990), and *I Wanted to See Angels* (1992). But the difference in Bodrov's use of amateurs here is signal, for their roughhewn, red-cheeked faces make up a kind of human scenery that underscores this picture with history—with the history of similar faces that populated the isolated, stubborn, struggling region of Chechnya before the czars as well as throughout their reign, and which subsequently survived the seventy-odd years of the so-called New Soviet Order.

    The people remain, and their *aul* or village in *Prisoner of the Mountains* remains much as it was when Tolstoy was a soldier there: a place of flinty, unpaved roads and clay huts with earthen floors, where wheat is still threshed by mules, men still travel on horseback, and dress codes, gender roles, the veneration of ancestors, and the rule of elders have persevered, unchanged, for many generations. These Chechnyans may not be prisoner to the Caucasus mountains, like their Russian captives, but they are in awe of the cruelly beautiful, grandly gaunt peaks that look down at them in stunning images (photographed by Pavel Lebeshev) with a chilling hint of blue-green. So much so that, in *Prisoner of the Mountains*, the Chechnyans step out onto their roofs in a paradoxical gesture of both deference and self-assertion toward the majestically uncompromising starkness that surrounds them. And so in awe are they that they have composed a plaintive yet celebratory ode to the Caucasus which forms half of the film's musical score: "We are the children of the mountains," the villagers sing, "The mountains will protect us."

    The other half of the film's score counterpoints the first: beloved songs from past Russian military campaigns, such as the pre-Revolutionary "On the Hills of Manchuria" and World War II's "The Blue Kerchief," both of which are here ironically deployed. There is no such irony in the story "Prisoner of the Caucasus," which the elderly Tolstoy oddly thought was one of his two best pieces of fiction (together with "God Sees the Truth, But Waits," which was written at about the same time—1872—but is quite different in subject, if similar in intended theme: enlightenment through imprisonment); nor is the short story's portrayal of Russians and Caucasians as balanced as the motion picture's. Tolstoy's central concern was almost exclusively with the experience of one of his two Russian soldiers, the dashing, courageous officer Vania Zhílin, captured along with another officer, the stout and dullish Sasha Kostílin, in an ambush by raiding "Tartar" mountaineers.

"A Prisoner of the Caucasus" is related in the third person, from Vania's point of view. This means, of course, that we get his interpretation of people and events with virtually no narrative intervention from the inveterately economical Tolstoy, as in the following:

> Zhílin was very thirsty . . ., and he thought: "If only they would come and so much as look at me!" Then . . . [t]he red-bearded Tartar entered, and with him was . . . a smaller man, dark, with bright black eyes . . . and a short beard. He had a merry face and was always laughing. . . . The red-bearded Tartar . . . stood . . . playing with his dagger and glaring askance at Zhílin, like a wolf. The dark one . . . came straight up to Zhílin, squatted down in front of him, . . . and began to talk very fast in his own language. His teeth showed, and he kept winking, clicking his tongue, and repeating, "Good Russ, good Russ." Zhílin could not understand a word, but said, "Drink! Give me water to drink!" The dark man only laughed. (Tolstoy, 16-17)

Bodrov's cinematic adaptation does not employ such third-person narration—few fiction films do, of course, for the more we hear such a non-participating narrator on the soundtrack, the more we feel that we might as well be reading the story or novel itself. (Third-person narration is most often found in documentaries.) *Prisoner of the Mountains* slips naturally into the omniscient form endemic to the camera-eye, and it is this omniscience—the power to regard character and action from multiple points of view, or an all-encompassing perspective—that enables Bodrov fully to articulate elements of the drama which Tolstoy only touches upon, sometimes with a touch of heaviness. The relationship between Vania and Sasha is a case in point.

The screenplay demotes Vania from a bold, debonair officer to a newly conscripted private, naïve and reticent, while it changes his fellow captive from a plodding, overweight officer to a veteran, non-commissioned one, a sergeant who is at once clever, cynical, garrulous, and reckless as well as ruthless. Several objectives are thereby achieved: (1) greater contrast between two already different prisoners; (2) more balance in their relationship, since the film, unlike the story, depicts an enterprising Sasha as the initiator of escape, not a resourceful Vania, whereas the latter remains the one, on film as in fiction, who develops an affection for Dína, the girl who brings the Russians their daily rations; (3) greater dramatic tension in the scenario as a whole—a tension that itself stands in contrast to the film's almost leisurely observation of archaic Muslim customs and age-old Caucasian vistas—since the boyish Vania's affection for his "enemy," the thirteen-year-old Dína, dangerously if plausibly verges on love-cum-marriage in Bodrov's adaptation (and in the Caucasus, where girls still routinely marry in their early teens); and (4) less contrast or difference between the Russian prisoners and their Chechnyan captors, because the former are no longer members of an elite, not to say aristocratic, class of commissioned officers (who, in these days of high technology and helicopter evacuation, the Russian brass might have been more eager to rescue), even if they are citizens of a great military power, while their chief jailer—the fiftyish Abdul-Murat, Dína's father—is unquestionably a village patriarch.

The similarities between these rivals extend to parallelism in the plot and beyond, for, in *Prisoner of the Mountains*, the stern and proud Abdul-Murat does not kill his two Russian prisoners (only one of whom he wanted) after the guerrilla ambush because he hopes to exchange them for his schoolteacher-son, Dzaramat, a prisoner of the *Russians* whom he has not been able to ransom with money. In Tolstoy's story, Abdul-Murat is less sympathetic, for he has no son and is interested only in ransoming Vania and Sasha for monetary gain. Furthermore, in "A Prisoner of the Caucasus" there is no character called Hasan, a dumb eunuch whom Bodrov and his collaborators write into the script. Hasan guards the already shackled Russians, more or less around the clock, for Abdul-Murat, to whom he appears almost to be in indentured servitude. This added figure's real significance, however, lies in the genesis of his condition, which says as much as his Chechnyan master as it does about the Russian imperialists. For Hasan lost the power of speech as a prison inmate in Siberia, where he was sent for the murder of his adulterous wife, who was also Abdul-Murat's daughter and Dína's older sister—and where his Russian captors cut out his tongue, in addition to castrating him, because they felt he talked and sang too much.

The Chechnyan captors of Vania and Sasha do not castrate them, and they do not cut out their tongues—indeed, they could be said to give the Russians a voice in their own fates. After a failed attempt to exchange the two soldiers for Dzaramat—failed because Russian forces tried to trick Abdul-Murat, whom they consider to be just another scheming Chechnyan—the patriarch ignores pressure from his fellow villagers to butcher the Russians and instead makes his prisoners write letters to their mothers urging them to intercede on their sons' behalf. Vania does so, and his widowed schoolteacher-mother comes to his aid; Sasha writes home, too, but he knows his letter will never get a response, as he grew up in an orphanage where no one will remember him now, anyway. The letter-writing in the story, by contrast, is only an appeal for ransom money, and there the swaggering Vania deliberately misaddresses his letter so that it will not reach its destination, whereas the pathetic Sasha writes home a second time in Tolstoy's fiction in a desperate attempt to raise the rubles necessary for his release.

Maslov, commander of the Russian garrison in the nearby, occupied town where Dzaramat is being held, refuses to let Abdul-Murat see his son, and the military chief meets with Vania's mother only to advise her not to negotiate with the shifty locals. She does so anyway, yet to no avail: Abdul-Murat tells his fellow parent merely that he will try again to arrange a prisoner exchange. Then, immediately afterwards, Sasha and Vania escape—apparently inspired by a radio broadcast of "Go Down Moses" (ironically so, with its equation of the Chechnyan struggle with those of the ancient Israelites and Egyptians and, by implication, of Americans blacks with their white racist oppressors) as performed by Louis Armstrong. In the process of fleeing, Sasha kills both Hasan and a shepherd whose rifle he steals; but the rifle turns out to be useless, as it contains only one bullet and the bumbling Vania fires it by accident, thus giving away his and his comrade's position to the pursuing Chechnyan rebels. Both Russians are recaptured, yet only Private Zhílin is returned to his Muslim master; Sergeant Kostílin gets his throat cut for the crime of murder.

Nonetheless, Sasha does not disappear completely from the film. Through shared adversity, the bond of trust between him and Vania has grown so great (so great that, sensing his imminent execution after their botched escape, Sasha asks Vania to help support a son he had out of wedlock), despite the sergeant's at first utter contempt for his otherwise earnest subordinate, that Vania twice has visions in which a serene and solicitous Sasha appears. Are these visions attributable in part to the place where they occur, a Muslim place conceivably more mystical or spiritual than Russia proper, where religion was officially suppressed for decades under the rule of the Soviets? Bodrov wisely does not comment on this matter, but one can infer that Vania's visions are at least in some measure a result of the remote, mountainous location, his long, enforced isolation, and his gradual, sentient education not only into the ways of his superior officer but also into those of a non-materialistic culture very different from his own.

As for Abdul Murat's son, he too is killed shortly after Sasha in an escape attempt—this one prompted by the shooting of a Chechnyan collaborator, Mamed, by his own father, who especially buys a Russian pistol from a pawnshop in order to do the job. This old man, according to Abdul-Murat in Tolstoy's story,

> "was the bravest of our fellows; he killed many Russians, and was at one time very rich. He had three wives and eight sons, and they all lived in one village. Then the Russians came and killed seven of his sons. Only one son was left, and he gave himself up to the Russians. . . After [shooting and killing him, the old man] left off fighting and went to Mecca to pray to God; that is why he wears a turban [and] is called 'Hadji' . . . He does not like you fellows [Vania and Sasha]. He tells me to kill you." (Tolstoy, 26-27)

Indeed, this village elder called Hadji has taken at least one shot of his own at the two Russian prisoners, in the story as well as the film. That one missed, but the one aimed at Mamed struck not only him but, figuratively speaking, the loyal Dzaramat as well. For the latter—who, to repeat, does not appear in Tolstoy's "Prisoner of the Caucasus"—conceived the idea to escape only during the pandemonium surrounding the slaying of Hadji's traitorous son, and, in the act of fleeing, Abdul-Murat's own son gets hit by a bullet to the back as, tellingly, *Vania's* long-suffering mother looks on in horror.

Because of Dzaramat's death, Dína reports to Vania in the solitary confinement of a stinking pit, he will be executed the next day. She then betrays her father—or, depending on your point of view, honors her burgeoning affection for Vania—by giving the Russian the key to his shackles. In order to protect Dína, however, he refuses to run away in Bodrov's adaptation, and is subsequently taken into the mountains to be shot by Abdul-Murat. But this father cannot shoot a stricken mother's only son, or his beloved daughter's own love, so he fires into the air, then turns around and starts walking home. As a stunned Vania wanders away on the vast Caucasian slopes, four Russian helicopters (gunships) appear overhead, on their way to a retaliatory strike against Abdul-Murat's village—not to a merciful rescue of the lone Private Zhílin.

While martial music blares on the soundtrack, the repatriated and in some ways still innocent Vania fondly recollects, in voiceover, his experiences as a "guest" of the Chechnyan people. To some of them he became deeply and unforgettably attached, he says, while for many of their customs he developed an increasing respect, even as they did for his "alien" skills as a mender of watches and a crafter of bric-à-brac. One of those crafted items, all of them presented to Dína, is a beautiful wooden bird with movable wings, which the grateful girl hangs from the ceiling of her and her father's small home, and which plainly symbolizes not only Vania and Sasha's will to freedom but also the Chechnyan people's.

The Vania of Tolstoy's story carves gifts for Dína as well, but they are dolls without the symbolic import of the bird, which is to say without an import that attaches equally to Russians and Chechnyans alike. This is the problem with the short story in general: it displays something less than mutual compassion for the combatants in this longstanding regional conflict. Tolstoy called "A Prisoner of the Caucasus," together with "God Sees the Truth, But Waits," a "Tale for Children." And in its uncomplicated view of the world, along with its emphasis on Dína's material accumulation as opposed to her spiritual bonding, "A Prisoner of the Caucasus" certainly seems designed to appeal to the child in all of us, particularly as its ending differs from the resoundingly poignant one of the film version.

In the story, Sasha is not slain after he and Vania are recaptured, because the former did not kill an innocent shepherd or Hasan. Afraid that her father will give in to his compatriots' demands that he cut Vania's throat, Dína frees him from his outdoor dungeon after fattening her favorite with cakes and cherries and cheese, while Sasha remains shackled in the pit on account of illness and fatigue. Then Vania successfully escapes, arriving back at his Russian fort after an all-night journey and an averted skirmish with at least three enemy horsemen. "He went on serving in the Caucasus," Tolstoy flatly concludes, and "a month later Kostílin was released after paying five thousand rubles ransom" (Tolstoy, 43). As for Vania's last-minute promise to Dína that he would never forget her, no further mention of it is made in the story—unlike the film—nor of the girl herself or, most importantly, of her father's reaction to her perfidious act.

Since the Dína-Vania relationship provides the gist of Bodrov's narrative, if not Tolstoy's, it was imperative that both roles be well cast. Bodrov found Susanna Mekhralieva in a school in Dagestan, not far from Chechnya, and her performance as Dína is exemplary in its ease, simplicity, and understatement. The director naturally found Sergei Bodrov, Jr., in his own family, and, as Vania, he gives an equally unsentimentalized but tremendously affecting performance of great faith—youthful faith in a caring universe—reminiscent of the World War II-draftee from Grigori Chukhrai's *Ballad of a Soldier* (1959), another young Russian (played by Vladimir Ivashev) thrown into the maelstrom before he has had time to live. This was Bodrov, Jr.'s, screen début (he was killed in 2002 in a rock-and-ice slide while shooting a film in the mountains of North Ossetia), which was followed by his role as the combat veteran-become-civilian-murderer in both parts of Balabanov's *Brother* (1997,

2000)—a chilling gloss on the possible fate of his character in *Prisoner of the Mountains*.

Oleg Menshikov, for his part, went on to become one of the biggest stars in Russian cinema. Prior to *Prisoner of the Mountains*, this actor was familiar to American audiences through his sterling work as the Stalinist policeman in Nikita Mikhalkov's otherwise languid *Burnt by the Sun*, which won the Academy Award for Best Foreign-Language Film in 1994 (part II was released in 2010). Here, playing the quite different character of Sasha, Menshikov brings to the role the doomed raillery and easeful cocksureness of a man convinced at once of his own superiority and his common mortality: a combination Errol Flynn and Martin Sheen, as it were.

Oleg Menshikov and Sergei Bodrov, Jr., deservedly shared the prize for Best Actor at the Sochi Kinotavr, today the leading Russian film festival, where *Prisoner of the Mountains* won the Grand Prix for best picture, which it also garnered, along with four other awards, at the 1997 Nikas (the Russian Oscars). This powerfully affecting film received, in addition, the Crystal Globe at the Karlovy Vary International Festival, as well as the International Critics' Prize and the Public Prize at Cannes, but it was subsequently beaten out for the 1997 Academy Award for Best Foreign-Language Film by the Czech director Jan Sverák's insipid *Kolya* (another tale about the encounter between two initially incompatible people, in this instance a man and a little boy).

The choice of *Kolya* over *Prisoner of the Mountains* should not surprise anyone, though, given the Academy's predilection for the maudlin and mannered over the measured yet moving, whatever a motion picture's national origin may be. In fact, had Sergei Bodrov made a *faithful* adaptation of Tolstoy's tendentious, sometimes puerile "Prisoner of the Caucasus," his *Prisoner of the Mountains* might well have won the Oscar—an irony perhaps grimmer, in the end, than the film itself.

Work Cited

Tolstoy, Leo. *Twenty-Three Tales*. Trans. Aylmer Maude. London: Oxford University Press, 1928.

Oblomov (1980, Nikita Mikhalkov)

One surprise about *Oblomov* is that, as far as I can tell, it had never been filmed before 1980 (except as a TV movie). The name of the protagonist, as well as the generic "Oblomovism," has passed into several languages, yet this Soviet picture is the first one based on the book. A second surprise is that it's a good film: surprising chiefly because the previous work I've seen by Nikita Mikhalkov, the director—*A Slave of Love* (1976), *Dark Eyes* (1987), *Burnt by the Sun* (1994)— was blatantly prettified. *Oblomov* isn't free of director's intrusions, but on the whole it's a moving, atmospherically authentic distillation of a great, highly significant novel. One byproduct of the picture's arrival may be to turn people to Ivan Goncharov's 1859 book; everyone knows his and its name, but many have it only on their Must Read Some Time list—where it has been for some time.

Our hero—a ridiculous use of the term if ever there was one—is in his early thirties and lives in St. Petersburg in the 1850s on the income of a badly run estate, which he rarely visits. What Oblomov does mostly is sleep. Or at least lie down. In his large, dowdy apartment, attended by a manservant, he reclines in his bed or on his sofa, calls for what he wants, grumbles when he gets it, overeats, and resists the efforts of friends to activate him. But if that were all, Oblomov (accent his name on the second syllable) would be only a Gogol cartoon out of *The Inspector General* (1836).

What makes the novel as important as it is good is that it's one of the early appearances in European literature of the dramatic power of disaffection. *Oblomov* had been preceded by Georg Büchner's *Leonce and Lena* (1836) and Alfred de Musset's *Fantasio* (1872). Russian critics have pointed out the connection with Alexander Pushkin's *Eugene Onegin* (1833) and the hero of Mikhail Lermontov's *A Hero of Our Time* (1840). But what about Ivan Turgenev's *Diary of a Superfluous Man* (1850)? And what about—ineluctably—Samuel Beckett's *Waiting for Godot* (1953)?

Why then did the USSR decide, in 1980, to make a film on this theme—from a novel supremely embodying this theme? The answer may lie in the attitude that Soviet theaters often took toward Chekhov: that the plays describe a past lassitude and are therefore cautionary tales. This misguided belief about Chekhov *and* the Soviet present of the last quarter of the twentieth century may be the ill wind that has blown to this film's good. As for the ill wind, the screenplay by Mikhalkov and Aleksander Adabashyan rearranges the material somewhat, Soviet-style: the script begins with Oblomov as a small boy, cosseted by mommy on the country estate, and there are flashbacks throughout to this pampered boyhood. Possibly we are to infer that he was the spoiled scion of wealthy bourgeoisie; and that the encouragement of idleness leads, inevitably, to the sofa, literally or figuratively. Outside the Soviet paradigm, however, *Oblomov* poses less soluble questions.

As in the novel, the film is not simply about a man who won't get up and busy himself: it's about why he won't. He is convinced that any activity by him, any existence by him, doesn't much matter in the cosmic scheme—in fact, that there isn't much of a cosmic scheme. His life is futile and therefore may as well be unobtrusive to others and pleasant to himself. The one possibility for his life to be altered galvanically is his love for the young and beautiful Olga. It looks as if that love may be fulfilled: but the complications of self-doubt cede her to Oblomov's close friend, Stolz. (He's another of those partly German Russians of the nineteenth century, like Tusenbach in Chekhov's *Three Sisters* [1901].) Oblomov sinks back into lethargy, eventually marries his housekeeper, has a son, and dies—rather, disappears *completely*. With an echo of the opening, the film ends with his little son running across fields to greet his mother. (Oddly, the child seems to run well over a mile—just to sustain the final image.) The inescapable implication is that Oblomov *fils* is headed eventually for the Oblomov sofa.

This isn't the emphasis of the book, though the film's sources are in Goncharov; still, the movie has lovely flavor and nicely muted poignancy. When Mikhalkov relaxes, when he isn't fretting to be visually inventive by moving the camera in or out without necessity, when he isn't searching for an odd angle—in short, when he relies on his actors and his story—the picture holds well. Occasionally he can put invention truly at the service of the story. Near the end, in the Stolz home, there's a shot with Stolz at his desk in another room, left background; his wife, Olga, sewing in an adjacent room, foreground; and an old friend in the room with her, right background. The triangle, involving two rooms, fixes an old relationship by means of the arrangement of space.

As in all Soviet films, the color here ranges from the dull to the insufficiently clarified to the gorgeous. The music is good; early on, Olga, an amateur singer, does "Casta diva" from Bellini's *Norma* (1831) after dinner, and it finds its way onto the soundtrack as a binding theme. Olga is played by Elena Solovei, who was the heroine of *A Slave of Love*, and Solovei is winning and puzzled and vulnerable—much more appealing than she was in the earlier film. Yuri Bogatyryev, for his part, is staunch and generous as Stolz, a friend in the full nineteenth-century sense.

Inevitably the picture depends on Oblomov, and Oleg Tabakov is excellent. He gets the prosaic but real yearning, the insufficient confidence without silliness, the pudgy but delicate dignity that make him withdraw from what Robert Penn Warren calls the "slur of the world's weather" (Warren, 320). *Oblomov* had to wait surprisingly long for filming: it has been here now for over forty years, and it will remain.

Work Cited

Warren, Robert Penn. "Birth of Love." In *The Collected Poems of Robert Penn Warren*. Ed. John Burt. Baton Rouge: Louisiana State University Press, 1998. 319-320.

The Brothers Karamazov (1958, Richard Brooks) & *The Eternal Husband* (1946, Pierre Billon)

The only sensible way to approach a film made from a gigantic work like *The Brothers Karamazov* is with good wishes and moderate hopes. Obviously, the matter of length alone prevents a film from encompassing this 1879 novel with anything like completeness. The tests one may reasonably expect such a picture to meet are: does it present an acceptable microcosm of Fyodor Dostoevsky's universe, and is the presentation itself satisfactory?

On both scores the 1958 MGM color production, directed by Richard Brooks and produced by Pandro S. Berman, deserves considerable praise. Brooks, who published several novels before devoting himself to film work, wrote his own screenplay from an adaptation by the playwrights Julius J. and Philip G. Epstein. As might be foreseen, the script is principally devoted to the more easily externalized encounters and conflicts in the novel, as it streamlines or foreshortens the story to an account of the joys and tribulations of Dmitri: Dmitri's love relationships, his father's debauchery, the murder, and the trial. Much of Dostoevsky's dialogue (in Constance Garnett's translation) has been retained, and within the scope of these episodes an honest and intelligent effort was made to develop the characters in depth.

In the matter of presentation, the picture is handsomely mounted and beautifully costumed. The interiors, particularly that of the Karamazov house, give exactly the right atmosphere of cultural frontiersmen, of a people rich in talents, avid for experience, belatedly joining the course of Western culture. There is a fairly close parallel (as a number of commentators have pointed out) between nineteenth-century Russia and nineteenth-century America *vis-à-vis* western Europe. In the picture the streets of Ryevsk rightly remind us of a raw Kansas town; the cloying luxury of the Karamazov home might, in essence, be that of any Midwestern robber baron's mansion.

Beyond this, and much more important, several of the performances are fine. As the elder Karamazov, Lee J. Cobb triumphs. In other film and television performances at the time, Cobb seemed to trade heavily on a kind of ostentatious honesty, a conscious air of abandonment of trickery, which in itself is an affectation. In Karamazov, Cobb has discarded a theory about acting in order to act. He has used empathy and imagination, and the result is a valid, valuable artistic creation.

It is true, of course, that he has the best "part" in the book. Audiences always respond to an intelligent scoundrel. But it is easy for a performance of Karamazov to dissolve in a welter of bombast. Cobb gives us this gross character with subtlety: the feral cunning, the sudden fears, the surprising perceptions. It is a graphic portrait of a huge glutton, greedy for self-gratification and power and equally greedy for respect and love and salvation.

Yul Brynner, whose background includes considerable training in the French theater, shows the benefits of that training in a well-sustained and sensitive performance as the eldest son, the impulsive Dmitri. One quickly forgives him his silly baldpate trademark as he shows us the schizoid torment of this man torn between his heredity and his vision, who can find a measure of peace only by accepting moral responsibility for a crime he did not commit. Brynner's face does as much to create the right ambience for the picture as any other factor; his repose and silences tell as much as his outbursts.

Claire Bloom, as Katya, delineates crisply an upper-class girl whose conventionality is not only her code but her burden and her weapon. (It is true that she offers herself to Dmitri in return for a crucial loan to her father; but she falls in love with him because he does "the decent thing".) We feel her straining at the bonds of her upbringing to reach Dmitri, and we understand the outrage of her little soul when her seeming generosity toward Grushenka is spurned.

But in spite of all the virtues cited above, one leaves the film with a sense of disappointment. Part of this is due to the shortcomings of the script. One is prepared for some tailoring of the ending, for, in plot though not in theme, the novel is notoriously indeterminate. But Brooks felt it necessary to show Dmitri escaping with Grushenka and even interrupting his flight to visit the bedside of the dying boy Ilyusha; then to have Ivan discover God on the witness stand before snubbing Katya at the close. (Presumably MGM is punishing her for having helped to convict Dmitri.) These seem excessive concessions to popular sentimentality and theatrical neatness.

Beyond this, although it is remarkable to hear any serious mention in a Hollywood film of such matters as the nature of sin, the effect of religious belief on ethics, and the shape of a national soul, these themes are treated with the breathless haste of a television adaptation. To take the love and murder elements so far out of their social and religious context is to synopsize, not to condense. One does not expect to find the whole "Russian Monk" section in the film or to hear Ivan tell the story of the Grand Inquisitor, but—to cite three examples—the skimpiness of the Father Zossima and Snegiryov episodes and the *reductio ad absurdum* of Ivan's philosophy make us conscious of surgery, not Dostoevsky.

Apart from various defects in the script, the production makes use of blatantly symbolic lighting. Characters step out of amber into green at patly appropriate moments; beds are bathed in purple. In fact (as in the contemporaneous film of *A Farewell to Arms* [1957, Charles Vidor]), stagy lighting effects sometimes interfere with scenes that might otherwise be credible. One more point about the direction: there are a number of wild parties in the picture, tiresome because the handling of them is predictable. Although these scenes may be accurate enough, they remain clichés.

Yet even with the same script, the same lighting and editing, this film could have been much more successful if four of the leading roles had been well played. Maria Schell, in the late 1950s, was rapidly becoming the most overrated actress of her time. As Grushenka, she grins or she does not grin; there isn't a great deal more to her performance. Here, in this Slavic Carmen, Dostoevsky has given us a marvelous portrait of a woman whose being is in her passions, who will live for them only, without pity for herself or anyone else: shrewd, defiant, fatalistic. Schell possesses the color and fire of an Alpine milkmaid. Her Grushenka simply does not flame; and without an enthralling Grushenka the plot lacks a fulcrum.

Richard Basehart paws ineffectually at the exterior of Ivan, the articulate atheist; the net effect is simply of a pleasant young man pinching his eyebrows together to indicate deep thought and inner turmoil. As Alyosha, the young embodiment of Russian mystic fervor, William Shatner (yes, that William Shatner) is a nullity; his bland face and voice contradict everything he says and does. As Smerdyakov, the Caliban in the house, Albert Salmi concentrates so thoroughly on superficial melodramatics that he evokes little true horror. With competent performances in these three parts, in addition to Schell's, we would not only be more moved, we would—in spite of the truncations—understand more of the author's underlying meanings.

After Dostoevsky's death, Tolstoy wrote: "I never saw this man and never had any direct relations with him, and suddenly, when he died, I understood that he was the closest, dearest, and most necessary man to me" (Simmons, 17). It is what one feels after reading such a monumental work—that Dostoevsky was a redeemer in art who was born and suffered that men might be, at least to the limits of the author's experience, further exalted. Buried somewhere among the good and bad things in the film of *The Brothers Karamazov* is a vague, fumbling hint that this might be true. But the inadequacies block the channel, and what is "most necessary"—in the book, in Dostoevsky— never quite reaches and rewards us.

Something similar could be said about Pierre Billon's *The Eternal Husband* (1946), taken from the 1870 novella by Dostoevsky. This French film, with Raimu (a.k.a. Jules Auguste Muraire) in the title role, poses a recurrent critical problem for which there is no satisfactory solution. The picture is a striking example of the screen adaptation that, in itself a production superior to the run of movies, falls far short of the original author's intent and penetration. If one condemns such a work for not rising to its great occasion (always a temptation, since the very decision to adapt a work of genius is an act of arrogance), one is apt to drive readers away from a production that would please them more than most; on the other hand, to praise the film on its own terms and with no reference to the model is to be a party to vulgarization.

The Eternal Husband as Dostoevsky wrote it is a masterpiece. It is short and does not attempt to do a great deal, but its atmosphere of unseemly excitement, its delicate shifting of the moral balance from one protagonist to the other, its conflict established directly between the souls of men—all of this comprehends as much about guilt and love and the motives impelling the human spirit as any writer has ever accomplished in a like form.

The film does not change the story; it lowers it, clarifies it, plots it. Where the novelist saw a complex of motives, the movie makes a choice; where the book makes its point by unresolved emotion, the picture drives its argument home with a finger in the ribs. Dostoevsky's husband is not a readily understood or very likable fellow; he is not to be tolerated and yet he must be loved. In the guise of Raimu, however, he is both easily comprehended and directly sympathetic.

As the movie unreels the story of an elderly cuckold who comes to Petersburg to punish, perhaps to execute, his dead wife's lover; as he sacrifices the child that is his in name to this purpose; as he dissipates and plays the fool in a new betrothal, one feels again and again that one should cry out, "Yes, that's the way it all happened, but you film people *still* don't understand." The facts are there very much as Dostoevsky wrote them; the feeling is mostly gone.

Raimu plays well the part as it was given to him; it is not his fault if that falls short of what the novelist had in mind. He is formidable where the original was feverish, ominous where the other was possessed, absurd where the real husband was terrifying. Still, this actor produces a full-bodied and plausible character, one far more individual than the screen customarily offers. He shows the hatred and he demonstrates the revenge; he cannot, for a number of reasons, show the love and prove the triumph. The film of *The Eternal Husband*, the last one before his death in 1946, is good for our memory of Raimu. As for the memory of Dostoevsky, it is in no immediate danger from Pierre Billon's picture—or from Richard Brooks's *The Brothers Karamazov*.

Work Cited

Simmons, Ernest J. *Leo Tolstoy*. Vol. 2: *The Years of Maturity, 1880-1910*. 1946. New York: Vintage, 1960.

Une Femme douce (1969, Robert Bresson)

All of Robert Bresson's features after *Angels of the Streets* (1943) have literary antecedents of one form or another. Two are from Dostoevsky (*Une Femme douce* [*A Gentle Creature*, 1969], *Four Nights of a Dreamer* [1971]), two from Bernanos (*Mouchette* [1967], *Diary of a Country Priest* [1951]), one from Tolstoy (*L'Argent* [1983]), and one from Diderot (*Les Dames du Bois de Boulogne* [1945]), while *A Man Escaped* (1956) and *The Trial of Joan of Arc* (1962) are based on written accounts of true events. In addition, *Pickpocket* (1959) is clearly influenced by Dostoevsky's *Crime and Punishment* and *Au hasard, Balthazar* (1966) has a premise similar to the same author's *The Idiot*. *Lancelot du Lac* (1974), for its part, is derived from Sir Thomas Malory's Arthurian legends, while *The Devil Probably* (1977) was inspired by a newspaper report, as stated at the start of the film. Even a longstanding, unrealized film project of Bresson's was to come from a literary source—in this case, the Book of Genesis (*Genèse*).

By the time he completed the adaptation of *L'Argent* (*Money*) in 1983, Bresson (1901-1999) was probably the oldest active director in the world. But his evolution had been in striking contrast to that of his contemporaries. Even if we do not take into account those filmmakers whose declines had been conspicuous, most of the senior statesmen of the cinema showed in their later phases a serenity of style, an autumnal detachment from reality, which compares with that of elder artists in other genres such as the drama, the novel, and poetry. Not so with Bresson. *L'Argent*, his thirteenth and final film (freely adapted from Tolstoy's 1905 novella *The Counterfeit Note*), was made in essentially the same strict, tense, controlled style—here used in the depiction of extraordinary violence—that he used in *Les Anges du péché* (*Angels of the Streets*) in 1943.

I would like to reconsider here what I believe to be Bresson's most underrated film from a literary source: *Une Femme douce*, or *A Gentle Creature*, his first work in color and his ninth film, after the 1876 novella by Dostoevsky (sometimes called *A Gentle Spirit*). Bresson regarded Dostoevsky as the world's greatest novelist, doubtless for his spiritual strain—an almost existential one, in contrast with the sentimental religiosity of Tolstoy—because Bresson avoids the Russian's preoccupation with truth and his probing of human psychology. Put another way, this most Catholic of filmmakers (French or otherwise) always forbids the surface as well as the depths of naturalism from distracting us from the mystical moments in his films, which cannot be explicated or revealed in any positivistic manner.

Those moments, to be sure, involve cinematic characters, but Bresson makes us focus, not on the story in the human beings on screen, but on the human beings in the story and their sometimes complete lack of connection to or understanding of what happens to them. Bresson almost disconnects character from story in this way. His is an extreme reaction to decades of "dramatic" pictures, where character is action and action character; "action" movies, in which the characters are designed to fit the exciting plot; and films "of character," where the plot is designed to present interesting characters—those with a "story," that is. To the oversimplifications of character of the cinema before him, Bresson responds by not simplifying anything, by explaining almost nothing. To the self-obsession of the Hollywood star system, the "dream factory," Bresson responds in the extreme by calling for complete self-denial on the part of his actors. (Hence his designation of them as "models" [Bresson, 1].)

Let us begin simply with the plot of *A Gentle Creature,* so that we can instructively compare what Bresson and Dostoevsky do with more or less the same series of events. A contemporary young woman, unnamed, of uncertain background and insufficient means, for no apparent reason marries a pawnbroker, also unnamed, whom she meets in his shop. She tells this man that she does not love him, and she makes it very clear that she disdains his, and all, money; if she is marrying to escape her origins, it remains unclear exactly what those origins were and why she is choosing to escape them in this particular way. The woman (as she is called in the credits, like "the man") and her husband go through periods of much unhappiness—we even see her with another man at one point, but we cannot be sure that she has been unfaithful—and some calm. Then she nearly shoots her spouse to death in his sleep. Later she becomes quite ill, and, once she recovers, matters appear to be righting themselves between her and her husband. Nonetheless, she proceeds to jump to her death from the balcony of their Paris apartment.

The plot of Dostoevsky's novella, *A Gentle Spirit*, is substantially similar to this one, allowing for differences in time (mid-to-late nineteenth century) and place (the harsh Russian countryside), with one major exception: the young wife in Dostoevsky's narrative is initially very loving toward her husband, with the result that the main turns of the above plot are easily explained. The husband in the novella—he is the narrator both of the novella and of Bresson's film—distrusts, out of his own perverse obsession with verifiable as opposed to intuited truth (his Dostoevskyan surge, if you will), his wife's love for him, so he decides to test it. He is cold toward her and holds over her head the fact that he has rescued her from her poor beginnings. For these reasons, she eventually comes to hate her husband and almost to commit adultery. Finally, she is even ready to shoot him. With his wife's gun at his temple, the man awakens but does not move. Yet, she cannot fire. A religious woman, she feels great remorse and atones for her "sin" by leaping to her death while clutching a Christian icon. The wife in fact is lying on her bier at the beginning of the novella with her husband at her side, reviewing his marriage in an attempt to understand why she committed suicide. What he winds up understanding is that his own contrariness is the cause of all his unhappiness, and that all men live in unbreachable solitude.

Any such explanations of what happens in *A Gentle Creature*, however, pale beside the facts—and the facts are almost all Bresson gives us (here as elsewhere in his *oeuvre*) and all that we should consider if we are to be able to interpret his film justly. One fact that critics have inexplicably ignored, and that I take to be the foundation of any sound interpretation of *A Gentle Creature*, is the young woman's declaration in the beginning that she does not love the man she intends to marry. Put another way, it is not at all clear *why* she marries him (*her* Dostoevskyan surge, in opposition to the husband's in Dostoevsky's novella), and certainly the sum of the evidence points to the conclusion that they are so different from each other as to be nearly exact opposites. (No, the "opposites attract" theory of romance does not work here, for nothing the young woman does indicates that she is even attracted to the pawnbroker, let alone in love with him.) The pawnbroker, for his part, although he may wish to marry this woman, does not make known why, after so many years of bachelorhood, he suddenly wants to wed someone about whom he knows so little. (Bresson makes him forty or so and gives him a live-in maid-cum-assistant whom, significantly, he does not dismiss after his marriage.) Certainly he gets little or no response from his fiancée, however much he may think he loves her, and they could hardly be said to carry on anything resembling a courtship.

In a word, these two are simply not meant for each other, and I am maintaining that Bresson makes sure we know this right from the start. Bresson's subject is thus not the rise and fall of a modern marriage, say, on account of financial problems or sexual infidelity (as it is Germaine Dulac's subject in *La souriante Madame Beudet* [1922], a kind of early feminist film that deals with the problem of a husband's economic domination of his wife, and to which, in letter but not in spirit, *A Gentle Creature* bears some resemblance). The couple in *A Gentle Creature* do not even fall out in direct conflict with each other over a genuine issue that is raised in the film: the spiritually transcendent way of life over the material driven one. These two are fallen out, as it were, when they first meet.

What Bresson does in *A Gentle Creature,* then, is the reverse of what Dostoevsky does in *A Gentle Spirit.* The latter has the husband test the love of his wife and conclude that all human beings live in unbreachable solitude. Bresson has the husband and wife living in unbreachable solitude from the start and tests the duty, if not the love, toward them of the maid Anna, the character whom Bresson adds and purposefully names so that she will stand in for us, the audience. (Although Bresson could just as easily have had the husband narrate the story of his marriage alone and unseen, in intermittent voiceover, he has us watch the husband tell it to Anna in the same room where his wife's corpse lies on their marital bed; like the wife's body lying in the street after she jumps to her death, which we see at the *start* of the film, this is another telling image—the dead woman juxtaposed against the (re)union of man and maid—of the end-of-the-marriage-in-its-beginning.) Whereas Dostoevsky had used the spiritual to express the nihilistic, Bresson thus uses the nihilistic to express the spiritual.

Let me go into some detail as to how he does this, chiefly by concentrating on the contrast between the figures of the man and the woman. Since most of what we learn about her is designed solely to establish how different from the pawnbroker she is, she does not add up to a unified character of depth and originality, or "color," with whom we can readily identify. She walks into the pawnbroker's shop, and immediately the otherwise beautiful Dominique Sanda, in her first screen role (and giving more of a "performance" here than Bresson usually allowed his "models"), is unsympathetic: her clothing is drab, her hair is disheveled, she makes very little eye-contact with anyone, and her walk has about it at the same time a timidity and an urgency that make it unnerving.

The pawnbroker, by contrast, is meticulous in appearance, sparing in gesture, and steady in his walk; he looks directly at all whom he encounters (whereas his customers avert his gaze), but with eyes that one cannot look into and a face that, eerily, is neither handsome nor plain. This is clearly a man (as "modeled" by Guy Frangin) who "understands" the world and how to get along in it, as opposed to being "had" by it: money is everything to him, and what cannot be seen, touched, and stored is not worth talking about (which is one of the reasons, as he himself says, that he is unable to pray). He accumulates item after item in his pawnshop, yet we never see him sell anything: he likes his money, but apparently he likes his "things," too. His wife, on the other hand, gives away his money for worthless objects when she is working in the pawnshop; before she was married, she pawned her own last possessions in order to get a few more books to read. Her husband, for his part, has shelves of books, not one of which we ever see him take down to read.

He likes them for their "thingness," yet he will not read those books so as to rise above the world of things. The woman longs to do so, but realizes that, as a human being, she can only achieve her goal to a limited extent. She indirectly reveals this knowledge when, early in *A Gentle Creature,* she declares, "We're all—men and animals—composed of the same matter, the same raw materials." Later we have this truism visually confirmed when the young woman and her husband visit a museum of natural history, where she goes on to ask, "Do birds learn to sing from their parents, or is the ability to sing present in them at birth?"

189

The wife yearns beyond a universe in which all is such nature, nurture, *matter*, and where human beings themselves frequently seem to behave in a preconditioned manner: preconditioned to beautify the self, to marry, to reproduce, to gather wealth and possessions, to enter society, et cetera.

Throughout the film the suggestion is that, himself obsessed with possessing matter (including his wife, or her body), the husband responds to situations in a preconditioned or "correct" manner, whereas his wife responds in the most unforeseen, and sometimes bizarre, of ways. Indeed, almost all her behavior in *A Gentle Creature* is choreographed according to this ideal of the unexpected or the gratuitous. When she and her husband enter their bedroom on their wedding night, for example, the young woman quickly turns on the television set but does not watch it. The man does, but what he sees could be called the image of his own dead-end behavior pattern: cars racing in a circle. (He drives an automobile, she does not.) Later the husband will watch *horses* racing around a track on the same television, then World War II fighter planes themselves flying round in endless circles as they try to out-maneuver one another in dogfights.

Meanwhile, incongruously, the wife nearly runs about the room in preparation for bed, wrapped in a towel that dislodges itself by accident as opposed to being dislodged in an act of sexual enticement. At one point she carelessly tosses her nightgown onto the bed, in much the same way she will leave underclothes strewn about it during the day and scatters her books everywhere, showing no respect for the material, for objects or possessions. At another point, this young woman takes a bath but does not drain the dirty water and even leaves the faucet running, which her husband then turns off. Moreover, she spurns money yet likes to eat fancy pastries; she enjoys jazz but plays Bach and Purcell, too. The wife wants a bouquet so much she goes as far as to pick sunflowers alongside a road, then quickly tosses them away when she sees that, nearby, some couples are gathering their own bouquets of sunflowers.

This woman is different even in dying. (Her suicide ends as well as begins the film.) We do not get her point of view of the street before she leaps from the balcony, nor do we await her fall from below, from the position where she will soon find herself. As the wife jumps in daylight, we "innocently" see a potted plant fall off the small table from which she leaped, we watch the table topple over, and we are given a slow-motion shot of her shawl floating discursively to the ground after her—as if it were both her surviving soul or spirit and a final reminder of the unpredictability of her human nature—to be followed by a series of shadows and feet that flutter toward her dead body. (She placed a white shawl around her shoulders before jumping, even as she fingered the Christ figure retained from the gold crucifix she had pawned at her future husband's shop.) Off-camera during her fall, the young woman lands in the street, cars screech to a halt, and we await her husband's discovery of her death.

If, even in suicide, the wife's behavior has not been categorizable, has once again been somewhere "in between"—we can never predict quite where, we do not know quite why—then Bresson's camera itself is always literally somewhere in between, except when it is teasing us with a subjective camera-placement or point-of-view shot. (As when the man and woman, together with us, attend a French movie called *Benjamin* [1968, Michel Deville]—a costume drama trading on the wiles of love—and a production of *Hamlet*, i.e., the kinds of narratives or dramas, unlike *A Gentle Creature*, we are accustomed to seeing and hearing, in which we are more or less easily able to identify with the characters, their worlds, their experiences.) There are many shots of doors, of empty stairways, of the objects filling the pawnbroker's shop and his apartment. The camera is also "in between" in its representation of people: we get hands and arms cut off bodies, bodies cut off from heads, just torsos, just feet. As usual in his work, Bresson thus makes matter of the human body, even as he films the material world, the literal distance between the husband and the wife, as much to bring this matter to (spiritual) life as to emphasize the fact that these two people live in unbreachable solitude, on either side of a great chasm. The last shot of *A Gentle Creature* is of the lid to the woman's coffin being screwed tight, as the material world—the actual coffin lid, the world of things which she has at last transcended—continues to separate her, in death, from her husband, just as it did in life.

If these two characters are so permanently "separated" or irreconcilably different, one might ask, why did they choose to get married? I do not know; I do not think that they know (if they do, they do not tell us); and Bresson does not care because, as I have more than suggested, this couple's "psychology" is not the focus of *A Gentle Creature*. Perhaps the man and the woman get together out of their own perversity, but the film does not contain this idea: it just does not contradict it. Just as it does not contradict the possibility that the young woman marries the pawnbroker only because it is the unexpected thing to do. For Bresson, then, their marriage is not a relationship to be explored, but instead a device to be used.

To wit: marriage is universally perceived to be the most intimate state in which two people can live, and Bresson counterpoints this perception of ours with the almost total lack of intimacy that exists between the husband and the wife in his film. In other words, the director does not allow us to identify with the marriage of the pawnbroker and the young woman, to see ourselves in them, because he does not indicate that they marry for the reasons *we* usually associate with marrying: love, money, convenience, convention, children. They wed, they are unhappy, they reach a fragile understanding, then she kills herself. The husband, in his narration—it is not narration in the proper sense, but more on this later—attempts to discover why his wife committed suicide, but he cannot find an answer. He does not know why she killed herself, nor do we, and neither does Bresson.

My point is not that every human action in *A Gentle Creature* is without explanation, without cause or motive—for instance, the wife's near murder of her husband after he discovers her with another man *can* be accounted for—but that these individual explanations become beside the point when one considers that there is no explanation in the film as to why the pawnbroker and the young woman got married in the first place. What becomes important, therefore, is not so much their relationship with each other as our relationship with each of them, and Anna's with the pawnbroker. This is why the camera shifts periodically from *its* illustration of past events to the husband pacing back and forth in the bedroom in the present, telling *his* story of the marriage: not only to point up that *neither* narrative account provides the "answers," but also to emphasize that this man, as character or person apart from his story, is the proper focus of our concerns. As is his wife, literally apart from her story in death, lying in the road at the beginning of the film even as she lies there at its conclusion.

Clearly, then, Bresson wants more from us than our "understanding" of the husband and wife's relationship, our feeling sorry for them for their frailties and obsessions, because ultimately this is only feeling sorry for ourselves; or it is making these characters do the work of our living, which is too easy. The remarkable aspect of this film is that we do much of the feeling and querying for the actors, not in identification with them as they do it, but *in their place*: we feel and query for them as we imagine they would. And this has the effect of making us think absolutely about their situation, instead of about theirs plus our own. Bresson, in this way, wants us to feel for and care about characters whom we do not "recognize," who reveal as little that is "like us" as possible, namely, the heights and depths of strong emotion: love, hate, anger, regret, happiness, sadness.

To this end, Bresson forces his actors to deny themselves in their portrayal of their characters. He denies *himself* in his shooting of these characters: for the most part, the camera is held steady in the middle distance, there is no panning or tracking, and there are no high- and low-angle shots— objectivity or distance that Bresson can afford because of the very lack of appeal of his main characters. The director asks us in turn to deny ourselves in our perception of these characters and their actions. He demands that we pay attention to the husband and wife for themselves, no matter how uninviting or inexpressive they may appear, no matter how their story resembles little more than a skimpy newspaper report.

The fact that, as in the case of *A Gentle Creature*, Bresson almost always made his films from preexisting texts should be a signal that he was not interested in the creation of original character for its own sake, or even in the re-creation of traditionally arresting and appealing character (which is one reason we never learn the name of the husband or wife). The fact that he frequently began his films by telling us what would happen at the end should be a signal, as well: that he was not primarily concerned to tell stories for the suspense they could create. Related to this, the effect of having the husband narrate parts of the story to Anna, the enactment of which parts we then see in flashback, is less to show us discrepancies in the husband's version as compared with "what really happened," than to obliterate the newness or freshness of story, the interest in it per se—precisely through the filming of both the husband's narration and its subsequent repetition in action instead of words.

Bresson asks us, not to fully fathom this "double-narrative," to decipher the how and why of the whole story, but simply to believe that it occurred and to take witness if not pity. His is a nearly perverse demand, which is to say a kind of religious one. If we can comply and perform the requisite act of faith, of utter selflessness, together with a leap of the imagination, *A Gentle Creature* becomes for us something resembling a religious or spiritual experience. It becomes an experience, moreover, that also teaches an important aesthetic lesson: that we must acknowledge the existence of the inexplicable in, as well as beyond, art.

According to this view, it is art's job not to make people and the world more intelligible than they are, but instead to re-present their mystery or ineffableness, their integrity or irreducibility, if you will, their connection to something irretrievably their own or some other's—like God himself. (I am not the first to assert that Bresson invokes mystery or "otherness" in *A Gentle Creature*, as in a number of his films; but I differ with other critics in my suggestion that Bresson is invoking mystery not for mystery's sake alone, but for the sake of exalting the human, of calling his audience's attention at once to the magisterially divine and the intrinsically worthy in all human beings.) All may not be grace for the young woman at the end of *A Gentle Creature*, then, as it was for the *curé* of Ambricourt at the conclusion of Bresson's *Diary of a Country Priest*, who utters these words of spiritual certitude ("All is grace") as he is dying. But all is not nothingness, either.

Anna the maid seems to have learned the lesson of inexplicability or irreducibility from life rather than art, for she knows as little as we do about the motives for, and causes of, the husband's and the wife's behavior, yet she utters not one querying or querulous word to either of them in the course of the picture. Indeed, Anna utters only a few lines through all of *A Gentle Creature*. Yes, she is the couple's maid, but her silence and impassivity (especially as she is played by Jane Lobré) here appear to go beyond the call of a servant's duty. Before the end of the film, Anna leaves the room in which she has quietly listened to the husband's narrative of his and his wife's relationship, but she will not leave him. She will remain with him during and after the funeral of the young woman because, as the husband himself admits, *he will need her*.

Bresson, by implication, asks the same of us: that, figuratively speaking, we do not desert this man in his time of need, that we recognize his humanity despite the fact we cannot comprehend his, or his marriage's deepest secrets. If there is anyone in *A Gentle Creature* with whom we should "identify," then, it is Anna. And if it can be said we identify with the husband and wife at all, it is in the sense, as I have implied, that they seem as puzzled by what is happening to them as we are. This is not only character almost disconnected from story, it is character nearly disconnected from *self*. Thus, are we disconnected from *our* selves, our certain egos, and made to look, not for the moral or balance in the story, the symmetry of feeling and form, of ideas and execution, but simply and inescapably for the only remaining tie that binds us to the characters depicted on screen: the human one, or the only one that cannot be explained away.

As one can doubtless deduce from my concentration above on *A Gentle Creature*'s method, Bresson's films are even more distinguished for their method or their style than for their individual subject matter. That is because Bresson's subjects pale beside his treatment of them, so much so that it is almost as if the director were making the same movie time after time. How ironic, or perhaps appropriate, that he filmed number nine in color (though elegantly understated or "innocent" color it is, as photographed by Ghislain Cloquet) because, as he later wrote in *Notes on Cinematography* (1975), he felt color was more true to life (Bresson, 55). Like André Bazin's true filmmaker, Bresson thus attained his power through his method, which is less a thing literally to be described or expressed (as in such terms as color, deep focus, handheld camerawork, and long takes) than an inner orientation enabling an outward quest. That quest, in Bresson's case, is (this is not too strong) to honor God's universe by using film to render the reality of that universe, and, through its reality, both the miracle of its creation and the mystery of its being.

Works Cited

Bresson, Robert. *Notes on Cinematography*. 1975. Trans. Jonathan Griffin. New York: Urizen Books, 1977.

Dostoevsky, Fyodor. *A Gentle Spirit: A Fantastic Story*. Trans. Constance Garnett. New York: Minton, Balch, and Company, 1931.

The Red Badge of Courage (1951, John Huston)

It is easy to say of John Huston's 1951 production of Stephen Crane's *The Red Badge of Courage* that it is a pictorially striking, often quite beautiful picture; beyond that it is not at all easy to know what to say.

Stephen Crane's 1895 novel presents formidable problems for the dramatic adapter. In the first place, and despite the violent, multitudinous events it records, the true action of the story occurs within the mind of the youth, Henry Fleming. The heart of the book is a long interior monologue, and that is not readily staged (particularly with the inexperienced and impassive Audie Murphy in the role). Nor do you escape the difficulty by having passages—well selected, to be sure—from Crane's text read by a commentator.

Second, Crane's dialogue is not the best side of his art. His instinct for realism, his wish to make books talk as men talk, was sounder than his ear, and the conversations of his soldiers are not only antique; they are often preposterous. Furthermore, Murphy and his partner in this film, Bill Mauldin, are so obviously unwilling to believe in oaths like "by the eternal thunders" and "gee rod" that their lines fall cold at their feet. The more experienced members of their supporting cast, John Dierkes and Andy Devine in particular, handle their improbable speeches a good deal better, but it is still hapless dialogue.

There remains, finally, the problem of projecting the moral struggle and the moral victory onto the screen. Why did the youth who fled in panic yesterday, return today a possessed and inspiring hero? Was it merely possession, a hysteria induced by shame and desperation and exhaustion? That is what it looks to be in this picture, but surely that is not what Crane meant. "He had been to touch the great death and found that, after all, it was but the great death." Or as writers have been saying ever since Crane, it is the fear of fear that makes us cowards.

The change in the youth is a thing you can experience from the novel, for you not only see what he sees but know what the sights are doing to him: Crane and his hero were very close and the reader partakes of that intimacy. But on the screen, Henry is a distant and tragic figure, first running, crazed, away from battle and then running, still crazed, into battle. The direction of flight seems immaterial; the fact that he survives seems ridiculous. And the voice reciting Crane is not much assistance—you cannot listen to prose, even beautiful prose, as you watch men leap and scream and die in torment.

It strikes me that Huston saw all these problems and attempted to escape them by making a tapestry of *The Red Badge of Courage*. It is a film of exquisitely heightened reality, so clear, so detailed, so lovingly designed that it looks again and again like a series of Civil War engravings brought magically to life. If you think of Huston's movie as a sort of dance-poem inspired by *The Red Badge*, and if you come to it fresh enough from a reading of the book to remember what the youth felt as the noise and terror and pain swept toward him, engulfed him, and finally receded and left him whole, the production may be an exciting experience. But as a dramatization of the novel in any sense of being its equivalent, it is baffling, often unconvincing, in the end unsatisfying.

Moby Dick (1956, John Huston)

John Huston's *Moby Dick* (1956) so closely parallels the events in Herman Melville's 1851 novel that it might well be a chronicle of the very voyage that impelled the writer to his masterwork. The three mates are on hand—Flask, Stubb, and Starbuck—and the three savage harpoonists, as well. Ishmael gazes out from the masthead, the carpenter planes Queequeg's coffin planks by candlelight, and the ivory-pegged captain paces the dark deck as the crew below listens in admiration and fear. The white whale is sighted, chased, lost, sighted again. The harpoons and the lances are driven home, Ahab flings himself to death on the hulk of his dying enemy, and the beast turns on the *Pequod* and drives her under the sea, leaving only Ishmael to bring back the news. Countless such histories were brought back to the people of New Bedford, Massachusetts.

The picture is scrupulously cast and performed with respect for the strength and courage of the sea hunters. Huston has no time for characterization at any depth; but he gives the men of the *Pequod* the grace of their terrible trade and stays quite clear of the quaintness that cheapens so many period films. His straightforward and uncluttered photography is shot in a subdued Technicolor that at last brings the spectrum down to a range that the mind will accept as true color. This is good work and possibly it is as much of *Moby Dick* as can he transferred to the screen. Huston obviously was trying to convey more than mere chronicle. Otherwise he would not have devoted a disproportionate space to the prophetic sermon on Jonah and God's will; nor have retained—when so much else is cut—Elijah's ominous warning or Captain Ahab's speech on the spirit of crippling evil he pursues through and behind the body of the white whale.

But what Huston hopes to imply beyond the events does not really register—too much else has been jettisoned, the style of the picture is too circumstantial, the voyage too plainly a hunt, not a quest. And Ahab himself is so mishandled as to prevent the picture from reaching beyond a tale of high sensation. The sound of the captain overhead in the night, his closed cabin door, his sudden appearance to presage the first sighting of whales—these details begin to build an image that could be Melville's Ahab. But then the director remembers the close-up and suddenly you are staring rudely into the twitching face of Gregory Peck. It is not Peck's fault—he does what he is told to do, which is roll up the whites of his eyes, break into a cold sweat, and talk with voice from the grave.

The fault is in the Hollywood convention that emotion should be communicated by close-ups. Humor can be communicated so, and occasionally passive loveliness. But passion always evaporates in embarrassment when you can count the hairs in an actor's eyebrows. Actors have arms and legs, back and shoulders; they have been taught, or should have been, to move to more purpose than other men. These are the tools of their trade. But Hollywood sells faces— six feet high and two inches from your nose. An actor thus becomes a trademark and is robbed of the chance to create an idea.

Ahab may have been a man possessed or he may have been a fallen angel; in any case, he was not one to be stared at like a lunatic in a cage. I don't know that Peck could have created, or any other actor could create, the idea of Ahab, but given the courtesy of distance he might at least have suggested the "more" that Huston hoped his *Moby Dick* would contain.

The Sun Also Rises (1957, Henry King) & Other Hemingway Fiction

There has always been something so deceptively simple about Ernest Hemingway's prose style, with its terse, pungent statements and vivid choice of adjectives, which critics liked to describe it as cinematic. His novels, even his short stories, they said, resembled movie scripts—all dialogue and quick description, colloquial rather than literary. (This was not always intended as praise.) It remained for the movie companies, however, to put this to the test. And the results have, in most instances, merely underscored the obvious, that Hemingway had created a literary form very much his own, with only the most superficial resemblance to film. As Edmund Wilson noted as long ago as 1924, Hemingway's seeming simplicity "serves actually to convey profound emotions and complex states of mind" (Wilson, 340). The pictures drawn from his works have tended to stay on the surface, preserving the sound while missing the substance. Presumably, most of them were as embarrassing to Hemingway (if he ever saw them) as to his admirers.

One thing that attracted the studios to Hemingway's books long before he became established either as a bestselling or a prizewinning novelist was his instinct for a good title. In fact, for the first Hemingway title to hit the screen, *Men Without Women*, Fox tossed out the 1927 book altogether and concocted a submarine yarn from scratch (1930, John Ford). The 1932 film version (Frank Borzage) of the 1929 novel *A Farewell to Arms* (made with Gary Cooper and Helen Hayes—and with an alternate happy ending in which Catherine survives) sweetened the original so much that Hemingway shied away from the movie companies completely for the next decade. Then *For Whom the Bell Tolls* (1943, Sam Wood) scrupulously avoided every political implication in the 1940 novel; and *To Have and Have Not* (1944, Howard Hawks) retained so little of his original, 1937 narrative that Warner Brothers was able to do it all over again in 1950 as *The Breaking Point* (this time, ironically, playing it considerably closer to the author's intentions), as directed by Michael Curtiz. Both *The Killers* (1946, Robert Siodmak) and *The Snows of Kilimanjaro* (1952, Henry King) were built from short stories (1927 and 1936, respectively) with materials not even suggested in the originals—and in *Snows* a last-minute air evacuation of the dying Harry Street was tossed in for good measure. Small wonder that Hemingway often looked askance at Hollywood.

Let's take "My Old Man" (1923) as a case study in ill-adaptation. This title runs to fourteen-and-a-half pages in the Modern Library edition (1938) of Hemingway's short stories. It is a spare tale, much of it told by implication. A boy recalls the days when he tagged along after his father, a jockey reduced by age and an unsavory reputation to riding third-rate horses on the tenth-rate tracks of Italy and France. He recalls also his desolation when, a few minutes after the "old man" was killed in a steeplechase, he heard two strangers speak of his father with hatred and contempt.

"My Old Man" is a very good story, but there was not enough factual meat in it to provide Hollywood with a feature picture. Casey Robinson, who adapted it for Twentieth Century-Fox into something called *Under My Skin* (1950, Jean Negulesco), therefore had to do a major job of embroidery. He invented a nightclub singer, a Hollywood-coated version of Edith Piaf with a weakness for heels; he blew up a couple of passing sentences from the narrative into a sadistic killer bent on exterminating the jockey; Robinson built the shadowy horseman-father into a robust, two-fisted braggart, big enough but not interesting enough to be played by John Garfield; and he interpolated a number of horse races.

None of this works any improvement on Hemingway, but it can perhaps be excused on the ground that Hollywood had to supply what the reader could only imagine. What cannot be excused is that the story should be debased into a kind of sordid *Sorrell and Son* (1925, Warwick Deeping), with the father battling his bad luck and worst impulses to protect his manly little tyke from unwholesome influences—and at the end killing himself in a supreme effort to regain his son's respect. *Under My Skin* is a sentimental tearjerker, a kind of entertainment to which Hemingway was not at all addicted.

Only once, in the memorable *The Old Man and the Sea* (1958, John Sturges; from the 1952 novel), did the studios earnestly attempt to capture both the spirit and the letter of his writings. Even so, despite the persistent attempts of screenwriters to "lick" the Hemingway stories into acceptable formulas for film entertainment, the vigor of his characters and the intriguing situations that he invented for them continued to fascinate the studios. However much they might have shied away from his ethical concerns, his testing of the nature of courage and the meaning of defeat, they recognized that in his best works he set in motion real people, people whose lives reflected the tensions and traumas of a real world. In a word, they were the kind of people the screen needed. If, as James Agee pointed out, the film version of *To Have and Have Not* "jettisoned a solid 90 per cent of the novel" (Agee, 353), if *The Macomber Affair* (1947, from the 1936 short story) and *The Snows of Kilimanjaro* were tidied up with meaningless endings (or rather, endings that negated their meanings), nevertheless, intrinsic to characters like Harry Morgan, Francis Macomber, and Harry Street was an indestructible fiber, an ingrained attitude toward life that carried through an astonishing amount of Hemingway's intention. Not even the superannuated stars of *The Sun Also Rises* (1957, Henry King; from the 1926 novel) could wholly mask the youthful disenchantment and despair of his death-seeking quintet of expatriates—although they *did* wear their masks a bit uncomfortably.

Indeed, the producers should have done Hemingway the courtesy of putting another title on *The Sun Also Rises*. Something like *The Nymph and the Masochists* would get the idea across better and at the same time suggest that this is not really the book that lighted the way for a whole generation of fiction and jelled for many a definition of expatriate rootlessness that even a second world war could not entirely dissolve. The picture is not only not Hemingway's novel, it is not much of a story in its own terms. It has been made as a romance between Jake Barnes and Lady Brett, but what kind of romance can it be when the army doctor has solemnly sworn that poor Jake will never make love again? There is no way of resolving the situation, and the picture fritters off into an account of how Brett is so restless that she jilts Robert Cohn, jilts Mike Campbell, jilts Romero, the amorous bullfighter, while Jake waits around to take her on evening walks between bouts. The characters keep assuring one another that they are the lost generation, but the only thing this crowd has lost is Jake's potency. The symbol has been taken for the content, with predictably ludicrous results.

It is always disconcerting when stars with faces as familiar as your own are used to impersonate famous fictional characters. It would never have occurred to me that Jake Barnes looked like Tyrone Power or that Robert Cohn had as elegant a profile as Mel Ferrer. Errol Flynn, as Mike Campbell, the alcoholic highland chief, is more plausible—at least you are more impressed by the fact that he is very large and very drunk than that he is Errol Flynn. Ava Gardner suffers the disadvantage of being presented as the woman no man can resist, a statement that immediately sets you to wondering why it should be so. She gives the impression of being a good-natured, not very experienced, American working girl on an awful binge. In fact, all of Hemingway's sadly wise young people turn out to be surprisingly healthy and unscarred. When the liquor and the bulls were finally used up, I felt (when I saw the film in college) that we should all report to the dean's office for a stern lecture on loose behavior in the dormitories.

Perhaps the greatest obstacle to getting Hemingway *qua* Hemingway on the screen, however, was neither the myopia of producers, the obduracy of censors, nor the insensitivity of script writers, but Hemingway's own literary style. He once said that "a writer of fiction has to invent out of what he knows in order to make something not photographic, or naturalistic, or realistic, which will be something entirely new and invented out of his own knowledge" (Bruccoli, 77). At his best, he succeeded all too well—so well, indeed, as to make his writing seem photographic nonetheless. But the secret of Brett and her star-crossed companions was not to be found in externals, not in the bistros and bullfights to which the cameras assiduously accompanied them. It lay in the overtones of words on paper, as Hemingway had learned to use them. The sense of a scene was imbedded neither in the speeches nor in the action, the special provinces of the microphone and the camera, but in the clang of connotations rising from Hemingway's language, sentence structure, and even punctuation. As a result, although the film version of *The Sun Also Rises* used many scenes from the book, and retained a considerable amount of the dialogue as well, their deeper implications were missing.

Works Cited

Agee, James. Review of Howard Hawks's film of Hemingway's *To Have and Have Not. Agee on Film: Reviews and Comments*. New York: McDowell Obolensky, 1958. 353.

Bruccoli, Matthew J., ed. *Conversations with Ernest Hemingway*. Jackson: University Press of Mississippi, 1986.

Wilson, Edmund. "Hemingway: *Three Stories and Ten Poems* (1923) and *In Our Time* (1924)." *The Dial*, 77 (Oct. 1924): 340-341.

Sanctuary (1961, Tony Richardson) & Other Faulkner Fiction

Faulkner country may not be everybody's cup of tea, but it fast became anybody's game, and the inhabitants of Yoknapatawpha (which lies in the environs of Oxford, Mississippi) the modern counterparts of the Jukes and the Kallikaks—cultural shorthand for the rural poor of the southern United States. The fictional bloodlines of the Sartorises, the Snopeses, and the Drakes subsequently coursed across the screen on several occasions in the mid-twentieth century, traced by a variety of writers, directors, and producers—and not always with the blessing of their creator.

William Faulkner, in his relation to the movies, was content to take the cash and let the credit go. One can only hope that for *Sanctuary*, the 1961 filmic incursion into Yoknapatawpha (from Faulkner's 1931 novel), he was well paid. Temple Drake's tawdry story, of course, was never the brightest jewel in Faulkner's crown (although that has not kept it from being perhaps the most widely read). An outright shocker, it combined lurid sex with one of the most fascinating portraits of pure evil in modern fiction: the impotent, sadistic, stunted Popeye. The movie, as might be expected, retains a good many of the racier situations; but it is completely unable to cope with Popeye.

Given the more euphonious sobriquet of Candy, and played by Yves Montand, he emerges as a dime-novel embodiment of illicit romance—so much so that when he springs, phoenix-like, into the second half of the picture (based on 1951's *Requiem for a Nun*) some five years later, Temple rushes off to bed with him. Curiously, this masculation of Popeye serves as the final flattener to a film already turgid with the tangled motivations and synthetic dénouements wrung from *Requiem*. Despite earnest performances by Lee Remick, Bradford Dillman, and Odetta Holmes—plus standout work from many of the atmospheric "bit" players—the picture comes to life only fitfully, and then in scenes that are at best tangential to the story itself. Tony Richardson, the director, seems to have steeped himself in the look and feel of the Deep South in the late 1920s, but was unable to cope with his—or Faulkner's—characters.

Faulkner country, his mythical Yoknapatawpha County, is the scene of almost a dozen of his books and innumerable short stories, including the 1940 novel *The Hamlet*. In 1958, three years before the film of *Sanctuary*, a film called *The Long, Hot Summer* (Martin Ritt) was based chiefly on *The Hamlet*, together with Faulkner's 1931 novella *Spotted Horses* and his 1939 short story "Barn Burning." (*The Tarnished Angels* [Douglas Sirk], adapted from the 1935 novel *Pylon*, was made in 1957 but also released in 1958, and *The Sound and the Fury* [Martin Ritt], from the 1929 novel of the same name, arrived in 1959.)

The Long, Hot Summer is, to put it mildly, a free adaptation of Faulkner. The filmmakers changed the name, of course, so people wouldn't confuse the picture with that other *Hamlet*. But *The Hamlet*, too, had to be considerably changed before they could even begin to make a film out of it. Actually, Faulkner's novel is little more than a series of loosely connected stories dealing with the weasel-like Snopeses, white-trash parvenus who spread like a sickness throughout Yoknapatawpha at the turn of the twentieth century. From *The Hamlet* the screenwriters borrowed scenes or situations, incorporating them into an overall narrative framework of their own devising. But Faulkner is full of ideas, and this picture spins with incidents. They have been homogenized to produce a fable of togetherness, yet, even so, the original inventive energy of Faulkner's fiction manages to work its way to the surface.

The resulting picture closely resembles William Inge's *Picnic* (play, 1953), with bits of Tennessee Williams' *Baby Doll* (film, 1956) leering around the edges and a pinch of Eudora Welty tossed in for seasoning. I don't mind the free and easy use of Faulkner, but I wish the adaptation hadn't come out looking so much like the work of other people. As a yarn spinner, Faulkner differs from Inge and Williams (if not Welty) by measure of a biting wit, and some of the material used here was wickedly funny in its first form. The film is full of wild laughter and ribald suggestion, but the effect is more country-club sexy than back-country Rabelaisian. The whole affair might have come closer to Faulkner's rough folkways if the Technicolor cinematography (by Joseph LaShelle) had not varnished Yoknapatawpha County as prettily as a travel-magazine excursion.

In the movie version, Flem Snopes (or Ben Quick) is transformed into a far more sympathetic character, the domineering Will Varner given a dimension of broad humor, and the time updated to the present of the 1950s. Orson Welles (got up with plastic nose and a terrible wheeze) plays the aging stud Varner with such roaring high spirits that one keeps expecting the other members of the cast to address him as "Big Daddy"—the larger-than-life character from Williams' 1955 play *Cat on a Hot Tin Roof*. Indeed, the actors in *The Long, Hot Summer* tend to precede frank passages with a slight gulp and a popping of the eyes. Welles cuts about like a veteran of the Grand Ole Opry; Paul Newman, as the provocative stranger Quick, faces up to him with the Method. It's a good match in personality projection, even if it seems a little studied for first-rate acting.

The long, hot summer of 1958, then, may have been when the movies discovered—or undiscovered—William Faulkner. I should say "fully discovered," because another, perhaps more fortunate film adaptation of the Mississippi master preceded those discussed above: *Intruder in the Dust* (1949, Clarence Brown).

Now few of Faulkner's readers could have been happy about his novel of the same title, published only a year before the making of the movie version. It was an awkward book written to demonstrate an awkward point of view. Faulkner, a man of highly developed moral awareness, was sincere in his belief that the South has an inalienable mandate to make its peace with the black man in its own time and with no interference or persuasion from outsiders; he did not recognize, certainly, the killing sterility of his credo that "we alone in the United States are a homogeneous people . . . that only from homogeneity comes anything of a people or for a people of durable and lasting value" (Faulkner, 153-154). Nevertheless, his novel betrays him.

The plot is implausibly melodramatic even for a writer who customarily employs garish incident with an easy persuasiveness (a fresh grave is violated, not once but three times, in the span of a day). One principal character is a black, Lucas Beauchamp, whom an illegitimate but aristocratic heritage has endowed with both the appearance and the personality of an eagle. For decades, Beauchamp has been permitted—improbably, or at least most atypically—to display a royal contempt for white men in a community where blacks are not permitted to lift their eyes. Only by being caught with a gun in his hand and a body at his feet is he finally brought to bay.

The other main figure is Chick, a high-school boy, through whose mind—as he desperately digs up corpses in an attempt to save Beauchamp from a lynch mob—passes a twisted panorama of Southern guilt and glory. The boy is haunted, but the ghosts are not his: they are Faulkner's. A third personality, Chick's uncle, is merely the author, walking by the boy's side and confusing him with a lecture that mixes civil rights and due process of law with a mystique of the blood that will never produce either. The book has beauty of detail—in insights and images—as has almost all of Faulkner's work, but as a whole it makes one wonder if his genius was nourished or depleted by the long years of isolation in Oxford, Mississippi.

This novel Metro-Goldwyn-Mayer has brought to the screen with partial fidelity and an almost excessive reverence. The plot has been simplified (one murder and one midnight exhumation have been eliminated), and it is a reflection on Faulkner's craftsmanship that the tailoring has done his narrative no harm. On the other hand, the implications of the novel are made to fade. What remains are the statements that a small group of honorable Southerners, given luck and a most unusual set of circumstances, can frustrate the hunger of a lynch mob, and that as long as lynching remains even a possibility, the conscience of the South cannot be clean. That, to be fair, is quite a lot for a picture to say, but it only begins to carry forward Faulkner's argument.

The film is admirably staged (in and around Oxford) by director Clarence Brown, but it was made by people who knew they were walking on eggs. Awe for Faulkner and a regard for the sensitivity of both North and South to the kind of discussion at hand produce a movie in which the characters move stiffly between guide ropes and recite lines that are placed in their mouths. The only actors who carry out their roles with relaxed conviction are Juano Hernandez, as Beauchamp, and Claude Jarman Jr., as the boy, Chick. The others, among them David Brian, Elizabeth Patterson, and Will Geer, seem time after time to be catching themselves up, anxiously watching for signals as they go about their work.

It is yet true that *Intruder in the Dust* is a skillful, baleful thriller with overtones of the South's moldering conscience. This is a picture so well-intentioned that one is astonished by the inexcusable detail of mongrelizing Chick's black chum Aleck (Elzie Emanuel) into a comic type whose eyes roll in the presence of tombstones. Faulkner does not make that kind of vulgar mistake. The movies *did* in the decades preceding the Civil Rights movement . . . and beyond.

Work Cited

Faulkner, William. *Intruder in the Dust.* New York: Vintage, 1996.

The Great Gatsby (1949, Elliot Nugent; 1974, Jack Clayton)

"So we beat on, boats against the current, borne back ceaselessly into the past" (Fitzgerald, 180). As college boys, a lot of us used to quote that line, the closing sentence of *The Great Gatsby* (1925). None of us knew quite what it meant, but it sounded more meaningful to us than any single line printed since the death of Shakespeare. It fitted a mood of melancholic self-disgust stemming partly from our own youth (as members of the Vietnam generation), but also reflecting the lackluster excesses and revulsions of the much older generation to which Fitzgerald belonged. Like all his books, *The Great Gatsby* was Fitzgerald's attempt to write an obituary for his decade and thus, perhaps, to lay its ghost to rest. But he did not live to get the words quite right, and though the answer may have been in Jay Gatsby, the book never worked very well as a key.

In 1949 *Gatsby* was made into a movie (Elliot Nugent) for the first time, a quite literal transposition that manages to lose the whole book. Gatsby, that figure of a self-destroyed man who had stolen even his illusions, appears as an example of young American resourcefulness, trim and ready for anything, and tripped up only because he didn't realize that nice people also play dirty. As Alan Ladd acts him, a little tough, a little boyish, quite definitely noble, he is a man to pity. But who ever had the resources or the effrontery to pity Gatsby?

Well, the times changed, and by 1949 people had become lost in different ways. But the color of Gatsby could have been recaptured by a company that understood his peculiar innocence, the naïveté of a man who kills himself and then starts planning a honeymoon. Still, as pictures go, *The Great Gatsby* is good enough. The brittle, inconsequential plot makes a clearly defined scenario and Betty Field, Ruth Hussey, MacDonald Carey, and Howard Da Silva play well opposite Ladd in what they understand to be a morbid melodrama of Long Island society. The monstrous spectacles of Dr. T. J. Eckleburg, glaring over the garbage dumps, don't seem to mean much anymore, but the story has been given a small subsidiary happy ending. What you lose one way, you gain another. Sort of.

The 1974 film adaptation of *The Great Gatsby* makes the 1949 version and Herbert Brenon's 1926 silent version before it (the 2013 adaptation, by Baz Luhrmann, is beneath comment) look like twin pinnacles of art. (For me, *Gatsby* on film is my memory of Warner Baxter in the 1926 adaptation, floating on his deserted pool in a moment of lonely, autumnal melancholy just before he is shot.) Every single aspect of the 1974 film is bad. Even Robert Redford, fine actor and attractive man, presents a Gatsby who is a dopey mooner instead of a subtle, large exponent of an American tragedy—a man for whom the romances of Money and Romance are inseparable, a compulsive feeder on illusions who insists that they must be true because the facts of his worldly accomplishments are true, and, saddest of all, a believer in "the green light, the orgiastic future that year by year recedes before us" (Fitzgerald, 180).

Redford, then, is at once too handsome and too dull (Gatsby was awkward, but hardly dull). However, he probably does as well as anyone could, since Gatsby is an impossible figure, an illusion in a pink suit who somehow sums up all that was endearing, outrageous, and fatally optimistic about the 1920s. Gatsby, naturally enough, is the figure in the book who never comes quite clear. He never comes clear to Nick Carraway, the narrator, and almost all we know of him is Nick's attempt to get down on paper Gatsby's wild romanticism and faintly sinister reticence, his shockingly accurate understanding of what America means by success and his pathetically immature infatuation with what lyric writers mean by love.

If Redford ultimately fails as Gatsby, then failure is too kind a word for Mia Farrow as Daisy Buchanan, a skeleton in *amour*; or Bruce Dern as her husband, Tom Buchanan, supposedly a well-bred gentleman who despises his *parvenu* neighbor, Gatsby, but who looks and sounds like a shoe clerk with cold manners and mean eyes. (I wish Tom hadn't been made to run through the public rooms of the Plaza Hotel, screaming threats and insults at Gatsby. Tom was a bully, but he staged his scenes in private.) Then there's Lois Chiles as Jordan, another cover girl trying to be an actress; or Karen Black as Myrtle, a writing gargoyle; or Sam Waterston, who looks right enough as Nick but whose voice is stultifyingly boring. Since he does a great deal of voice-over narration, Waterston hurts the picture a great deal.

The '74 *Great Gatsby* is a meticulous job of adaptation, as such things go, the plot and indeed much of the dialogue having been lifted (by screenwriter Francis Ford Coppola) intact from Fitzgerald's novel, the surroundings having been re-created at God knows what cost, and the cast having been coached by the director, Jack Clayton, into at least a superficial impersonation of rich and desperate people back in those Calvin Coolidge days of Prohibition. This is respectful work, yet it is appalling. Perhaps the quickest way to explain what is wrong with the picture is to say that it was, and is, unnecessary. When it sticks close to the original, it adds nothing; when it deviates, it puts a heavy foot into Fitzgerald's magic, turning his suggestions into visual blatancies. Overall, this version's most conspicuous weakness is that it cannot handle vulgarity or ostentation without itself becoming vulgar or ostentatious.

A couple of examples: when Nick Carraway goes over to East Egg to renew a friendship with his cousin, Daisy, Tom greets him by riding up on a polo pony. In the book, Tom is in riding clothes, but Fitzgerald didn't think it necessary to supply a horse. In the film, Nick goes for the first time to one of Gatsby's parties, is tapped on the shoulder by a grim-faced bodyguard, taken upstairs in a private elevator, and thrust into an Abercrombie & Fitch gent's study to meet his host. In the book, Nick, talking with a stranger at a table in the garden, says: "This is an unusual party for me. I haven't even seen the host" (Fitzgerald, 47). And the other replies: "I'm Gatsby. . . . I thought you knew, old sport" (Fitzgerald, 48). Why spoil that with the gangster flummery, as if we were witnessing a scene out of *The Godfather* (1972)? Because in fact we only think we know that Gatsby was a gangster: the whole dreamlike, terrifying, and infinitely sad tone of the book hangs precisely on the point that we don't really know anything about Gatsby, and yet he is by far the most real presence in the story.

Gatsby imposes himself unforgettably because he is as much a symbol of those post-World War I years of elaborate masquerade and unjustified gaiety as are the empty eyes of Dr. Eckleburg, staring out on the purgatory of auto junkyards and burning rubbish that one had to cross to get from Manhattan to the strip of wealthy playground that once edged the North Shore of Long Island. Fitzgerald wrote an aquatint of a story, very light, very deft, a little indistinct, leaving a good deal to the reader's understanding of the several levels of Hell, but with details that leap from the page and haunt you forever. The movie people turned this, in 1974, into a mammoth painting in oils, making every Fitzgerald allusion into a fact, helping the author by filling in any areas that he did not cover with his pencil, proving point by point that theirs is the authentic, permanent record of a work that, despite its delicacy, still shows no sign of fading. *The Great Gatsby* is a short book—astonishingly short and unassuming, when you think what it has meant to us now for close to 100 years. You can read it in less time than you would spend in a movie theater, watching Fitzgerald's pastel threnody turned into acetate.

Much of the movie's failure must be held accountable to the producer, David Merrick, but at least as much is accountable to the director. Jack Clayton accepted the above collection of incompetencies and inadequacies, and he directed the wretched performances. He once made a good picture—*Room at the Top*, in 1959, from the 1957 novel by John Braine. How Clayton's undistinguished career since then led him to this job is one of Movieland's higher mysteries. Besides the tininess of ear he shows, he insists on an utterly inappropriate atmosphere of quasi-expressionist grotesquerie—sweaty faces, fish-eye lenses, Gatsby's parties as somewhat degenerate debauches—an atmosphere that stupidly controverts the reticence of Fitzgerald's novel. To make matters just a little worse, Clayton slams an enormous number of enormous close-ups at us, quite pointlessly, which is rather as if a music composer worked steadily in loud chords. Nelson Riddle's own music is even more heavy-handed—in fact ridiculous. Douglas Slocombe's color cinematography, previously encountered in *Jesus Christ Superstar* (1973, Norman Jewison), is equally subtle here.

In sum, this picture is a total failure of every requisite sensibility: a long, slow, sickening bore. When the filmmakers first thought about making it, they should simply have asked themselves, "How will we handle Gatsby?", realized that it couldn't be done, and taken their hands off Fitzgerald's fragile masterpiece. They didn't, and the result is that, over the years up to the present day, millions of people who have not read the book have seen, or will see, the movie and never know what they missed. It doesn't matter which movie—the 1974, 1949, 1926, or 2013 version of *The Great Gatsby*. None of them are the novel, and none of them could be; none of them transmute the novel, and—what's worse—none of them realized they couldn't.

Work Cited

Fitzgerald, F. Scott. *The Great Gatsby*. 1925. New York: Scribner, 2004.

Wise Blood (1979, John Huston)

John Huston's career was eclectically ambitious, in an idle way. He took on a number of good books, of widely different varieties, and wrestled some of them onto the screen successfully: *The Maltese Falcon* (1941), *The African Queen* (1951), *The Treasure of the Sierra Madre* (1948), and (a short story) *The Man Who Would Be King* (1975). On the other hand, he had no hesitation about tackling such numbers as *The Red Badge of Courage* (1951), *Moby Dick* (1956), and, if you please, *The Bible* (1966), all of which failed. One of the better things to be said about Huston is that he failed equally badly with dreck: *The Roots of Heaven* (1958), *The Barbarian and the Geisha* (1958), *The Unforgiven* (1960), *The List of Adrian Messenger* (1963), *Fat City* (1972). A middleweight, seemingly.

Except that he also had his failures in the middle ranges as well. Two of them were Southern Grotesque in provenance if not in setting: Tennessee Williams's *The Night of the Iguana* (filmed 1964) and Carson McCullers' *Reflections in a Golden Eye* (filmed 1967). (But note that, in the latter, Marlon Brando gave one of his best and least appreciated performances.) In *Wise Blood* (1979) it's Southern Grotesque time again, and again Huston fumbled.

Flannery O'Connor's 1952 novel *Wise Blood* is middling O'Connor, I think, far from the finest work by that often wonderful writer. But it's kept on a course of gravity, of taut contrast with a rational world and a healthy Christianity, by O'Connor's presence through her prose. The book is populated with distorted humans in baroque landscapes, but O'Connor's art manages, not easily, to keep it an *agon* instead of a freak show.

Huston was apparently unaware of this. Likewise his screenwriter, Benedict Fitzgerald. When Éric Rohmer made *The Marquise of O . . .* (1976), he evidently knew that he had to situate his film in a technique of composition that would reproduce in pure cinema the medium of Heinrich von Kleist's prose. But no such need ever crossed the Huston-Fitzgerald minds. They thought that (near) fidelity to the story and the dialogue would in itself re-create the book.

It doesn't, of course. What we get are the data of the book: a chamber of horrors and a mass of unexplained behavior. A few flashbacks, with some glimpses of Huston himself as the preaching grandfather, do not explain Hazel Motes's anti-clerical religiosity. (And Brad Dourif in the role doesn't explain Hazel's power over women.) Instead of a mad Protestant Stephen Dedalus with the cursed Jesuit strain injected backward, this Hazel is only a horny and homicidal psychopath. O'Connor, in a note written ten years after the book was first published, called Hazel "a Christian *malgré lui*" and said the book was "a comic novel" (Magee, 92). Neither point is made here.

Huston's direction shows no special fluency or ease in this instance. Gerry Fisher's cinematography—the pallidness deliberate, I suppose—makes the factitiousness more so. O'Connor wanted to show us one lode of the resident evangelical strain in American history. But Huston's film shows us only a South of nutty religious con men and their gulls.

Work Cited

Magee, Rosemary, M., ed. *Conversations with Flannery O'Connor*. Jackson: University Press of Mississippi, 1987.

Quartet (1981, James Ivory)

Ruth Prawer Jhabvala was a writer of clear distinction who lost it when she wrote screenplays. Her script for *Roseland* (1977, James Ivory) was a ragout of Movieland sentimentalities; her adaptation of *The Europeans* (1979, James Ivory) reduced James's work from a novel to a series of wooden scaffoldings. Then her screenplay of Jean Rhys's 1928 novel *Quartet* came as close to obliterating the book as is possible for an adaptation that sticks pretty much to the story and retains much of the dialogue.

All Jhabvala's screen work, as far as I know, was done for one director-producer team, James Ivory and Ismail Merchant, which may explain the trouble. Of the team's work that I've seen, only *Shakespeare Wallah* (1965) gave me much pleasure; in most of the others, the filmmaking itself has been stilted. But in *Quartet* (1981) Ivory-Merchant don't provide Jhabvala with that "excuse": Ivory's direction, with a top-drawer cast, is more secure than I can remember it, and the atmosphere—Paris of the expatriates in 1920—is vivid. It's the screenplay that unbalances Rhys. The novelist gives us the sense of a tiny but astonishingly hardy, narcissistic bird singing the song of its troubles during a prolonged battering by life. The effect of the film is just a lot of wailing.

Most of this wailing is done by Isabelle Adjani as the presumably autobiographical heroine. She is married to a handsome Pole who turns a swindling trick ineptly. After he is jailed, she is alone and broke. She is taken into the home of a rich English couple played by Alan Bates and Maggie Smith: he is an art patron, she a painter. (The Bates role is generally believed to be a portrait of the writer Ford Madox Ford, with *Quartet* as an account of Rhys's affair with him.) The bizarre coziness in the story is that Smith not only agrees to Adjani's presence in their home, she virtually assists her husband's affair with the guest. Apparently it's not the first time that Smith has helped her husband to acquire women; and Smith conveys that, though she is not delighted—nor bereft of his conjugal attentions—she does this to ensure the marriage.

Out of the ménage and its consequences, very little of interest develops other than the atmospherics, already familiar to us from painting and photography and literature. (We even get a character vaguely modeled on Hemingway, hovering vaguely on the edges of the story.) Where Rhys gives us loneliness and bewilderment and desperate strength in her heroine, the film just gives us Adjani crying a lot.

Bates, moustached, generally spectacled, always brusque, supplies the solipsism that equates moral values with gratification. Smith slithers through her dialogue the way she slithers in her slinky 1920s dresses, and she has the most memorable line. She and Bates and Adjani, whose character is named Marya, are sitting at a restaurant table one night, bored; and Smith suggests that they visit an amusement park. "We'll put Marya on the Joy Wheel," she says, "and watch her being banged about a bit."

Quartet lacks the interest of its source because of its basic failure, a familiar one: failure to understand that filming a good novel doesn't mean filming the story, it means transmutation of the entire work.

The Postman Always Rings Twice (1981, Bob Rafelson)

Cloning may be relatively new in science, but it's old in Hollywood. Got a successful star? Clone him or her. Sigourney Weaver was once patently being groomed to be another Jane Fonda. You didn't have to adore everything Fonda had done to be mild about Weaver's chances. Then came Jessica Lange, first noted in the remake of *King Kong* (1976, John Guillermin), whom some apparently saw as a new Faye Dunaway. Lange can wear clingy, cheap clothes provocatively and she has blunt sensual features, so in the film of *The Postman Always Rings Twice* she is put through a lot of sweat-cum-sultriness to remind us of the early Bonnie in *Bonnie and Clyde* (1967, Arthur Penn). But Dunaway—sometimes, anyway—was an actress of sustained power. No hint of this from Lange in this picture or any of those to follow in her lengthy career.

The 1981 *Postman* is another remake, from James M. Cain's novel *The Postman Always Rings Twice* (1934)—which makes eight rings because this is the fourth filming. The French did one in 1939 (*Le Dernier tournant*, Pierre Chenal); Luchino Visconti did one called *Ossessione* (1943) in Italy during World War II (without authorization; his producers may have been banking on an Axis victory so there'd never be trouble about the rights); and then there's the Lana Turner-John Garfield version from 1946 (Tay Garnett). The French version is the only one I haven't seen, but it would have to be abysmal to be the worst of the four, because the 1981 attempt is very bad.

We get a hint of this before we see anything. Under the credits Michael Small's music is so schmaltzy that it makes Max Steiner sound like Claudio Monteverdi. Yes, the picture is set in the 1930s, but nothing else in the film is intrinsically reflexive, so it's hard to believe that this hokey music is meant to set the period. Besides, later on when Jack Nicholson forces Lange to their first sexual encounter on a kitchen table, the music idles along with quiet lyricism, not with swing or jazz (the real signature of the '30s). This is one of the worst film scores I've ever heard—which is saying something where Hollywood is concerned.

Nicholson is almost becoming a clone of himself. Since *Easy Rider* (1969, Dennis Hopper), by no means his first picture, he has, almost alternately, shown and hidden great talent. His wool-capped clever maniac in *One Flew Over the Cuckoo's Nest* (1975, Miloš Forman) is one of the deeply etched icons in the American film gallery. But in *The Postman Always Rings Twice* he looks a good deal of the time as if he hadn't recovered from the *Cuckoo's Nest* lobotomy: his forehead seems to have moved permanently closer to his eyebrows—an impression fostered by his furrowed, feeble imitations of his previous force. Nicholson seems to be trying to remember how good he once was and how he got that way; he seems to be leaning on our memory of his past work. In short, he is his own clone.

The role of the stud vagabond, as written here, is stock; and Nicholson makes not one move to nudge it past platitude. Here he is, again (we feel), the raunchy footloose male, attractive through irresponsibility, who has raised hell with marriages in innumerable novels and films and plays. In a picture whose very being depends on our conviction that two people are drowning helplessly in a sexual tide, what we get are puppets—the musky wife, the fond-blind husband, the crotchy newcomer—taking up traditional positions and going through mechanical strophes.

The fact that the playwright David Mamet, the author up to this point of *The Duck Variations* (1972), *Sexual Perversity in Chicago* (1974), and *American Buffalo* (1975), had written the adaptation raised expectations on my part. Dashed. Admittedly, Cain's novel is not so good as one remembers: some of the writing lapses out of tension into slush. ("I kissed her. Her eyes were shining up at me like two blue stars. It was like being in church" [Cain, 24].) But the book has two qualities that still hold. The structure is like an arrow flight, except for the episode with the puma-hunting girl (which is worsened in the film). And Cain is careful to make his lovers pathetic—not sympathetic, which would kill things: pathetic victims of moral weakness. Mamet's screenplay destroys both these qualities. The structure is tugged out of shape (an episode in a bus station, for instance); the line of the lovers' involvement is zigged and zagged; and nothing of the woman's past is clarified. Puppets are what these two start as and remain. And some of the movie dialogue is quaint, to say the least. "You scum," Lange says to Nicholson, the man with whom she has planned and committed her husband's murder.

Moreover, the "twice" of the title is left out. The quintessential irony of the story is that a man who commits murder and gets away with it is later found guilty of a killing he did not commit. (It's the same twist as in C. S. Forester's *Payment Deferred*, which was written earlier—in 1926.) But this film ends with Lange's accidental death in a car crash, with nothing of what follows. The implication is less than faint that Nicholson will be arrested for murdering her, then be tried and executed.

But maybe that castrated ending was the director's idea, not Mamet's. The director was Bob Rafelson, and the film was another slope on *his* toboggan slide. His first film, *Head* (1968), had some zany charm. His next, *Five Easy Pieces* (1970), showed that he had really serious possibilities. Next came *The King of Marvin Gardens* (1972), which showed only imitative seriousness, then *Stay Hungry* (1976), which stayed hungry. Still, though it was hard to expect first-line work from Rafelson any longer by the 1980s, he had shown enough verve so that some good program pictures still seemed possible. But he sank *The Postman Always Rings Twice* with ineptitude and cheapness. (And he kept sinking pictures after that: *Black Widow* [1987], *Man Trouble* [1993, with Nicholson], *Blood and Wine* [1996, with Nicholson], *No Good Deed* [2002].)

For *Postman*, Rafelson engaged Ingmar Bergman's master cinematographer, Sven Nykvist, then encouraged or permitted Nykvist to shoot the film in plummy colors that visually contradict the story's lithe line. Over and over Rafelson (or Nykvist) repeats the device of having a character walk from the background into an immense close-up, which not only becomes a tedious movement but nullifies the effect of close-ups. Over and over, like Elia Kazan at his worst, he pushes the camera into the middle of physical violence, only to lessen immediacy.

For the sexual heat that ought to bake the film, Rafelson substitutes explicitness. Instead of sexual looks and sniffings, Rafelson *shows*. He shows us Nicholson's hand groping Lange's groin, he shows Nicholson performing cunnilingus. (That's the first time I had seen it, outside pornography, since *I Am Curious, Yellow* [1967, Vilgot Sjöman].) When Rafelson decides to be sexually symbolic, he's equally deft. After the first time that Lange has made love with Nicholson, she prepares for bed, later that night, with her husband; the unaware husband plays "La donna è mobile," from Verdi's opera *Rigoletto* (1851), on the phonograph. ("Woman is fickle," in case you missed it.) Then the director follows this with the seduction duet from Mozart's *Don Giovanni* (1787). *Then,* when Lange comes down to the kitchen for something, where Nicholson is sitting and listening, she carries a cat in her arms. The cat/pubis connection wasn't new when Erich von Stroheim used it in *Queen Kelly* (1928). Throughout, Rafelson's work is thus all grabs, no style, and most of the grabs are at pictures he remembers and at exploitations permissible by the last quarter of the twentieth century.

Cain's story, if you've forgotten, is about a Depression drifter who is hired as a mechanic by the Greek owner of a combination garage and diner in California. The Greek has a wife younger than himself and not Greek. (In the novel she has a lot of ethnic loathing for her husband, which at least helps to characterize and motivate her.) Cain wasn't concerned to show the hell into which two lovers plunge themselves by murdering the woman's husband, which was what Zola had done in *Thérèse Raquin* (1867); he wanted to dramatize the immorality of egotism, the fact that there is no reliable bar between gratification-as-ethics and murder. Rafelson and Mamet just reduce the lovers to objects of our smirking recognition ("Oho, so that's the set-up!"), abetted by the trite portrayal of the husband—John Colicos—as that same old wine-bibbing, life-loving European innocent strayed in from the film *They Knew What They Wanted* (1940, Garson Kanin).

All the people involved here, laboring diligently together, have nonetheless turned out an empty and odious film.

Work Cited

Cain, James M. *The Postman Always Rings Twice*. New York: Grosset & Dunlap, 1934.

The Natural (1984, Barry Levinson)

In *The Natural* (1984), Robert Redford is first seen as a Midwest farm youth in the late 1920s who goes to Chicago for a pitching tryout with the Cubs and seems bound to make good. A woman whom he met on the train invites him to her hotel room; she, demented, shoots him in the stomach, then commits suicide. After fifteen obscure years, most of them spent out of baseball, Redford is scouted by the New York Knights in a semi-pro game, comes to New York, and in time succeeds as a slugging outfielder. Again a beautiful woman threatens him with destruction—of a different sort. The sudden reappearance of a sweetheart from his farm-country past, accompanied by the adolescent son that Redford didn't know he had, bolsters him and brings him through to victory, then to the retirement that his health demands. He returns to the farmland of his boyhood; the last sequence is a replay of the opening sequence in a wheat field, except that Redford is throwing fly balls as his father once did and his son, not he, is now catching them.

As screen stories go, it's pretty good: with its Hemingwayesque use of contemporary sport as the locus of contemporary epic, with agreeable symmetries, and with a symbolic overlay of temptations and redemption. As screen adaptations go, this one really *goes*—far from the Bernard Malamud novel (1952) that is its source. Robert Towne and Phil Dusenberry, the screenwriters, have reworked much of the material of the novel, some of it quite unconventional, into a script that tries to retain the unconventional atmosphere while forging conventional form. To Malamud's symmetries they have added some of their own (the use of lightning, for instance); they have converted Malamud's malevolent forces into patent villains; and they have transformed his novel of haunting fate into a mystical story with a happy ending.

The Natural was Malamud's first novel (and has no Jews in it), but it contains several themes that run through his later books (all of which have Jews in them): actions have consequences; some mistakes are irreparable; happiness exists as a criterion, not as an achievable state; life, seen with ideal objectivity, is a complex joke but still a joke, even though, like the hero of *The Natural*, you may weep "many bitter tears" at the end of your story. The screenwriters have kept only hints of these themes.

I'm not raising here the antique complaint of the distortion of a novel (or play) by film, although there's no question that Malamud's novel *has* been distorted. Even if one places this book among its author's lesser works—my own opinion—one can't be blind either to the screen changes or the reasons for them. If *The Natural* is sacrosanct to you, stay away from the film (even at this late date) and reread the book. On the other hand, if you want to see how some competent craftsmen winnowed some cinematic elements out of the book and transmuted them to their own ends, the film has its rewards.

The first problem that the filmmakers faced, and dealt with adequately, was tone: how to balance and combine the hard, clear-cut talk and action of baseball with the numinous elements that overhang the story. (Curious, how baseball induces authors to use it as a locus for the fantastic. Some post-Malamud examples: Douglas Wallop's 1954 novel *The Year the Yankees Lost the Pennant*, which became the stage musical *Damn Yankees* (1955) and film musical of the same name [1958, George Abbott & Stanley Donen]; Robert Coover's 1968 novel

211

The Universal Baseball Association, Henry Waugh, Prop.; John Ford Noonan's 1969 play *The Year Boston Won the Pennant*; W. P. Kinsella's 1982 novel *Shoeless Joe*, which became the film *Field of Dreams* [1989, Phil Alden Robinson].)

The director, Barry Levinson, whose first film was *Diner* (1982), understood from the start that this matter of tone was primary; he and his cinematographer, the talented Caleb Deschanel, therefore tried to move and light the film so as to suggest that the bright world of the diamond is surrounded by mysterious forces. We have all seen the blimp shots, now TV commonplaces, of a brilliantly lighted playing field surrounded by oceanic darkness. That may have been a guiding metaphor for the film; and, except that Levinson uses slow motion too predictably for empyrean emphases of both fact and fantasy, he fulfills the metaphor much of the time.

Second, the filmmakers have frankly faced commercial considerations and, to their purposes, have made those considerations serve them. Having altered and condensed and rearranged the materials as they did all along the line, they had no alternative but to give the film a happy ending; so they gave it one that, in pop terms, is a good glow-making one. Once this film story is launched as it is, it takes on its own artistic responsibilities; any unhappy ending would have been jarring, even more arbitrary than what we see. Kenneth Burke's famous critical dictum tells us that form is the arousal and satisfaction of expectation. George M. Cohan's earthy equivalent was that the audience writes the last act. Malamud purists will shriek at the ending, but they will have been shrieking long before that. Those who can accept the idea that this is not the novel, in order to see what pleasures they may get from the transformation, will get those pleasures.

Oddly, the pleasure that comes first to mind is a scene of two men shaving. Just before the game that will decide the pennant race, the Knights manager and his bench coach are shaving side by side in a locker-room mirror. The manager is Wilford Brimley, familiar by this time from *Tender Mercies* (1983, Bruce Beresford) and *The Stone Boy* (1984, Christopher Cain). The coach is Richard Farnsworth, already beloved (I hope) because of *Comes a Horseman* (1978, Alan J. Pakula) and *The Grey Fox* (1982, Phillip Borsos). Those two laconic codgers scraping away, saying things I can't even remember, exemplify the fact that the right people doing even commonplace things at the right time—before an uncommon game—can make the screen interesting.

Or there's the scene in which Redford re-meets his boyhood sweetheart. He slips into a soda-fountain booth opposite her, and the first thing he says, after fifteen years, is, "Are you married?" (Malamud's line [152], transposed). Redford's look at the woman implies the quick rush through his mind of everything that had been between them; it also implies that he is still able to hope, and leads him directly to the question he wants to ask even more than he wants to say hello. This is a subtle, lovely moment. Then there's the contrasting, recurring presence of Robert Duvall as an almost literally diabolical sportswriter, insisting that the past continues, that the wolves of mortal malice are always at the door.

Redford, making his first screen appearance here in four years, reminds those who need reminding that he was one of the perfect male film stars. Like only a few other men—Paul Newman and Marcello Mastroianni—he is extraordinarily handsome, effortlessly fascinating, and enormously talented. His role here is not the most demanding of his career, not on the level of *The Candidate* (1972, Michael Ritchie) and *Jeremiah Johnson* (1972, Sydney Pollack), but it gives us ample chance to see another kind of natural in his element.

Glenn Close is the boyhood sweetheart, and, once again, she works honestly yet unappealingly. The costumes and settings, for their part, tell us graphically that we are in the 1930s, but we would know it anyway: there's not a black man on any of the ball teams. I didn't even see a black person in any of the ballpark crowds. (Was this why, at one of the ball-club parties, they sing "Darktown Strutters' Ball" [1917, Shelton Brooks]? Are we being told something about pre-Jackie-Robinson prejudice?)

Possibly I ought to feel guilty about not being more protective (as I often have been) of a novel by a good writer, but with all its alterations, the film of *The Natural* in itself gave me some fun. Which underscores my chief critical dictum: criticism is less a matter of dicta than of instances.

Work Cited

Malamud, Bernard. *The Natural*. New York: Noonday Press, 1961.

A Passage to India (1984, David Lean)

At the time of the release of *A Passage to India* (1984), I had been collecting reviews of the film by people who don't usually review films, and a curious lot these exhibits are. Noel Annan describes the meeting between David Lean, eventually the screenwriter-editor-director of the film, and the dons of King's College, Cambridge, which is E. M. Forster's executor. Annan says the dons had read a screenplay of the 1924 novel by Santha Rama Rau that reassured them enough about the eventual quality of the film such that they were willing to meet with Lean. But "as it turned out" (Annan, 5)—an odd phrase on Annan's part because the dons' reassurance had come from Rau's script—David Lean wrote his own screenplay. Says Annan, "It was not difficult to predict the result" (Annan, 5). Indeed it wasn't: Lean's film is for Annan a self-fulfilling prophecy. Lean made the film as it is, says Annan, because he has "little respect for [his audience]" (Annan, 5).

But what about Annan's respect for his readers? He makes two glaring and important misstatements of fact. He says that the film "begins with the arrival of the P & O liner that brings not only Mrs. Moore and Miss Quested to Bombay, but the Viceroy as well"; and that the film "ends in Srinagar with magnificent shots of the Himalayas." Neither of these statements is true. The film begins and ends in rainy London. This is something more than a detail: the start and finish are Lean's attempt to round off the themes, to transmute into cinematic form some of the ideas—especially at the end of the book—that he felt would not work on screen in Forster's form. With that frame of start and finish, Lean is trying to imply Britain's failures in India and India's inevitable triumphs. Annan doesn't deal with these attempts by Lean: he simply rules that they don't exist.

In the February 14, 1985, issue of the *New York Review of Books*, Frank Kermode himself writes that, as he recalls, Annan wasn't present at that Cambridge meeting (although the impression in Annan's article is otherwise) and that his report wasn't entirely accurate. Santha Rama Rau's screenplay could not have figured in the matter, says Kermode, because Lean had sent copies of his own screenplay to Cambridge in advance of the meeting. Again, where is Annan's respect for his readers? (Kermode feels he must note that he tested Lean's vaunted knowledge of the novel by asking him the name of Ronnie Heaslop's Hindu servant. On this weighty question, Lean flunked. So much for upstart film rabble.)

Then Christopher Hitchens weighed in with a three-page scathing review of the film of *A Passage to India* in the Spring 1985 issue of the journal *Grand Street*. An aggregate of about one page is devoted to quotations from Forster's letters and from Lean's indefensibly grandiose comments in interviews. This décor is insufficient for Hitchens, as he ends with rumor: "Rumors filtering from the set suggest that we were narrowly spared even worse—we hear of Alec Guinness walking off one scene, of Peggy Ashcroft's being invited to play the rendezvous in the mosque with more love interest" (Stape, 185). (Bother the fact that it's not a rendezvous, in novel or film; it's an accidental meeting.) Hitchens thus insists that even what we *don't* see proves that the film is bad.

Hitchens complains that Lean "manages to be unfair to everybody. The British are portrayed in stock terms, as brutes, duffers, or eccentrics, and the Indians as chattering *babus*, servile and cunning by turns" (Stape, 184). Tapan Raychaudhuri, who at the time was teaching Asian history at Oxford, disagrees about the source of the "stock terms" and Lean's use of them. In his review Raychaudhuri writes:

> The Indian characters in Forster's novel are not entirely convincing and are somewhat stereotyped, as are his British bureaucrats. . . . [Lean's] Anglo-Indians . . . appear more real in the novel, as much the creatures of historical circumstance as are the hapless lot they rule over. (Raychaudhuri, 384)

Though Raychaudhuri spots some startling gaffes in the film, he calls it "pure enchantment; a splendid film." Yet he, too, says: "A forced happy ending is the logical climax of [Lean's] vision of India." One might dispute this view of the concluding scenes in India, but—again—they are not the end of the film. It ends, not amidst snowy peaks but in Adela Quested's rain-curtained living room.

I'm hardly arguing that one must like the film. Some of my best friends didn't, and don't. The point is that, in these articles, those who dwell in strata high above the film world have deigned to descend to find support for their prejudices. Annan says: "Every great novel loses when dramatized because it conveys meaning that cannot be seen on the screen." In an isolated state, this platitude is inarguable, but all it does experientially is to prepare Annan and like thinkers to discount any film made from a great novel. Obviously no great novel *needs* to be filmed, but in the right hands—as experience proves soundly—a great novel can be filmed in a way that puts another art truly at its service, a way that conveys meanings visible on the screen. Examples: Robert Bresson's 1951 film of Georges Bernanos's novel *Diary of a Country Priest* (1936), Éric Rohmer's 1976 film of Kleist's novella *The Marquise of O . . .* (1808).

I don't contend that Lean's film is in their class; but I saw it again recently and, apart from Maurice Jarre's atrocious score (which won an Oscar!), I think even more firmly that the art in its making transmutes major elements of the novel into cinematic form, suggests other resonances, and honors Forster. With his view of film, he might not have acknowledged the honor; nonetheless, I think it was paid to him.

Works Cited

Annan, Noel. "The Unmysterious East." *New York Review of Books*, 31.21-22 (January 17, 1985): 5-6.

Hitchens, Christopher. "Busted Blue: *A Passage to India*." *Grand Street*, 4.3 (Spring 1985): 215-217.

Kermode, Frank. "A Passage to Cambridge." *New York Review of Books*, 32.2 (February 14, 1985): 40.

Raychaudhuri, Tapan. "A View of the Hills." *Times Literary Supplement* (London), no. 4279 (April 5, 1985): 384.

Stape, J. H. *E. M. Forster: Critical Assessments.* Vol. IV: *Relations and Aspects: The Modern Critical Response, 1945-1990.* London: Helm, 1998.

La Belle noiseuse (1991, Jacques Rivette)

La Belle noiseuse features two couples, the older of whom hosts the younger yet both of whom feed off each other, although in Jacques Rivette's 1991 film the hosts' motive is less sadomasochistic than, let us say, sadoartistic. Rivette has freely adapted *La Belle noiseuse* from Honoré de Balzac's story "The Unknown Masterpiece" (1831), transposing it from the seventeenth century to the present, adding characters as well as altering the role of others, changing the ending, and giving during the film's four hours—as only the cinema can do — the experience of real time, of duration, in the creative process of painting a picture. But Rivette's aim is similar to Balzac's, and different from that of the numerous bio-pics which romanticize the (historical) artist as tortured genius: to dramatize in a sober way the dangers and the triumphs that every artist courts in attempting to achieve the goal of art, which, even for the realist, is not merely to copy nature, but to express it.

Rivette has structured four of his (often very long) films around the rehearsals of plays: *Paris Belongs to Us* (1961), *L'Amour fou* (*Mad Love*, 1969), *Out One* (1971), and *L'Amour par terre* (*Love on the Ground*, 1984). As Luigi Pirandello knew, the theater (being a naturally reflexive form) is more concerned with questions of illusion and reality, lies and truth, than any other art, and Rivette's characters in these films sort out the painful truth about themselves in the process of arduously preparing plays for performance. In *La Belle noiseuse*, the theatrical rehearsals of the previous films are replaced by painting "rehearsals": ink or charcoal sketches of a clothed model, then of that same model naked; sketches of the model's whole body, only of her back, only of her face; one posing after another until, finally, the artist is ready to put oil to canvas. But, as in Rivette's "theatrical" films, the characters undergo a crucible during the artistic process, and here that crucible is connected to the crisis of representational painting subsequent to the invention of cinema: the need to demonstrate that, because the artist's vision is unmediated by a camera, a realistic canvas can capture the essence or soul of its subject whereas a film cannot, despite the ease with which it is able to manipulate light and space, color and mass.

In cinematic style and subject, *La Belle noiseuse* resembles the six "comedies and proverbs" of Éric Rohmer, which explore the interiority of women who fall in love with essences as opposed to surfaces. These films do so with a camera concerned to preserve the integrity of space—that is, with a camera that relies on the long take, the full shot, and deep focus, and that cuts mostly to suggest discord between characters, preferring to track in when it wishes to intensify our view of someone or to pull back when it wants to enhance our perspective on a scene. Such a cinematic style is, of course, ideally suited to a film about painting, about the protracted process of painting a picture—one stationary picture, on one continuous space—and its torturous effect on artist, model, lover. (This is also the style of Rivette's "theatrical" films, where its realism, its dependence on the long take and the full shot—which the cinema borrowed from the stage—seems equally appropriate.)

The writer Marianne (Balzac gives her no profession or occupation) is not the painter-protagonist Frenhofer's literal lover in La Belle noiseuse, but she is his figurative one in the sense that, by modeling for him, she restores his creative potency after ten years of inactivity punctuated by bouts of self-portraiture. Marianne's voice-over begins and ends the film, not to indicate that the narrative will be told from her point of view, but to underline her pivotal role in the action: here, as the object of both the camera's and Frenhofer's revelatory gaze rather than as the author of that gaze. In the story it is Marianne's boyfriend, the aspiring young artist Nicolas, who gets the emphasis along with Porbus, whom Rivette turns from a court painter into Frenhofer's dealer. In addition to shifting the focus from Nicolas to Marianne, Rivette gives Frenhofer a wife, Liz, a former architect whose life is now consumed by her relationship with her husband. Thus a nineteenth-century story, set in the seventeenth, about the nature of artistic creation becomes a twentieth-century film about the nature of artistic creation as it affects, not only artists, but also the women who live with, inspire, and even rival them.

La Belle noiseuse is set in southeastern France, where the renowned Frenhofer lives with his wife in a large chateau. Frenhofer's last attempt to paint someone other than himself was a portrait of "La Belle noiseuse," the sobriquet (out of Balzac) of a beautiful seventeenth-century courtesan named Catherine Lescault. The term translates as "the beautiful troublemaker," "the pretty nuisance," or "the lovely pain in the ass," and it was Liz who posed for this unfinished masterpiece. She tells why her husband abandoned what was meant to be his crowning achievement: "Because Frenhofer loved me, he stopped painting me. It was either me or the painting." Along come Nicolas and Marianne, who are staying at a nearby country inn and who are escorted to Frenhofer's chateau by Porbus. Nicolas wishes both to pay his respects to the master and to find out what, if anything, he has been working on; Porbus wants his client to resume work on "La Belle noiseuse," so that he can sell it; and both Nicolas and Porbus agree that Marianne should be Frenhofer's new model. She resists hotly at first, averse to the idea of posing nude and possibly suspicious that her lover is merely trying to ingratiate himself with the famous artist. But she makes the decision to pose, almost in spite of herself, and Frenhofer, with Liz's approval, is moved to take up his "Noiseuse" again.

Over the next five days he paints his masterpiece in the studio Marianne compares to a cathedral, and the camera gives us shots of him working far more than it does of his beautiful model. Mostly we watch Frenhofer's hands at work, in real time that is occasionally elided by a series of jump cuts but more often by slow dissolves. We never catch more than a glimpse of the completed painting, and the fact that it is not unveiled to the mediating camera confirms for us the sacred mystery of art as contrasted with the profane erotics of Marianne's naked body on screen, no matter how sculpturally she is lit by the cinematographer, William Lubtchansky. Liz and Marianne separately view the finished "Belle Noiseuse," with Liz feeling betrayed that Frenhofer has painted it over the earlier painting of herself, and with Marianne reacting angrily at the extent to which the painting has exploited her soul (not her body), has exposed her essence. She nonetheless seems transformed by the experience, as does Frenhofer, who remarks to Liz that completing his masterpiece has "killed" him.

Frenhofer makes sure that nobody but his wife, Marianne, and posterity will see the finished work, which seems at once to please and distress him: he bricks it up behind a wall in his studio, then quickly paints another, less inspired "Noiseuse" that his dealer likes all the same. At the end of Balzac's "Unknown Masterpiece," the artist ends up mad and burns every one of his canvases, including "La Belle noiseuse" (which no one sees, since he has concealed it beneath "a dead wall of paint"), before dying. Rivette's Frenhofer figuratively dies but literally lives to resume his shaken relationship with Liz, whom he has "betrayed" through his art, by "going all the way" with Marianne in the act of painting her. Frenhofer makes no sexual advances whatsoever toward his young model; still, she never quite sheds her resentment at his artistic "advances," never quite stops resisting them. This is one of the reasons he finds painting her such a challenge. Nicolas, for his part, is jealous of them both: of Frenhofer, for his fame and achievement as well as his communion with his naked subject; and of Marianne, for her growing independence as a woman and as an artist in her own right. Marianne's last word to Nicolas, and the last word of *La Belle noiseuse,* is "No," after he has suggested that it is time they return to Paris, whose constant bustle and pervasive grayness inspire him if the quiet and color of the sunlit countryside do not.

For all its clarity, that color is densely photographed by Lubtchansky, and for all its gentleness, that quiet is framed by pulsing strains from Igor Stravinsky's *Agon* (1957) and *Petrushka* (1911). A similar dichotomy exists in the acting of Michel Piccoli, who plays Frenhofer with just the right counterpoise between world-weariness and artistic awakening, intellectual complacency and animalistic obstinacy. The role of Frenhofer's wife is performed by the delicately spoken but undynamic Jane Birkin, who first got my attention as one of the two romping nude models in Michelangelo Antonioni's *Blow-Up* (1966). David Bursztein, previously unknown to me, is acceptable as Nicolas, which is really all that he need be.

It's Marianne who must be radiant, who must simultaneously radiate reluctance and curiosity, sensuality and discernment, self-assertion and self-denial. Emmanuelle Béart does all this and more. She makes us long to look, not at her naked body, but at Frenhofer's *painting* of that body, at the "Belle Noiseuse" that captures the divine flame inside her in a way the cinema, forever hamstrung by the very technology that gives it its being (even as fiction itself is restricted to the mind's eye), can only approximate.

The Handmaid's Tale (1990, Volker Schlöndorff)

The future has a long past. For centuries, writers of fiction and plays have shaped the future in various ways, and they were joined in the twentieth century by screenwriters. Almost always the future has been used to say something about the present, and occasionally it's memorable. If the work has inner consistency and vivifying imagination, it can often chill us, as we note how near and nearly inevitable a particular future seems.

There's no chill in the film (1990) made from Margaret Atwood's 1985 novel *The Handmaid's Tale*, because the consistency is thin and the imagination isn't vivid, even though the screenplay is by Harold Pinter. The setting is the near-future in a new state on the North American continent, a highly militarized state (besieged by rebels) in which machoism, racism, homophobia, and religious fundamentalism prevail. Those elements were certainly apparent enough, then as now, and possibly they could wax, but the Atwood-Pinter treatment of them is simultaneously mechanical and facile. Instead of being frightened by possibility, we almost nod in recognition as one scare topic after another is exploited somewhat smugly.

Issues like the ones in this film—issues of any kind—didn't much concern Pinter in his career. Mostly he devoted himself to playwriting of unique and exquisite surreality, with a vision that pierces the diurnal to disclose its mysteries. In a few short plays toward the end of his career—generally overrated, as if to congratulate Pinter for giving up all that nebulous stuff and getting down to issues—he dealt with political oppression. Perhaps it was as a reward for coming to his social senses that he was asked to do this screenplay. In any case, it is by far his worst. All his screenplays up to this point had been adaptations, of his own plays or of other people's novels, and they range in quality from the plain workmanship of *The Quiller Memorandum* (1966, Michael Anderson) to the genius of *The Proust Screenplay* (1977). It's certainly conceivable that Pinter might have improved *The Handmaid's Tale* with a fiery plunge into its essentials that realized its themes, mended its meanderings, and raised it out of sexy futurist soap opera. Instead, almost lazily, he has merely trailed after Atwood and produced garish science fiction.

Ryuichi Sakamoto's music starts us off with lots of lower-colon rumblings. We open in a snowy landscape as a young couple and their small child are trying to cross a border. Lights flash on, and an amplified voice warns them to stop. Dad, for no sane reason, ventures out alone and is gunned down. (Well, there is a reason: the script needs to get rid of him.) Then Mom, Natasha Richardson, rushes to him and is captured by troops. They drag her off and abandon the child. (Retrospectively this seems strange because the new regime is avid for children. However, it does provide chances, during the first hour, for the film to cut away from Richardson's adventures to the child wandering in the snow and calling "Mommy.")

We are introduced to the new regime—immense barracks, stockyard handling of human beings, many soldiers, many stern female guards armed with electric prods. Young white fertile women are isolated as brood mares; they are called handmaids and are all dressed identically in red. (Women of each group— wives, maids, etc.—are all dressed in one color.) Richardson, who forgets her dead husband and abandoned child unless the script reminds her of them from time to time, is assigned to the home of the Commander, Robert Duvall, because his wife, Faye Dunaway, is sterile. Dunaway is delighted that Richardson is going to bear Duvall's child; the state's ritual even demands that the wife be present at the impregnation attempts.

I interrupt this synopsis, which may make the film sound less ridiculous than it is, to note that Igor Luther, the cinematographer who did so well for Andrzej Wajda's *Danton* (1983), shoots everything in tones that are exceptionally precise, almost inhumanly exact, which is just right for the film. Luther's work is the film's best asset. But it can't redeem the whole, which seems like a more expensive and sophisticated spin-off from Saturday afternoon sci-fi serials.

One reason that all these characters, rulers and underlings, seem phony is that they are always being hustled through prisms of emotion. Especially Richardson. Anger, fear, longing, despair, whatever—they swish by like the spotlights that keep sweeping around at night. Nothing can really register because everything seems under the gun—not of the police but of the director. He is Volker Schlöndorff, the German who previously worked his dampening wiles on *The Tin Drum* (1979) and *Swann in Love* (1984). True, he has some sense of pace and space: nothing is languorous or remote. But he has no sense of the ridiculous. He doesn't know when an emotional encounter is so compressed that it seems funny—as are the swift series of such high-speed encounters in this picture.

Among the actors Richardson suffers most. I saw her first as Nina in a 1985 London production of *The Seagull* (1896, Anton Chekhov) that starred her mother, Vanessa Redgrave, and she was adequate. As of 1990, her film career had been less than happy. Her previous major part was the title role in *Patty Hearst* (1988, Paul Schrader), in which she was dim. Here she seems puny—but admittedly it's a part for a marionette. Dunaway, as the Commander's wife, does one more of her Dragon Ladies. Duvall, the Commander, shows only how an excellent actor can waste his time.

The Comfort of Strangers (1990, Paul Schrader)

Italy in general and Venice in particular have long fascinated English dramatists, from John Webster (*The Duchess of Malfi*, 1614) to Percy Shelley (*The Cenci*, 1819) to Harold Pinter (*Betrayal*, 1978). That's not to say that writers of other nationalities have not conducted their own "romance" with Italy, only that the priggish reserve of the English seems especially drawn to its opposite number, the torrid abandon of the Italians. Shakespeare himself understood the dramatic appeal of an Italian setting with its built-in extremes of courtliness and corruption, luxuriance and decay, eroticism and reprisal. And Pinter takes up the Venetian theme for the first time, not in *Betrayal*, but in his greatest play, *The Homecoming* (1965), where a man and his wife visit his family in London after a week's vacation in Venice apparently designed to revive their failing marriage. The Venetian vacation doesn't work for them, just as it finally does not work for Colin and Mary, the two English lovers in Ian McEwan's novel *The Comfort of Strangers* (1981), who have come to Venice on holiday in an attempt to decide whether to end or deepen their seven-year relationship.

Pinter, also an accomplished scenarist, was the perfect choice to adapt McEwan's novel to the screen, less because of both authors' attraction to Venice than because of their interest in the same themes: (sexual) dominance and subservience, the darkness and brutality lurking not only outside our doors but also inside the most ordinary of us, and the fundamental elusiveness of much human behavior. This last theme leads both men to write in an elliptical style that, even when ostensibly candid, eschews explanation or exposition and that, in Pinter's case, is heightened by his use not only of silence but also of incantatory language.

If Pinter was the ideal choice to write the screenplay for the film of *The Comfort of Strangers* (1990), Paul Schrader initially seems to be a less-than-ideal choice for its director. The product of a strictly Calvinistic background, he once said that "the common thread that runs through all my films is redemption, a belief in God, a belief that something must be sacrificed [in order to reach God]" (Wakeman, 994). While this is true of such films of Schrader's as *Hardcore* (1979) and *American Gigolo* (1980)—both of which deal with the subject of prostitution—it is also true that his cinematic style has been archly cool, detached, affectless, as if the director were attempting to transcend the very material he had deigned to treat. That is largely the style he brings to *The Comfort of Strangers,* and it meshes beautifully with McEwan's understated, amoral tale.

The Comfort of Strangers tells the story of Mary and Colin, she an actress whose women's theater group has just broken up over the issue of male membership, he someone who works in publishing. Even though these two have been lovers for seven years and Mary is legally divorced, they do not live together and no longer have a great passion for each other; when they talk of sex, it is of the *politics* of sex, not of their sexual relations. This is the second time Colin and Mary have chosen to vacation in Venice, so obviously the city has some appeal for them at the same time that it unfortunately has come to represent the stagnancy of their relationship—that is, until they meet Robert and Caroline.

Robert is an Italian who learned his English in London, where he grew up (his father was a diplomat), and who is married to a Canadian, Caroline. They reside in a sumptuous apartment, art-filled and book-lined, in a house that had once belonged to Robert's grandfather. Before we see Robert, we see his photographs of Colin and Mary, which he secretly takes as they walk about Venice, and which appear on screen as black-and-white stills that interrupt or break up the couple's stroll. Caroline and her husband have adorned one of their bedroom walls with pictures of the extremely handsome Colin (Mary is either not in the photographs or has been cut off at the hand, the elbow, or some insignificant portion of her face), which they use to stimulate their lovemaking. In fact Colin has unwittingly brought this involuntarily childless couple close together again, by which I mean that he has enabled them to make love in a conventional way after a long episode of sadomasochistic sex that had culminated in Caroline's hospitalization with a broken back, and that would have led to her death had Robert's beatings continued.

As Caroline puts it in the novel, "If you are in love with someone, you would even be prepared to let them kill you, if necessary" (McEwan, 66). Pinter's script breaks this line off after the word "prepared" in order to let the actress playing Caroline suggest on screen what McEwan has spelled out in hard prose, just as this actress is later called upon to insinuate what the novelist himself has only insinuated: that instead of killing Caroline in the name of love, Robert will, with his wife's complicity, be "sensible" and sacrifice a beautiful man to their love, first through framing him in a number of still photographs, then by murdering him. Why sacrifice a man instead of a woman? Because Robert is as attracted to men as Caroline is—his "hobby" is a gay bar he owns in Venice, where he enjoys being alone with males—an attraction that is fueled by his abhorrence of strong women in general and feminists in particular.

From earliest childhood, the world Robert saw was made by his imperious father, of whom everyone was afraid (his mother, his four sisters) *except* Robert, who was his favorite. Yet the only son was closest to his tender mother, in whose bed he slept when his father was away. And the combination of male and female, or in any event of heterosexual and homosexual, we see in his character is symbolized by a lapidarian account Robert gives of his father just once in the novel but three times in the film (in voice-over at the start, to Colin and Mary soon after he meets them, and to the police at the very end), so that it becomes a kind of mantra to his identity:

> My father was a very big man. All his life he wore a black moustache. When it turned grey he used a little brush to keep it black, such as ladies use for their eyes. Mascara. (McEwan, 3, 15-16, 51)

Robert tells this story to Colin and Mary at his bar, where he has taken them for drinks after arranging to intercept the couple one evening as they wandered, lost, through Venice's dark and labyrinthine streets. Finding (stalking?) them on the street again the next morning, he invites them to his apartment. There they meet Caroline, there Caroline talks to Mary about love and death and her husband makes derogatory comments to Colin about women— after which, suddenly, unprovoked and unanswered, Robert punches his guest in the stomach. There also Mary sees a photograph of Colin among a group of photos taken by Robert that he shows to her; Caroline launders her visitors' clothes while they nap but playfully refuses to give them back unless the couple agrees to stay for dinner, which they do; and Caroline admits to Mary that she observed her and Colin sleeping naked.

The cumulative effect of this series of incidents, paradoxically, is to awaken Mary and Colin's sexual desire for each other. After they emerge from Robert and Caroline's apartment, they go back to their hotel room and barely leave it for four days, so busy are they making love and exulting in their renewed passion. But that renewal has its dark side: not only does Colin and Mary's visit to the luxury flat arouse their dormant libidos, it also unearths a sadomasochistic component in their relationship. A benign sadomasochism in comparison with Robert and Caroline's, but a form of sadomasochism nonetheless:

> MARY. I'm going to hire a surgeon—a very handsome surgeon—to cut off your arms and legs. And then you'll be quite helpless, you see. I'll keep you in a room in my house . . . and use you just for sex, whenever I feel like it. And sometimes I'll lend you to my girlfriends . . . and they can do what they like with you . . . (McEwan, 35)
>
> . . .
>
> COLIN. I'm going to invent a machine . . . made of steel. It's powered by electricity. It has pistons and controls. It has straps and dials. It makes a low hum . . . like this . . . (*He hums.*) And you'll be strapped in . . . quite securely . . . tight . . . and the machine will fuck you—not just for hours and weeks but for years and years and years. For ever. (McEwan, 35-36)

Not long after making these statements, Mary tells Colin about the photograph of him she saw at Robert and Caroline's apartment, Colin tells her of the punch in the stomach Robert gave him, and they board a launch for a pleasure trip—only to get off at Robert and Caroline's stop, as if drawn back to this couple's parlous sensuality for reasons they can but dimly comprehend.

They are almost immediately spotted by Caroline from her balcony and waved up, to be greeted by Robert's "We were expecting you sooner" (McEwan, 42). Caroline says that she and her husband are going on holiday, but not only have they packed all their suitcases, they've also sold off the contents of their apartment. In addition, Robert is selling his bar to its manager and says he must go there to complete the deal; he takes Colin along, ignoring the Briton's questions about the photograph Mary had seen, touching him frequently, and telling his gay friends that Colin is his lover. While they are gone, Caroline serves Mary drugged tea as she matter-of-factly summarizes her sadomasochistic relationship with Robert, shows off their bedroom photographic shrine to Colin, and awaits her husband's return. By the time the men come back, Mary is too far gone to warn Colin as the couple approaches him for the kill, with Caroline stroking him and Robert manhandling him before abruptly slitting his throat with a razor. While Colin bleeds to death slumped against a wall, Caroline and Robert passionately kiss each other and Mary drifts off into troubled, interminable sleep.

The murderers are quickly apprehended, largely because of their seemingly willful carelessness, their apparent desire to be caught and punished. Caroline and Robert are separated for good at the end of *The Comfort of*

Strangers, each one sitting alone in a small interrogation room, each waiting to be put inside a prison cell. And it is as if they have wanted their own separation but could not effect it in any other way, have wanted to end the sadomasochistic relationship that signals their love-hate feelings toward each other as well as toward themselves. Something similar could be said about Colin and Mary: that the budding sadomasochistic element in their relationship is a sign of each one's love-hatred for the opposite sex in addition to equal parts of self-loathing and self-absorption.

Mary likes Caroline, and one reason is that she understands Caroline's desire to be hurt by men. Mary is treated by the police as if somehow she had acceded to Colin's slaying or at the very least been tainted by it, and this is because there is a part of her that curses the existence of men, that would have the lot of them—not merely those guilty of (sexual) violence against women—castrated or even exterminated. It is this part of her that resists remarriage, that puts off Colin right before their second visit to Robert and Caroline's when he suggests that they move in together and make a commitment. Mary has just been for a swim when Colin declares his total love for her, and the peaceful loneness of that swim only reinforces her desire to remain single. Even as, in the words of Cesare Pavese that McEwan uses as one of two epigraphs to his novel, "[Traveling] forces you to trust strangers and to lose sight of all that familiar comfort of home and friends " (McEwan, 8), marriage would force Mary to trust a man, essentially a stranger to her sex, and dwell simultaneously "in two worlds / the daughters and the mothers/ in the kingdom of the sons" (McEwan, 7). These last lines, from the poem "Sibling Mysteries" (1976) by Adrienne Rich, make up McEwan's other epigraph and succinctly express the idea of female estrangement in a man's world—a world from which women are nevertheless obliged to seek comfort (even when it comes in the form of pain), just as travelers are from their foreign hosts. By the end of *The Comfort of Strangers*, Mary is all alone, sundered forever from Colin's world and from the world of Caroline and Robert, whose own sundering will never again afford them the comfort of each other's strangeness.

Paul Schrader's cinematic style mirrors the attraction-repulsion of the sexes in *The Comfort of Strangers*. On the one hand, the camera is removed from the action, staying mostly in the medium-to-full range and opting at times for an overhead view of the action, just as McEwan's prose seems "removed" in its matter-of-fact or dispassionate recounting of increasingly bizarre events. On the other hand, the camera moves a lot—as if it were a voyeur magnifying Robert's own role as voyeur, yet not exactly adopting or advocating his point of view. This quality of motion, and hence of pursuit, is missing from McEwan's prose, which dwells on the narrative without giving the simultaneous impression that it must track down or stalk the characters along with their world.

That Venetian world, with its labyrinthine interiors as well as exteriors, is photographed by Dante Spinotti in a way that makes it appear at once inviting and forbidding, shimmering and shadowed, profuse and pallid. And Angelo Badalamenti's score, mostly for flute but occasionally for guitar, manages to suggest the Byzantine quality of Venice and the story taking place there at the same time that it acts as a momentary, melodic balm to our troubled senses. As for the performances of the principals—Rupert Everett (Colin), Natasha Richardson (Mary), Helen Mirren (Caroline), and Christopher Walken

(Robert)—it need only be said that they understand, or have been helped to understand by Schrader, the subtlety called for in the acting of such superficially smooth but intrinsically scabrous characters. Walken, in particular, uses his sonorous voice, and lets the camera use his androgynous face, to suggest a figure of menacing politeness coupled with chilling sexuality. Strange comfort, indeed.

Works Cited

McEwan, Ian. *The Comfort of Strangers*. London: Jonathan Cape, 1981.

Wakeman, John, ed. "Paul Schrader." In Wakeman's *World Film Directors*. Vol. 2, 1945-85. New York: H. W. Wilson, 1988. 991-995.

Orlando (1992, Sally Potter) & *Mrs. Dalloway* (1997, Marleen Gorris)

Some projects in art are doomed from the start. For instance, the ballet of *Hamlet* (1601) that I once saw. It wasn't done by Balanchine for Baryshnikov, but even if those men had been involved, though it would have been blessedly improved, the ballet still would have been doomed.

Sally Potter, a young Englishwoman of evident brains and talent, wrote and directed a film of *Orlando* in 1992. The film itself makes clear that she understood most of the difficulties involved in adapting Virginia Woolf's 1928 book. But the film also makes clear that she didn't quite grasp the inevitable: Woolf's work is in the form that it's in because that's what it is.

One basic problem, as Potter did see, is not so much with the story—which presents problems enough—but with the prose: how to transmute it into film. For instance, after Orlando calls aloud her lover's name: "The beautiful, glittering name fell out of the sky like a steel-blue feather" (Woolf, 558). "Film that, Potter!" she doubtlessly said to herself about that and about a hundred other instances in the book. She took steps. She engaged Alexei Rodionov, the very best of the Russian cinematographers whose work I had seen up to this point, and with him Potter contrived sequences that in themselves are gorgeous, evocative, austere, lush. Halations often crown scenes like aureoles.

The trouble is that all these sequences don't meld into the Woolf tissue, and without that tissue the book is only a fantastic tale. We can imagine that after Potter showed one or another sequence to people—possibly to backers—they said, "That's it. You've got it. Now for the whole thing." But the whole thing is precisely what isn't here. It probably couldn't be. Twenty-five years ago Mary Ellen Bute made a film modestly called *Passages* (1966) from James Joyce's *Finnegans Wake* (1939), and, within scale, she succeeded better in her venture than Potter does here.

I don't mean to rank Woolf with Joyce. For this reader, *Orlando* is a lesser work than some claim. In the course of the book the disparaging poet Nicholas Greene says of Sir Thomas Browne that "he was for writing poetry in prose, and people soon got tired of such conceits as that" (Woolf, 440). It was brave of Woolf to include that line because it states her own book's risk-taking—the reader's feeling after a while that a slog through a barnyard might be a welcome respite from the empyrean. Still, there is the empyrean in the book, and we're constantly aware of Potter's gifted but unavailing attempts to reach it.

There's another trouble, too, inherent in the move to film. Woolf's fantasy follows her protagonist from the Elizabethan age to the present (which here is sensibly moved to the present of 1992 from Woolf's 1928), with era stops along the way and with a gender change from male to female. For all these delicate impossibilities, Woolf enlists our collaboration simply by assuming that readers, taken by the manner of the telling, will work the necessary magic themselves. It's a cunning call to partnership with her, which flatters us and succeeds.

But film doesn't need that collaboration. Film is the very home of ascendancy over the literal, the earthbound. Changes of place and century and sex, in an instant, offer no problem whatsoever and need no kind of collaboration from the audience. Many decades of filmic miracles have left us, in a sense, imaginatively slothful because we needn't lift a figurative finger. Fantasy on film demands less. It's "normal." On the screen, therefore, *Orlando* almost gets jostled into the *Time Bandits* (1981, Terry Gilliam) genre.

Some lesser quibbles. Why is *Othello* (1604) misquoted? Why is Orlando's eventual son changed to a daughter? This upsets the gender cycle that Woolf presumably had in mind. Why insert such banal locutions as "Goodbye. Good luck"? On the other hand, some of Potter's touches are fine. Queen Elizabeth's arrival at Orlando's stately home is a really royal progress. A tea party that the eighteenth-century Orlando attends, with Swift and Addison and Pope, is good pastiche fun. The gauzy-mysterious palace of a Middle Eastern potentate has pleasant *Arabian Nights* languor.

Some of the performances are striking. Quentin Crisp, in a nod to the story's androgyny, plays Elizabeth and is grandly sour as the old queen. It's she who bids Orlando, her young favorite, never to age. (However, she certainly doesn't bid him to become female. That comes later.) Heathcote Williams, who himself had been a notable playwright, overenunciates amusingly as Greene, the Elizabethan literary malcontent, and in a witty casting maneuver, Greene also appears later as a modern money-minded publisher. John Wood, exquisite actor, is the Archduke Harry, looking like a Thomas Rowlandson cartoon. Charlotte Valandrey, as Sasha, Orlando's Russian light o' love, is enchanting. Billy Zane, as the female Orlando's nineteenth-century lover, here made an American, is a true romantic presence.

Tilda Swinton as Orlando is insufficient. She—here s/he might be permitted—fills the first need: she resembles Vita Sackville-West. Literary history's most open secret is that *Orlando* was an elegant love letter to Woolf's lesbian inamorata. (Three of the photographs in the book, supposedly of Orlando, are in fact of Sackville-West.) Swinton has subtlety—her line readings are sometimes almost chordal, freighted with more than one meaning. But she has no whiff of fire. This is a drastic loss in a character who, as male or female, goes lovemaking through the ages. Swinton's declarations of passion—for people, for poetry, for life—come right from the refrigerator.

Potter's directing itself often has freshness. At the very start she gives us a hint of it. The Elizabethan Orlando is striding back and forth under a great tree (the same tree under which the film ends), and Potter's camera, at a fair distance, moves counter to Orlando's striding, gliding left when he goes right and vice versa. She keeps him centered on the screen, but she avoids tracking him tritely. Potter's decision to have Orlando occasionally play to the camera is in fact the closest that the film comes to the invitations of Woolf's book. Moreover, the way that Potter takes Orlando through an immense maze in a formal garden, to emerge radically changed, has humor and verve.

But for all of this, for all the splendid costumes and the magnificence of such sequences as the festival on the frozen Thames, the film just keeps reaching and hoping. Which is not enough.

The same might be said of the 1997 film adaptation of Virginia Woolf's *Mrs. Dalloway* (1925), which also tries to cling close to its famous fiction forebear (unlike a free adaptation of a famous novel, such as Alfonso Cuarón's 1998 picture of Dickens' *Great Expectations* [1861].) Eileen Atkins wrote the screenplay of *Mrs. Dalloway*. An intelligent and inquiring English actress, Atkins had been working on Virginia Woolf projects for almost ten years prior to this film. First, in 1989, she did a one-woman adaptation of *A Room of One's Own*

(1929), which she played in London and New York and on tour. Then, in 1993, Atkins made a theater piece, not exactly a play, out of the correspondence between Woolf and her lover, Vita Sackville-West. In New York, Atkins played Virginia and Vanessa Redgrave played Vita. Clearly, then, Atkins would have recognized the problems in adapting so shimmery a novel as *Mrs. Dalloway*, but, alas, recognizing them is not enough. Those problems still obtrude.

Woolf's novel might be seen as a (much smaller) parallel to Joyce's *Ulysses* (1922). By closely following one day in the life of one quite ordinary woman, the book includes a social tapestry, a political index, a theological position, and something of the history that produced all these elements. Woolf knew Joyce's work (about which she had decidedly mixed feelings, especially because of Joyce's candor); but "stream of consciousness" technique was in the air at the time, and she might well have done what she did if Joyce had never existed. That technique works wonderfully well in the novel; but it is not a comfortable film mode.

The story deals with one June day in the London of 1923, from morning to the evening when Clarissa Dalloway gives a party in her house. She is wealthy and reticently elegant, the middle-aged wife of an Member of Parliament, a woman whose life is plainly pleasant and vacuous. Through her day of party preparations, several other stories wind. A former suitor of hers, Peter Walsh, returns after a long stay in India. He visits Clarissa, is still in some way affected by her, yet tells her of a current amorous involvement. And there is the story of a young man, a severely shell-shocked veteran of the Great War (as it was prematurely called), who has a devoted Italian wife. His story connects with Mrs. Dalloway because the physician who so signally fails to help him is a guest at her party that evening.

To accommodate the background of these and other encounters, Atkins has devised some flashback scenes, derived from Woolf. Also, those scenes serve the usual purpose of the past juxtaposed with the present, a pathos so inevitable that it hardly needs to be mentioned. When we see the young Peter asking the young Clarissa to marry him and thus break out of her cosseted life, when we see her opt instead for the quite conventional young Richard Dalloway, we understand how Clarissa's upbringing has crimped the possibilities for her life. She was reared to be a quite conventional lady, and that is what she has become.

This flashing-back is pretty to look at, and it flexes the narrative, but it works against the unification of the piece; and unification of the whole was patently what Woolf was after. Her prose makes the novel a holistic work even when the narrative shifts from one strand to another. This is impossible in the film, where the shifts are exactly that, breaks from the centrality of Mrs. Dalloway's day. There's a further disjuncture. Woolf's prose transmutes ordinary experience. One instance: when Big Ben strikes, she writes: "The leaden circles dissolved in the air" (Woolf, 129, 158, 188, 245). In the film, we simply hear the bells. In a sense Woolf might just as well not have written as she did. Any of us can hear bells; only Woolf could have thus transfigured the sound, and the film cheats us of her.

This is not remotely to argue a fixed superiority of literature over film, but it is to suggest that some novels resist adaptation to the core of their beings. Further, it suggests that an actress-writer can fall so much in love with a fine novel that she overlooks her own experience and knowledge. (For a quite contrary example, see Emma Thompson's screenplay of the 1995 film of *Sense and Sensibility* [Ang Lee].) And, unfortunately, that is not all. Most of Mrs. Dalloway's activity during that June day is inner—things that she thinks and feels. Atkins knew this, of course, and tried to enrich the outer, visible woman with some voice-over quotations from her thoughts. But those few quotations never have, could not have, the wholeness of the contrapuntal feeling in the book, the sense that the woman whom the world sees has a more interesting, invisible self constantly attending her.

This condition puts a dreadful burden on Vanessa Redgrave, as Clarissa. Up to this point, she had rarely had a role that demanded less of (let us please use the term) her genius. She moves through Mrs. Dalloway's house and the London streets like a great, beautiful ship sailing on urban seas, and when she speaks, she makes as much as she decently can of her clumps of standard chatter—banal slivers of politesse such as "How delightful to see you!" (Woolf, 233, 235) and the like. If the role weren't in the hands of an actress who is being underused, it would be intolerable. But even Redgrave can't make Mrs. Dalloway, in this form, a fascinating woman.

Her clothes, designed by Judy Pepperdine, are unostentatiously lovely, especially the hats. In the pre-war flashback scenes, the clothes bespeak their period cleverly. And in those clothes, the performances of the young Clarissa and Peter and Richard are vividly . . . young. As the older Peter, Michael Kitchen carries nicely an air of regret plus hope. But the most demanding performance, a demand well met, is by Rupert Graves as the unbalanced war veteran. This man's presence in both novel and film is obviously meant to give us a glimpse of the horror in the world through which Mrs. Dalloway has floated. Graves has to deal with abrupt swirls of mood and reality, and he does it movingly.

The director was Marleen Gorris, the Dutch woman whose previous film, *Antonia's Line* (1995), was smoothly fulfilled. (Incidentally, Gorris did an M.A. at an English university, and she has some feeling for the country.) In her hands we can be sure that the feminist aspects of Woolf's work will not be slighted. Moreover, Gorris understands the story as, in the truest sense, a woman's work. As in the case of Potter's *Orlando*, however, the handicaps that she could not overcome are the implacable ones of the screenplay.

Work Cited

Woolf, Virginia. *Selected Works of Virginia Woolf*. London: Wordsworth, 2007.

Germinal (1993, Claude Berri) & *Gervaise* (1956, René Clément)

In their journals the Goncourt brothers, Edmond and Jules, record that, on December 14, 1868, Émile Zola came to lunch:

> He talked about how hard his life was, how much he needed and would like to find a publisher who would give him 36,000 francs at the rate of 6,000 per year, so that he might be assured a livelihood for himself and his mother and thus be able to write the "history of a family" that he had in mind, a novel in eight volumes. (Goncourt, 264)

Things worked out for the twenty-eight-year-old Zola, and he wrote that history of a family, the Rougon-Macquarts, which in fact ran to twenty volumes (1871-93).

Those novels are of immense importance both to the rise of naturalism and to its assumption of a place amidst the resources of literature. (After a style has burst forth in any art, and has aroused discussion, it then mildly takes its place in the family of styles, along with others that once, too, ruled the roost when they were new.) But Zola's novels also had a marked effect on the theater and, in time, on film.

In 1902 the French director André Antoine produced a dramatization of one of them, *La Terre* (1887), at his theater, and after he moved into cinema, he filmed it in 1919. One of the first serious films I ever saw was *Gervaise* (1956, René Clément), made from *L'Assommoir* (1877), about a Paris washerwoman; she is the (absent) mother of the hero of the 1993 Zola film *Germinal* and is referred to in this picture by her son. *Germinal*, published in 1885, had previously "inspired" a French film in 1913 (Albert Capellani) and was itself filmed by Yves Allégret in 1963. All these are only a few instances of the way that Zola's fictional family's lineage has intertwined with the lineage of French theater and film.

Claude Berri, who directed the 1993 *Germinal*, continued his own evolving career with this picture. He began with such glop as the short *The Chicken* (1962) and *The Two of Us* (1967), but grew into a director of epic sweep comparable to Bertrand Tavernier. *Jean de Florette* (1986) and *Manon of the Spring* (1986) were large-sized in every good way, and *Uranus* (1990), set in postwar France, though it didn't quite succeed, had the same sense of size, understood and embraced.

With *Germinal*, the very first shot is reassuring. Night. A few lights. The camera pans slowly and discovers, at a distance, the works at a coal mine ahead, fires blazing, giant gaunt structures casting shadows, men and heavy horses moving like figures in a hell transposed to the surface of the earth. As we approach, we are stunned by the scene's stark, somehow complex simplicity. The cinematographer was Yves Angelo, who did *Tous les Matins du Monde* (1991, Alain Corneau), *The Accompanist* (1992, Claude Miller), and *Un Coeur en Hiver* (1992, Claude Sautet), all of which were refined work. Here Berri brings Angelo into a broad, spectacular mode, without abandoning his former delicacy. This opening sequence shows why naturalism and the theatrical were made for each other; later interiors, of miners' hovels and of managers' villas, are like the best traditional painting of the time.

That time is the late 1860s. The place is northern France. Berri, with a screenplay on which Arlette Langmann collaborated, carries us through Zola's account of Étienne Lantier, who arrives looking for work in the mine, is taken on as a hauler, then boards with a miner named Maheu, his wife, Maheude, and their family. Étienne soon plunges into the realities of mine work, the intricacies of socio-sexual relations among the miners and their women (some of whom work in the mine), the simmerings of revolt against the wretched and dangerous conditions of their lives. Counterpointing these elements are the lives of the bosses: ultra-luxe, elegant, frivolous. Eventually there is a strike; eventually, too, there are terror and bitter resolution. (A reminder here of another film about a labor struggle, Mario Monicelli's magnificent *The Organizer*, made in 1963.)

All of these components Berri handles with clarity, immediacy, and engaging pace. If we begin to feel uneasy about Berri's brusque juxtaposition of miners' grub with the pheasant and patisserie at the rich tables, we can remember that Berri is simply following Zola's blueprint. If the opposition looks too blunt here, it's not Berri's fault: it's because prose, the very being of prose itself, acts as buffer between contrasting elements; quick cutting from one place to another doesn't afford that kind of buffer in film, in the immediacy of film's images.

But, sadly to note, despite the patent sincerity of Berri's work, this rendering of *Germinal* isn't fulfilled—because (which is quite unlike him) there are three major miscastings. Étienne, Zola's twenty-year-old hero, is played by Renaud (a.k.a. Pierre Manuel Séchan), the mono-named popular singer who is much too old and, more importantly, dull. Renaud has no warmth or depth. For instance, he warns others about his fierce temper, but when it explodes, it is merely an action done on cue. Judith Henry plays Maheu's oldest daughter, with whom Étienne falls in love but who is involved with another miner, Chaval. She, too, is dull. The descriptions of her effect on her admirers, the violence she provokes between them, are not credible.

The biggest drawback, however, is the biggest name, Gérard Depardieu, who is Maheu. Many have remarked about his ample girth in this role of an underfed miner, but what's worse, he seems only a plump visitor to the film. Depardieu is an overwhelmingly gifted man with breathtaking range—the city man as farmer in *Jean de Florette*, the title role in **Andrzej Wajda's** *Danton* (1983), and the anguished priest in *Under the Sun of Satan* (1987, Maurice Pialat) are just a few instances. But sometimes Depardieu-the-reputation smothers Depardieu-the-actor, as in *Cyrano* (1990, Jean-Paul Rappeneau), which he merely bullied his way through, and as in *Germinal*. He seems here consciously the star willing to take a non-star role, becoming in some scenes a member of the mob, yet both bland and obtrusive as such.

These three people weaken a film that contains some fine acting: Miou-Miou (a.k.a. Sylvette Herry) as Maheude, who has to deal with three deaths in her family; Jean-Roger Milo as Chaval, rough and frightening as Étienne's rival; Jacques Dacqmine as the mine manager, full of craggy self-confidence in his dealings with the dissident men; Jean Carmet as the half-maddened old miner who coughs coal dust; Laurent Terzieff as the anarchist miner who despises his co-workers because they want merely to strike, not destroy.

But these performances, vivid though they are, are not positioned to give the film the central verity that it needs; and Berri's directing, as such, can't fill the gap. This is a fundamental, vitiating flaw. When we see Monicelli's *The Organizer*, we never ask why we needed a film about early labor struggles at such a late date: Marcello Mastroianni, Folco Lulli, and all the cast seize us, draw us in. But when *Germinal* ends, for all its assets, we do ask why we needed this picture in 1993. The question wouldn't arise if the principal actors had brushed it away.

Acting aside for the moment, the compliment one can pay the French film *Gervaise* (1956)—again, one of the first serious pictures I ever saw—is to say that it represents faithfully the novel on which it is based. The usual movie made from a book, like the film of Zola's 1880 novel *Nana* (Christian-Jaque, 1955), is generally a grab bag; the producer takes from the fiction what he thinks will fit his stars or his conception of assured popularity. This isn't true of the producer (Annie Dorfmann), the director (René Clément), and the screenwriters (Jean Aurenche and Pierre Bost) of *Gervaise.* Their purpose was simply to render a novel as film. Limited only by the inflexible differences between the two media, they succeeded.

L'Assommoir, it will be remembered, is a cornerstone in Émile Zola's immense Rougon-Macquart cycle of twenty novels. It was one of the first Zola novels—published in 1877—to achieve wide popularity. An American translation (under the title *Gervaise*, incidentally) appeared only two years later and was made from the *sixtieth* French edition. (Zola's title is difficult to translate and is variously rendered in English as *The Gin Palace*, *The Drunkard*, or *The Drinking Den*.) The book tells the story of Gervaise Macquart, a cripple from the south of France who comes to Paris with her lover and their two sons, works hard to support them all, is deserted by the lover, marries a roof mender by whom she has a daughter (Nana), and then has to support him, too, after he is injured in a fall. She opens a laundry shop, but her husband's drinking—encouraged by her lover, who returns and is welcomed into the house by the husband—brings about their eventual ruin. In the end the husband dies raving in a madhouse, the sons are scattered, Nana is gaily embarked on her own story, and Gervaise, her hope crushed, dies drunk and alone. Though it sounds austere, Angus Wilson once called this Zola's "most compassionate work" (Wilson, 127).

The book is in the film. The last quarter of the novel is drastically condensed but the spirit of it is not violated; instead of protracting the husband's delirious disintegration, Gervaise's decline, and the start of Nana's fancy career, the adapters let the first occur in the shop and clearly foreshadow the latter two. It is enough; two hours of any movie, even a refreshingly grim one, are enough. To reread *L'Assommoir* is to be struck by the fidelity of the film. The first view of the cheap hotel balcony, the steamy fight in the public laundry, the wedding party in the Louvre, the fall from the roof, the feast on Gervaise's saint's day—all these are in the film.

"I must show all the world trying to bring about her ruin, consciously or unconsciously" (Buckler, 124), Zola wrote about his heroine in a note to the novel. As Gervaise, Maria Schell embodies the giving soul looking for a worthy receiving soul who is heartlessly used, in the short or long run, by men whose egos are unable to withstand her generosity. There is in Schell's performance perhaps an ounce too much winsomeness—a winsomeness that she was to depend on, and therefore overdo, in later films—but here she moves us with her straightforward, simple affection. (Both her performance and the film won awards at the Venice Film Festival.) The rest of the cast, notably Suzy Delair as

233

Virginie, is always satisfactory. But the most notable triumphs of the film are those of the adapters and the director.

How do the European filmmakers, especially the French, evoke the past so convincingly in their pictures? The answer cannot be simply that their sets are ready-made. Old Paris streets are available to American filmmakers, as well. Part of the answer is in the actors, whose training and whose imaginations—cultivated by that training—enable them to breathe and bend in costume. Yet a larger part of the answer must lie with the directors, in this case René Clément. He made the world of *Gervaise*. What happens to his principals in a tavern or a marketplace or a music hall seems only a portion of what is happening there; certain characters are in the foreground only because it is their story that has been chosen to be told. Any of the people moving around them are equally real, equally interesting, just as busily engaged in following the unraveling threads of their own lives. There are no dress extras in this picture.

Clément also has a gift for unfolding a large scene from a small beginning. The scene that ends with the husband's wild, obscene smashing of the laundry begins with a close-up of little Nana looking through a glass that is about to be heated and affixed to her ailing father's back. The effect is one of slipping through a quiet keyhole into a gradually revealed house full of hell. The squeamish may at first object to the blatancy of the husband's bloodied back (when his delirium topples him against the wall, with cupping glasses on him), of a vomit-spattered bed, of nose-picking. But that objection cannot be held against the director: these things are true to the spirit of *L'Assommoir*. For at almost every point the film is strapped to the book; you cannot tug at the former without hitting up against the latter.

Here the reward of virtue is that the film's faults are Zola's faults. For all its excellences of acting, editing, photography, and direction, *Gervaise* leaves us with a feeling of pointlessness. We have watched a simple, hard-working woman beaten down by a clever, opportunistic lover whom she cannot resist, by a weak husband who turns to drink, by ceaseless toil, and by whimsical fate. This is not tragic; it is simply grinding. We are neither enlightened sociologically nor harrowed psychologically by her experience. As to the former, Zola's theories are cold, his revelations stale. His theory of scientific determinism may have been a valuable ingredient in the intellectual ferment of the Third Republic, but we now know enough about slums and poverty to understand that we must fight ceaselessly to eliminate them—and must not expect human character to be notably improved thereby.

We are not moved tragically by the heroine's fall because we are too conscious that she is a clinical example. "It is surely a lesson in morality" (Zola, ix), wrote Zola in his preface to the novel. Indeed, in the scene of the soiled bed he writes: "And this was the outcome of Drink, this was an example of the results of the passion for strong liquor: Man degraded to bestiality" (Zola, 273). In the film as in the book, the author, standing at the side with blackboard pointer, vitiates his own work as art. It is a slice of life, and we feel that the knife might have gone into any one of a million specimens.

If all this is true, why isn't Zola's film (for such it is) at the level of a franker soap opera of the nineteenth century? For the hallmark of soap opera is continual woe heaped on the unremittingly virtuous. What prevents *Gervaise* from being merely *Nana's Mama, or Too Poor to Be Sober*? There are, I think, two factors that keep us from being bored or from sniggering. The first is the titanic intensity of the mind that assembled these materials and is pointing this moral. His purpose may be didactic, but his perceptions, his sympathies, his energies, his instinct for architecture are enormous. His theories seem foolish, but Zola makes himself felt, here as in *Germinal*, despite them. The second factor is the result of the first: we find ourselves touched by a work written in anger at the obstacles men put in the path of their own perfectibility. In our world of more moderate expectations, we are moved, nostalgically, by the fire of a man to whom the farthest horizon was at once limitless and attainable.

Works Cited

Buckler, William E. *Novels in the Making*. New York: Houghton Mifflin, 1961.

Goncourt, Edmond de, & Jules de Goncourt. *The Goncourt Journals, 1851-1870*. Trans. Lewis Galantiere. 1937. New York: Doubleday, 1958.

Wilson, Angus. *Émile Zola: An Introductory Study of His Novels*. London: Secker & Warburg, 1964.

Zola, Émile. *L'Assommoir*. Ed. Ernest A. Vizetelly. New York: Marion Company, 1915.

Angels and Insects (1995, Philip Haas)

I approach my analysis of the film *Angels and Insects* (1995, Philip Haas) by way of the occupation of its leading male character. He is a naturalist, and what immediately struck me was the similarity between this profession and an apparently dissimilar one: that of the photographer. To wit, photography made every human being's face reproducible, not only the faces of those who could afford to engage a portrait painter, even as its logical extension, the cinema, placed the world at every individual's disposal, not just the disposal of the rich who could travel anywhere and see anything they wanted. In the same way as the photographer, a naturalist is committed to the objective study of all living organisms without passing value judgments on, or attributing moral, spiritual, or supernatural significance to, those animals and plants.

Naturalism in science, ethics, and philosophy led, of course, to naturalism in late-nineteenth-century European fiction and drama, where lower-class characters took center stage, heredity and environment became determinants of character, and human beings became animalistic objects for observation and control through artistic means comparable to those of the scientific method. Naturalism in the arts, together with—and often in direct combination with—its less fatalistic or more ameliorative middle-class relative called realism, has been with us ever since, as I trust the ugly, even repulsive, domestic matter of *Angels and Insects* will show. This picture was directed by the American Philip Haas, who adapted its screenplay, along with his wife, Belinda (who is also his editor), from A. S. Byatt's novella "Morpho Eugenia," which is one of two novellas in Byatt's collection titled *Angels and Insects* (1992).

The Haases are fairly faithful to Byatt's novella, with one significant exception, which I shall note later. The film *Angels and Insects* tells of an impoverished young entomologist of working-class background, William Adamson, who is taken into the country home of Sir Harald Alabaster, a wealthy, middle-aged clergyman and amateur scientist. William has lately returned to England (the year is 1859) from ten years in the Amazon country, where he lived among natives and risked his life to study the local butterflies. Shipwrecked on his homeward voyage, he lost all his belongings, including his many specimens—except, that is, for two butterflies from the species classified as Morpho Eugenia. William is grateful to Sir Harald for rescuing him from penury, and returns the favor by agreeing to organize Alabaster's own collection of insect life, as well as to tutor the reverend's younger children in natural history. The reverend and Lady Alabaster's older children are a grown son, Edgar, and two grown daughters, Rowena and Eugenia.

The correspondence between Eugenia's name and that of William Adamson's two lovely butterfly specimens is naturally no accident. Indeed, Eugenia and the other Alabaster women are exquisitely gowned (by the designer Paul Brown) in the riotous colors of the butterfly world, so that there can be no mistaking the film's (and the novella's) ironic parallels between the blond, patrician Alabasters and the low life of insects. Butterflies may be beautiful, but they are still insects, and here their flitting about is certainly meant to suggest the frivolous behavior of aristocratic women chiefly occupied with the pursuit of pleasure.

Insects other than butterflies populate the Haases' movie and Byatt's fiction, however, and they are of the unappealing kind. William breeds moths and is writing a book about red-ant colonies; moreover, during walks he takes with the Alabaster youngsters, he overturns rocks and dead branches to show them the maggots and worms underneath. A maid carries a bucket full of beetles up from the cellar of the Alabasters' great house, called Bredely Hall in a thinly disguised reference to the various kinds of breeding that take place there. And moths are visibly drawn to the pallidly beautiful silk of one of Eugenia's evening dresses.

The connection is made throughout, then, between the Alabasters and unclean insects—not, as one might guess from the meaning of "alabaster," between these aristocrats and pristine angels. And the symbolic pronouncement of this connection becomes clear: that beneath the seeming decorum, even primness, of the Victorian social order lurks a repressed sexuality that has the potential to create moral anarchy. The entomologist William Adamson nonetheless doesn't perceive the equation of Alabaster and insect until he is nearly crushed by its force, for he gets drawn early into his host family's web through a quiet attraction to the angelically beautiful Eugenia. Grimly aware of his poverty and low social standing, William falls deeply in love with the melancholy Eugenia despite himself. He is subsequently surprised, albeit delighted, to learn of her willingness to marry him, and the marriage goes forward, over Edgar's vehement objections, with the kindly approval of Sir Harald.

In spite of the fact that William and Eugenia's union results, over a three-year period, in the birth of two sets of female twins and one son, there remains an ominous uneasiness at the heart of their marriage. In the novella, this uneasiness is intimated by narration such as the following:

> He was unhappy for many reasons.... [I]n the midst of the enclosed and complicated society of the country house, he was lonely ... He had no place inside the female society of kitchen, nursery, or pretty parlour.... His wife dozed and sewed and her attendants fed and groomed her. The other girls were away doing this and that ... The young men were not often there, and when they were, were smoky and noisy.... If he had a place, it was in the spaces between the cushioned family softnesses and the closed-away servile hierarchies in the attics and cellars and back rooms. (Byatt, 84-87)

The effect of Byatt's third-person narration here is to isolate William in his thoughts, and so to convey both his psychological and even physical isolation on the manor to which he was *not* born—and where his enforced separation from Eugenia during her pregnancies would only remove him further from the possibility of spiritual intimacy with her.

That separation is visually conveyed three times in the Haases' film by the emphatic closing of the door to Eugenia's private bedroom; and the cumulative effect of the successive images of this barring door is inauspiciously to suggest something more than mere coital abstinence, as Byatt's single verbal description of the ritual of exclusion does not by itself do. In addition, whenever Eugenia and her husband do have sex in this picture, the malady at the core of their marriage is expressed through visual metaphor rather than verbal portent. That is, the Haases make the direct point, through the sensational juxtaposition of images, that William Adamson's problem at Bredely Hall goes beyond his own emotional isolation or spiritual disjunction to the very nature of his connubial alliance with Eugenia Alabaster. We watch this couple's lovemaking four times in *Angels and Insects,* and in the first three of these instances—two of which result in the impregnation of Eugenia, ostensibly by William—the act of intercourse is followed almost at once by a shot of insects feeding, breeding, or bleeding. When we see him copulate with his wife for the fourth time, moreover—a copulation that is succeeded by the birth of Eugenia's second set of twins—William simultaneously recalls someone's hand in the act of drawing warrior ants.

The "someone" doing the sketches of ants is the dark-haired, drably dressed Matty Crompton, a poor but somewhat educated relation of the Alabasters who has charge of the family's younger children. She fashions herself a socialist, and is curious to study, with William, the behavior of ant colonies—of slave ants and their masters—for what it can teach humans about their own practices. Matty refers explicitly to the Civil War "being waged at present across the Atlantic, to secure not only the liberation of the unfortunate slaves," she says, "but the moral salvation of those whose leisure and enrichment are sustained by their cruel labors" (Byatt, 115-116). She means by those masters not merely the plantation owners of the southern United States, but also the Alabasters themselves, whose family wealth comes from the Lancashire cotton trade, which itself depends on the American slave trade. So Matty has been observing Alabasters as well as ants, and she knows that, even as master red ants crossbreed with their worker black-and-brown ants, Edgar has been ravishing the servant girl, Amy. She gets pregnant and is dismissed from Bredely Hall, but Matty Crompton recognizes that another young woman remains with whom Edgar has also been breeding.

He has been inbreeding with Eugenia, and remarkably appears to have sired all five of her children, each of which looks to the bemused William like "an Alabaster, a pale, clean-cut, nervous creature" (Byatt, 84). Matty herself has known about Edgar and Eugenia's taboo relationship for some time. But it is a stable lad, not Matty, who calls William back from a fox hunt—ironically, the first "gentlemanly" pursuit in which we see him engaged—to look in on his wife, whom he finds in bed with her brother. William will not kill Edgar or harm Eugenia, however, nor even reveal the truth about their "secret" to Sir Harald. He will instead flee Bredely House for good and set out on another expedition to the Amazon, this time with Matty Crompton as his loving companion-cum-collaborator. The Alabasters must now live by—and with—themselves, with all that Edgar and Eugenia have wrought. Because they cannot survive otherwise, this family must also continue to live with its "worker ants," the lowly servants who nevertheless know everything that goes on in the great house and sometimes anonymously choose to bare the truth.

As for the equating of the Alabasters and the British aristocracy in general with insects, all I can say is that Byatt's novella does this far less melodramatically than the Haases' movie. Nor does "Morpho Eugenia" seriously make the contrary parallel between angels and the Amazonian natives who befriended William Adamson, as Belinda Haas does through her editing of the film's credit sequence. In the very first shots, we see and hear these natives singing, drumming, and dancing orgiastically around a fire, to be momentarily interrupted by the superimposition of the word "Angels" on the screen. "And" appears as the image dissolves to a different kind of dance, a measured ball at Bredely Hall featuring couples moving in telling circles, which is duly followed by the superimposition of the word "Insects." Haas's intercutting the title "Insects" here is, of course, the verbal equivalent of her visual counterpointing of William and Eugenia's sexual intercourse—and, by implication, the latter's incestuous defiling of their conjugal knot—with the ignoble life of insects. The opposite verbal effect is achieved not only through the superimposition of the title "Angels," but also through William's association in the screenplay of the Amazon country and its indigenous inhabitants with paradise as it is depicted in John Milton's *Paradise Lost* (1667).

In the novella, however, Byatt goes out of her way to associate the Amazonians, not with angels, but instead with the slave-making Amazonian ants, as this passage from William's forthcoming book, *The Swarming City*, reveals: "[T]he Amazons . . . Their name is probably bestowed because like the classical Amazon warriors, . . . [these ants] have substituted belligerence for the delicate domestic virtues associated with the female sex" (Byatt, 115). Moreover, it is the Amazonian Indians, not the aristocratic Anglicans, who resemble insects in that the men, like male butterflies, dress in brilliant colors, while the females of the species display plainer coverings or surfaces.

The point of the novella, then, is that *all* human life is somewhat insect-like, if only in the sense that people and insects alike are animals. While it is true that some of the Alabasters behave like "insects," it is equally true that their purely patrician breeding is more a human than an animal or insect phenomenon. The real intention of Byatt's title *Angels and Insects* is thus not simplistically to divide the world into angels and insects, into noble savagery and base civilization. Rather, that intention is to designate the change the world had undergone in the nineteenth century from an age of religion, when the line between good and evil was clearly drawn, theologically revealed, and aristocratically confirmed, to an age of science. This was the age of Charles Darwin and Auguste Comte, of Karl Marx and later Sigmund Freud, in which the line between good and evil became blurred if not beside the point in a brave new world devoted to methodically explaining the behavior of humans in particular, and animals in general, in terms of genetics and milieu, evolution and conditioning, biology and psychology in tandem with sociology, economics, and politics. No longer was man considered a special or divine order of creation, but instead just another creature subject to the same basic needs and impelled by the same basic drives as all other creatures.

The cinematography of *Angels and Insects* happens to convey the idea of a world under the measured sway of impartial modern science, as opposed to the absolutist rule of parochial Christian theology or lately of vilifying liberal-labor politics, better than the Haases' scenario does. Bernard Zitzermann, who shot their first movie, *The Music of Chance* (1993), lights this film in such a way that sunlight doesn't always bring with it a cheery brightness, nor does candlelight always warm the cockles of one's heart. Whatever the light in a particular scene, it is subtly shaded, and the effect is to create a complex but whole picture of the world rather than an easy carving of it along partisan lines.

The wholeness of this picture is necessarily enhanced by the cool, painterly detachment of Zitzermann's camera, which eschews excessive cutting for the equipoise of the fully framed composition. That equipoise is sometimes disturbed, however, by the filmmakers' predilection for high-angle shots of the aristocrats, such as the one of fat Lady Alabaster, asleep outside on the sprawling lawn after having gorged herself on strawberries and cream, the remnants of which are now swarming with ants. Shots like this obviously diminish the stature of the English upper class at the same time as they emphasize its increasing vulnerability, but they amount to a species of overkill in this picture.

The mostly appropriate music is by Alexander Balanescu, and it alternates between two contrasting themes, sometimes uniquely combining them into the same piece of accompaniment: a delicate, sprightly one, epitomizing by turns the play of innocence and the habit of purblindness, and a moderately melancholic, never manifestly maudlin, melody that evokes the passing if not the decadence of a way of life. Symbolizing the new order or the new man, of course, is William Adamson, understatedly yet sensitively played by Mark Rylance. He manages to shade his character in such a way that this externally dour plebeian comes off at once as someone animated as much by submerged passion and intensity as by mannered protocol and inhibition.

Adamson may be at the center of the drama of *Angels and Insects,* but he is flanked by three figures whose own drama sets his in relief and therefore requires acting of a particularly illuminating yet unself-conscious kind: the well-meaning but intellectually naïve Sir Harald (Jeremy Kemp), who also remains naïve about his children's incestuous relationship; the class-arrogant, sexually predatory Edgar (Douglas Henshall), who has not a mitigating ounce of kindness in his character; and the tremulously alluring female of the family, Eugenia (Patsy Kensit), who shows herself to be an amoral and finally amorphous being. As the somber Matty, William's complement rather than his foil, Kristin Scott-Thomas proves that she is Rylance's equal in the ability to suggest a depth of feeling and range of ambition beneath a tightly wound, narrowly focused surface.

In sum what *Angels and Insects* does—in fiction as in film but with more immediacy, and therefore more power, on screen—is centrally examine the life of an ordinary but affecting human being (William Adamson) under a microscope, if you will, and microscopes have a way of both opening up dirty little pores and extenuating or alleviating the big bright colors of life's spectrum. In other words, "microscopic" art such as that found in *Angels and Insects* paradoxically enlarges our humanity at the same time as it reduces us all to our least common denominator.

Work Cited

Byatt, A. S. *Angels and Insects: Two Novellas.* 1992. New York: Vintage, 1994.

Washington Square (1997, Agnieszka Holland)

In November of 1880 William James read two new novels by his brother Henry, one of which was *Washington Square*, and sent him a congratulatory letter. Henry replied:

> Thank you for what you say about my two novels. The young man in *Washington Square* is not a portrait—he is sketched from the outside merely & not *fouillé*. The only good thing in the story is the girl. (Skrupskelis, 128)

Too modest, many of us might say. Few would put this novel in the first James rank, but the young man is sufficiently explored to make him entirely credible, and Dr. Sloper, the girl's father, has fascinations. His complexities, his modes of wreaking vengeance on his daughter because her birth caused the death of his beloved wife, have a range that includes the sexual. (There's a slight reminder here of the relationship between Elizabeth Barrett and her own father.)

In the William Wyler film (1949), some suggestion of the sensual touched Ralph Richardson's performance of Dr. Sloper, the eminent New York physician who thinks irony a useful tone to employ toward a daughter who is failing to come forward as rapidly as he had hoped. That screenplay was by Ruth and Augustus Goetz, who derived it from their 1947 dramatization of the book for the theater (it was revived successfully in 1995 on Broadway). Their version gave the story a vindictive conclusion. Wyler's film, like the Goetz play, was called *The Heiress*, and the jilted heiress had a biter-bit last scene in which, after some years, the jilter was jilted.

The picture was admirably done, a superior entertainment with excellent performances; but it was also a literal translation of a play that was itself a dubious adaptation—an approximation, if you will, of an acknowledged work of art. The authors of *The Heiress*, in order to fashion something that would "play," had to coarsen a story whose quality lay in the delicacy of its perception and the quietness of its torments. Emotional violence was introduced to provide action, and the characters, particularly Catherine Sloper (played by Olivia de Havilland, opposite Montgomery Clift as Morris Townsend), were forced into implausible gestures to provide good curtains.

In 1997, James's 1880 novel was filmed again and called *Washington Square*, but the Goetz version is not in evidence. In this screenplay by Carol Doyle, the tyrannical rich father is again, through his wealth, successful in dissuading his daughter's suitor, but the ending is much closer to James (despite a sugary touch with a child). Catherine Sloper wreaks no vengeance; she simply dismisses the returned Morris Townsend. She has become the queen of her self, of her pride, in a way that her now-deceased father might not have imagined.

But, despite its more Jamesian conclusion, this film flounders. First, the casting. Jennifer Jason Leigh, as Catherine, is a reclusive, damaged, tight-lipped worrier, with no hint in her of thwarted possibilities for fullness. In Wyler's film Olivia de Havilland was a prisoner; Leigh is a neurotic. Ben Chaplin, as Morris, may have been chosen because he has a vague resemblance to Montgomery Clift, de Havilland's too amiable suitor; but Chaplin has no hint of Clift's temperament or depth. Morris needs to convince us of his genuine feeling for Catherine, despite the genuineness of his need for her wealth. Chaplin is simply around a lot in the film, with not much power.

The gifted Maggie Smith plays Catherine's aunt, but the colorful Smith is straitjacketed in this doting-aunt role. The biggest disappointment, because of high hopes for him, is Albert Finney as Dr. Sloper. Most of what he does here seems first-take acting—though it may have been twentieth-take or more. Finney curls his lines in the air like a slave-driver's whip, but the whole part is, as theater lingo has it, indicated. Nothing that Finney says or does comes from a realized man.

The cinematographer was Jerzy Zielinski, who manages to frame compositions without planes or emphasis. Except for the two-shots and close-ups, we frequently see frames in which there is little distinction between the flowers on the table, the pictures on the wall, the curtains on the windows, and the characters in the scene. Yes, domestic clutter was a sign of the *bon ton* of the time, but to include the characters in the clutter doesn't much help the drama. And Zielinski's colors would be the envy of any postcard manufacturer.

The director was the Polish-born, Czech-trained Agnieszka Holland, who won some renown for *Europa, Europa* (1990) and a few other films. If before *Washington Square* her work sometimes seemed overbearing, here it seems ill at ease, uncomfortable, straining for effect. She falls back on the sorriest of clichés. Is there a scene between the two lovers in a park near a fountain? Then we must have at least one shot of the lovers seen through the fountain spray. Does Morris abandon Catherine and drive off, with her running after the carriage through the muddy street? Then of course Catherine must trip and fall headlong into the mud. And naturally Holland is ultimately responsible for the general superficiality of the acting throughout.

Washington Square doesn't begin to answer the question that attends all re-makes: Why?

Work Cited

Skrupskelis, Ignas, & Elizabeth M. Berkeley, eds. *William and Henry James: Selected Letters*. Charlottesville: University Press of Virginia, 1997.

The Hours (2002, Stephen Daldry)

"More matter, less art," is what kept running through my mind as I watched Stephen Daldry's *The Hours* (2002), which aims to be a mainstream art-house movie based on a postmodern novel (of the same title, written by the American Michael Cunningham and published in 1998). That novel was inspired by an earlier work—Virginia Woolf's *Mrs. Dalloway* (1925)—itself a modernist experiment in the use of stream-of-consciousness technique to plumb the depths of one woman's character. So, in a sense, *The Hours*, which was the working title of *Mrs. Dalloway*, has three authors: Woolf, Cunningham, and the British playwright-cum-filmmaker David Hare, who wrote the scenario and has written comparable characters in the drama *Plenty* (1978) and the movie *Strapless* (1989). That is to say, this picture has no one author and therefore no single voice. Let's call it adaptation *à la mode*, art by committee, or an instance of the aesthetics of incest. *The Hours* even has a cinematic relation: Marleen Gorris's 1997 adaptation of Woolf's novel, also titled *Mrs. Dalloway*, which starred Vanessa Redgrave.

Mrs. Dalloway, the book, spans a single day in the life of its titular character, a London society hostess married to Richard, a conventional chap who is an unremarkable member of Parliament as well. As she prepares for a lavish party, Clarissa Dalloway appears irritatingly chirpy, so much so that we sense her happy face masks a deep, inner weariness or dissatisfaction. In the course of her day, she is invaded by memories of two lost loves—one male, one female—from a time when everything still seemed possible. Clarissa is haunted, then, by the sense of a life misspent, of opportunities missed, but she is able to endure, despite her flashes of loneliness, because she can cling to the present moment and its "ordinary pleasures" (Cunningham, 211)— unlike Virginia Woolf herself, the bisexual visionary artist doomed to hearing voices in her head, to suffering from depression, and ultimately to committing suicide-by-drowning. Simultaneously in the novel, a shell-shocked veteran of World War I shares Mrs. Dalloway's unease in tragically heightened form— opting in the end to kill himself—though the two characters never meet.

Three women are the chief subjects of Michael Cunningham's novel, which is a suite of variations on the fiction of, and facts about, Virginia Woolf. This book, like the movie, begins with a snapshot prologue presenting Woolf's death in 1941; then both novel and film, flashing back to 1923, follow her through a single day as she labors at the manuscript of her fourth—and first major—novel, *Mrs. Dalloway*, under the lovingly watchful if hopelessly resigned eye of her husband, Leonard; until finally each work flashes forward, in a kind of epilogue, to that fateful day in 1941 when the English novelist ended her life in the River Ouse, her pockets stuffed with rocks. Alternating with Woolf's story in the novel as well as the film of *The Hours*, in the manner of the parallel story lines in *Mrs. Dalloway* itself, are two other narrative strands examining comparable days in the lives of two other women.

The first is Laura Brown, a pregnant, suburban Los Angeles housewife in 1951 who is reading *Mrs. Dalloway*, who may be a repressed lesbian, whose doting if doltish spouse is a veteran of World War II, and whose adoring young son tries to help his otherwise withdrawn mother as she bakes a cake for her husband's birthday celebration. The second woman is

Clarissa Vaughan, a fiftyish New York book-publisher's editor in the present in the midst of fastidiously preparing a party to celebrate the poetry prize that her ex-lover, Richard—who has teasingly nicknamed Clarissa "Mrs. Dalloway"—has just received. She is now a "partnered" lesbian with a grown-up daughter, he a single or abandoned homosexual afflicted with AIDS in its agonizing final stages.

Cunningham's novel uses multiple points of view and stream-of-consciousness technique (in addition to a time-jumping structure) to tell the stories of Woolf, Brown, and Vaughan, but David Hare wisely rejected the idea of three different, first-person voice-overs as too confusing, as well as the device of an off-screen omniscient narrator as over-literary. He knew he had to make his screen characters speak out loud, to other people, thoughts that were implicit or submerged in the book. The result is not, as one might have guessed, to the film's detriment, for Hare's streamlining of all three narratives meant that he had to mute the novel's concern with gay and feminist sexual politics. Indeed, the novel of *The Hours* sometimes seems like a veiled but insistent lament for the closeted homosexual, in which Woolf's plangent voice is used to inflate a more limited (and dourly sentimental) agenda: one that valorizes gay higher consciousness. (I was therefore not surprised to learn that Michael Cunningham had originally intended to make his modern, female Dalloways homosexual men.) And according to this agenda, being "out," as Clarissa and Richard are, somehow makes you uniquely self-aware— even if "outing" in the end, particularly for gay men, leads only to the freedom to contract AIDS more readily or openly.

It may be Richard, in the film, who presciently warns Clarissa, "When I die you'll have to think of your own life," and who illuminates the title after his former (female) lover tells him that he doesn't have to come to the party in his honor if he does not want to: "But there are still the hours, aren't there? One and then another, and you get through that one and then, my God, there's another." Yet, since the movie is no political screed on behalf of gay superiority, intellectual or otherwise, these lines point to larger issues that are also present in Woolf's *Mrs. Dalloway*: how one chooses to live one's life or not live it, and what it actually means to be alive; why we connect with some people but not others, as well as the ultimate disconnection from others that is their death or ours; the ubiquitous presence in our lives of our own mortality, along with the fleetingness of human experience juxtaposed against the infinitude of disembodied time.

Richard escapes the infinitude of time by the same means as the war veteran in *Mrs. Dalloway*. Still, Woolf's own death is of far greater importance to the atmosphere of the film than her novel. It's the image of her methodically stuffing stones into her pockets that is essential to *The Hours*, not her fictional portrait of Clarissa Dalloway. Thus Daldry and Hare's movie lives in an adduced gravity. Virginia Woolf's finish, just because it is Woolf's finish, is used to aggrandize the other two stories (even as the dramatist Edward Albee used just her name to aggrandize his own inflated 1962 play *Who's Afraid of Virginia Woolf?*). Her suicide in 1941 has nothing to do with Clarissa's life, unless one argues, absurdly, that Woolf would not have killed herself had she "married" the poet and novelist Vita Sackville-West, with whom she had once been romantically involved. Woolf's death has even less to do with Richard's fate, for his trouble is physical more than mental: were he not racked by AIDS, he would not be so concerned with living out the hours before his premature death.

Laura Brown may be closer to Woolf's Mrs. Dalloway than is the contemporary Clarissa of New York, and she may even be somewhat more of a refraction of Woolf herself, allowing for the "reduction" in her socioeconomic stature. Nonetheless, her own drama relies almost impertinently on Virginia Woolf the person rather than the author, particularly when one considers that Laura's potential suicide, along with the actual suicides of Woolf and Richard, provides the atmosphere of both the book and film of *The Hours*. Paradoxically, then, it is the immanence of death—again, the fact that life is attended throughout by the possibility of sudden, intentional exit—not the life of Clarissa Dalloway, that gives the story its pulse. As when Laura one day leaves her little boy in the care of a neighbor, takes a purse full of pills along with a copy of Woolf's book to a hotel room (at last, a room of her own), lies down, bares her pregnant belly, and considers her pills—which she does not take.

As we learn, she undergoes a different change, which is revealed eventually through the fate of her son. That son is the poet Richard, whom she abandoned, together with his father and her infant daughter, right after giving birth for the second time. These two strands of the story, seemingly disparate, finally integrate (as the two strands in *Mrs. Dalloway* do not) when the older Laura Brown arrives at Clarissa Vaughan's Greenwich Village apartment in the wake of Richard's suicide—to explain herself and, implicitly, to trace Richard's homosexuality to the same repressive hetero-domesticity that she herself escaped. The third strand then completes *The Hours* and reiterates its thematic emphasis, or reintroduces what I have termed its adduced gravity, as Virginia Woolf wades into the water that will irrevocably end her psychological torment—as well as the brilliant literary career that gave us, subsequent to *Mrs. Dalloway*, *To the Lighthouse* (1927), *Orlando* (1928), and *The Waves* (1931).

So, once more, suicide in a work of art—particularly when it "quotes" the suicide of a fabled artist—proves to be a good investment, since it virtually guarantees that, whatever the ultimate view of the work, it will be taken seriously. Michael Cunningham's novel deserved serious consideration partly because his *Hours* was helped by the unifying device of its prose, which "channels" Woolf's rippling cadences at the same time as it curves gracefully into one historical present after another. For Cunningham tells the stories of Woolf, Brown, and Vaughan in discrete, alternating chapters, whereas Daldry and Hare do a fair amount of skipping around in time, moving freely among the three strands through the use of match cuts that, sometimes banally, sometimes ponderously, draw parallels between Woolf and her "descendants."

The ringing of an alarm clock, the placing of flowers in a vase—each of these actions is mundanely used as a springboard in the movie to move the action back and forth between eras. But when Virginia Woolf lies on the ground to stare into the black eyes of a dead bird, and that bird morphs seamlessly—nay, transcendently—into the emotionally dead Laura Brown, we know we're in the presence of two characters in search of an author, not a film editor. The cinematographer, Seamus McGarvey, can't help them, because he has obviously been instructed to give each place and time period of *The Hours*—Britain between the two world wars, Southern California in the early fifties, New York City just after the turn of the millennium—a different look: mildly misty to sepia sunny to subtly shaded or shadowed.

The minimalist composer Philip Glass attempts to create the continuous rush and swirl of Cunningham's prose with an insistent score for alternately somber and sobbing strings, but the insistence of this music borders on intrusion and its over-amplification amounts to overcompensation. As for the film's director, Stephen Daldry, he manages to keep the ambience close and confidential throughout, as if secrets were in the air, without resorting (or without being permitted to resort, by Hare's carefully pruned script) to the sentiment that marred his *Billy Elliot* (2000)—oddly enough, itself a movie about a "closeted" character, trapped in a northern British mining town and mourning his dead mother, who longs to reinvent himself as a dancer.

The question remains, does the acting in *The Hours* help to unify this picture by the very uniformity of its excellence? Almost. The biggest problem, in the role of Clarissa Dalloway, is Meryl Streep, who feels compelled to fill in every second of screen time with fussy bits of stage business that are designed to reveal what we already know about her character. It's as if Streep were gesturally running by us everything she has ever learned about acting or characterization, and such stunting doesn't work here—it hadn't worked for her, in my view, for some time—where she should organically *be* more than artificially *do*, where Clarissa's very connection with Woolf and Brown is in her sheer unemancipated female being, despite all the external trappings of emancipation in this middle-aged woman's professional as well as personal life.

As for Nicole Kidman in the part of Virginia Woolf, she is unrecognizable beneath a prosthetic nose and layers of makeup, which means that for once in a film, she can attempt to create a character rather than be a star. And Kidman succeeds, in no small measure because everything is painfully apparent on the surface of the character she has created; she need actively reveal nothing—which in the past had led to her overacting—only physically perform the little that the role of the remote or removed Woolf calls on her to do. Julianne Moore, for her part, is more than recognizable as Laura Brown, a character akin to the fifties housewife she played in Todd Haynes's virtually simultaneous *Far from Heaven* (2002)—except that in *The Hours* the polish is off (if the crude old-age makeup is not in her meeting with Clarissa Vaughan) and Moore's character is exposed in all her vulnerability. This talented and lovely actress is not helped, however, by the casting of the homely John C. Reilly as her benighted husband: Laura Brown's feelings of entrapment and despair are thus almost superficially explained, or explained away. (The novel's Laura, by contrast, is somewhat plain, but has a conventionally handsome husband.)

As for the artifice of *The Hours*, then, I reject it. It is a fundamentally feckless and self-indulgent, if not cannibalistic, exercise of the kind that film as well as fiction artists should eschew at all cost—or is it conscience?

Work Cited

Cunningham, Michael. *The Hours*. New York: Picador/Farrar, Straus, and Giroux, 1998.

STUDY QUESTIONS

1. Did the adapted film in question add anything (plot elements, for instance) that was not in the original narrative or dramatic version? Why do you think the individuals who made the film added those parts?

2. What parts of the original narrative or drama were left out of the adapted film? Why do you think the people who made the film left out those parts?

3. Did you like the source version—the novel, short story, or play—better than the adapted film itself? Why?

4. When reading the original novel, story, or play, did you imagine the characters differently from the way in which they were portrayed on screen? Why? What caused your imagination—or the adaptation itself—to "fail"?

5. Why do you think movie producers and directors often change the original narrative or dramatic version of a work (so much so that sometimes the work's fundamental theme or thesis itself changes) when they adapt it to the screen?

6. In the case of a *play* versus its film version, how did the film change—or not change—the lighting, setting, and time period of the dramatic source?

7. Think about the setting (including the time period) of the original *fiction narrative* of a work that has been adapted to the screen. Did the setting in the film look as you had imagined it? If not, how was it different and why were changes made?

8. Think about the main character as transposed from page or stage to screen. How was he or she different from what you had imagined? How was he or she the same?

9. Were there any major changes in the cast of characters—deletions, additions—between the narrative or dramatic source and the adapted film? Why do you think the people who made the film would leave out or add a character?

10. Do you think the individuals who made the adapted film in question did a good job of staying true to the spirit, if not the letter, of the narrative or dramatic source? Why or why not?

11. Do you agree with the idea that theater cannot be as psychologically "deep" as cinema, due to film's ability to express or even enforce a subjective point of view through the narrative device of the camera?

12. Agree or disagree with the following statement: "Film scripts are frequently published, but it is evident that very few of them can rank as literature."

13. It has been observed that theater is bound by sequential causality, whereas film is not. How accurate is this observation? Is avant-garde theater bound by causality?

14. Which of the following two questions would you choose to ask, and why? "How does literary adaptation serve the cinema?" Or, "How does film adaptation serve literature?"

15. A critic once said that "film criticism can usually afford to disregard actors in a film's total effect." Do you agree or disagree? Consider, in your answer, why such a statement could never be made about theater criticism.

16. "The screenplay is as far from the drama, on the one hand, as it is from the novel, on the other. Its nearest analogy in literature is the short story or the lyric poem." Analyze these two statements, using actual (not theoretical) examples from fiction, drama, poetry, and cinema to buttress your argument.

17. "Everything can be transferred to the screen, everything expressed through an image." Is this an argument for the utter "adaptability" of the cinema, for film's overall superiority to the other arts, or both?

18. "The role of the audience at a canned drama is a passive one. Its reaction cannot affect the movie product. In the live theater, on the other hand, the audience's role is creative. Every audience evokes from the actors the performance that it deserves." Do you agree that the audience of a play has a creative, contributory role in the theatrical production (and that the audience therefore gets the performance it deserves)? Is this an argument that authors should write for the stage—where they and their performers can get more help or support, so to speak—rather than for the screen?

19. "The movies are the great mass art of our times, the people's art, the international theater of the twentieth century, and drama that knows no boundaries." In the twenty-first century, is this statement still true? Is the cinema being replaced by another, more "adaptable" mass art? If so, which one, and what are its sources?

20. Can the adapted film in question stand alone, or is it necessary to have read the original novel, story, or play to understand and appreciate the film? If the adaptation *can* stand alone, is it a quality film in its own right?

21. Why does the cinema engage in so much adaptation of other people's work? Wouldn't it simply be easier (and perhaps cheaper) to commission the writing of original screenplays? What forces are at work here—and have been at work since 1906, when *The Story of the Kelly Gang*, based on Arnold Denham's 1899 play *The Kelly Gang*, opened at the Athenaeum Theatre in Melbourne, Australia?

22. Purely from the point of view of aesthetics, do you think it is better to read a film's literary or dramatic source before, or after, a screening of the adaptation itself?

23. Agree or disagree with the following statement: "The movies, being basically a visual art form, give the audience more work to do and consequently more scope for the imagination; the theater and fiction, since they must rely almost solely on dramatic dialogue and/or verbal narration, subject the audience to a constant and unnatural flow of words, words, words."

24. "Adaptations of great works of art can hardly fail to be damaging reductions of the originals. It is scarcely reasonable to suppose that the

249

work of adapting Shakespeare or Ibsen, Jane Austen or Thomas Hardy, will be done by persons of comparable genius." Is this a legitimate argument against adapting great works of art to the screen? Why or why not?

25. If you were a writer today, would you write directly for the screen; would you write for the stage; would you try to have your fiction published; or . . . ? What is your choice—and why?

Adaptation: An English-Language Bibliography

Books

Albrecht-Crane, Christa, & Dennis Ray Cutchins, eds. *Adaptation Studies: New Approaches*. Rutherford, N.J.: Fairleigh Dickinson University Press, 2010

Allen, Graham. *Intertextuality*. London: Routledge, 2011.

Allen, Robert C. *Vaudeville and Film, 1895–1915: A Study in Media Interaction*. New York: Arno, 1980.

Andrews, Cyril Bruyn. *The Theatre, the Cinema, and Ourselves*. London: Clarence House, 1947.

Aragay, Mireia, ed. *Books in Motion: Adaptation, Intertextuality, Authorship*. Amsterdam: Rodopi, 2005.

Axelrod, Mark. *I Read It at the Movies: The Follies and Foibles of Screen Adaptation*. Portsmouth, N.H.: Heinemann, 2007.

Aycock, Wendell, & Michael Schoenecke, eds. *Film and Literature: Classic Comparisons to Adaptation*. Lubbock: Texas Tech University Press, 1988.

Bacon, Henry. *Continuity and Transformation: The Influence of Literature and Drama on Cinema as a Process of Cultural Continuity and Renewal*. Helsinki, Fin.: Suomalainen Tiedeakatemia, 1994.

Baetens, Jan. *Novelization: From Film to Novel*. Columbus: Ohio State University Press, 2018.

Baskin, Ellen, & Mandy Hicken, eds. *Enser's Filmed Books and Plays: A List of Books and Plays from Which Films Have Been Made, 1928–2001*. 1968. Aldershot, U.K.: Ashgate, 2003.

Beja, Morris. *Film and Literature: An Introduction*. New York: Longman, 1979.

Bluestone, George. *Novels into Film*. 1957. Baltimore: Johns Hopkins University Press, 2003.

Bolter, Jay David, & Richard Grusin. *Remediation: Understanding New Media*. Cambridge, Mass.: Massachusetts Institute of Technology Press, 1999.

Boozer, Jack, ed. *Authorship in Film Adaptation*. Austin: University of Texas Press, 2008.

Boyum, Joy Gould. *Double Exposure: Fiction into Film*. New York: New American Library, 1985.

Brady, Ben. *Principles of Adaptation for Film and Television*. Austin: University of Texas Press, 1994

Brewster, Ben, & Lea Jacobs. *Theatre to Cinema: Stage Pictorialism and the Early Feature Film*. New York: Oxford University Press, 1997.

Brown, John Russell, ed. *Drama and Theatre, with Radio, Film, and Television*. London: Routledge & Kegan Paul, 1971.

Brown, Kathleen L. *Teaching Literary Theory Using Film Adaptations*. Jefferson, N.C.: McFarland, 2006.

Bruhn, Jorgen, *et al.*, eds. *Adaptation Studies: New Challenges, New Directions*. London: Bloomsbury, 2013.

Bryant, John. *The Fluid Text: A Theory of Revision and Editing for Book and Screen*. Ann Arbor: University of Michigan Press, 2002.

Burke, Liam. *The Comic Book Film Adaptation: Exploring Modern Hollywood's Leading Genre*. Jackson: University Press of Mississippi, 2015.

Cahir, Linda Costanzo. *Literature into Film: Theory and Practical Approaches*. Jefferson, N.C.: McFarland, 2006.

Cardullo, Bert. *Screening the Stage: Studies in Cinedramatic Art*. New York: Peter Lang, 2006.

----------. *Formal Matters: Studies in Film Adaptation and (Re)Evaluation*. Washington, D.C.: New Academia, 2011.

----------, ed. *Stage and Screen: Adaptation Theory from 1916 to 2000*. New York: Continuum, 2012.

Cardwell, Sarah. *Adaptation Revisited: Television and the Classic Novel*. Manchester, U.K.: Manchester University Press, 2002.

Carroll, Rachel, ed. *Adaptation in Contemporary Culture: Textual Infidelities*. New York: Continuum, 2009.

----------, ed. *Adaptation in Contemporary Culture: Textual Infidelities*. Continuum, 2009.

Cartmell, Deborah, *et al.*, eds. *Pulping Fictions: Consuming Culture Across the Literature/Media Divide*. London: Pluto Press, 1996.

Cartmell, Deborah, & Imelda Whelehan, eds. *Adaptations: From Text to Screen, Screen to Text*. New York: Routledge, 1999.

----------, eds. *Adaptations: From Text to Screen, Screen to Text*. New York: Routledge, 1999.

Cartmell, Deborah, *et al.*, eds. *Classics in Film and Fiction*. London: Pluto Press, 2000.

----------, eds. *Retrovisions: Reinventing the Past in Film and Fiction*. London: Pluto Press, 2001.

Cartmell, Deborah, ed. *The Cambridge Companion to Literature on Screen*. New York: Cambridge University Press, 2007.

Cartmell, Deborah, & Imelda Whelehan, eds. *Screen Adaptation: Impure Cinema*. New York: Palgrave Macmillan, 2010.

Cartmell, Deborah. *A Companion to Literature, Film, and Adaptation*. Malden, Mass.: Wiley, 2012.

----------. *Adaptations in the Sound Era: 1927-37*. London: Bloomsbury, 2014.

Cartmell, Deborah, & Imelda Whelehan, eds. *Teaching Adaptation*. New York: Palgrave Macmillan, 2014.

Cattrysse, Patrick. *Descriptive Adaptation Studies: Epistemological and Methodological Issues*. Antwerp: Garant, 2014.

Chatman, Seymour. *Story and Discourse: Narrative Structure in Fiction and Film*. Ithaca, N.Y.: Cornell University Press, 1978.

----------. *Coming to Terms: The Rhetoric of Narrative in Fiction and Film*. Ithaca, N.Y.: Cornell University Press, 1990.

Cohen, Keith. *Film and Fiction: The Dynamics of Exchange*. New Haven, Conn.: Yale University Press, 1979.

Collier, Jo Leslie. *From Wagner to Murnau: The Transposition of Romanticism from Stage to Screen*. Ann Arbor, Mich.: UMI Research Press, 1988.

Conger, Syndy, & Janice Welsch, eds. *Narrative Strategies: Essays in Film and Prose Fiction*. Macomb, Ill.: Western Illinois Press, 1980.

Constandinides, Costas. *From Film Adaptation to Post-Celluloid Adaptation: Rethinking the Transition of Popular Narratives and Characters across Old and New Media*. London: Bloomsbury, 2012.

Corrigan, Timothy. *Film and Literature: An Introduction and Reader*. 1999. New York: Routledge, 2012.

Costello, Tom, ed. *International Guide to Literature on Film*. London: Bowker-Saur, 1994.

Cronin, Bernadette, et al., eds. *Adaptation Considered as a Collaborative Art: Process and Practice*. Cham, Switz.: Palgrave Macmillan, 2020.

Cutchins, Dennis, *et al.*, eds. *The Pedagogy of Adaptation*. Lanham, Md.: Scarecrow Press, 2010.

----------, eds. *Redefining Adaptation Studies*. Lanham, Md.: Scarecrow Press, 2010.

----------, eds. *The Routledge Companion to Adaptation*. 2018. London: Routledge, 2020.

Davidson, Phebe. *Film and Literature: Points of Intersection*. Lewiston, N.Y.: Edwin Mellen, 1997.

Davis, Patrice. *Analyzing Performance: Theater, Dance, and Film*. Trans. David Williams. Ann Arbor: University of Michigan Press, 2003.

Dean, D. Alan. *Novels into Film: Adaptations & Interpretations*. Vol. 1. Ipswich, Mass.: Salem Press, 2018.

----------. *Novels into Film: Adaptations & Interpretations*. Vol. 2. Ipswich, Mass.: Salem Press, 2021.

DeBona, Guerric. *Film Adaptation in the Hollywood Studio Era*. Urbana: University of Illinois Press, 2010.

Deltchava, Roumiana, ed. *Literature and Film: Modes of Adaptation*. Toronto: University of Toronto Press, 1994.

Dench, Ernest A. *Playwriting for the Cinema*. London: A. & C. Black, 1914.

Desmond, John M., & Peter Hawkes. *Adaptation: Studying Film and Literature*. 2006. Boston: McGraw-Hill, 2017.

Eidsvik, Charles. *Cineliteracy: Film Among the Arts*. New York: Random House, 1978.

Elliott, Kamilla. *Rethinking the Novel/Film Debate*. Cambridge, U.K.: Cambridge University Press, 2003.

----------. *Theorizing Adaptation*. New York: Oxford University Press, 2020.

Erskine, Thomas L., & James M. Welsh, eds. *Video Versions: Film Adaptations of Plays on Video*. Westport, Conn.: Greenwood Press, 2000.

Esslin, Martin. *The Field of Drama: How the Signs of Drama Create Meaning on Stage and Screen*. London: Methuen, 1987.

Frus, Phyllis, & Christy Williams, eds. *Beyond Adaptation: Essays on Radical Transformations of Original Works*. Jefferson, N.C.: McFarland, 2010.

Genette, Gerard. *Palimpsests: Literature in the Second Degree*. Lincoln: University of Nebraska Press, 1997.

Geraghty, Christine. *Now A Major Motion Picture: Film Adaptations of Literature and Drama*. Lanham, Md.: Rowman & Littlefield, 2008.

Giddings, Robert. *Screening the Novel: the Theory and Practice of Literary Dramatization*. New York: St. Martin's Press, 1990.

Gifford, Denis. *Books and Plays in Films, 1896-1915: Literary, Theatrical, and Artistic Sources of the First Twenty Years of Motion Pictures*. Jefferson, N.C.: McFarland, 1991.

Gillespie, David. *The History of Russian Literature on Film*. London: Bloomsbury, 2022.

Goble, Alan, ed. *The Complete Index to Literary Sources in Film*. New Providence, N.J.: Bowker, 1999.

Grant, Barry Keith. *Books to Film; Volume 1: Cinematic Adaptations of Literary Works*. Farmington Hills, Mich.: Gale, 2018.

Griffiths, James. *Adaptations as Imitations*. Newark: University of Delaware Press, 1997.

Griffiths, Kate. *The History of French Literature on Film*. New York: Bloomsbury, 2021.

Griggs, Yvonne. *The Bloomsbury Introduction to Adaptation Studies: Adapting the Canon in Film, TV, Novels, and Popular Culture*. London: Bloomsbury, 2020.

Grossman, Julie, & R. Barton Palmer, eds. *Adaptation in Visual Culture: Images, Texts, and Their Multiple Worlds*. London: Palgrave Macmillan, 2017.

Hannon, William M. *The Photodrama: Its Place Among the Fine Arts*. New Orleans: Ruskin, 1915.

Harrington, John, ed. *Film and/as Literature*. Englewood Cliffs, N.J.: Prentice-Hall, 1977.

Hassler-Forrest, Dan, & Pascal Nicklas, eds. *The Politics of Adaptation: New Media Convergence and Ideology*. London: Palgrave Macmillan, 2015.

Hermansson, Casie, & Janet Zepernick, eds. *Where Is Adaptation? Mapping Cultures, Texts, and Contexts*. Amsterdam: John Benjamins, 2018.

Hischak, Thomas S. *American Plays and Musicals on Screen: 650 Stage Productions and Their Film and Television Adaptations*. Jefferson, N.C.: McFarland, 2005.

Hitt, Jim. *Words and Shadows: Literature on the Screen*. Secaucus, N.J.: Carol Publishing Group, 1992.

Hodgkins, John. *The Drift: Affect, Adaptation, and New Perspectives on Fidelity*. London: Bloomsbury, 2013.

Hopton, Tricia, *et al.*, eds. *Pockets of Change: Adaptation and Cultural Transition*. Lanham, Md.: Lexington Books, 2011.

Horton, Andrew S., & Joan Magretta, eds. *Modern European Filmmakers and the Art of Adaptation*. New York: Ungar, 1981.

Housel, Rebecca, ed. *From Camera Lens to Critical Lens: A Collection of Best Essays on Film Adaptation*. Newcastle-upon-Tyne, U.K.: Cambridge Scholars, 2009.

Huhtamo, Erkki, & Jussi Parikka, eds. *Media Archaeology: Approaches, Applications, and Implications*. Berkeley: University of California Press, 2011.

Hunter, Jefferson. *English Filming, English Writing*. Bloomington: Indiana University Press, 2010.

Hurt, James, ed. *Focus on Film and Theatre*. Englewood Cliffs, N.J.: Prentice-Hall, 1974.

Hulfish, D. S. *The Motion Picture: Its Making and Its Theatre*. Chicago: Electricity Magazine Corporation, 1909.

Hutcheon, Linda. *A Theory of Adaptation*. 2006. New York: Routledge, 2013.

Jenkins, Henry. *What Made Pistachio Nuts? Early Sound Comedy and the Vaudeville Aesthetic*. New York: Columbia University Press, 1992.

Jinks, William. *The Celluloid Literature: Film in the Humanities*. Riverside, N.J.: Glencoe, 1971.

Kaklamanidou, Betty, ed. *New Approaches to Contemporary Adaptation*. Detroit: Wayne State University Press, 2020.

Kennedy-Karpat, Colleen, & Eric Sandberg, eds. *Adaptation, Awards Culture, and the Value of Prestige*. London: Palgrave Macmillan, 2017.

Kittredge, William, & Steven M. Krauzer. *Stories into Film*. New York: Harper & Row, 1979.

Klein, Michael, & Gillian Parker, eds. *The English Novel and the Movies*. New York: Ungar, 1981.

Knopf, Robert, ed. *Theater and Film: A Comparative Anthology*. New Haven, Conn.: Yale University Press, 2004.

Kranz, David L., & Nancy C. Mellerski, eds. *In/fidelity: Essays on Film Adaptation*. Newcastle-upon-Tyne, U.K.: Cambridge Scholars, 2008.

Krebs, Katya. *Translation and Adaptation in Theatre and Film*. London: Routledge, 2013.

Kroeber, Karl. *Make-Believe in Film and Fiction: Visual vs. Verbal Storytelling*. New York: Palgrave Macmillan, 2006.

Langman, Larry. *Writers on the American Screen: A Guide to Film Adaptations of American and Foreign Literary Works*. New York: Garland, 1986.

Leitch, Thomas. *Film Adaptation and its Discontents*. Baltimore: Johns Hopkins University Press, 2007.

----------, ed. *The Oxford Handbook of Adaptation Studies*. 2017. New York: Oxford University Press, 2020.

----------. *The History of American Literature on Film*. London: Bloomsbury Press, 2019.

Leonard, William Torbert. *Theatre: Stage to Screen to Television*. 2 vols. Metuchen, N.J.: Scarecrow Press, 1981.

Lind, Paula Baldwin, ed. *Telling and Re-telling Stories: Studies on Literary Adaptation to Film*. Newcastle-upon-Tyne, U.K.: Cambridge Scholars, 2016.

Lindner, Oliver, & Pascal Nicklas, eds. *Adaptation and Cultural Appropriation: Literature, Film, and the Arts*. Berlin: De Gruyter, 2012.

Lothe, Jakob. *Narrative in Fiction and Film: An Introduction*. New York : Oxford University Press, 2000.

Lupack, Barbara Tepa, ed. *Take Two: Adapting the Contemporary American Novel to Film*. Bowling Green, Ohio: Bowling Green State University Popular Press, 1994.

MacArthur, Michelle, *et al.*, eds. *Performing Adaptations: Essays and Conversations on the Theory and Practice of Adaptation*. Newcastle-upon-Tyne, U.K.: Cambridge Scholars, 2009.

Magill, Frank N., ed. *The Novel into Film*. Pasadena, Calif.: Salem Press, 1980.

Manvell, Roger. *Theater and Film: A Comparative Study of the Two Forms of Dramatic Art, and of the Problems of Adaptation of Stage Plays into Films*. Rutherford, N.J.: Fairleigh Dickinson University Press, 1979.

Marcus, Fred H., ed. *Film and Literature: Contrasts in Media*. Scranton, Pa.: Chandler, 1971.

Marill, Alvin H. *More Theatre: Stage to Screen to Television*. Metuchen, N.J.: Scarecrow Press, 1993.

McCabe, Colin, *et al.*, eds. *True to the Spirit: Film Adaptation and the Question of Fidelity*. Oxford, U.K.: Oxford University Press, 2011.

McConnell, Frank D. *The Spoken Seen: Film and the Romantic Imagination*. Baltimore: John Hopkins University Press, 1975.

McDougal, Stuart Y. *Made into Movies: From Literature to Film*. New York: Holt, Reinhart, & Winston, 1985.

McFarlane, Brian. *Novel to Film: An Introduction to the Theory of Adaptation*. Oxford, U.K.: Oxford University Press, 1996.

McHugh, Dominic, ed. *The Oxford Handbook of Musical-Theatre Screen Adaptations*. New York: Oxford University Press, 2019.

Meikle, Kyle. *Adaptations in the Franchise Era: 2001-16*. London: Bloomsbury Press, 2019.

Miller, Gabriel. *Screening the Novel: Rediscovered American Fiction in Film*. 1980. New York: Bloomsbury, 2020.

Mittel, Jason. *Narrative Theory and Adaptation*. London: Bloomsbury, 2017.

Mooney, William H. *Adaptation and the New Art Film: Remaking the Classics in the Twilight of Cinema*. Cham, Switz.: Palgrave Macmillan, 2021.

Morrissette, Bruce. *Novel and Film: Essays in Two Genres*. Chicago: University of Chicago Press, 1985.

Moses, Gavriel. *The Nickel Was for the Movies: Film in the Novel from Pirandello to Puig*. Berkeley: University of California Press, 1995.

Murphet, Julian, & Lydia Rainford, eds. *Literature and Visual Technologies: Writing after Cinema*. New York: Palgrave Macmillan, 2003.

Murray, Simone. *The Adaptation Industry: The Cultural Economy of Contemporary Literary Adaptation*. London: Routledge, 2013.

Nagib, Lúcia, & Anne Jerslev, eds. *Impure Cinema: Intermedial and Intercultural Approaches to Film*. London: I. B. Tauris, 2014.

Naremore, James, ed. *Film Adaptation*. New Brunswick, N.J.: Rutgers University Press, 2000.

Nicoll, Allardyce. *Film and Theatre*. 1936. New York: Arno, 1972.

Orr, John, & Colin Nicholson, eds. *Cinema and Fiction: New Modes of Adapting, 1950-1990*. Edinburgh: Edinburgh University Press, 1992.

Orr, Mary. *Intertextuality: Debates and Contexts*. Cambridge, U.K.: Polity, 2003.

Owen, Alistair. *The Art of Screen Adaptation*. Harpenden, U.K.: Kamera Books, 2020.

Peary, Gerald, & Roger Schatzkin, eds. *The Classical American Novel and the Movies*. New York: Ungar, 1977.

----------, eds. *The Modern American Novel and the Movies*. New York: Ungar, 1978.

Pettey, Homer B., & R. Barton Palmer, eds. *French Literature on Screen*. Manchester, U.K.: Manchester University Press, 2019.

Portnoy, Kenneth. *Screen Adaptation: A Scriptwriting Handbook*. 2nd ed. Waltham, Mass.: Focal Press, 1998.

Quinn, Maureen. *The Adaptation of a Literary Text to Film: Problems and Cases in Adaptation Criticism*. Lewiston, N.Y.: Edwin Mellen, 2007.

Raw, Laurence. *Translation, Adaptation, and Transformation*. London: Bloomsbury, 2014.

----------. *Expanding Adaptation Studies*. Basingstoke, U.K.: Palgrave Macmillan, 2020.

Redmon, Allen H., ed. *Next-Generation Adaptation: Spectatorship and Process*. Jackson: University Press of Mississippi, 2021.

Reynolds, Peter, ed. *Novel Images: Literature in Performance*. London: Routledge, 1993.

Richard, David Evan. *Film Phenomenology and Adaptation: Sensuous Elaboration*. Amsterdam: Amsterdam University Press, 2021.

Richardson, Robert. *Literature and Film*. Bloomington: Indiana University Press, 1969.

Ross, Harris. *Film as Literature, Literature as Film: An Introduction to and Bibliography of Film's Relationship to Literature*. New York: Greenwood, 1987.

Ryan, Marie-Laure. *Narrative Across Media: The Languages of Storytelling*. Lincoln: University of Nebraska Press, 2004.

Sanders, Julie. *Adaptation and Appropriation*. 2006. London: Routledge, 2016.

Schoenfeld, Christiane. *The History of German Literature on Film*. London: Bloomsbury, 2021.

Seed, David, ed. *Literature and the Visual Media*. Rochester, N.Y.: D. S. Brewer, 2005.

Seger, Linda. *The Art of Adaptation: Turning Fact and Fiction into Film*. New York: Henry Holt, 1992.

Semenza, Greg M. Colón, & Bob Hasenfratz. *The History of British Literature on Film, 1895-2015*. London: Bloomsbury Press, 2015.

Shelley, Frank. *Stage and Screen*. London: Pendulum, 1946.

Sinyard, Neil. *Filming Literature: The Art of Screen Adaptation*. London: Croom Helm, 1986.

Slethaug, Gordon E. *Adaptation Theory and Criticism: Postmodern Literature and Cinema in the USA*. London: Bloomsbury, 2014.

Spiegel, Alan. *Fiction and the Camera Eye: Visual Consciousness in Film and the Modern Novel*. Charlottesville: University of Virginia Press, 1975.

Stam, Robert. *Literature through Film: Realism, Magic, and the Art of Adaptation*. Malden, Mass.: Blackwell, 2005.

----------, & Alessandra Raengo, eds. *Literature and Film: A Guide to the Theory and Practice of Film Adaptation*. Malden, Mass.: Wiley, 2004.

----------, eds. *A Companion to Literature and Film*. 2004. Malden, Mass.: Blackwell, 2008.

Stewart, Michael, & Robert Munro, eds. *Intercultural Screen Adaptation: British and Global Case Studies*. Edinburgh, U.K.: Edinburgh University Press, 2020.

Tibbetts, John C, & James M. Welsh, eds. *The Encyclopedia of Stage Plays into Film*. New York: Facts on File, 2001.

----------, eds. *The Encyclopedia of Novels into Film*. 2nd ed. New York: Checkmark Books, 2005.

Toles, George E., ed. *Film/Literature*. Winnipeg: University of Manitoba Press, 1983.

Vardac, A. Nicholas. *Stage to Screen: Theatrical Method from Garrick to Griffith*. Cambridge, Mass.: Harvard University Press, 1949. Reprint: *Stage to Screen: Theatrical Origins of Early Film, David Garrick to D. W. Griffith*. 1968. New York: Da Capo, 1987.

Verrone, William. *Adaptation and the Avant-Garde: Alternative Perspectives on Adaptation Theory and Practice*. London: Bloomsbury, 2011.

Vincendeau, Ginette. *Film/Literature/Heritage*. London: British Film Institute, 2001.

Wagner, Geoffrey. *The Novel and the Cinema*. Rutherford, N.J.: Fairleigh Dickinson University Press, 1975.

Waller, Gregory A. *The Stage/Screen Debate: A Study in Popular Aesthetics*. New York: Garland, 1983.

Welch, James M., & Peter Lev, eds. *The Literature/Film Reader: Issues of Adaptation*. Lanham, Md.: Scarecrow Press, 2007.

Welch, Jeffrey Egan. *Literature and Film: An Annotated Bibliography, 1900–1977*. New York: Garland, 1981.

----------. *Literature and Film: An Annotated Bibliography, 1978-1988*. New York: Garland, 1993.

Wurth, Kiene Brillenburg, ed. *Between Page and Screen: Remaking Literature through Cinema and Cyberspace*. New York: Fordham University Press, 2012.

Young, James O. *Cultural Appropriation and the Arts*. Malden, Mass.: Blackwell, 2010.

Zatlin, Phyllis. *Theatrical Translation and Film Adaptation: A Practitioner's View*. Buffalo, N.Y.: Multilingual Matters, 2005.

Journals

Adaptation. Published by Oxford University Press, U.K. 2008-present.

Journal of Adaptation in Film and Performance. Published by Intellect, U.K. 2008-present.

Literature/Film Quarterly. Published by Salisbury University, U.S. 1973-present.

Shakespeare on Film: An English-Language Bibliography

Aebischer, Pascale, Esche, Edward J., & Nigel Wheale, eds. *Remaking Shakespeare: Performance Across Media, Genres, and Cultures*. Basingstoke, U.K.: Palgrave Macmillan, 2003.

Aebischer, Pascale. *Shakespeare's Violated Bodies: Stage and Screen Performance*. Cambridge, U.K.: Cambridge University Press, 2004.

Anderegg, Michael. *Cinematic Shakespeare*. Lanham, Md.: Rowman & Littlefield, 2004.

Atkinson, E. J. Ruppert. *Key to the Adaptation of the Best of Shakespeare's Plays to the Stage—Cinema Interaction Process for the Production of Drama*. New York: Knickerbocker, 1920.

Ball, Robert Hamilton. *Shakespeare on Silent Film: A Strange Eventful History*. London: George Allen & Unwin, 1968.

Béchervaise, Neil E., *et al.*, eds. *Shakespeare on Celluloid*. Rozelle, Austral.: St. Clair Press, 1999.

Béchervaise, Neil E., ed. *Constructing Shakespeare on Screen*. Rozelle, Austral.: St. Clair Press, 2003.

Bevington, David, Welsh, Anne Marie, & Michael L. Greenwald. *Shakespeare: Script, Stage, Screen*. New York: Pearson/Longman, 2006.

Bickley, Pamela, & Jennifer Stevens. *Studying Shakespeare Adaptation: From Restoration Theatre to YouTube*. London: Arden Shakespeare, 2021.

Boose, Lynda E., & Richard Burt, eds. *Shakespeare, the Movie: Popularizing the Plays on Film, Television, and Video*. New York: Routledge, 1997.

----------, eds. *Shakespeare, the Movie, II: Popularizing the Plays on Film, Television, and Video*. New York: Routledge, 2003.

Brode, Douglas. *Shakespeare in the Movies: From the Silent Era to* Shakespeare in Love. New York: Oxford University Press, 2000.

Brusberg-Kiermeier, Stefani, & Jörg Helbig, eds. *Shakespeare in the Media: From the Globe Theatre to the World Wide Web*. New York: Peter Lang, 2004.

Buchanan, Judith. *Shakespeare on Silent Film: An Excellent Dumb Discourse*. New York: Cambridge University Press, 2009.

----------. *Shakespeare on Film*. 2005. London: Routledge, 2014.

Buchman, Lorne M. *Still in Movement: Shakespeare on Screen.* New York: Oxford University Press, 1991.

Buhler, Stephen M. *Shakespeare in the Cinema: Ocular Proof.* Albany: State University of New York Press, 2002.

Bulman, James C., & H. R. Coursen, eds. *Shakespeare on Television: An Anthology of Essays and Reviews.* Hanover, N.H.: University Press of New England, 1988.

Burnett, Mark T., & Ramona Wray, eds. *Shakespeare, Film, Fin de Siècle.* New York: St. Martin's, 2000.

----------, eds. *Screening Shakespeare in the Twenty-First Century.* Edinburgh: Edinburgh University Press, 2006.

Burnett, Mark T. *Filming Shakespeare in the Global Marketplace.* New York: Palgrave Macmillan, 2007.

----------. *Shakespeare and World Cinema.* New York: Cambridge University Press, 2013.

Burt, Richard, ed. *Shakespeare after Mass Media.* New York: Palgrave, 2002.

----------, ed. *Shakespeares after Shakespeare: An Encyclopedia of the Bard in Mass Media and Popular Culture.* Westport, Conn.: Greenwood Press, 2007.

Calbi, Maurizio. *Spectral Shakespeares: Media Adaptations in the Twenty-First Century.* New York: Palgrave Macmillan, 2013.

Cartelli, Thomas, & Katherine Rowe. *New Wave Shakespeare on Screen.* Cambridge, U.K.: Polity Press, 2007.

Cartmell, Deborah. *Interpreting Shakespeare on Screen.* New York: St. Martin's, 2000.

Cochran, Peter. *Small-Screen Shakespeare.* Newcastle-upon-Tyne, U.K.: Cambridge Scholars, 2013.

Cohn, Ruby. *Modern Shakespeare Offshoots.* Princeton, N.J.: Princeton University Press, 1976.

Collick, John. *Shakespeare, Cinema, and Society.* Manchester, U.K.: Manchester University Press, 1989.

Coursen, Herbert R. *Watching Shakespeare on Television.* Cranbury, N.J.: Fairleigh Dickinson University Press, 1993.

----------. *Shakespeare in Space: Recent Shakespearean Productions on Screen.* New York: Peter Lang, 2002.

264

----------. *Shakespeare Translated: Derivatives on Film and Television*. New York: Peter Lang, 2005.

----------. *Teaching Shakespeare with Film and Television: A Guide*. 1997. Charlotte, N.C.: Information Age, 2009.

Croteau, Melissa, & Carolyn Jess-Cooke, eds. *Apocalyptic Shakespeare: Essays on Visions of Chaos and Revelation in Recent Film Adaptations*. Jefferson, N.C.: McFarland, 2009.

Croteau, Melissa. *Reforming Shakespeare: Adaptations and Appropriations of the Bard in Millennial Film and Popular Culture*. Saarbrücken, Gny.: Lambert, 2013.

Crowl, Samuel. *Shakespeare Observed: Studies in Performance on Stage and Screen*. Athens: Ohio University Press, 1992.

----------. *Shakespeare at the Cineplex: The Kenneth Branagh Era*. Athens: Ohio University Press, 2003.

----------. *Shakespeare and Film: A Norton Guide*. New York: W. W. Norton, 2008.

Dakin, Mary Ellen. *Reading Shakespeare Film First*. Urbana, Ill.: National Council of Teachers of English, 2013.

Davies, Anthony. *Filming Shakespeare's Plays: The Adaptations of Laurence Olivier, Orson Welles, Peter Brook, and Akira Kurosawa*. Cambridge, U.K.: Cambridge University Press, 1988.

----------, & Stanley Wells, eds. *Shakespeare and the Moving Image: The Plays on Film and Television*. 1987. Cambridge, U.K.: Cambridge University Press, 1994.

Dionne, Craig, & Parmita Kapadia, eds. *Bollywood Shakespeare*. New York: Palgrave Macmillan, 2014.

Donaldson, Peter S. *Shakespearean Films/Shakespearean Directors*. Boston: Unwin Hyman, 1990.

Eckert, Charles W., ed. *Focus on Shakespearean Films*. Englewood Cliffs, N.J.: Prentice-Hall, 1972.

Fischlin, Daniel. *OuterSpeares: Shakespeare, Intermedia, and the Limits of Adaptation*. Toronto: University of Toronto Press, 2014.

French, Emma. *Selling Shakespeare to Hollywood: The Marketing of Filmed Shakespeare Adaptations from 1989 into the New Millennium*. Hatfield, U.K.: University of Hertfordshire Press, 2006.

Geal, Robert. *Anamorphic Authorship in Canonical Film Adaptation: A Case Study of Shakespearean Films*. Cham, Switz.: Palgrave Macmillan, 2019.

Gielgud, John, & John Miller. *Shakespeare: Hit or Miss?* London: Sidgwick & Jackson, 1991.

Guneratne, Anthony R. *Shakespeare, Film Studies, and the Visual Cultures of Modernity.* New York: Palgrave Macmillan, 2008.

Harold, Madd. *An Actor's Guide to Performing Shakespeare: For Film, Television, and Theatre.* Lanham, Md.: Lone Eagle, 2002.

Hatchuel, Sarah. *A Companion to the Shakespearean Films of Kenneth Branagh.* Winnipeg, Can.: Blizzard, 1999.

----------. *Shakespeare: From Stage to Screen.* Cambridge, U.K.: Cambridge University Press, 2004.

Henderson, Diana E. *Collaborations with the Past: Reshaping Shakespeare Across Time and Media.* Ithaca, N.Y.: Cornell University Press, 2006.

----------, ed. *A Concise Companion to Shakespeare on Screen.* Malden, Mass.: Blackwell, 2006.

----------, & Stephen O'Neill, eds. *The Arden Research Handbook of Shakespeare and Adaptation.* London: Arden Shakespeare, 2022.

Hindle, Maurice. *Studying Shakespeare on Film.* 2007. Basingstoke, U.K.: Palgrave Macmillan, 2015.

Hodgdon, Barbara. *The Shakespeare Trade: Performances & Appropriations.* Philadelphia: University of Pennsylvania Press, 1998.

Holderness, Graham. *Visual Shakespeare: Essays in Film and Television.* Hatfield, U.K.: University of Hertfordshire Press, 2002.

Hopkins, Lisa. *Relocating Shakespeare and Austen on Screen.* Basingstoke, U.K.: Palgrave Macmillan, 2009.

Howlett, Kathy M. *Framing Shakespeare on Film.* Athens: Ohio University Press, 2000.

Jackson, Russell. *Shakespeare Films in the Making: Vision, Production, and Reception.* New York: Cambridge University Press, 2007.

----------, ed. *The Cambridge Companion to Shakespeare on Film.* 2007. Cambridge, U.K.: Cambridge University Press, 2020.

Jackson, Russell. *Shakespeare and the English-Speaking Cinema.* Oxford, U.K.: Oxford University Press, 2014.

Jess-Cooke, Carolyn. *Shakespeare on Film: Such Things as Dreams Are Made Of.* London: Wallflower, 2007.

Jorgens, Jack J. *Shakespeare on Film.* 1977. Lanham, Md.: University Press of America, 1991.

Keller, James R., & Leslie Stratyner, eds. *Almost Shakespeare: Reinventing His Works for Cinema and Television.* Jefferson, N.C.: McFarland, 2004.

Kelly, F. M. *Shakespearean Costume for Stage and Screen.* London: A. & C. Black, 1970.

Kirwan, Peter, & Kathryn Prince, eds. *Arden Research Handbook of Shakespeare and Adaptation.* London: Bloomsbury, 2021.

Klein, Holger, & James L. Harner, eds. *Shakespeare and the Visual Arts. Shakespeare Yearbook*, 11 (2000).

Lehmann, Courtney. *Shakespeare Remains: Theatre to Film, Early to Postmodern.* Ithaca, N.Y.: Cornell University Press, 2002.

Lippmann, Max, ed. *Shakespeare in Film.* Wiesbaden, Gny.: Saaten Verlag, 1964.

Manvell, Roger. *Shakespeare and the Film.* 1971. New York: A. S. Barnes, 1979.

Massai, Sonia, ed. *World-Wide Shakespeares: Local Appropriations in Film and Performance.* London: Routledge, 2005.

McKernan, Luke, & Olwen Terris, eds. *Walking Shadows: Shakespeare in the National Film and Television Archive.* London: British Film Institute, 1994.

McKernan, Luke, Oesterlen, Eve-Marie, & Olwen Terris, eds. *The Researcher's Guide to Shakespeare on Film, Television, and Radio.* London: BUFVC (British University Film and Video Council), 2008.

McMurtry, Jo. *Shakespeare Films in the Classroom: A Descriptive Guide.* Hamden, Conn.: Archon Books, 1994.

Moeller, Victor J. *Socrates Does Shakespeare: Seminars and Film.* Lanham, Md.: Rowman & Littlefield, 2005.

Morris, Peter, ed. *Shakespeare on Film.* Ottawa: Canadian Film Institute, 1972.

Owens, Rebekah. *Studying Shakespeare on Film.* Oxford, U.K.: Auteur, 2021.

Parker, Barry M. *The Folger Shakespeare Filmography: A Directory of Feature Films Based on the Works of William Shakespeare.* Washington, D.C.: Folger Shakespeare Library, 1979.

Pilkington, Ace G. *Screening Shakespeare from* Richard II *to* Henry V. Newark: University of Delaware Press, 1991.

Pittman, L. Monique. *Authorizing Shakespeare on Film and Television: Gender, Class, and Ethnicity in Adaptation.* New York: Peter Lang, 2011.

Rasmus, Agnieszka. *Filming Shakespeare, from Metatheatre to Metacinema.* New York: Peter Lang, 2008.

Rosenthal, Daniel M. *Shakespeare on Screen.* London: Hamlyn, 2000.

----------. *100 Shakespeare Films.* London: British Film Institute, 2007.

Rothwell, Kenneth S. *Early Shakespeare Movies: How the Spurned Spawned Art.* Chipping Campden, U.K.: Clouds Hill Printers, 2000.

----------. *A History of Shakespeare on Screen: A Century of Film and Television.* 1999. Cambridge, U.K.: Cambridge University Press, 2004.

Ryle, Simon. *Shakespeare, Cinema, and Desire: Adaptation and Other Futures of Shakespeare's Language.* Basingstoke, U.K.: Palgrave Macmillan, 2014.

Sammons, Eddie. *Shakespeare: A Hundred Years on Film.* Lanham, Md.: Scarecrow Press, 2004.

Sen, Suddhaseel. *Shakespeare in the World: Cross-Cultural Adaptation in Europe and Colonial India, 1850-1900.* New York: Routledge, 2021.

Shaughnessy, Robert, ed. *Shakespeare on Film: Contemporary Critical Essays.* New York: St. Martin's, 1998.

Skovmand, Michael, ed. *Screen Shakespeare.* Aarhus, Dnk.: Aarhus University Press, 1994.

Starks, Lisa S., & Courtney Lehmann, eds. *The Reel Shakespeare: Alternative Cinema and Theory.* Madison, N.J.: Fairleigh Dickinson University Press, 2002.

----------, eds. *Spectacular Shakespeare: Critical Theory and Popular Cinema.* Madison, N.J.: Fairleigh Dickinson University Press, 2002.

Weiss, Tanja. *Shakespeare on the Screen: Kenneth Branagh's Adaptations of* Henry V, Much Ado about Nothing, *and* Hamlet. 1999. New York: Peter Lang, 2000.

Welsh, James M., & Richard Vela, eds. *Shakespeare into Film.* New York: Checkmark, 2002.

Widdicombe, Toby, & Michael Greer. 2002. *Screening Shakespeare: Understanding the Plays through Film.* New York: Pearson/Longman, 2010.

Willis, Susan. *The BBC Shakespeare Plays: Making the Televised Canon*. Chapel Hill: University of North Carolina Press, 1991.

Willson, Robert F. *Shakespeare in Hollywood, 1929-1956*. Madison, N.J.: Fairleigh Dickinson University Press, 2000.

Poetry on Film

Few if any feature films are based entirely on poems—"inspired," "triggered," or "provoked" would be better words in this case. By contrast, many films are based on stories, novels, or plays, and their numbers are far too great to list here. What follows is a select listing of the appearance of recognizable, often canonical, poems—or excerpts from poems—in full-length films.

Addison, Joseph

"The Campaign"
My Darling Clementine, 1946

Apollinaire, Guillaume

"L'amour" ["Love"]
Peau d'âne [*Donkey Skin*], 1970

Arnold, Matthew

"Dover Beach"
Without Love, 1945
The Anniversary Party, 2001

Auden, W. H.

"Night Mail"
Night Mail, 1936

"Funeral Blues"
Four Weddings and a Funeral, 1994

"As I Walked Out One Evening"
Before Sunrise, 1995

Baudelaire, Charles

"The Albatross"
A Very Long Engagement, 2004

"The Jewels"
La Letrice [*The Reader*], 1988

Bishop, Elizabeth

"One Art"
In Her Shoes, 2005

Blake, William

"The Tyger"
The End of the Affair, 1955
The Horse's Mouth, 1958
Blade Runner, 1982
The Dangerous Lives of Altar Boys, 2002

"America: A Prophecy"
"The Fly"
Blade Runner, 1982

From "Milton" ["And did those feet in ancient time"]
The Loneliness of the Long-Distance Runner, 1962
Privilege, 1967
Chariots of Fire, 1981
Calendar Girls, 2003

"The Sick Rose"
Educating Rita, 1983

"The Marriage of Heaven and Hell"
Bull Durham, 1988

"The Everlasting Gospel" ["The vision of Christ that thou dost see . . ."]
"The Marriage of Heaven and Hell"
Dead Man, 1995

"Auguries of Innocence"
Dead Man, 1995
In the Bedroom, 2001
Lara Croft: Tomb Raider, 2001

"The Little Black Boy"
The Horse's Mouth, 1958

Bradstreet, Anne

"To My Dear and Loving Husband"
Le Divorce, 2003

Brecht, Bertolt

"Germany Pale Mother"
Germany Pale Mother, 1980

"Die Moritat von Mackie Messer" ["The Ballad of Mack the Knife"]
Quiz Show, 1994

Browning, Elizabeth Barrett

"Aurora Leigh," Second Book
Take the High Ground, 1953

"A Child's Grave at Florence"
Tea with Mussolini, 1999

Browning, Robert

"Sordello"
The Barretts of Wimpole Street, 1934

"The Pied Piper of Hamelin"
The Sweet Hereafter, 1997

Bukowski, Charles

"2 p.m. Beer"
"Old Man, Dead in a Room"
Barfly, 1987

Burns, Robert

"A Red, Red Rose"
Side Street, 1950

"Afton Water" ["Flow gently, sweet Afton . . ."]
Pride and Prejudice, 1940

Byron, Lord George Gordon

"She Walks in Beauty"
Blockade, 1938
Jamaica Inn, 1939

Childe Harold's Pilgrimage, IV.178 ["There is a pleasure in the pathless woods"]
The Bridges of Madison County, 1995

Don Juan
Don Juan de Marco, 1995

Carroll, Lewis

"The Walrus and the Carpenter"
Today We Live, 1933
The Clairvoyant, 1934

Chaucer, Geoffrey

"Prologue"
"Wife of Bath's Tale" ["the woe that is in marriage"]
Sylvia, 2003

Cocteau, Jean

"Les Muses" [*The Muses*]
Peau d'âne, 1970 [*Donkey Skin*]

Coleridge, Samuel Taylor

"Kubla Khan"
Citizen Kane, 1941
Pandaemonium, 2000

"The Rime of the Ancient Mariner"
Out of Africa, 1985

Congreve, William

from *The Mourning Bride*, Act 3, Scene 8 ["Heaven has no rage like love to hatred turned . . ."]
Adam's Rib, 1949

Corso, Gregory

"Marriage"
Reality Bites, 1994

Cowper, William

"The Castaway"
Sense and Sensibility, 1995

Cummings, E. E.

"i carry your heart with me"
In Her Shoes, 2005

"somewhere i have never travelled,gladly beyond"
Hannah and Her Sisters, 1986

"she being brand"
Plain Clothes, 1988

Dante Alighieri

"Vita Nuova, III"
Hannibal, 2001

Dickinson, Emily

"Ample make this Bed"
Sophie's Choice, 1982

"Because I could not stop for Death"
Crimes and Misdemeanors, 1989
Sophie's Choice, 1982

"'Hope' is the thing with feathers"
Quiz Show, 1994
Autumn in New York, 2000

"Two Butterflies went out at Noon"
Autumn in New York, 2000

"We never know how high we are"
Seabiscuit, 2003

Donne, John

"Holy Sonnet X" ["Death Be Not Proud"]
The Exorcist III, 1990
Wit, 2001

Douglas, Lord Alfred

"In Summer"
"Two Loves"
Wilde, 1997

Dowson, Ernest

"Vitae Summa Brevis Spem Nos Vetat Incohare Longam" ["They are not long /
They are not long, the weeping and the laughter"]
Days of Wine and Roses, 1962

Dryden, John

Horace, Book 3, Ode 29 ["Happy the man, and happy he alone . . ."]
Tom Jones, 1963

Eliot, T. S.

"East Coker"
Butley, 1974

"The Hollow Men"
Apocalypse Now, 1979

"The Love Song of J. Alfred Prufrock"
Love and Death, 1975
Apocalypse Now, 1979
Till Human Voices Wake Us, 2002
The Fog of War, 2003

"Little Gidding" ["We shall not cease from exploration"]
The Fog of War, 2003

"Old Possum's Book of Practical Cats"
Logan's Run, 1976

"The Waste Land" ["April is the cruelest month . . ."]
Without Love, 1945

Éluard, Paul

"Nudité de la vérité" ["The nakedness of truth"]
Alphaville, 1965

Frost, Robert

"Death of the Hired Man"
Frenzy, 1972

"Stopping by Woods on a Snowy Evening"
Telefon, 1977
Dreamcatcher, 2003

"Nothing Gold Can Stay"
The Outsiders, 1983

"The Road Not Taken" [in Italian]
Down by Law, 1986

Ginsberg, Allen

"Howl"
Hairspray, 1988
Howl, 2010

Goethe, Johann Wolfgang von

"Erlkönig" ("Elf King")
Burning Secret, 1988

Gray, Thomas

"Elegy (Written in a Country Churchyard)"
Bull Durham, 1988

Gregory, [Isabella Augusta] Lady

"Donal Óg" ["Young Donald"]
The Dead, 1987

Hardy, Thomas

"Drummer Hodge"
The History Boys, 2006

Herrick, Robert

"To the Virgins, to Make Much of Time" ["Gather ye Rose-Buds while ye may"]
A Prairie Home Companion, 2006

"Upon Julia's Clothes"
Julia, 1977

Hood, Thomas

"Silence"
The Piano, 1993

Hopkins, Gerard Manley

"Spring and Fall"
Vision Quest, 1985

Housman, A. E.

From *A Shropshire Lad* (XL) ["Into my heart an air that kills"]
Walkabout, 1971

"To an Athlete Dying Young"
Out of Africa, 1985

From *A Shropshire Lad* (XIII) ["When I was one-and-twenty"]
Stage Struck, 1958

Hughes, Langston

"Montage of a Dream Deferred"
A Raisin in the Sun, 1961

Jonson, Ben

"Song to Celia" ["Drink to me only with thine eyes"]
Ghosts on the Loose,1943

Keats, John

Endymion ["A thing of beauty is a joy forever"]
Portrait of Jenny, 1948
White Men Can't Jump, 1992

"To Autumn"
The Prime of Miss Jean Brodie, 1969
Bridget Jones's Diary, 2001

"La Belle Dame Sans Merci" ["The Beautiful Lady with No Mercy"]
In the Cut, 2003

"When I Have Fears that I May Cease to Be"
Brief Encounter, 1945

Khayyám, Omar

The Rubáiyát, 7 ["The Bird of Time has but a little way . . ."]
Morning Glory, 1933

Unfaithful, 2002

The Rubáiyát, 46 ["O threats of hell and hopes of Paradise . . ."]
Duel in the Sun, 1946

Kipling, Rudyard

"Gunga Din"
Gunga Din, 1939
Two-Way Stretch, 1959
Sylvia, 2003

"The Conundrum of the Workshops"
F for Fake, 1974

"Tomlinson" ["the sin they do by two and two they must pay for one by one"]
Lifeboat, 1944

"If—"
St. Martin's Lane, 1938

Larkin, Philip

"Ignorance"
Holy Smoke, 1999

Lawrence, D. H.

"Self-Pity"
G.I. Jane, 1997

Lazarus, Emma

"The New Colossus"
Saboteur, 1942
Since You Went Away, 1944

Levertov, Denise

"At David's Grave"
Any Mother's Son, 1997

Longfellow, Henry Wadsworth

"The Song of Hiawatha"
Here We Go Again, 1942

Hiawatha, 1952
Desk Set, 1957
Spider Man 2, 2004

"My Lost Youth"
In the Bedroom, 2001

Lorca, Federico García

"Ballad of a Sleepwalker"
Revenge, 1990

"Backwaters"
In the Cut, 2003

"Poem of the Soleá"
Little Ashes, 2009

Lowell, James Russell

"The Present Crisis" ["Once to every man and nation . . ."]
Kid Glove Killer, 1942

Marlowe, Christopher

"The Passionate Shepherd to His Love"
The Private Lives of Elizabeth and Essex, 1939
Come Live with Me, 1941
Richard III, 1995

"Hero and Leander" ["Whoever loved that loved not at first sight"]
Intolerable Cruelty, 2003

The Tragical History of the Life and Death of Doctor Faustus, V, 100 [". . . make me immortal with a kiss"]
The Ruling Class, 1972

Marvell, Andrew

"To His Coy Mistress"
A Farewell to Arms, 1932
A Matter of Life and Death, 1946
The 25th Hour, 2002

"The Definition of Love"
The Daytrippers, 1996

Millay, Edna St. Vincent

"Sonnet: Love Is Not All"
Take the High Ground, 1953

"First Fig"
A River Runs through It, 1992

"God's World"
"To a Young Poet"
Autumn in New York, 2000

"Elaine"
Without Love, 1945

Milton, John

"Lycidas" ["Tomorrow to fresh woods, and pastures new"]
The Horse's Mouth, 1958

Paradise Lost, IV. 846 ["Abashed the devil stood and felt how awful goodness is"]
The Crow, 1994

from *Comus* ["Sabrina fair . . ."]
Sabrina, 1995

Neruda, Pablo

"The Dead Woman"
Truly Madly Deeply, 1991

"The Enigmas"
Mindwalk, 1991

"Sonnet 17"
Patch Adams, 1998

Various poems by Antonio Skármeta and Pablo Neruda
Il Postino [*The Postman*], 1994

Owen, Wilfred

"The Parable of the Old Man and the Young"
"Dulce et Decorum Est" ["It Is Sweet and Fitting"]
"Greater Love"
Regeneration, 1997

Parker, Dorothy

"Resume"
Girl, Interrupted, 1999

"Midnight"
Autumn in New York, 2000

Poe, Edgar Allan

"The Raven"
The Raven, 1935, 1963
Young Guns, 1988
The Crow, 1994

"Ulalume"
Lolita, 1962
The Ladykillers, 2004

"El Dorado" ["That Which Is Golden"]
El Dorado, 1967

"Alone"
The Krays, 1990

"Annabel Lee"
Stage Struck, 1958
Play Misty for Me, 1971
Holes, 2003

"To Helen"
The Ladykillers, 2004

Pope, Alexander

"Eloisa to Abelard"
Eternal Sunshine of the Spotless Mind, 2004

Raleigh, Sir Walter

"His Pilgrimage"
A Matter of Life and Death, 1946

"The Nymph's Reply to the Shepherd"
The Private Lives of Elizabeth and Essex, 1939
Richard III, 1995

Rilke, Rainer Maria

"The Panther"
Another Woman, 1988
Awakenings, 1990

"Archaic Torso of Apollo"
Another Woman, 1988

Rossetti, Christina

"Remember"
Kiss Me Deadly, 1955

Sassoon, Siegfried

"Base Details"
Regeneration, 1997

Scott, Sir Walter

Marmion, VI.30 ["O woman! in our hours of ease"]
The Prisoner of Zenda, 1937

Marmion, VI.532-3 ["O what a tangled web we weave"]
The Perfect Man, 2005

"Love as a Theme of Poets"
A Matter of Life and Death, 1946

"Patriotism"
Groundhog Day, 1993

Shakespeare, William

Hamlet, Act 1, Scene 2 ["How weary, stale, flat, and unprofitable . . ."]
Lola Montes, 1955

Hamlet, Act 2, Scene 1 ["To be or not to be"]
Morning Glory, 1933
My Darling Clementine, 1946
Star Trek VI: The Undiscovered Country, 1991

Henry IV, Part 1
My Own Private Idaho, 1991

Henry V, Act 3, Scene 1
Too Much, Too Soon, 1958

Henry V [Saint Crispin's Day speech, Act 4, Scene 3]
Too Much, Too Soon, 1958
Renaissance Man, 1994

Julius Caesar, Act 1, Scene 2 ["The fault, dear Brutus, is not in our stars"]
Intolerable Cruelty, 2003
Good Night and Good Luck, 2005

Julius Caesar, Act 2, Scene 2 ["Cowards die many times before their deaths"]
The Human Stain, 2003

Julius Caesar, Act 3, Scene 2
Pinero, 2001

Macbeth, Act 5, Scene 5 ["Tomorrow and tomorrow . . ."]
Smoke, 1995

A Midsummer Night's Dream, Act 3, Scene 2 ["Jack shall have Jill"]
The Anniversary Party, 2001

Othello, Act 3, Scene 3 ["Oh, curse of marriage . . ."]
The Unfaithful, 1947

Richard II, Act 2, Scene 1
The Scarlet Pimpernel, 1934

Romeo and Juliet, Act 2, Scene 2 ["O Romeo, Romeo . . ."]
Morning Glory, 1933
This Land is Mine, 1943
Tea with Mussolini, 1999

Romeo and Juliet, various passages by William Shakespeare
Stage Struck, 1958
Tumbleweeds, 1999

The Tempest, Act 3, Scene 2 ["The isle is full of noises . . ."]
The Four Feathers, 1939

Twelfth Night, Act 2, Scene 5 ["Some are born great . . ."]
The Miracle of Morgan's Creek, 1944

"Sonnet 29" ["When, in disgrace with Fortune and men's eyes"]
In a Lonely Place, 1950

"Sonnet 94" ["They that have power to hurt and will do none"]
A Map of the World, 1999

"Sonnet 116" ["Let me not to the marriage of true minds"]
The Trouble with Harry, 1955
Sense and Sensibility, 1995

"Venus and Adonis" ["Dismiss your vows, your feigned tears"]
Intolerable Cruelty, 2003

Shelley, Percy Bysshe

"Adonais," stanza 40 ["He has outsoared the shadow of our night"]
The Thin Man Goes Home, 1944

"Love's Philosophy"
In & Out, 1997

Spenser, Edmund

The Faerie Queene, V.ii.39 ["For whatsoever from one place doth fall . . ."]
Sense and Sensibility, 1995

Stevenson, Robert Louis

"Requiem"
They Were Expendable, 1945
The Horse's Mouth, 1958

"My House, I Say"
Undercurrent, 1946

"My Wife"
Tender Comrade, 1943

Tennyson, [Alfred] Lord

"The Charge of the Light Brigade"
The Charge of the Light Brigade, 1936, 1968
The Bridge on the River Kwai, 1957
The Falcon and the Snowman, 1985

"Maud," III. 23-5
The Thin Man Goes Home, 1944

"Crossing the Bar"
Finding Graceland, 1998

"The Lady of Shalott"
The Mirror Crack'd, 1980

"Tithonus"
Shadow of the Vampire, 2000

Thomas, Dylan

"Do Not Go Gentle into That Good Night"
Back to School, 1986
Dangerous Minds, 1995

"And Death Shall Have No Dominion"
The Weight of Water, 2000
Solaris, 2002

Valéry, Paul

"Le Cimetière marin" ["Graveyard by the Sea"]
The Victors, 1963

Verlaine, Paul

"Song of Autumn"
The Longest Day

Whitman, Walt

"The Untold Want"
Now, Voyager, 1942
Love and Death on Long Island, 1997

"I Sing the Body Electric"
Bull Durham, 1988

"Song of Myself"
Beautiful Dreamers, 1990

"O Captain! My Captain!"
Dead Poets' Society, 1989

"Out of the Cradle, Endlessly Rocking"
Intolerance, 1916
L.I.E., 2001

"Spontaneous Me"
The Notebook, 2004

"So Long"
The Notebook, 2004

"Passage to India" ["Sail forth, steer for the deep waters only"]
Street Scene, 1931

Wilde, Oscar

"The Sphinx"
The Picture of Dorian Gray, 1945

"The Ballad of Reading Gaol [Jail]"
Wilde, 1997

Williams, William Carlos

Paterson
Paterson, 2016

Wordsworth, William

"Ode: Intimations of Immortality"
Splendor in the Grass, 1961
Alice in Wonderland, 1966
A River Runs Through It, 1992

"Tintern Abbey"
Pandaemonium, 2000

Yeats, W. B.

"An Irish Airman Foresees his Death"
Memphis Belle, 1990

"The Young Man's Song" ["Ah, penny, brown penny, brown penny . . ."]
Must Love Dogs, 2005

"When You are Old"
Peggy Sue Got Married, 1986

"Aedh Wishes for the Cloths of Heaven"
84 Charing Cross Road, 1987

"The Song of Wandering Aengus"
Bridges of Madison County, 1995

"The Stolen Child"
A. I.: Artificial Intelligence, 2001

"The Stolen Child"
A. I.: Artificial Intelligence, 2001
Blue Car, 2002

"The Sorrow of Love"
Sylvia, 2003

"The Lake Isle of Innisfree"
Million-Dollar Baby, 2004

Index